Access 2002 Programming

BY EXAMPLE

201 West 103rd Street
Indianapolis, Indiana 46290

Bob Villareal

Access 2002 Programming by Example

Copyright © 2002 by Que® Corporation

International Standard Book Number: 0-7897-2594-0

Library of Congress Catalog Card Number: 2001096466

Printed in the United States of America

First Printing: Febrary 2002

04   03   02   01   4   3   2   1

Trademarks

Warning and Disclaimer

Publisher
David Culverwell

Acquisitions Editor
Loretta Yates

Development Editor
Susan Hobbs

Managing Editor
Thomas F. Hayes

Project Editor
Tonya Simpson

Copy Editor
Nancy Sixsmith

Indexer
D&G Limited, LLC

Proofreader
D&G Limited, LLC

Technical Editor
Lawrence P. Steele

Team Coordinator
Cindy Teeters

Interior Designer
Karen Ruggles

Cover Designer
Rader Design

Page Layout
D&G Limited, LLC

Contents at a Glance

Table of Contents

About the Author

Bob Villareal has been working with microcomputers since 1981 and has nearly 10 years experience with VBA programming in both Access and Excel. Bob has written many tracking and management applications and has been developing databases for a large insurance firm for well over a decade.

Bob also does freelance programming and instruction. He is a contributor to the monthly publication and Web journal, *Inside Microsoft Access*, as well as a Microsoft Access instructor at Tulsa Community College in Tulsa, Oklahoma. Bob earned his Bachelor of Science degree in Communications from the University of Tulsa.

Dedication

I would like to dedicate this book to my parents, Morey and Lou Villareal, whose support and encouragement have guided me throughout my life.

Acknowledgments

First of all, I would like to thank Loretta Yates, acquisitions editor for Que Publishing, who was a huge motivator and encourager throughout the writing of this book. Another great encourager was Greg Perry, a successful Pearson author, who helped me "learn the ropes," so to speak, of writing. I couldn't have done it without Sue Hobbs, development editor, whose talent and support have been instrumental along the journey from writing to publishing. Larry Steele, technical editor, gave me a good balance of constructive criticism and encouragement. His input has definitely helped shape this book. And finally, I'd like to thank my friends and family, who seemed almost as excited as I was at the prospect of seeing this book published.

Tell Us What You Think!

As the reader of this book, *you* are our most important critic and commentator. We value your opinion and want to know what we're doing right, what we could do better, what areas you'd like to see us publish in, and any other words of wisdom you're willing to pass our way.

As a publisher for Que, I welcome your comments. You can fax, email, or write me directly to let me know what you did or didn't like about this book—as well as what we can do to make our books stronger.

Please note that I cannot help you with technical problems related to the topic of this book, and that due to the high volume of mail I receive, I might not be able to reply to every message.

When you write, please be sure to include this book's title and author as well as your name and phone or fax number. I will carefully review your comments and share them with the author and editors who worked on the book.

Fax: 317-581-4666

E-mail: feedback@quepublishing.com

Mail: David Culverwell
            Que Publishing
            201 West 103rd Street
            Indianapolis, IN 46290 USA

Introduction

Although Microsoft Access is a powerful platform for database development, it takes considerable time to fully grasp its capabilities and unlock its power. Like any other learning process, you must first understand the fundamentals of database design, so you can build a solid foundation on which to build.

This book does not intend to be comprehensive. Even the more advanced books covering Microsoft Access development would not dare to assume to cover everything there is to know about Access. What it does intend to do is give you a "jump start" into the database development process. How can this be accomplished? We intend to give you clear-cut, easy-to-understand examples; and yes, you will learn a great deal about Access in the process.

Why By Example?

It has often been said that "a picture is worth a thousand words." It's one thing to talk about golf theory, for example. You can talk about your grip, your stance, and the fundamentals of the swing. These are all necessary. But when you see someone walk up to the ball and knock it down the fairway, much can be learned from observing the swing fundamentals "by example."

Most people are visual learners. Of course, you will have many images of dialog boxes and other graphics to help you visualize the techniques involved, but you also will have "real-world" examples of situations that often are encountered in a business or home environment. Other computer books claim to have real-world examples. But most of our examples will come directly from the business world—the world of everyday computing. In other words, you won't find much "theory" here, except when we talk about fundamentals.

This means that after a new concept is introduced, you immediately have a hands-on example of how to implement the concept. Using the learning-by-example approach, we try to start with the simple and then gradually introduce the more complex. This way, you should never feel overwhelmed. You tackle each topic a little bit at a time. Each chapter is an entity in itself; yet, you will be building on a foundation with each new technique you learn.

What This Book Should Accomplish

What I hope to accomplish by writing this book is simple. I want to present a book that is easy to understand and easy to put into action. This is where the rubber meets the road. I am well aware of the fact that there are other Access books out there, but many of them are difficult to understand and even harder to put into action. Others have many techniques but no cohesiveness to help you fit the pieces together. This book will help you discover the "why" behind the techniques, so that you will understand which situation is best for what technique, and how various techniques relate to each other. Comparisons are used extensively to help you understand the distinctions between various Access terms.

I also hope to give you the tools that are important. The beginning programmer can encounter many obstacles and pitfalls. An experienced programmer might say, "Had I known then what I know now, I could have accomplished so much more." I want to give you those tools now, so you won't have to fumble through Web sites and help menus looking for answers. It becomes very logical when you know what you are doing. Even if one of the tools doesn't seem to be useful or relevant at first glance, just wait. Sooner or later, you will run into a situation that will require the exact technique that you learned in this book.

What I Assume You Know

It is assumed that you are a novice developer. It is helpful if you have some basic knowledge of Microsoft Access and a familiarity with Windows, but even that is not absolutely necessary because the book covers some Access basics as well. It is also assumed that you are serious about learning to get the most out of Microsoft Access in every way. This book will take you from a beginner to an intermediate (and in some cases, advanced) user of Access.

What I Assume You Don't Know

You certainly don't need to be an expert in Microsoft Access. No knowledge of macros, Visual Basic for Applications (VBA), or programming in general is required. I assume that you are a complete novice. Therefore, any knowledge that you might have in any programming language will be a plus, but it certainly will not be required.

Source Files and How to Access Them

To take advantage of the many examples presented in this book, first create a folder on your C drive called AccessByExample. Then, visit www.QuePublishing.com and download AccExamp.exe to your AccessByExample folder. Several compressed databases are included in the download, so it might take some time, depending on the type of Internet connection you're using. These databases and files are used throughout the book as a hands-on way of teaching you by example.

Conventions Used Throughout the Book

NOTE
Notes clarify or expand a concept in each chapter.

TIP

A tip provides a shortcut or solution that either relates to a problem or offers an alternative to the common approach. Tips are time-saving and practical.

CAUTION

Cautions give you warnings about potential problems or pitfalls that can arise as you complete the many hands-on exercises and examples throughout the book.

Naming Conventions

Some people follow the Reddick VBA naming convention for naming Access objects. For example, all tables would have a tbl prefix, whereas all queries would have a qry prefix. So, the Customer table would become tblCustomer. This is handy from one aspect. Access does not allow you to have a table and a query with the same name. In addition, you can tell at a glance what kind of object is in view. You are certainly free to use this naming convention. This convention is often used in this book, especially in procedures.

Another popular naming convention is to use capital letters to distinguish words while avoiding spaces in object titles. For example, instead of Last Name for a field title, you would instead use LastName. This avoids having to use brackets in query criteria as well as in VBA. Instead of typing `[Customer]![Last Name]` for the expression criteria, you just type `Customer!LastName` and the brackets are automatically inserted for you. Access allows spaces in field, table, form, report, and query names. However, except in rare instances, you will use this convention.

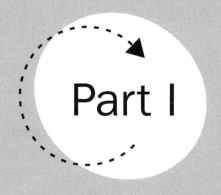

Part I

Tables and Queries

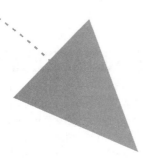

Planning and Designing Your Access Database

Can you imagine building a house without a blueprint or an automobile without a design? Common sense tells us that it won't happen. Likewise, it only makes good sense to take the time to plan and design your database before building it. It will save time in the long run because you are spared the frustration of fixing the inherent problems of a poorly designed application. This chapter focuses on how to employ sound database principles in your design. Specifically, you learn

- about obtaining data from outside sources
- why relational tables are important
- about database design and normalization
- why you should avoid duplicate data
- about normalization fundamentals
- about the first, second, and third normal forms
- how to let Access automatically normalize for you

Consider Your Data Before Designing Your Database

When this book speaks of obtaining data from outside sources, it is referring to a broader scope than customers, clients, WAN, e-mail, external mainframe, or Internet sources. Outside sources can be within your company or even within your department. The term "outside" refers to anything outside of Microsoft Access. What do you do with data that you have not personally tested for consistency, accuracy, and integrity? Even if you created the data yourself with a program like Microsoft Excel, how do you know that it conforms to the rules of "database normalization" (discussed in "Avoiding Duplicate Data" later in this chapter) for database design when imported into Access?

More specifically, are the ZIP Codes complete and accurate? Does a comma always separate the city and state? Does the data need to be parsed (separated) into separate fields? Has the data been validated? For example, do all the social security numbers have the same number of characters? Microsoft Access provides validation for data that has been input into Access databases, but what about data that has been input in other software packages?

Here's some good news for you: Microsoft Access has many tools to help you validate data even "after the fact." This book shows you methods to prepare data to be part of a consistent and well-planned application. After using the tools to analyze and clean up the data in preparation for becoming part of your application, there are still design principles that must be clearly understood and applied to ensure data consistency and integrity. So before we go outside, let's go inside.

Why Relational Tables?

Now let's talk about database design. Why is it so important to have relational tables in databases? Why can't you just use them like we use spreadsheets—in two dimensional tables? Can't you calculate and add records this way?

Well, it's because *real-world* situations usually aren't arranged that way. How many customers will only order one item? How many employees will only have one project? How many students will take only one course? We live in a "one-to-many" three-dimensional world. Although two dimensions might work in a spreadsheet, databases have much more rigid structures; and this extra dimension can be a big advantage.

A flat file database is a two-dimensional model. What does that mean? If you think of a table like a spreadsheet, with rows as records and fields as columns, you are only looking at one view, so to speak. A relational database adds the third dimension. You can think of it as length, width and depth. The row is the width, the column is the length, and the relation is the depth (see Figure 1.1).

Region	1997	1998	1999	2000
SW Region	150,000	195,000	253,500	329,550
Central Region	145,000	186,500	245,050	318,565
Southern Region	175,000	227,500	295,750	384,475

Record: 1 of 3

Figure 1.1: *This three-dimensional spreadsheet shows the region as the width, the year column as the length, and the relational progression of year data as the depth.*

At first glance, this looks like a two-dimensional model. In fact, it *is* a two-dimensional model if you think of it in terms of rows and columns. But the data in the financial columns are three dimensional if you conceptualize them properly as shown in Figure 1.2.

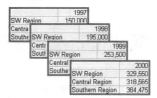

Figure 1.2: *The best way to conceptualize the table data is to use a three-dimensional view.*

The column headers all have one thing in common: They are all years. In a database, you want to keep common information in categories called *fields*. This will be discussed in greater detail later, but the design in Figures 1.1 and 1.2 is not a good database model.

For example, if you wanted a total for the financials in the SW Region, you could easily place a formula in a cell off to the side in a spreadsheet. But in a database, you need a calculated field to total four columns. Placing these kinds of totals in a field are not usually a good database design strategy anyway. And if you want to total all financial fields, though it is possible, it is not the quickest or most efficient way to set up your query. The example in Figure 1.3 is a better design for a database, yet it's still flawed. Notice that the years are placed in a field called Year and the financial data is labeled Sales.

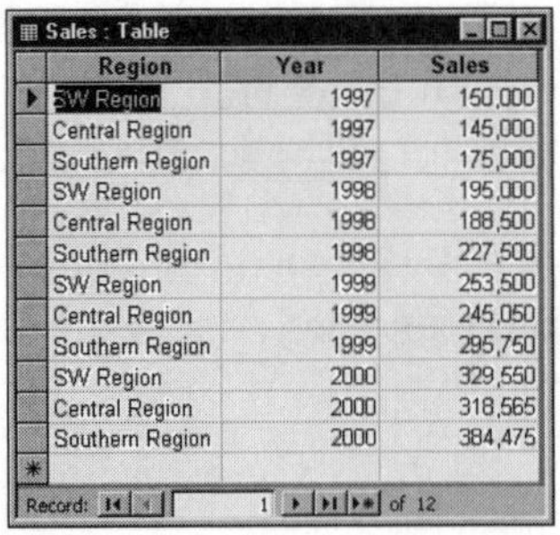

Region	Year	Sales
SW Region	1997	150,000
Central Region	1997	145,000
Southern Region	1997	175,000
SW Region	1998	195,000
Central Region	1998	188,500
Southern Region	1998	227,500
SW Region	1999	253,500
Central Region	1999	245,050
Southern Region	1999	295,750
SW Region	2000	329,550
Central Region	2000	318,565
Southern Region	2000	384,475

Figure 1.3: *A better, but still flawed three-dimensional table showing Year and Sales as separate fields.*

At least now the user knows what kind of information he or she is dealing with. The user can query by group and easily find the total for each year or each region, or a combination of both. The only problem is that the example shows redundant (duplicate) information. In contrast, every value is different in a unique field. The only way to establish a unique field in the previous scenario is to combine the first two fields into one. There must be a better way.

Database Design and Normalization

By now, you should know that a database is a collection of information related to a specific purpose. But how do you organize this information for maximum efficiency? A good database design is the key.

The table is the heart of the database. It is where most of your database work focuses either directly or indirectly. But just because you have several tables that relate to each other in your database doesn't necessarily mean that they are ready for database functionality.

Considerations related to database design include

- the purpose of the database
- necessary tables and fields
- necessary relationships between tables
- how to avoid data redundancy
- how to ensure data consistency

When you examine these considerations, you quickly come to realize the advantages of data *normalization*, which is the process of simplifying the design of the database to obtain maximum efficiency and uniformity. Some say that normalization is the process of detecting and eliminating redundant data and the anomalies associated with them in a database. Others say that normalization is the process of breaking tables down into smaller components for optimization. Some combination of these definitions could get you fairly close. To ensure a good database design and proper table structure, two design flaws need to be avoided at all cost: redundancy and inconsistency.

If you have a table with an excessive number of fields, or if you have a table with a great deal of redundant (duplicate) data, chances are you need to normalize. By breaking down your tables into smaller tables while providing a link between the related tables, you accomplish several things, which include

- avoiding duplicate data both within the table itself and between the tables that are related

- maximizing the speed and efficiency of your database

- ensuring that the same data never had to be entered into more than one place

- saving disk space by avoiding redundant data

- ensuring data consistency and uniformity, whether the data is being input or output

- creating a design that is far easier than unnormalized data to maintain and manipulate

- creating a mechanism for conditional lookups in queries, forms, and reports

Now let's explore these topics by example.

Avoiding Duplicate Data

When you store data in more than one place (either in the same table or in two or more tables), you create *data redundancy*. Why is redundancy so undesirable in database design? If you have a supplier who moves from Houston to Dallas and fifty rows of data containing their address, you have to change all fifty rows. This is called an *update anomaly*. To make things worse, if you delete a part related to that supplier in a non-relational model, you delete the supplier as well. Fortunately, there is a better approach to achieve optimal database design.

From this point forward the term *internal redundancy* to refers to redundancy within a table whereas the term *external redundancy* refers to the same information (other than key fields) that is in more than one table. External redundancies are common with spreadsheets. This is because you are not punished for storing the same information in multiple tables, sheets, or workbooks.

The table in Figure 1.4 shows examples of redundancy.

Project ID	Name	Age	SSN
1	Jane	50	444-44-4444
2	Jane	50	444-44-4444
3	Jane	50	444-44-4444

Figure 1.4: *This redundant table has only one unique field—the Project ID field.*

First of all, imagine the table in Figure 1.4 without the first column. What can you do with it? When Jane's age changes, you have to change three records instead of changing just one. Without the first column, you can't link this table with anything because you have no "hook" or pointer with which to link information; therefore, the information becomes virtually meaningless. The first column is the only column in the table that is unique. Even with the first column, the design is not functionally flawless.

The Project ID provides the "hook." This key (unique) field can be linked with another table called Projects, which can contain all sorts of information about each project. All you have to do to eliminate redundancy is to assign a unique Employee ID to Jane (because Jane is not a very unique name) and place her in an Employee table. You can even use her social security number because you know that this number is unique. You can then link her to a Clients table, Prospects table, or others; the list goes on. Note the results of eliminating redundancy in Figure 1.5.

EmployeeID	ProjectID	Name	Age	SSN
000123	1	Jane	50	444-44-4444
000456	1	Ralph	40	777-77-7777
000789	2	Sally	30	888-88-8888

Figure 1.5: *This table shows Jane with a unique Employee ID placed in a table with her coworkers.*

Normalization Fundamentals

In 1969, a man named E.F. Codd founded the relational database model. To achieve optimal structure he created *normal forms,* a progression of rules you apply to your database with each normal form level attaining a better overall design.

If you wanted to put together an employee database to track their clients, you might arrange the fields as they are in Figure 1.6.

Employee ID	Employee Name	Employee Position	Client ID 1	Client Name 1	Client ID 2	Client Name 2
10	Hargus	Producer	6710	Inroad Trucking	7745	Ace Engineering
14	Maggie	Controller	2811	Key Realty		
17	Stanley	Sales	3033	Triad Development	8018	Coley Personnel
34	Willard	IT Specialist	9921	United Tool	1144	Allied Rental
44	Elwood	Sales	2780	Acme Services		

Employee Clients : Table — Record: 1 of 5

Figure 1.6: *This unnormalized table has internal redundancy and repeating fields.*

Figure 1.6 is an unnormalized table. The first problem, which is at the *field* level, is obvious. What if you want to track more than two clients per employee? More specifically, what if Stanley, who already has two clients, gains another client? Adding another field is not a good option because this is only making the table more complicated and inefficient.

In the *first normal form,* there should be *no repeating groups* (of columns), so we must deal with the fact that we have two repeating fields. To put it another way, you should not have multiple fields in the same category. That's what a field is, for the most part: a category. With two client ID fields and two client name fields, it becomes difficult to select, sort, and track information properly. As a rule, there is no need to have two or more fields containing the same type of information. The problems can be summarized as follows:

- null values when employee has only one client
- cannot track more than two clients
- repeating groups (difficult to track)
- same type of data in more than one field

The only good thing you can say about the table in Figure 1.6 is that the employee information is unique.

First Normal Form—Eliminate Repeating Groups

How do you fix repeating groups and other problems associated with unnormalized tables while assuring that you can track clients the way you want to track them? Examine Figure 1.7, which shows the same information in a different arrangement, with one exception.

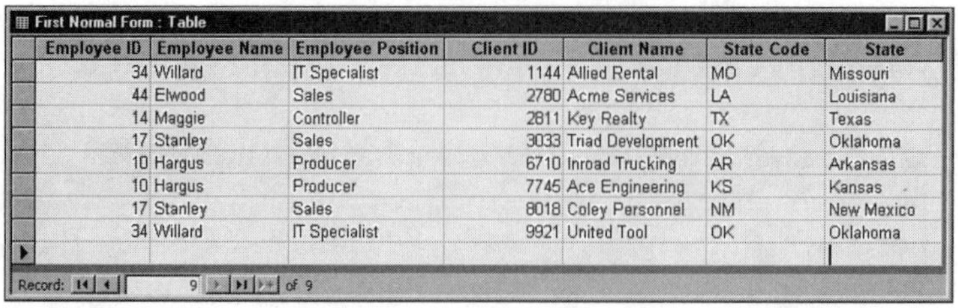

Employee ID	Employee Name	Employee Position	Client ID	Client Name	State Code	State
34	Willard	IT Specialist	1144	Allied Rental	MO	Missouri
44	Elwood	Sales	2780	Acme Services	LA	Louisiana
14	Maggie	Controller	2811	Key Realty	TX	Texas
17	Stanley	Sales	3033	Triad Development	OK	Oklahoma
10	Hargus	Producer	6710	Inroad Trucking	AR	Arkansas
10	Hargus	Producer	7745	Ace Engineering	KS	Kansas
17	Stanley	Sales	8018	Coley Personnel	NM	New Mexico
34	Willard	IT Specialist	9921	United Tool	OK	Oklahoma

Record: 9 of 9

Figure 1.7: Although the first normal form corrects some problems, it is still flawed.

The state code information in Figure 1.7 is added for each client. With this new arrangement, the table can support any number of clients for each employee. But fixing one problem has created a new problem, which is at the *record* level. The table now has internal redundancy in the employee information. You have reached the *first normal form* level, which is a better design than you started with, but you still haven't achieved the *optimum* design. You have yet to establish a primary key. Although the employee information in the unnormalized table is unique, the new design has redundant employee information. On the other hand, notice that one field tracks the same information that two fields did before. That makes this form superior to the preceding form, but it's not yet perfect.

PRIMARY KEY

A *primary key* is a field (or set of fields) that uniquely identifies each record in a table. Access does not allow duplicate values in a primary key field. Furthermore, you are forced to enter a value in every record of a primary key field to ensure that you do not have any records without values. This is what the relational model demands. It makes good sense. You certainly don't want duplicate customer numbers if you want to identify a customer. Access does not mandate creating a primary key in every table, but it is strongly recommended because it is to your advantage that you do so. Your situation might vary, but this is a general principle.

Because the Employee ID field is not unique, you need to create a *composite* (two fields acting as one) field, which acts as a key to create uniqueness. In this case, you could put the Employee ID and the Client ID fields together. Notice that if you combined these two fields into one field, it would create a unique field. In other words, the two fields joined together would not repeat themselves. Why would they repeat themselves? Why would you need to track an employee with the same client twice? Even though the first normal form allows the establishment of a primary key, the fact that it is a composite key is an indication that you have not yet achieved the second normal form.

If you split this table into two or more tables, you still haven't resolved the redundancy problem; that is, until you go to the next level. You might have situations where redundancy is next to impossible to avoid. In the preceding example, suppose that instead of one employee having many clients, one client utilized many employees who had other clients as well. This scenario, which is entirely possible, creates redundancy. But keep in mind that you are just stating the "norm" here. Perhaps that's why these are called *normal* forms.

Along the same lines, the *Access 97 Developer's Handbook*, by Paul Litwin, Ken Getz and Mike Gilbert and published by Sybex, states that there are situations in which it is acceptable to *denormalize*. In these rare cases, there are general rules to follow to "break the rules" properly. These rules include documenting every step in the denormalization process and making the necessary adjustments in the application to avoid anomalies and inconsistencies.

INCONSISTENT DATA   *Redundancy → anomalies → inconsistencies*

Redundancy creates anomalies and anomalies create *inconsistencies*. Suppose you have order numbers for which there is no customer. This happens if the Customer table is not linked and a customer number has changed, or if the customer's information is deleted from an Orders table. This customer's orders are like "lost data" floating around, taking up space without a link. This is because the order is *dependant* on the customer.

Another type of inconsistency, which was mentioned previously, is created when you enter data in more than one place. A person's name might be spelled correctly in one place, but not in another. In this way, normalization minimizes human error. But with the first normal form, you have still not eliminated redundancy or inconsistency.

Table 1.1 shows what can and cannot be done with the first normal form.

Table 1.1: First Normal Form Capabilities

Things You Can't Do	Things You Can Do
Eliminate redundancy	Break the table down into smaller tables
Eliminate inconsistency	Establish a primary key (composite only)
Have either repeated groups (of columns) or more than one value in the intersection of a row and a column (such as a cell in a spreadsheet)	Eliminate repeating groups
Have a primary key that is not composite	

Second Normal Form—Eliminate Redundancy

For a table to be in second normal form, it must first be in first normal form. Another qualification is that every non-key column must be fully dependent on the entire primary key. This means that if you have a composite primary key the other non-key fields must fully depend on the primary instead of partially depending on it. Figure 1.8 illustrates full dependencies in the second normal form.

Employees Second : Table

Employee ID	Employee Name	Employee Position
10	Hargus	Producer
14	Maggie	Controller
17	Stanley	Sales
34	Willard	IT Specialist
44	Elwood	Sales

Record: 1 of 5

Clients Second : Table

Client ID	Employee ID	Client Name	State Code	State
1144	34	Allied Rental	MO	Missouri
2780	44	Acme Services	LA	Louisiana
2811	14	Key Realty	TX	Texas
3033	17	Triad Development	OK	Oklahoma
6710	10	Inroad Trucking	AR	Arkansas
7745	10	Ace Engineering	KS	Kansas
8018	17	Coley Personnel	NM	New Mexico
9921	34	United Tool	OK	Oklahoma

Record: 9 of 9

Figure 1.8: *To be in second normal form, you cannot have any partial dependencies.*

Partial Dependencies

A *partial dependency* depends on only *part* of the primary key rather than on the *entire* primary key. Therefore, if you have a composite key, there is a good chance that you have partial dependencies and are in first normal form. Notice in Figure 1.8 that the Employee Name is fully dependant on Employee ID, rather than being dependent on Employee ID and some other field making up a composite. So you can conclude that Figure 1.8, which is a second normal form example, does not contain any partial dependencies. We can also assert that a relation is *automatically* in second normal form if it contains a single attribute (non-composite) primary key.

Note the reduction of duplication. Employee IDs 34, 10, and 17 are stored once instead of twice, as they were in the previous form shown in Figure 1.7.

One-to-Many

common field → foreign key

The Employees table is the primary table and the *one* in the one-to-many relationship. Thus you have one employee with many clients. Because the Employee ID field is in both tables, it is called a *common* field. However, the Employee ID in the Clients (related) table is called a *foreign* key. Also note that the commonality rests not so much in the identical field names; it is more important that the data within the fields match. Linking the Employee ID fields of the two example tables is what establishes a one-to-many relationship. You can view relationships between tables in the Relationships window.

> ✔ To learn more about the Relationships window, see "Referential Integrity" in Chapter 2, "Joins and Cascades."

You might suppose that, because the second normal form has so many advantages, it is the highest form, but this is not the case. In fact, Codd established the third normal form and several other higher forms. This chapter discusses the third normal form because the others don't return enough extra benefit over the third normal form for the additional effort. To reach the third normal form, you still have a design flaw to correct.

Third Normal Form—Eliminate Non-Key Columns Not Dependent on the Key

What about the state data that you added? There is only one duplicate record. So is it correct? In the third normal form you look for non-key columns that are not dependent on the primary key of the table. Don't confuse an association with a dependency. The State Code key is associated with the Client data but not functionally dependent on it. This is called *transient dependency*. It's not surprising that you have duplicate values because two or more clients could be from the same state. The State Code field could function on its own in a lookup table without the Client data. Another way to look at this is that the State field is dependent on a non-key field (State Code). If a company moves and the State Code changes, the State also changes. This does not conform to the third normal form. *Good point.*

In the second normal form you eliminated partial dependencies; in the third normal form, you eliminate transient dependencies. This is an important distinction. The State Code information needs to be moved to a new table and used as a look-up table.

In the third normal form, you have eliminated redundancy, with two exceptions. The first is in the Employee ID field. This is acceptable to maintain the one-to-many relationship. The second is in the State Code field in the Client ID table. This is also acceptable since it can be maintained as a lookup if needed. The "many" side of a one-to-many relation or the "one" side of a many-to-one relation are both acceptable field values to duplicate since we are only talking about one field. The whole idea is to conserve space by using one field to link to as much information in related tables as you need. Notice in Figure 1.9 that the State Code lookup field in the Clients table is left as a link.

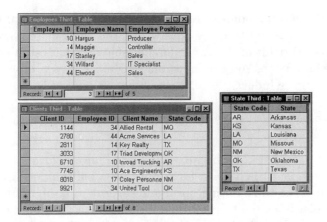

Figure 1.9: *This example of third normal form shows the elimination of transient dependencies.*

Normalizing in Access

Now you are ready for some hands on instruction. This should be easy and fun. Download ADBE.zip from www.QuePublishing.com. Unzip the files to a folder called AccessByExample on the C: drive. Open the Normalize.mdb database from the AccessByExample folder with the CustOrder table shown in Figure 1.10. This table will be analyzed by the Table Analyzer Wizard, which follows the principles of normalization presented in this chapter.

Figure 1.10: *This is the CustOrd table that will be examined by the table analyzer.*

To allow Access to automatically normalize your table for you, follow these steps:

1. Choose Tools, Analyze Table, from the Access menu to open the first page of the Table Analyzer Wizard, as shown in Figure 1.11.

NOTE

Don't let the term "Analyzer" fool you. The Table Analyzer Wizard does more than just analyze your table. It actually divides your table into smaller tables if that is what is needed. Don't worry: Your original table is always saved.

AccExamp.exe

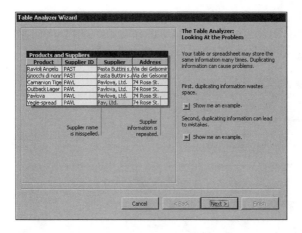

1800
382 3419

Figure 1.11: *The first page of the Table Analyzer Wizard offers examples of duplication that you are trying to avoid.*

2. The first page of the Table Analyzer Wizard contains buttons you can click for examples of duplication. Click the Show Me An Example buttons. After reading the information that the buttons retrieve, click Next. The next page, shown in Figure 1.12, is like the first one, simply instructional. Click Next after reviewing the sample buttons to open page 3 of the wizard.

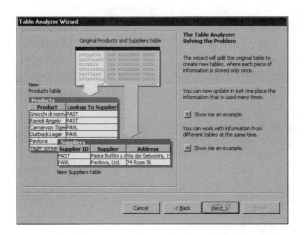

Figure 1.12: *The second page of the Table Analyzer Wizard explains that one table may be split into two or more tables.*

3. On page 3 of the wizard, choose CustOrder, and then click Next to open page 4 of the wizard. You can let the wizard decide or you can decide what fields go in what tables. For this exercise, let the wizard decide. Choose that option, and then click Next to open page 5 of the wizard.

4. Page 5 of the wizard is a diagram representing tables, fields, and relationships visually. Click the CustName field in Table3 and drag it back to Table2, as shown in Figure 1.13.

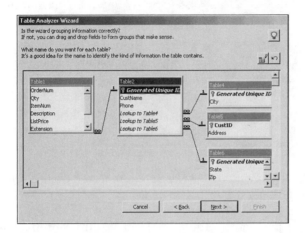

Figure 1.13: *You can move fields between tables in page 5 of the Table Analyzer Wizard.*

5. Using the same method, move every field from Table4 through Table6 to Table2. The horizontal and vertical scrollbars can also be used. Rearrange the fields to the proper order: CustID, OrderNum, CustName, Address, City, State, Zip, and Phone. Just click, hold, and drag each one to its proper place to look like Figure 1.14.

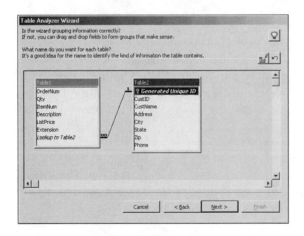

Figure 1.14: *When the fields are rearranged, you can rename the tables.*

6. Now double-click the title bar of Table2 and rename it Customers. Using the same method, rename Table1 Orders. Flip-flop the tables horizontally by dragging them with the title bar so that Customers is on the left. Accept the one-to-many relationship that Access has defined for you, and click Next to open Page 6 of the wizard.

7. When page 6 opens, you have a chance to identify primary keys in either table. Click CustID in the Customers table, and then click the Set Unique Identifier button shown in Figure 1.15. This should remove the Generated Unique ID primary key in the Customers table. Click Next to open page 7 of the wizard.

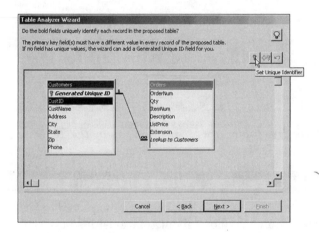

Figure 1.15: *You can set a primary key on page 6 of the Table Analyzer Wizard.*

8. Page 7 asks you if you want a query. Click No, Don't Create the Query, and then click Finish. Close the help screen after reading to view the two tables shown in Figure 1.16. That's all there is to it!

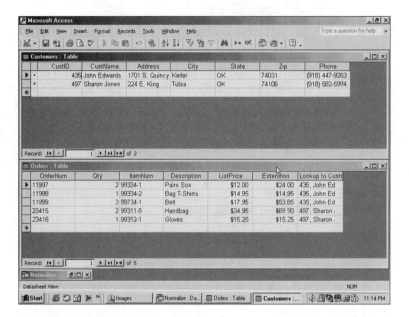

Figure 1.16: *Two tables are created for you by the Table Analyzer Wizard.*

What's Next

The fundamentals of database design were explored in this chapter. In the next chapter, you learn more about relationships between tables. Examples of joins, cascades, and referential integrity give you practical knowledge of these important topics.

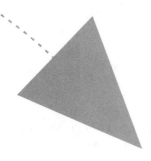

2

Joins and Cascades

Chapter 1 explored sound database design principles. You learned that you might need to break up a large table into smaller tables for better efficiency and data integrity. This chapter focuses more on the relationships between tables. To properly understand the way Access handles relationships between tables, you need to understand joins and cascades. To be more specific, you learn

- what joins are and why you should use them

- what referential integrity is

- what cascading updates and deletes are

- how to define referential integrity and cascades in the Relationships window

What are joins and why use them? Before these questions can be answered, you need to understand where to use them. The primary places in Access that you use join lines are in the query design, which can be accessed in forms and reports, and in the Relationships window. However, you can also use joins practically anywhere else in the Access workspace using SQL (Structured Query Language).

✔ For a more detailed discussion of SQL, see "Introduction to SQL" in Chapter 4, "Unleashing the Power of Queries."

You use join lines, which simply represent what is going on behind the scenes in SQL, in the query design to produce various kinds of relational results, such as conditional lookups or pre-report comparisons. You use join lines in the Relationships window to set up more permanent (though they can be changed) global joins on table relationships. The term "global" is used for joins that affect many objects in Access, such as forms, reports, and queries. For example, when you design a form in the Form Wizard and choose fields from two tables that are joined in the Relationships window, Access automatically asks you if you want a sub-form for the second table so that a one-to-many relationship can be shown. This is a handy way to enter orders for customers because you can see both the customer and his orders at a glance.

Returning to the original questions, *Access joins* are SQL operations that enable you to retrieve records from two tables that have relationships defined by two columns in those tables being linked. These relationships are one-to-one, one-to-many, or many-to-many. Functionally, a join matches records in two tables. The common field or join field must reside in both tables and have matching data. A join is most typically part of a *select* query.

Why should you use joins? Access doesn't force you to use them. However, they are a must for people who are serious about getting the most out of the relational capability of Access. Although it is possible to design some powerful queries using more than one table *without* using joins, you can get yourself into trouble if you don't know how to properly construct these types of queries.

An improperly designed query using two or more tables without joins can produce what is called a Cartesian product, which is seldom useful or desirable. The Cartesian product obtained its name from French mathematician and philosopher Rene Descartes. Although you normally produce a Cartesian product without joins, if you joined every row of one table with every row of another, you would be producing a Cartesian join, which is essentially a Cartesian product. Under normal circumstances, why would you want such a join?

If you fail to create a join between tables, these types of queries display all possible combinations of rows from every table represented in your query. To illustrate, two 60-row tables set up this way in a query produce 3,600 row results. This is because 60 times 60 equals 3,600. Without a join or a where clause in a query containing two or more tables, you can easily get confused with the results. In short, joins usually are the easiest, most efficient method of comparing and linking tables.

If you let Access normalize your tables, it creates joins for you in the Relationships window. Because it is in your best interest to get familiar with this window, take the following guided tour of what it offers.

1. From your AccessByExample folder, open the Northwind database (NWIND.MDB or NORTHWIND.MDB). You also can copy it from the Access/Office CD-ROM.

2. When you see the Northwind introductory screen, click OK, and then click the Display Database Window button.

While in Access, if you click the Relationships button (which is two buttons to the left of the question mark), you enter the Relationships window. Take a look at the tables laid out in a one-to-many relationship.

Notice that there are join lines joining the various tables. Also notice the "1" on the "one" side of the relationship and a sideways figure 8 representing the many side of the relationship, as shown in Figure 2.1.

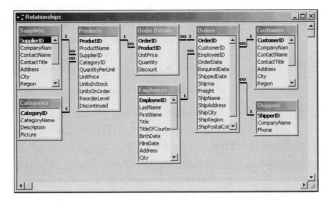

Figure 2.1: *The join lines in the Relationships window give a graphical representation of the one-to-many relationships between tables.*

3. Double-click the join line between Customers and Orders to open the Edit Relationships dialog box.

4. Click the Join Type button. The Join Properties dialog box appears, as seen in Figure 2.2.

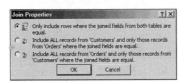

Figure 2.2: *The Join Properties dialog box shows three options that correspond to three join types available in Access.*

This is the same dialog box that you see when you join tables in a query. It is important that you understand what each of these options means so that you can properly set up your relationships between tables, whether they are between tables in the relationships window or between tables in a query.

The options in this dialog box include

1: Only Include Rows Where the Joined Fields from Both Tables are Equal—This is called an *inner join* or *equi-join*. It simply means that the values in the joined fields from both tables must be equal or match for their records to be retrieved. This is the most common type of join. It can also be used to look up values.

2: Include ALL Records From Customers and Only Those Records from Orders Where the Joined Fields are Equal—This is a *left outer join*. This means that all the records in the left table are included, but records in the right table are included only if their joined field has matching values in the joined field of the left table.

3: Include ALL Records from Orders and Only Those Records from Customers Where the Joined Fields are Equal—This is a *right outer join*. This means that all the records in the right table are included, but records in the left table are included only if their joined field has matching values in the joined field of the right table.

So in what situations would you use either of these outer join types? Suppose you had a Customers table and an Orders table that you wanted to query. The Customers was the "one" side of the "one-to-many" on the left and the "Orders" table was the "many" side of the relationship on the right. Suppose again that you want to see only the Customers that have orders. In that case, you use an inner join. But if you want to see all the orders that match and all the Customers, whether they have orders or not, then you would use a left join.

5. Close the Northwind database.

Because most people are visual learners, the following is a simple illustration by example that should help you visualize what is going on in an outer join.

1. Open Microsoft Access. If you already have Microsoft Access open, switch to the Database window.

2. Click File, New and Blank Database from the menu. Name the database Joins and then place it in the AccessByExample folder.

3. Under Objects, click Tables; then click Create Table in Design View from the Database window toolbar to open a blank table Design view.

4. After you're in Table Design view, type Value for the first field name, and press the Tab key. Type a in the Data Type field and watch

"autonumber" appear as shown in Figure 2.3. Click in the Field Name column on the blank row under Value.

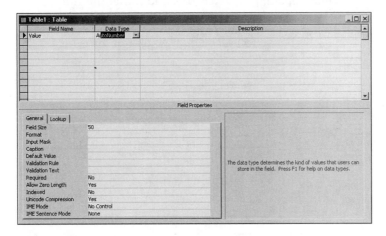

Figure 2.3: *When you type* a *in the Data Type column, AutoNumber is automatically inserted.*

5. For the next field, type Result, and make it a text field with a field size of 20. Press F6 to enter the Field Properties section and the Field Size field.

6. Click the Value field, and click the Primary Key button at the top of the screen, as shown in Figure 2.4 to make the Value field a primary key. Now you are ready to enter data.

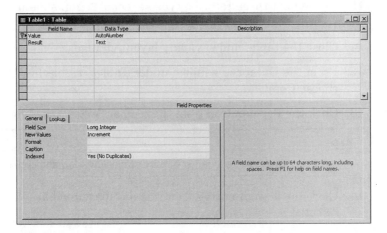

Figure 2.4: *The Primary Key button assumes that you are only entering unique values in the field in which the button is applied.*

7. Click the View button from the Database toolbar under the File menu shown in Figure 2.5. When Access prompts you to save your table before opening it, select Yes and name the file "A."

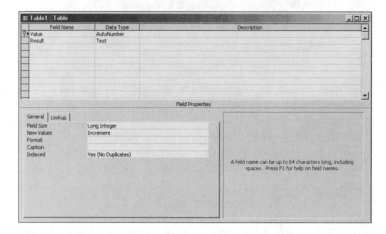

Figure 2.5: *The View button saves a step by opening the table immediately after saving it.*

8. The Value field enters sequential values automatically because it is autonumber. Type doesn't match B in the Result field.

9. While in that field, cursor down to the next record and press Ctrl+' (apostrophe) simultaneously to duplicate the previous record; then do the same for the next record.

10. In the next three records, type matches B. You should now have six records that look like Figure 2.6.

11. Close the table, and save any layout changes.

12. From the Database window under Tables, right-click table A and choose Copy.

13. Click the Paste button from the toolbar. When asked for a name, type B.

TIP

You also can right-click the Title bar of the Database window and click Paste.

---

14. Click the Design button from the database toolbar while the B table is selected.

15. Change the Value field's Data Type to Number and click the Primary Key button to remove the primary key.

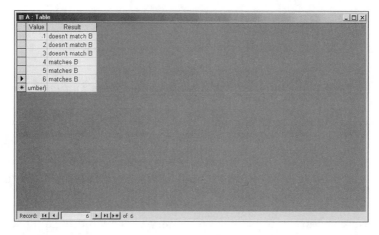

Figure 2.6: *The A table shows you which records match records from the B table.*

16. In the Field Properties section, change the Indexed field at the bottom to Yes (Duplicates OK). Click the View button and save changes.

17. You should be ready to input data, but in this case you change data. Highlight the first three rows by clicking the row selector on the left; then hold and drag it down three rows as shown in Figure 2.7.

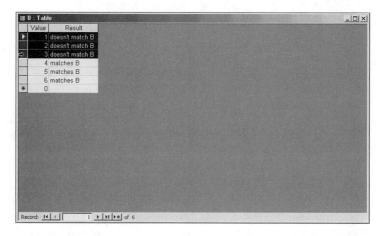

Figure 2.7: *Move the first three records in table B to a new position.*

18. Press Ctrl+X or click the Cut button from the toolbar and then click Yes to the message shown in Figure 2.8. Select the entire row from the New Record (*) position, and then click Paste from the Toolbar.

Figure 2.8: *Changing the B table to be able to join with the A table.*

19. Change the 1 through 3 in the Value field to 7 through 9.

20. Change the B in the Result field of each record to A. The numbers in the Value field should increment from 4 through 9. The text in the Result field records should either say "matches A" or "doesn't match A." Close the table.

Now you are ready to set up a query to see what is going on with joins.

1. Under Objects, click Queries, and choose New to open the New Query window.

2. Click Design View and then click OK to open the Show Table dialog box. Click A and then click the Add button. Double-click B so that you can see both methods to add tables. Choose Close.

   The Join Properties dialog box appears, as shown in Figure 2.9, later in the chapter. Notice that the Value field is automatically joined for you.

NOTE

You can turn the auto join feature on and off by clicking Tools, Options, Tables/Queries and then selecting (or deselecting) Enable Auto Join.

---

3. Double-click the Result field in the B table to copy it to the query grid.

   Notice that the "figure 8" one-to-many representation is missing. This is because a one-to-many relationship was never established in the relationships window.

4. Click the Run icon.

   Although there are six records in the B table, you should only see three matching records because those are the only records that match. They should all display matches A. What you see is an inner or equi-join. This is a one-to-one match so far.

5. Click the View button to get back to the design grid.

6. Click the drop-down box in the Result field and Table: row, change the table to A, and click the Run icon. You should retrieve three records displaying matches B.

7. After clicking back to Design view, right-click the line between tables and then choose Join Properties to open the Join Properties dialog box. You can also double-click the line, but the line must be thick (like boldface) before you double-click. If it is not thick, right-click.

8. Choose the second option (see Figure 2.9). Read what it says in option 2. You are to include ALL records from table A and only those records from table B where the join fields are equal. This is a left outer join.

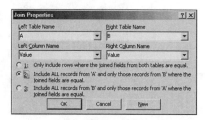

Figure 2.9: *The second option, which includes all records from the left table, represents a left outer join.*

9. Click OK and run the query. Notice that you can now see all the records, not just the records that match.

10. After returning to Design view, right-click the join line, choose join properties, and change the properties to option 3. Rerun the query.

    At this point, you should see three records with "matches B" in the Result field and three blank records.

11. Return to Design view, change the properties back to option 2 and click OK. Click the Save icon and then name the query Join. Close the query by clicking the X.

12. Click the Relationships button shown in Figure 2.10, and then click the Show Table button (a thick yellow plus sign) within the Relationships window to select the tables.

13. Select the A and B tables the way you did in the query design show table dialog box.

14. Click, hold, and drag the Value field from table A to table B, thus entering the Edit Relationships dialog box, as shown in Figure 2.11.

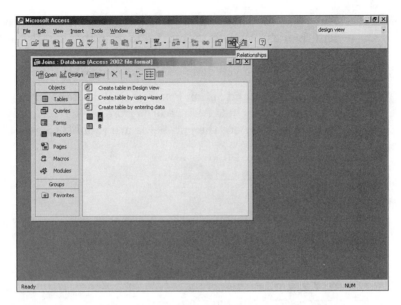

Figure 2.10: *The Relationships button opens the Relationships window, where you can define relationships in your database.*

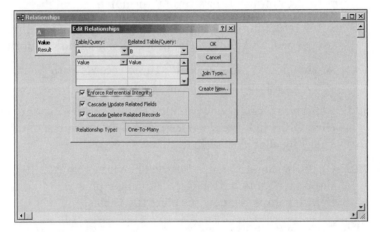

Figure 2.11: *The Edit Relationships dialog box allows you to define relationships between tables.*

15. Click the Create New button to enter the Create New dialog box, as shown in Figure 2.12. You can click the appropriate drop-down box to enter table and column names.

Figure 2.12: *The Create New dialog box shows the left and right table name as well as the fields that are the basis of the join.*

16. Click Cancel and then click the Enforce Referential Integrity check box. Click the Create button.

17. A message box explaining that referential integrity cannot be enforced displays. The reason the relationship cannot be created is that the B table violates the referential integrity rules.

18. Click OK in response to the message, and then click Cancel. Close the Relationships window and then click No to discard the changes.

Referential Integrity

Notice in Figure 2.13 that the only records that match are 4 through 6. If you hook up the two tables with a left join, then you are going to have three dangling records in table B. If table A is Customers and table B is Orders, you have orders without Customers.

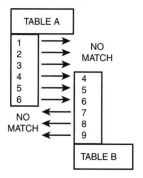

Figure 2.13: *This diagram shows that table B has no matching records for records 1 through 3 in table A.*

✳ *Referential integrity* states that a value may not be added to a table with a foreign key without a corresponding value existing in the table being referenced. In layman's terms, a matching value must exist in table A before it can be entered in table B. If a value in table A is changed, the corresponding value in table B cannot be *orphaned*. Figure 2.13 shows the referential integrity violation. If you want a left join, there are no matching records in table B for records 1 through 3 in table A.

Referential integrity should not be confused with *entity integrity*, which states that primary keys cannot contain any null values. This makes perfect sense when you consider that there is no way to have unique values if the primary key can be null.

Notice that Figure 2.13 shows both tables having values that don't match. If table A is the primary table, then non-matching values are allowed. But what about table B? Table B has orphaned records in a left join.

So what must you do to solve this dilemma? You must change records in table B to correspond to table A. To do so, follow these steps:

1. Open table B.

2. Change records with values 7 through 9 to 4 through 6. This duplicates the Value field, but that's acceptable in the related table.

3. Change the result column records that currently read doesn't match A to matches A. (You can duplicate by using Ctrl+' as you did earlier.) Exit and save the layout.

Now try enforcing referential integrity again.

1. Open the Relationships window.

2. Click on the Show Tables button, double-click table A and table B to bring them into the window. Click Close.

3. Click, hold, and drag the value field from table A to table B.

4. Click Enforce Referential Integrity, and then click the Cascade Update Related Fields and Cascade Delete Related Records options check boxes in the Edit Relationships dialog box.

5. Click the Create button, and Close the Relationships window.

6. Select Yes to save the changes.

Congratulations! You have now corrected the problem and established referential integrity. If you were not successful, go back and retrace the steps and make sure that everything was entered correctly.

Cascades

What are *cascades*? You can think of it this way: If you change a value in one table, it is automatically cascaded or updated in another table, regardless of how many records are tied to that record in the other table. Similarly, if you delete a value in one table, the corresponding records in the other table are also deleted. The former works at the field level, and the latter works at the record level. So, when you change primary key values or delete records in a primary table, Access automatically makes necessary changes to related tables so that referential integrity is preserved.

If you change a customer's number, you want his orders to be updated to reflect this change. Otherwise, his orders are not synchronized. In the same manner, if you delete this customer, you also want his orders deleted. This is another distinction from the query design.

Now let's see this principle in action by demonstrating cascading by example. First, remove the Autonumber data type property of the Value field in table A. You should do this because you cannot change an autonumber field; at least you can't do it without getting into some advanced programming.

1. With table A selected, click the Design button.

2. In the Data Type column of the Value field, click the drop-down box and then choose Number. Leave the field size as Long Integer.

   You should receive a message telling you that you cannot change the data type because it is part of one or more relationships. The solution is to temporarily delete the relationship. Click OK in response to the message and close the table without saving.

3. Open the Relationships window, click the join line between A and B, and press the delete key. Click Yes to the question that follows and close the Relationships window.

Now we can change the Value key in table A to Number (Long Integer).

1. Click the Design button of table A, change the Value field Data Type to Number and then close and save the Table.

2. Click the Relationships button to open the Relationships window.

3. Choose Join Type. Select the second option to include all records from table A and only those records from table B that match. Click OK.

4. Click the Enforce Referential Integrity box, and then click Cascade Update Related Fields and Cascade Delete Related Records.

5. Click Create. Close the Relationships window.

6. Double-click table A. Change Value 4 in table A to 7 and then open table B.

Notice two things. There is no Value 4. Two records have been replaced by Value 7. The reason that you can cascade your change now is that you selected cascade update related fields.

7. Open table A, and click the expand button (+)—sometimes referred to as the drill down button—on Value 7 to view the records that are linked. Click (-) collapse to return to normal. Then click the record selector button to the left of Value 7 and press the delete key, answering Yes to the following question about cascading deletes. Close the table.

8. Open table B.

Two corresponding records with a value of 7 in the Value column of table B were automatically deleted when you deleted one record with a value of 7 in the Value column from table A as shown in Figure 2.14. This is due to the enforcement of cascading deletes.

Figure 2.14: *If you delete a value in the one side of the relationship, cascading deletes makes sure that any corresponding values in the many side of the relationship are deleted as well.*

Printing the Relationships Window

As you build more and more relationships in your database, it becomes more difficult to see all the relationships from the window without scrolling. Access offers an easy way to print a hard copy of the Relationships window that shows all the relationships in your entire database. The graphical results are in the form of a report that can be saved. The following steps show you how:

1. Click the Relationships button; then click File, Print Relationships.

2. A report is created for you in Design view. Click the Printer icon at the top of the screen to print the relationships.

3. Access asks you if you want to save the report. If you choose to save it, it is in Reports under Objects in the Database window.

What's Next

Now that you have a better understanding of joins and cascades, the focus of the next chapter turns to the table, the heart of a database. You explore the internal structure of a table by learning what data types are all about. You also learn how to create a table and add data to it.

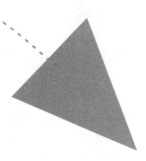

3

The Table—The Heart of Any Database

In Chapter 2, you learned about relationships between tables. This chapter explains the table and its structure, which is made up of fields. The table is the heart of a database because virtually everything that happens in the database revolves around the table. When you run a query, it is based on a table or a query based on a table. When you open a form, it is based on a table or query. You get the picture. Specifically, you learn

- about tables and the fields that make up tables
- the advantages of the rigidity of a table
- how to know what data type to use in a field
- about formats for fields
- how to test your formats

Fields—The Building Blocks of Tables

If the table is the heart of a database, then it might be said that the field is the heart of a table. A record is simply a collection of fields. Yet, if you search the Internet for a definition of a field, you'd be hard pressed to find one that adequately describes what a field is, much less what a field does. Some say that a field is the smallest database unit, but this is hardly descriptive. On the other hand, the fact that the field is so small when compared to the magnitude of today's databases gives one cause to reflect.

The cell is the smallest organic unit in the human body, yet scientists are just beginning to understand the significance of the cell in terms of diagnosing and treating a broad spectrum of human diseases. Similarly, the field is crucial to the health of a database. A *field* is simply a category, or a grouping of common values. You would not put a city in a state field, nor would you place a last name in a first name field. These categories must be meticulously maintained for accuracy.

Although Excel has introduced validity checks, you can still get away with inaccuracy and inconsistency more easily in a spreadsheet than you can in a database. In fact, this is one of the primary advantages of a database. Although databases have much more rigid structures than spreadsheets, they are far less prone to error. In addition, databases can handle large volumes of information much quicker and with much less effort than a spreadsheet, especially when they are set up and maintained properly.

The rigid structure pays dividends by forcing accuracy in input. This mostly occurs at the field level. Because the field is where you calculate, update, modify, refine, and compare data, it is not surprising that Access supplies a nice array of validity checks that you can apply to fields to maintain accuracy. For example, suppose you were entering social security numbers into a table. If you happened to enter eight instead of nine digits, you would want to know that a digit was missing. The Access input mask feature takes care of this while insuring that the dashes go in the right places.

Normalization, along with common sense, can help you determine what fields go in which tables. Common sense tells us to have all the fields in a table pertaining to only *one* subject. You don't want an employee phone number in a customer table, for example. But how much information should each field contain?

Database purists tell us that aggregate information (multiple categories) should not be in one field. For example, the city, state, and ZIP information should not be in one field. Similarly, the first name and last name should not appear in the same field. Of course, Access provides the tools to separate (*parse*) and bring together (*concatenate*) data rather easily. But you should try to keep field data in *one* category as much as possible.

A good rule of thumb is to have table data only pertain to *one* subject, and field data only pertain to *one* category. If you must break these rules, be sure you have a valid reason for doing so. A good test case is an address list. Some people like the "address1, address2" approach. This way you don't have to worry about those pesky blank lines that appear in reports. With this approach, you enter an address similar to the following:

Customer:	Ralph Jones
Address1:	2742 North Cedar
Address2:	Suite 200
Address3:	Indianapolis, IN 46290

At first, this seems like a logical reason to break the rules. You won't have to worry about the blank line when there is no second address. You just type as many address lines as you need. But what if you want to sort by ZIP code? Or what if you want to see a list of all your customers in Indiana? You can't do it without programming. It seems that you have solved one problem only to create another. This is just another reason why good design principles must be employed, and it applies not only to the organization of data in each field, but also to the type of data in each field.

Access 2002 Data Types

How do you know which data type to use for each field? Access enables you to use the text data type (default) for every field if you want to do that. But, in this instance, that approach is not wise for several reasons. You would not be able to sort numeric data properly and you would not be able to calculate the number of days between two dates at all. And this is just the tip of the iceberg.

The solution is to know the reason you are using the various data types. Let's examine these and then put them into action by example. Figure 3.1 shows the Text data type being applied. It also shows the other data types that you can use.

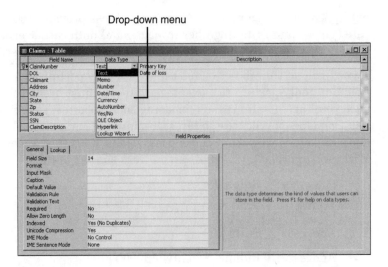

Figure 3.1: *A drop-down menu in table design showing the data type options available.*

Text

Text is probably the most common data type used in Access. It is great for address information. The default 50-character field width accommodates most addresses. It is also great for short description fields. You also can use this field for numeric data that does not require calculations, such as phone numbers and ZIP codes. But what if you have a field that is over 255 characters? Then you would go to the next data type.

Memo

The memo data type is for any fields that exceed 255 characters. A good example would be a long description field. You can type an entire paragraph or more in this field with no problem. A memo field can store up to 65,535 characters, which equates to roughly 32 pages of text. If you want to store formatted text or long documents, the OLE data type is preferred.

Number

After you select the Number data type, several settings are available for your use under the Field Size property in the Field Properties section in Design view. Table 3.1 shows which attribute to use.

Table 3.1: Numeric Field Settings

Setting	Number Size	Bytes	Description
Byte	0–255	1	Uses the least space
Integer	–32,768 to 32,767	2	Whole numbers with no decimals
Long Integer	–2,147,483,648 to 2,147,483,647	4	Larger whole numbers with no decimals
Single	Large numbers to seven decimals	4	Larger than Long Integer
Double	Huge numbers to 15 decimals	8	Larger than Single
Replication ID	Globally unique identifier	16	Establishes a unique identifier.
Decimal	Numbers from –10^28-1 through 10^28-1. To 28 decimal places	12	To 28 decimal places.

You can insert up to 27 digits on the left side of the decimal with single precision using standard formatting. Double precision goes off the scale. Let's put it this way: Unless you are a scientist or statistician, you won't even get close to exceeding the number of digits you need with double precision.

Some might say, "Why not just use double precision for every number?" They reason that by doing it that way, they will never run out of digits. The only problem with that reasoning is that they waste too much space. If you have an Autonumber field that you know will never exceed two billion, there is no reason to use Double precision. In that case, the Long Integer setting is fine.

Even if you have an abundance of space, it is not a good habit to be wasteful. When your databases grow too large, they take longer to compact, run queries, and perform calculations. If space limitations don't get your attention, then the slower speed will.

Just remember that integers are whole numbers with no decimals. When you don't need decimals and the numbers are not huge, by all means, use integers.

Date/Time

You can enter dates from January 1st, 100 to December 31st 9999. There are several date formats offered by Access, but you can also enter your own custom date formats. For example, you could enter m.d.yyyy for a custom date format, which would return 1.21.2001 format for that date. Slashes, dashes, periods, or whatever other delimiter you choose, can automatically be entered for you with an input mask. You can sort on these dates from latest to earliest if you choose ascending order and you can calculate the time span between two periods.

> ✔ To learn more about custom formatting that includes dates, see "Testing and Using Custom Formats," later in this chapter.

Currency

You can use the Currency data type if you plan to perform calculations on a field that contains data with up to fifteen digits on the left side of the decimal and up to four digits on the right side of the decimal. Whereas Single and Double precision requires floating-point calculation, the Currency data type uses a faster fixed-point calculation.

AutoNumber

You can specify sequential numbering or random numbering on integer values using this data type by selecting either option in the New Values property of the field. Access automatically inserts a value in the field for each new record. This guarantees uniqueness in the field. However, if you delete a sequential record, this field type does not renumber or reassign the deleted value. The deleted value is missing.

Yes/No

This data type limits the values entered to yes/no, on/off, or true/false. It only takes up one character of space. For example, if you want to know if an invoice was paid, you could create a Paid field that is either checked yes or no. You end up with a "toggle" field that uses only one of two possible conditions.

OLE Object

You can use this type of field to bring in objects from other programs, such as images, photographs, drawings, charts, voice mail messages, sound files, spreadsheets, and word processing documents. If you have an Employees table and want to include a picture of each employee, this is the data type to use.

Hyperlink

This is an alphanumeric field that is used as a hyperlink address to connect you to the Internet. However, you are not limited to just URLs (Universal Resource Locators). You can connect to an e-mail address, a Microsoft Office document, a table, query, form, report, or data access page. To use the hyperlink datatype for e-mail, enter `mailto://` followed by the address. For example, type `mailto://JohnSmith@hotmail.com`.

Lookup Wizard

This wizard creates a Lookup field that helps you when you have a long list of codes. This way, you can see at a glance which value goes with what code. If you want to know the code for a certain customer, for example, and you are in the order table, use this data type to look up customers.

> ✔ To learn about other ways to look up values, see "How to Use DAO and ADO to Manipulate Data" in Chapter 12, "Access Visual Basic Tools, Tips, and Techniques."

Testing and Using Custom Formats

Suppose you have a nonstandard date or number format that you want to use. Tables 3.2 and 3.3 help you understand the symbols used to create custom date and number formats.

Table 3.2: Date Formats

Symbol	Represents
/ (slash), – (dash), or . (period)	Separators to delimit date values
d	Day of the month in numbers with no zero added for single digit days
dd	Day of the month in numbers with zero added for single digit days
ddd	The first three letters of the weekday (Sun through Sat)
dddd	The full name of the weekday (Sunday through Saturday)
w	Day of the week (1–7)
ww	Week of the year (1–53)
m	Month of the year in numbers with no zero added for single digit months
mm	Month of the year in numbers with zero added for single digit months
mmm	The first three letters of the month (Jan through Dec)
mmmm	The full name of the month (January through December)
yy	The last two digits of the year (01 through 99)
yyyy	The full year (2001 through 9999)

Table 3.3: Number Formats

Symbol	Represents
. (period)	Decimal separator
, (comma)	Thousand separator
0	Number if a number, nothing if blank (null), 0 if zero
#	Number if a number, nothing if blank, nothing if zero
$	Literal character $
%	Percentage value times 100 with percent sign added

Now let's demonstrate a method to test your formats before you enter them into a table, form, or report. After you try a few of these formats, the charts become more meaningful.

Testing Your Formats

In the following example, an old basic convention is used. The question mark (?) represents Print. You are simply saying, "Print the following to the screen." In functions, commas separate arguments.

An *argument* is a value passed to the function, which can be another function, a field, a constant, a variable, or an expression. A *constant* is simply a raw number or alpha value that does not change, as opposed to a variable. A *variable* acts as a container that holds changing values. An *expression* in Access can contain a combination of fields, functions, constants, and operators resulting in a formula. An example of an expression is [InvoiceAmt] * .08. [InvoiceAmt] is a field, * is an operator, and .08 is a constant.

In the function format(date, "mm/dd/yy"), format is the function. Date is another function used as an argument. In the second argument, mm, dd, and yy are used as variables, while the slashes (/) are used as constants.

1. While in the Access Database window, press Ctrl+G. This takes you into the Immediate window of Visual Basic.

2. Type ? format(date, "dddd, mmmm dd, yyyy") and press Enter. For St. Patrick's Day of 2001, this should return Saturday, March 17, 2001. Your date will differ, but the format should be similar.

3. Type ? format(date, "m/d/yyyy") and press Enter. This should return 3/17/2001 for St. Patrick's Day. If your date was 12/02/2001, it would return 12/2/2001. Check Table 3.2.

4. Type ? format(date, "dd-mmm-yy") and press Enter. This should return 17-Mar-01 or something similar for your date.

5. Finally, type ? format(date, "mm.dd.yyyy.") and press Enter. This should return 03.17.2001 for that date.

6. Now for some number formats. Type ? `format(2000.00, "#,##0")` and press Enter. This should return 2,000.

7. Type ? `format(00, "0.00")` and press Enter. This should return 0.00. Notice the first zero is gone. Type ? `format(00, "#.##")` and press Enter. What's the difference? This last format is not suggested, but it gives you an idea of what's happening.

8. Type ? `format(9864, "$#,##0.00")` and press Enter. This should return $9,864.00. Close the Immediate window.

Using the Immediate window to practice has given you several advantages:

- You now can enter custom formats with confidence because you understand the inner workings of the formats.

- You have an introduction to the Immediate window, which you will use later to test functions.

- You have an understanding of how the built-in Access function format works.

Building an Access 2002 Table

The following steps lead you through building this table from scratch using different quality checks and data types:

1. Open the Claims.mdb database from your AccessByExample folder.

2. Under Objects, click Tables; then click New to open the New Table dialog box.

3. Click the second option, Design View, when the next window appears, and then click OK to open table Design view.

4. After typing `ClaimNumber`, tab to the Data Type column. Notice that a down arrow automatically appears. You can choose any of the data types after clicking the down arrow. In this case, accept the default.

5. Click the Primary Key button to make it a primary key and then click on Field Size in the lower part of the window (or press F6).

6. Set the field size to 14, and then click on the blank space in the Field Name column under ClaimNumber. Type `DOL` (date of loss) for the next field.

7. Tab to the Data Type column, but this time start typing the `d` in Date/Time and watch it appear. Accept this data type by tabbing to the Description column type "Date of Loss," as shown in Figure 3.2.

Acronym

What the acronym
stands for

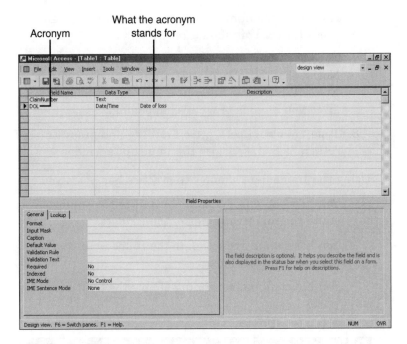

Figure 3.2: *In fields that have an acronym, you can type what the acronym stands for in the description field as a reminder.*

8. Press F6 to enter the Field Properties section. Click the drop-down box in the Format field; then choose Short Date. Click the Validation Rule field in the Field Properties section.

NOTE

A validation rule is used as a basis against which field data can be checked when the user leaves the field. This is one of the things that sets a database apart. It's much easier to prevent the user from entering invalid data during data entry than to go back after the fact and correct every mistake.

---

9. Click the expression builder (...) and then type not > date() in the window. Click OK.

10. Click Validation Text, and type Enter a date that is equal to or less than today's date in the box, as shown in Figure 3.3.

11. Press F6 or click to the blank row under DOL. Type Claimant in the Field Name column, and then cursor down to the next field. Notice that it automatically places a default value of Text data type with a 50-character field length (unless you have set another default field size in Tools, Options, Tables/Queries).

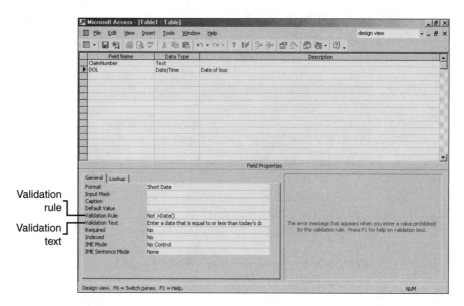

Figure 3.3: *You can use the Validate rule to be sure the input data is correct and the Validation text to notify the user what the proper value should be.*

12. In the Field Name column under Claimant, type Address. Click the Required field in the Field Properties section. (The default field size will be entered.) Notice that a down arrow appears. Click the drop-down box and choose Yes. This means you cannot avoid entering information in this field.

TIP

Double-clicking also toggles the yes/no state.

---

13. Type City in the blank row below Address, and then cursor down to the blank row below. Type State, press F6, and change the Field Size to 2.

14. In the blank row below State, type Zip, and press F6 and change the Field Size to 10. Click the blank row below Zip, type Status. Press F6 to go the Field Size box and change it to 1.

15. Click the Default Value field and type O for open. This value is automatically inserted into a new record; however, it can be changed.

16. Type SSN in the blank row under Status. Click the Field Size box, and change it to 11.

17. In the Field Properties section, click the input mask and then on the ellipses (...) on the side. Click Yes when asked if you want to save the

table first and save the table as Claims. The Input Mask Wizard opens. Click the Social Security option and try it with your own Social Security number, as shown in Figure 3.4.

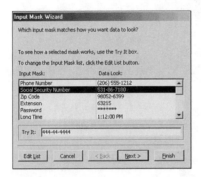

Figure 3.4: *The Input Mask Wizard enables you to try the mask while still in table Design view.*

18. Click Next and then finish the wizard.

19. Under SSN, type ClaimDescription. Press Tab and change the Data Type to Memo.

20. Under ClaimDescription, type ClaimAmount. Press Tab and change the data type to Number; then click Field Size and change it to Double.

21. Under the Field Size box, click Format and change it to Standard.

22. Under the Format box, change Decimal Places to 0, and then click the Save button.

23. Click the View button. This is actually a short cut. Rather than having to Exit design view and open the table, this is a one-click procedure to prepare you to enter data.

Entering Data

Because the most essential component of any database is the data itself, the importance of data entry should not be underestimated. When data is properly validated, errors are minimized.

In the next example, you can play the role of a data entry typist to test the validation checks that you have configured at each field. The goal is to fill in the data to match Figure 3.5, tabbing immediately after each entry.

Figure 3.5: *Entering data into a newly created table to test the validation checks and data types.*

1. Type 12345 in the ClaimNumber field, and then press Tab.

2. When you reach the DOL column, enter tomorrow's date. For example, if today is 3/15/2001, enter 3/16/2001. Press Tab. You should receive the message that you typed in the Validation Text field in table Design view. Go back and enter today's date.

3. Enter John Smith in the Claimant field and press the Tab key. In the Address field, tab to the next field without entering data. Nothing should happen. Return to the Address field and enter 123 N. Main.

NOTE

If you do not enter data in a field, you create a null field entry. The reason that nothing happens when you press Tab is that the Required property is enforced at the table level by Jet. However, you do get an error message if you try to exit the table or move to the next record.

4. In the City column type Anywhere, and in the State column, type OK. In the Zip column, type 74107, and in the Status column, press Tab. The "O" should be inserted automatically because Status is a default field.

5. Type in the SSN. Type only 444-44-444 and press Tab. You should receive a validation message telling you that the value you entered is not appropriate. Click OK; then go back and type the last 4.

6. In the ClaimDescription column, type Claimant fell from ladder and broke his leg. You can type on and on in this column. You won't run out of space because this is a Memo field. Press Tab.

7. Type 3000.00 in the ClaimAmount column and click the ClaimDescription column. The two decimal places should disappear.

NOTE

A number between 2999.50 and 2999.99 rounds to 3000. On the other hand, any number between 2999.01 and 2999.49 rounds to 2999. Because this number was formatted with the Standard format with no decimal places, the two zeros after the decimal are dropped.

8. Exit the table by clicking the X at the top-right corner of the table title bar.

CAUTION

If you try to enter another record with the same Claim number, you will generate an error message. That's because the ClaimNumber field is a primary key.

Explanation of Limitations

Why would you place so many restrictions on the table you just created? You want your data to be as error-free as possible. You will discover that there are provisions in Access to check data after the fact, but why not check data as you input it? The users aren't annoyed with any messages *unless* they type something that is incorrect. If the current month is March, it's easy to accidentally type a 4 instead of a 3 for the month. Access doesn't allow that entry with the validation rule you established. The user is notified of the problem and when it is corrected, he or she can continue.

Although you can't totally eliminate human error, you can minimize the chances of errors occurring. When large amounts of data are entered, input speed can also be increased. For example, if a typist is entering social security numbers, having the dashes automatically entered into the field can increase typing speed. Even if it increases the speed by just a fraction of a second on every record, those fractions add up over a long period of typing.

The Table Is the Center

Returning to our original proposition, why is the table the heart of the database? Simply put, the table is the center of everything in the database. Queries, forms, reports, macros, and modules all revolve around the table. Just as a table should be about one subject, a database should be about one theme. For example, within a client database, you might have an Employees table that shows you which employees work with which clients. But you might also include a Projects table. The theme is clients, but there might be many aspects of that theme. Or you can look at it as the database being about one main topic and the tables contained therein being about subtopics.

Access has added another tool to help you further delineate your database. Now you can group your tables, reports, and forms that are related to the same or similar category. Even though a field is a category, this is a category of a broader scope. Just as a field is a category of common values, an Access group is a category of common objects. For example, you can have all the reports related to invoices in one group, or all the tables related to projects in another group. You can mix and match tables, reports, forms, and modules into a group. You determine the commonality of the objects.

It all boils down to organizing and categorizing information. The table is the best tool to do that. But tables must be organized, as well. The forms primarily help you with inputting the information, and the reports help you with outputting the information.

What's Next

In the next chapter, you discover how to get the most out of your tables using queries. You see, a database is not only about organizing information. It is also about controlling, manipulating, comparing, summarizing, and forecasting information. The query is a powerful tool that can enable you to do it all.

controlling
manipulating
comparing
summarizing
forecasting information

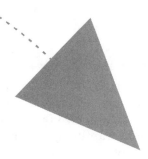

Unleashing the Power of Queries

In Chapter 3, "The Table: The Heart of Any Database," you learned how to build a table and prepare it for data entry. This chapter focuses on why a query is so invaluable when it comes to updating and manipulating table data.

In this chapter, you learn how to

- create queries using the Access query grid
- use query types
- use the SQL language
- sort and group
- use wildcards

Queries Ask Questions

You discovered in the last chapter that the table is the heart of the database. A good database plan can help you organize your table data. But organization is not the only function of a database. You might need to compare last year's table with this year's table. Or you might want to update one field's data throughout the entire table. Or you might need to compute the sales tax on all the invoices in the table. And the list goes on. In other words, you need a vehicle that can manipulate and examine data in a variety of different ways.

What is a *query*? It is simply a program that asks a question pertaining to table data. You can consider a query a description of the records you want to retrieve from your table data. That description usually includes a *criterion* (plural, criteria), which is a condition or a test by which record selection is determined. This condition in the query takes the form of an expression, which was covered in Chapter 3. How many claims in the state of Missouri are more than $5,000 in the period between July 1, 1994, and June 30, 1995? This is a typical question that could easily be converted to a criterion for a query.

Queries Access Records

The query is the perfect tool to manipulate tables. So far, substantial space has been devoted to topics involving fields and tables. But what about records? With queries, records come to the forefront. A table is a set of records, whereas a record is a set of fields. You might not need to see all the records or fields in a particular table. With a query, you pick and choose which records and fields you want to see.

Queries produce *subsets*, which are the records that match the query conditions. A table is a set of records; a subset is a *set of a set* of records. You might not need to see every state in your table. What if you just want to examine the Texas records? Or what if you want to see totals of all the states? Queries powerfully handle these kinds of requests.

The subsets are viewed as *datasheets*, which look exactly like table datasheets. There is, however, one important distinction: Query datasheets are temporary; table datasheets are permanent. Table datasheets represent stored data on a disk or similar storage media. The temporary nature of query datasheets can work to your advantage because you can bring two or more tables together in a query producing a large table that doesn't have to be stored, thus taking up disk space. It can then be brought into a form or report.

The Query Grid

The query grid has a table-like structure. You can select and move fields around in a grid using the same technique you used to move fields in tables. But first you must select which table(s) you want in the query. From there, you double-click or drag the fields you want down to the grid. The field order that you select is the same order that is reflected in the results. Unlike a table, you don't see individual records, but you do have the ability to describe which fields and records you want to retrieve.

The QBE (Query By Example) design is much easier to implement than directly writing or issuing SQL code. There's no need to write SQL code manually, because QBE creates SQL code for you. But in Design view, you simply cursor to the appropriate field(s), type in a sample criterion, and click the Run icon to view your results. Figure 4.1 shows an example of a QBE criterion that is ready to be run.

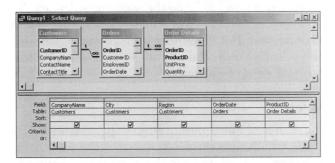

Figure 4.1: *Use Query By Example in the query Design view to create your criteria.*

Understanding Query Types

Although Access displays six query types in its drop-down menu, you can divide those into three categories: select queries, action queries, and crosstab queries. Select queries produce subsets displayed as datasheets. These datasheets might or might not be updateable, depending on several factors. The select query, in and of itself, does not change table data. It simply allows you to view and possibly edit subset data (after the query is run) from a variety of different perspectives. You can pull the results of the query into a form or report. It is the most common query type.

✔ To learn more about updating datasheets, see "Understanding Dynasets and Their Underlying Tables," later in this chapter.

The action query, on the other hand, changes a set of records in just one operation. There are four types of action queries: make-table, update, append, and delete. The make-table query makes a new table from one or more tables in the query design. The update table changes field data in the underlying table. The append query copies (adds) records from one table into another. The delete query deletes records from a table based on criteria.

Think of a crosstab query as a way to look at a table from a different perspective. It performs aggregate calculations on the values of a database field using one or more fields as row headings and one field's data as column headings.

Query Types

Which type of query should you use? It depends on what you want to do. You have to be more careful with action queries because they have the capability to change large volumes of information almost effortlessly. However, there is no way to undo these changes. In fact, before running any action query, Access displays a message warning you that the changes cannot be undeleted. But if you just want to ask questions and print the results, the select query is the way to go. Let's examine the various query types in greater detail by example.

Select Query

Behind the scenes of query design is an SQL statement. The SELECT statement in SQL, which runs the select query, is the driving force behind SQL. The word "select" is used because the queries select records. While you're at it, take a peek behind the Select query to see the SQL code that controls it. The following steps will introduce you to both the query grid and SQL. You can think of them as two ways to view your query before it is run.

1. From the AccessByExample folder, open the Claims database.

2. Under Objects in the Database window, click Queries to view a list of queries, as shown in Figure 4.2.

3. Click the New button to open the New Query dialog box, as shown in Figure 4.3.

4. Be sure that Design is selected, and then click OK. The Show Table dialog box opens, as shown in Figure 4.4.

5. Choose the Tables tab, if necessary. Double-click the Losses table, click the Close button to close the Show tables dialog box, and display the Losses table (see Figure 4.5).

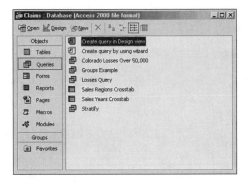

Figure 4.2: *When you click on Queries under Objects in the database window, you see a list of stored queries.*

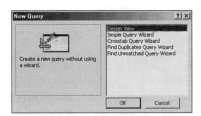

Figure 4.3: *You can either click Design view from the list of options in the New Query dialog box or choose from a list of wizards to run.*

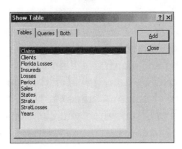

Figure 4.4: *The Show Table dialog box displays a list of tables and queries that can be added to your query Design window.*

6. Double-click the title bar of the Losses table to select all the fields.

7. Click, hold, and drag the selected fields in the table as shown in Figure 4.6 to bring all the fields down to the query grid.

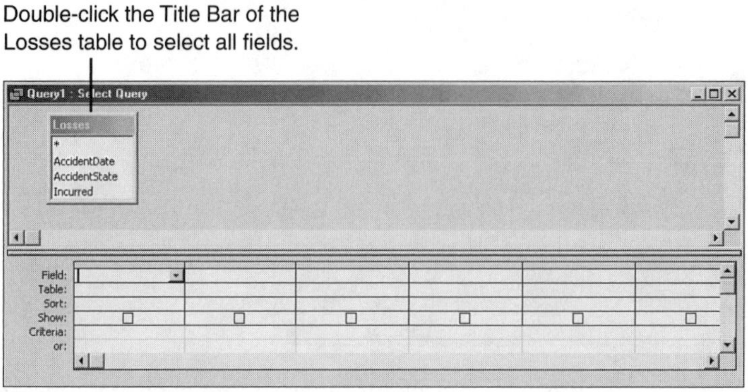

Double-click the Title Bar of the
Losses table to select all fields.

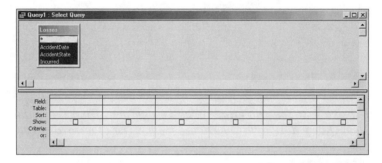

Figure 4.5: *Once you add a table to the query Design view, you can select any field listed to add to the query Design grid.*

Figure 4.6: *When the fields are selected, drag them down to the query grid.*

8. In the criteria section of the `AccidentDate` field type `>=7/1/97 AND <7/1/98` to display the records that are greater than or equal to 7/1/97 and less than 7/1/98. Notice the pound signs (#) that Access requires for dates are automatically entered when you click or cursor to another field.

CAUTION

Even though the pound signs (#) are automatically inserted when a date or date expression is entered as criterion in the query grid, keep in mind that the query grid is the only place in Access that enters the pound signs automatically. For that reason, it's not a bad idea to get in the habit of entering the pound signs manually.

You now have a date range criteria as shown in Figure 4.7. Any dates that fall within the range of 7/1/97 and 6/30/98 will be included. However, 7/1/98 will not be included because the criterion reads "<" or less than 7/1/98. Using "between 7/1/97 and 6/30/98" includes 6/30/98 because this clause is inclusive on both sides of the "And" operator.

Click the View button
to access SQL view

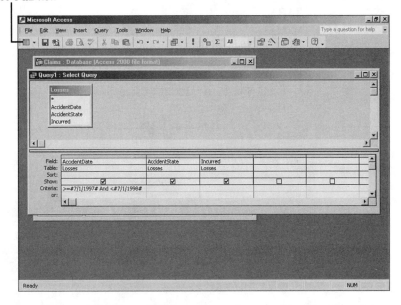

Figure 4.7: *You can enter a date expression that is a description of records between two dates that will be retrieved.*

To examine the query in SQL view, click View, and then choose SQL View. Notice the date range in the criteria as shown in Figure 4.8.

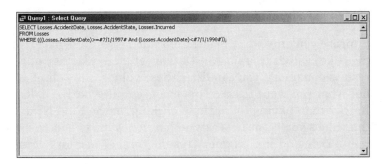

Figure 4.8: *The SQL view of the date range query shows the SQL statement behind the query Design view.*

Now you can take a look at the query results by running the query. To discover how you can manipulate data after the query is run, follow these steps:

1. Switch back to the Design view by clicking View, Design.

TIP

You can run the Query from either view. For example, you can either click Run or click Datasheet View on the View menu to see the query results, regardless of whether you are in query Design view or SQL view.

---

2. Click the Run button to run the query. You should see the results of the query, as shown in Figure 4.9. This is the subset mentioned previously and shown in Datasheet view.

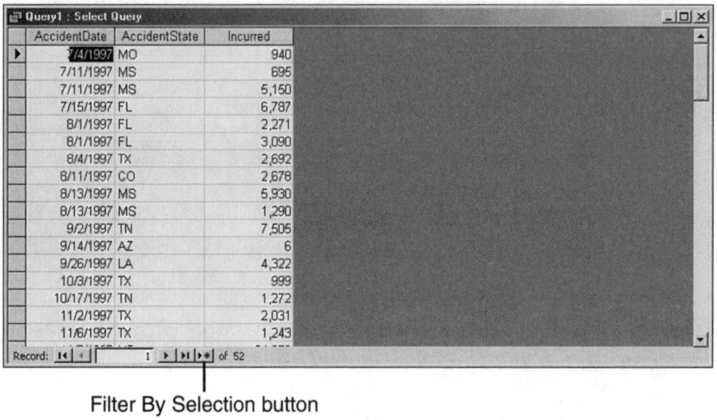

Filter By Selection button

Figure 4.9: *You can change the way you look at the data even after the query has run.*

Suppose you only want to see Colorado losses. Whenever you have repeating "like" values in a field in Datasheet view, whether in a table or in the results of a query, you can *filter* these values, thus eliminating everything but what you want to see. This is a great alternative to looking up values. Rather than having to continue clicking on the Find Next button, just filter the values you want to see, whether you want to edit them or just examine them. Using a filter on query results further narrows down your selection of records.

The following steps show how easy it is to apply a temporary filter so you can focus on only one state:

1. Click any CO value in the AccidentState field (refer to Figure 4.9, if necessary.

2. Click the Filter By Selection button. Notice, as shown in Figure 4.10, that the results are filtered, which is indicated at the bottom of the window.

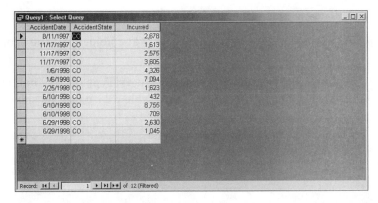

Figure 4.10: *After applying the Filter By Selection button, you see only the Colorado records in the datasheet.*

3. Click the Remove Filter button to remove the filter and return to the original subset.

4. Close the query, and then save it as Select Example.

Make Table Query

The Make Table query is the only Access query type that actually creates another table from the table on which your query is based. The resulting table usually is smaller than the source table. For example, suppose your boss approaches you and tells you that he needs a table with all the losses over or equal to $10,000 to pull into a spreadsheet for statistical analysis. He needs it sorted by date (latest claims first), and he also needs to see the state. Whether he realizes it or not, he is asking you to create a query that turns out results based on his criteria into a table.

A smaller table is also a faster table. This can be a great tool to use when working with large tables. To create a make table query, follow these steps:

1. Under Objects, click Queries.

2. Double-click Create query in Design view, and then double-click the Losses table from the Show Table dialog box that appears. Close the Show Tables dialog box.

3. Double-click the title bar of the Losses table to select all the fields.

4. Click, hold, and drag the selected fields in the table down to the query grid.

5. Cursor to or click the Incurred field in the Criteria row of the query grid.

6. Type >=10000 (four zeros) for a criterion.

7. In the sort row of the AccidentState field, click the drop-down box, and then choose Ascending.

8. Click the drop-down box of the Query Type button, and choose Make Table Query to open the Make Table dialog box, as shown in Figure 4.11.

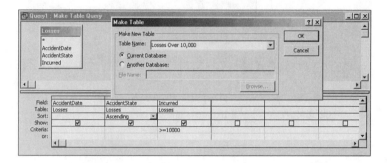

Figure 4.11: *The Make Table query dialog box produces another table based on the criteria you enter in the query grid.*

9. Type Losses Over 10,000 in the Table Name text box, and then click OK.

10. Run the query. A message box opens to inform you that you are about to paste 47 rows into a new table to warn you that you cannot reverse these changes.

11. Click Yes to finish the query; then close and save the query as Make Table Example.

12. Click Tables and double-click Losses Over 10,000 to view the results of the query.

Append Query

An Append query copies records from one table into another table, "appending" them after the last record. It is important to keep in mind that you are not removing records from the original table. To illustrate, your boss tells you that the Florida division of the company was sold. It is not needed in the claims analysis, but he would like to preserve it in a separate table by extracting it from the Losses table for later archiving. This requires two queries. First, place a copy of those records in another table, then delete them from the original table to complete the extract, which is similar to cutting and pasting them into another table.

1. Click Tables under Objects; then right-click the Losses table, and choose Copy.

2. Click the Paste button, and choose Structure Only under Paste Options.

3. Name the Table Florida Losses and then click OK.

4. Under Objects, click Queries.

5. Double-click Create Query in Design view. When the Show Tables dialog box appears, choose the Losses table by double-clicking it. Close the Show Tables dialog box.

6. Double-click the title bar of the Losses table to select all the fields.

7. Click, hold, and drag the selected fields in the table down to the query grid.

8. Type FL in the criteria row for AccidentState.

9. Click the drop-down box of the Query Type button.

10. Choose Append as your query type. When the Append dialog box appears, choose the Florida Losses table from the Table Name drop-down box and click OK.

The correct field names are automatically inserted in the Append To row from the Florida Losses table in the grid (see Figure 4.12). This happens because the field names match. You are appending to an empty table, but you can just as easily append to a table with records. Neither the number of fields nor the field names in both tables have to match. You can even get away with some data type conversion, but be careful. For example, you can create another table that has an identical structure to the Florida Losses table except that the Incurred field is textual rather than numeric. Access enables you to append from the Florida Losses table to this table or vice versa. But be aware that you could lose decimal places in the process.

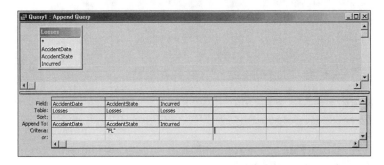

Figure 4.12: *Because you enter FL as criterion for the Append query, only Florida records are appended into the Florida Losses table.*

When you run the query, you will be copying the Florida records from the Losses table into the newly created Florida Losses table. Remember that you only copied <u>the structure</u> of the Losses table and named it Florida Losses. Therefore, the Florida Losses table is blank and ready to receive records. The following steps will accomplish this:

1. Run the query. A message box appears, asking if you are sure you want to append the selected rows. Click Yes.

2. Click the Save button and save the query as Append Example. Stay in the query.

Now that you have appended the data, you need to delete it from the old table. These two queries combined (the one you just ran [Append query] and the one you are about to run [Delete query]) constitute moving rather than copying data from one table to another.

Delete Query

The delete query actually removes records from a table based on criterion. In this case, you already have the correct criterion for your delete query; you just need to change the query type. This deletes the very records that you just copied (appended) to another table, thus completing the process:

1. Click the drop-down box of the Query Type button.

2. Change the type to Delete Query.

3. Run the query. Again, a message box opens, asking if you are sure you want to delete the selected records, as shown in Figure 4.13. Click Yes.

Figure 4.13: *As with all action queries, the delete query has a warning message informing you that the changes cannot be reversed.*

4. Click File, Save As, and then save it as Delete Example. Click OK, and close the query.

Update Query

The update query actually changes *existing* underlying table data while the other action queries change by either adding or subtracting data, or by creating an entirely new table. Consequently, update queries are a powerful tool that enables you to modify large volumes of data very quickly.

Be forewarned, however, that although the original condition of tables from other action queries can be recovered rather easily, this action query could cost you some recovery time. And because this action cannot be undone, it's wise to make a habit of copying the table you want to change every time you run this query. The following steps show how to create an Update query based on two tables:

1. Make a copy of the Losses table, calling it Losses Backup. As you did in the append example, right-click and choose Copy. Click the Paste button, but this time accept the default of Structure and Data as you name the table to Losses Backup.

2. Click Queries under Objects and double-click Create Query in Design view.

3. This time, when the Show Tables dialog box appears, double-click the States table and the Losses Backup table before closing the Show Tables dialog box.

4. As shown in Figure 4.14, click, hold, and drag the Code field in the States table over to the AccidentState field in the Losses Backup table and release the left mouse button. This creates an inner join between the two fields signified graphically by the line between fields in the two tables.

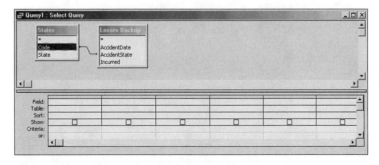

Figure 4.14: *Dragging the* Code *field in the States table to the* AccidentDate *field in the Losses Backup table creates an inner join between the tables.*

5. Double-click the AccidentState field in the Losses Backup table to bring it to the query grid.

6. Choose Update Query from the drop-down Query Type button. Note that the Update To: row is automatically inserted.

7. In the Update To: row type `states!state` and press the down-arrow key. Notice that the brackets are automatically inserted, as shown in Figure 4.15.

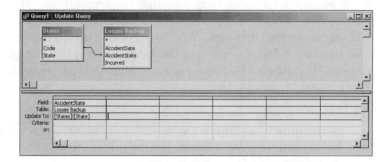

Figure 4.15: *The inner join can be used in an Update query to change field data in the right table based on the data in the left table.*

You are telling the query to match the `Code` field from the States table with the `AccidentState` field (abbreviations) in the Losses table. Figure 4.16 shows what information is in the States table. This confirms that the field names do not have to match, but the data should match in a join. You are telling the computer, "When the codes match, substitute the full state name for the abbreviation." If the code is CO, the program will substitute Colorado.

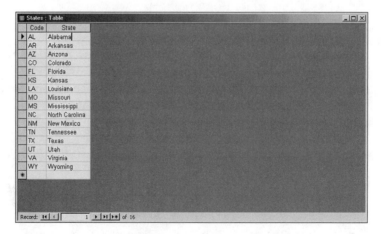

Figure 4.16: *This information in the States table is used to update the information in the Losses Backup table.*

8. Run the query, and close the query saving it as Update Example.

9. Click on Tables, and then double-click the Losses Backup table to view the results as shown in Figure 4.17.

AccidentDate	AccidentState	Incurred
6/29/1993	Mississippi	514
6/29/1993	Mississippi	1,523
6/29/1993	Mississippi	1,135
6/29/1993	Mississippi	746
7/20/1993	Colorado	4,840
8/20/1993	Colorado	73,025
8/20/1993	Colorado	39,305
8/20/1993	Florida	1,215
8/20/1993	Colorado	67,772
8/20/1993	Florida	457
8/20/1993	Colorado	88,191
8/20/1993	Wyoming	376,807
8/22/1993	Colorado	8,198
8/22/1993	Colorado	11,708
8/22/1993	Colorado	5,963
8/23/1993	Colorado	4,874
8/24/1993	Florida	1,301
8/25/1993	Colorado	9,013
9/8/1993	Wyoming	5,150
9/14/1993	Texas	2,822
10/15/1993	Colorado	30,900
10/15/1993	Colorado	4,458

Figure 4.17: The AccidentState *field in the Losses Backup table after update to full state names.*

Crosstab Query

This query is unique in several ways. No other query type turns a field's table data into column headings. This is in contrast to Excel's Paste Special, Transpose command where the columns become rows and the rows become columns but the data stays the same, adjusted for the new coordinates. The Crosstab query uses one or more columns for the row headings on the left while using another column's *data* for the column headings on the top. It uses Aggregate functions such as Sum or Count to produce a spreadsheet-like result. No other query type so drastically changes the way you view the data. Rows and columns can be readjusted to suit your individual needs.

1. Under Objects, click Queries.

2. Click New, and then double-click the Crosstab Query Wizard from the New Query dialog box.

3. On page 1 of the wizard, click Table: Sales to select it, and click Next to open page 2.

4. On page 2 of the wizard, choose the Region field as a row heading by double-clicking it, and click Next.

5. On page 3, choose the Year field as a column heading (it should already be selected) and click Next (see Figure 4.18).

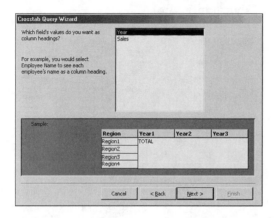

Figure 4.18: *Selecting column headings is easy using the Crosstab Query Wizard.*

6. On page 4, the Sales field is selected, but choose Sum under Functions on the right, as shown in Figure 4.19, and click Next.

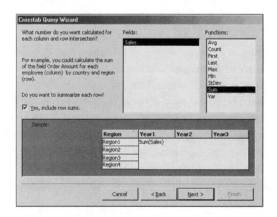

Figure 4.19: *By choosing Sum for the Sales field, you create an aggregate total.*

7. Accept the default of View Query, but delete the underline on the query name substituting Years to read Sales Years Crosstab, and click Finish to view the results.

8. Click View (the blue triangle) to switch to Design view. On the Field row in the grid, click Sales, and then right-click and choose Properties. Under format, type #,##0. Close the Field Properties sheet.

9. On the field row of the Total of Sales column, right-click and choose Properties. Under format, type #,##0.

TIP

Rather than closing the Field Properties sheet and one field and then right-clicking the next field, you can click the next field in the grid that you want to format (assuming that the Field Properties sheet is sized small enough to see the query grid) while you have the first field's property sheet open. The next field's property sheet will open.

---

10. Click Run to see the formatting results; then Click Save (since you have already supplied the name, you are just saving the formatting) and close the query.

Although the next Crosstab query is similar to the previous query, it uses different fields for a totally different perspective. The following steps guide you through the creation of the query:

1. Under Objects, choose Queries.

2. Click New, click Crosstab Query Wizard, and click OK.

3. On page 1 of the wizard, choose Table:Sales and click Next.

4. On page 2, double-click Year and choose Next.

5. On page 3, leave Region highlighted and click Next.

6. One page 4, click Sum under Functions for the Sales field and click Next.

7. Name the query Sales Regions Crosstab and click Finish to view the query.

8. To format the fields, complete steps 8 through 11 for the Sales Regions Crosstab query.

9. Compare the two queries paying special attention to the column headings.

10. Compare your results to Figure 4.20.

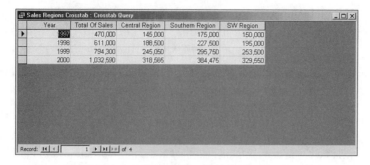

Figure 4.20: *In the transformed perspective of the crosstab query results, table data turns into column titles.*

Introduction to SQL

Now that you have had a glimpse of what SQL can do, let's take a closer look. SQL is a standard for which every major relational database management system (DBMS) has a version. After you learn it, it's not difficult to begin learning and using the SQL versions of other database systems.

You can construct queries directly in the SQL, but strict syntax (language rules) must be applied if you want to run your query. One of the things that sets Access SQL apart is its capability to interpret queries in both directions. This means that you can type SQL statements directly into the SQL window and immediately see the equivalent QBE Design view before running the query. Likewise, you can construct a QBE query and immediately see its counterpart in the SQL window.

Consider what this means. An SQL expert can learn Access QBE very quickly by constructing SQL queries and examining the query design counterpart. Conversely, a user who has mastered QBE can begin to learn and use SQL by examining the equivalent SQL commands.

Another SQL advantage is that you can cut and paste SQL code into Visual Basic with just a few modifications. This is not the only place that SQL can be used in Access, as you shall see, but it is a powerful way to consecutively run multiple queries, which in turn can be used to automate important repetitive tasks.

The beginner sometimes finds SQL intimidating, but the basics are fairly straightforward. The best place to start is the SELECT statement. Table 4.1 shows the basic SQL syntax. Italics represent optional statements for this example only; not for actual code.

Table 4.1: SQL Clause Explanations

Clause	Clause Counterpart	Function
SELECT	Field list	Fields to include
FROM	Table list	Tables or queries from which to select records
WHERE	Expression	Description of restrictions (criterion)
ORDER BY	Field list or Expression	Sort Order

If you want to see *all* the fields and records in the Claims table, enter the following SELECT statement:

```
SELECT *
FROM Claims;
```

Is this simple enough? If you only want to view the CustomerName and the CustomerPhone columns from the Customer table, use the following syntax:

```
SELECT CustomerName, CustomerPhone
FROM Customer
```

When and When Not to Use Brackets in Queries

If you have spaces or nonalphanumeric characters in field names, you must enclose the fields in square brackets like the following example:

```
[Customer#], [Customer Name], [Customer Phone]
```

The following are rules about select queries:

- Separate field, table, and sort key names by commas.

- End the statement with a semicolon.

- If a field, table, or sort key name has spaces, enclose them in brackets.

- To include the table name, precede the field name with the table name, connecting them with a period (for example, Customer.Phone)

By using SQL, you are defining what you want to see in your results. In contrast to the query design grid, you are writing instead of building your query. The following steps will guide you through the process of creating an SQL query:

1. Under Queries, double-click Create query in Design view.

2. Click Close at the Show Table dialog box.

3. On the View button, click SQL.

4. Place your cursor after the "T" in SELECT, and type

   ```
   SELECT AccidentDate
   FROM Losses;
   ```

5. Run the query. Click the View button (blue triangle) to open Design view (QBE).

6. Click the drop-down box of the View button and select SQL View. Edit the SELECT statement to read:

```
SELECT AccidentDate, Incurred
FROM Losses
WHERE Incurred >=1000
ORDER BY Incurred DESC;
```

7. Run the query. Click the View button, and close without saving.

Understanding "Ands" and "Ors" in the Query Grid

If you want to construct a query with multiple criteria, you need to understand the difference between the logical operators And and Or. Although these operators can combine more than two conditions, for the sake of simplicity, let's use just two. Start with the premise that an And operator selects records only if *both* conditions in a two-condition query are met. In contrast, an Or operator selects records only if one *or* the other condition in a two condition query are met. In other words, at least one condition in an Or query must be met.

This is where it gets a little tricky. Suppose you want to see both the Colorado and the Mississippi losses in the Losses table. You would think that you could just type CO And MS in the AccidentState column and retrieve those records. This criteria retrieves nothing. How can this be? You must think of it on a record-by-record basis. SQL examines *each* record to see if both conditions are met. Of course, it finds nothing because there is not a single record that has *both* Colorado *and* Mississippi values in the AccidentState field. This is why you would normally use two or more fields to create an And condition in the query grid.

Retrieving Two Values from the Same Field

So, how can you retrieve two states in the preceding example? You can use the Or operator because you want both values in the same field. Consistent with Or operations, at least one condition was true. In this case, both conditions are true, but not on an individual record examination basis. So, we have to use the Or operator. In contrast, with the And operator, both conditions can be true in the same record, because the conditions are in two different fields.

It is easy to deduce from the previous comments that you should always use the Or operator in a single field in the grid, and use the And operator in two or more different fields. However, this is not always true. In keeping with our two-condition format, you can use the Or operator in two fields by placing the second condition in the second field on a different row in the query design. Let's illustrate before going any further.

Creating an And Condition Query

When you have conditions in two or more fields in the same row of the criteria section of the query grid, you have an And condition. Follow these steps to produce this type of query:

1. Under Queries, double-click Create query in Design view.

2. Double-click the Losses table, and then click Close.

3. Bring all the fields to the query grid by double-clicking the title bar of the Losses table and dragging the fields down to the grid.

4. Type CO in the Criteria row of the AccidentState field.

5. Tab to the Incurred column, and type >= 50000 (four zeros) on the criteria row.

6. Click the Run button to run the query. This retrieves Colorado records with Incurred losses greater than or equal to $50,000. Stay in the query.

We have now established an And condition by typing two criteria in two different fields. This constitutes an AND clause. Notice in Figure 4.21 that they are in the same row.

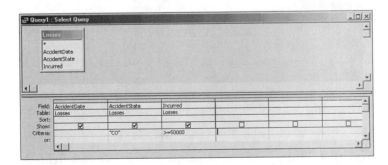

Figure 4.21: *Two conditions in two different fields constitutes an "And" condition.*

Just to be sure, click View and choose SQL View. Notice the AND in the criteria as shown in Figure 4.22.

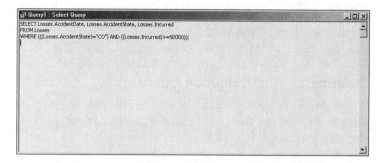

Figure 4.22: *You can verify that you have an* And *clause by checking in SQL view.*

Keep in mind that both conditions must be true *per record* in an And query. You can easily take this query and turn it into a multi-column Or query.

The following steps show how to change an And query into a multi-field Or query just by changing one field. This will help you understand query design.

1. Click Design view, and then select CO in the Criteria row. Press Ctrl+X to cut the criterion to the clipboard.

2. Cursor down to the Or: row of the AccidentState field and press Ctrl+V to paste as shown in Figure 4.23.

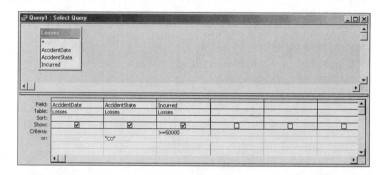

Figure 4.23: *You can construct an* Or *query on two fields by placing one of the conditions in the "Or:" row of the design grid.*

3. Run the query. Stay in the query.

Now you are directing the query to find records that are either in Colorado *or* have losses greater than or equal to $50,000. This is quite different. A loss could occur in Colorado, but not be $50,000 or more. Conversely, a loss could be $50,000 or more, but not be in Colorado. Another possibility would be that a loss could be $50,000 or more *and* occur in Colorado. At least one of the conditions must be true. Check the SQL View to verify the Or condition. It is also possible to create a query that has an And condition and an Or condition in the same query. The following steps convert the Or query to an And/Or query:

1. Click Design view and cursor to the blank space in the Criteria row above CO.

2. Type MS for the criterion. Notice that this is on the same row as >=50000 as shown in Figure 4.24.

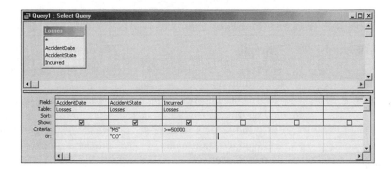

Figure 4.24: *The multiple conditions of this query constitute an And/Or query.*

3. Run the query.

Still another condition has been added, making this an And/Or query. You are telling the query to find every loss in Mississippi that has a $50,000 or above value. But the Or part of the criteria is telling the query to find every loss in Colorado, regardless of what value it has. Check the SQL View to verify the And/Or condition. Close the query, naming it And Or Example.

It almost seems that in Access, there is no exception to the rule that there is an exception to every rule. The And and Or operations provide an illustration. Generally speaking, if you place two criteria in the same field in different rows in the grid, you have just created an Or condition. Likewise, if you place two criteria on the same row, but in different fields, you have created an And condition. However, subqueries and functions can create And conditions in the same field and Or conditions in different fields in the same row.

✔ For more information about subqueries, see "Using Subqueries to Unleash the Power of Queries" in Chapter 16, "Overcoming the Limitations of Queries."

Even without these programs, you can simply type multiple Or declarations on the same row. For example you could type TX Or FL in the AccidentState column as criteria rather than type these values on separate rows in the grid.

Understanding Wildcards

There might be times when you do not need an exact match reflected in the records you are retrieving. Suppose, for example, that you want to see all the states in your table that begin with the letters "AR." After examining Table 4.2 let's try some wildcard queries by example.

Table 4.2: Wildcard Character Examples

Wildcard	Example	Operation
*	tr* selects train, translate, try, and so on	Match any number of characters
?	?at selects bat, cat, rat, and so on	Match any single character
[]	[bfk]ind selects bind, find, and kind, but not mind, hind, and wind	Match any single character within brackets
!	[!bfk]ind selects mind, hind, and wind, but not bind, find, and kind	Do not match any single character within brackets
-	[b-k]ind selects bind, find and kind, but not mind, hind, and wind	Match any character within a range of characters
#	#92 selects 192, 892, 492, and so on	Match any single digit

Selecting Records Using Wildcards

Perhaps the best time to use wildcards is when you don't remember the name of an individual or company. Suppose you were looking for a certain company, and you couldn't remember the full company name, but you knew it started with "United." You could just type United* for criterion, and the query would pull up United Trucking, United Rental, and so on. If you want all words that had four characters that started with "S," you can type "S???" (with quotes) for your criterion because "S" is one of the four characters. The other three characters can be any characters. The following steps lead you through the process of creating a query using wildcards:

1. Under Queries, double-click Create Query in Design view.

2. Double-click the States table, and then choose Close.

3. Bring both the Code and State fields to the Query grid by double-clicking them.

4. In the Criteria row of the Code field, type "?S" (with the quotes).

5. Tab to the State field and notice the Like operator is automatically inserted. Run the query.

   You should see Mississippi and Kansas records because both codes have "S" as the second letter.

6. Click View to return to Design view.

7. Select the criteria in the Code column and then delete it.

8. Tab to the State field criteria row and then type AR* and press Tab.

9. Run the query. You should see both Arkansas and Arizona, as shown in Figure 4.25.

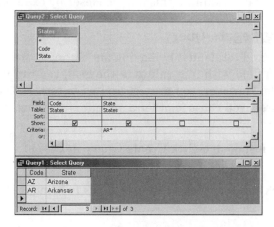

Figure 4.25: *Because the wildcard criterion started with the letters AR, both Arkansas and Arizona are retrieved by the query.*

10. Close the query without saving.

Understanding Grouping and Sorting

The Group By clause in Access queries provides a quick and easy way to run aggregate calculations, such as totals, on groups of like values. The DSUM function in Excel is the counterpart to a Sum calculated with the Group By clause in an Access query. However, this function is cumbersome when compared to ease of running its counterpart in Access. You could sort and subtotal in Excel, but again, the Access method is more streamlined.

In Table 4.3, notice that there are two losses for both Florida and Colorado. Because the AccidentState field has the like values and the Incurred field has the values you want to add for a total, place the Group By clause in the AccidentState field and the Sum aggregate calculation in the Incurred field. You do not want to group the Incurred field because there are no like values in this example. And you do not want to try to sum a field with text values, such as AccidentState.

Table 4.3: Sample Table for the **Group By** *Operator*

Accident State	Incurred
FL	500
FL	493
CO	209
CO	1,215

If you prefer to count all the values, you simply change the Sum aggregate function to Count. Let's examine this a little closer by example.

Creating an Aggregate Query

You can create grand totals just by having one financial field in the design grid. If you add a field with like values to the grid, you can produce group (aggregate) totals. However, you are not limited to totals. As the following example illustrates, you can use other aggregate functions, such as count and average:

1. Under Queries, double-click Create Query in Design view. Choose the Losses table and click Close.

2. Double-click the Incurred field *three times* to bring it to the design grid.

3. Click the Totals button to bring up the Total: row.

4. Change the first Group By operator to Sum by clicking the down arrow that appears when you click in the Total: row of the first instance of the field and choosing Sum.

5. Repeat the previous step on the next two instances of the field, but choose Count and Average (consecutively and in that order) on those fields as Figure 4.26 illustrates.

6. Run the query to view the results. You should see a sum, a count, and an average in one record. Don't worry about the formatting yet.

7. Click the View button to return to Design view. Then, double-click the AccidentState field to bring it to the grid.

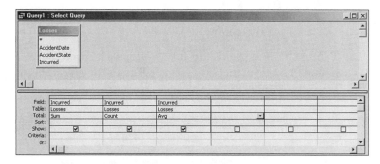

Figure 4.26: *You can insert multiple instances of the same field for a variety of aggregate functions.*

8. Place your cursor above the AccidentState field until the cursor changes to an arrow pointing down. Click to select the field as shown in Figure 4.27.

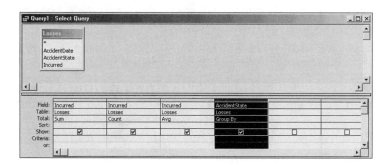

Figure 4.27: *When you select the AccidentState field, you can move it to a new location.*

9. Click, hold, and drag the field over to the first position in the table. Leave the Group By operator. Run the query, and return to Design view.

10. Right-click the first instance of the Incurred field in the Field: row. Choose Properties from the menu.

11. Under Format, type #,##0 and then click the X to close.

12. If Incurred is not highlighted, press the HOME key in the field to move the cursor before the first character in the field name. Otherwise, click before the "I" in "Incurred."

13. Type Sum: before the word Incurred. Don't forget the colon.

14. Tab to the next Incurred field. Type `Count:` before the word Incurred. Don't forget the colon.

15. Tab to the next field and follow steps 11 through 12. Type `Average:` before the word Incurred. Don't forget the colon. Your query should look like Figure 4.28.

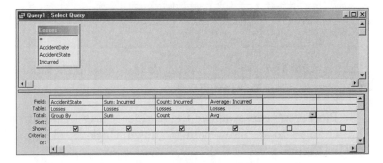

Figure 4.28: *Like values in the* `AccidentState` *field become the basis for the group calculations on Incurred values.*

16. Run the query and then save the query as `Groups Example`.

Observe some things about the query you just created. Each state is summarized by sum, count, and average. Even with the formatting, you created the query very quickly. You renamed three fields (on the fly) very easily. Previously, you created a grand total, a count grand total, and an average for the same field. You transformed the query into a summary of each state just by adding a field.

Sorting Fields in Queries

You can sort an Access query as you run the query and after you run the query. Sorting in the datasheets results in a very simple process. You just click the Sort Ascending button on the toolbar while in the selected column, if you want an ascending sort on the column. By contrast, in the query grid, you must click the appropriate field in the sort row and choose either ascending or descending order. Then you must run the query. Although sorting in the query grid is not quite as easy, it has better functionality.

So, it boils down to what you want to do. If you want a quick and easy way to sort one or more fields, choose the datasheet method. But if you have nonadjacent fields or two or more fields that have different sort orders, choose the query design method.

Before you analyze these sort techniques by example, be sure you understand what a multiple sort involves. Table 4.4 is a multi-level sort—or a sort within a sort. The first level, or primary sort field, is AccidentState. You can tell that this field is in alphabetical order because the "O" entries come before the "T" entries. The secondary sort field is Incurred. Although AccidentState is in ascending order, Incurred is in descending order. You might want to see the most severe losses first in each state. Because you have repeating values in the AccidentState column, you can do a subsort, or secondary sort, in the Incurred column.

Table 4.4: Sort Within a Sort Table

AccidentState	Incurred
OK	5,000
OK	4,000
OK	3,000
TX	7,000
TX	6,000
TX	5,000

Sorting While and After Running the Query

A multi-level sort has to do with the order in which you want to view records. As the following example illustrates, a secondary sort ("sort within a sort") can be in the opposite order of the primary sort. Complete the following steps to see "by example" how to sort both while and after running the query:

1. Under Queries, double-click Create Query in Design view. Choose the Losses table and click Close.

2. Double-click the AccidentState and Incurred fields to bring them to the grid. On the sort row of the AccidentState field, select Ascending.

3. On the sort row of the Incurred field, select Descending. Now you have a multi-level sort as shown in Figure 4.29.

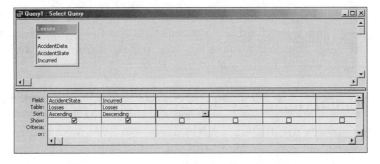

Figure 4.29: *The AccidentState field is in ascending order while the Incurred field is in descending order in this multi-level sort query.*

4. Run the query.

5. Select both columns by placing the cursor above the AccidentState column. When the cursor changes to a down arrow, select the column and click, hold, and drag your cursor across the Incurred column. If you performed this correctly, both columns should be highlighted.

6. Click the Sort Ascending button on the toolbar to sort the fields. Note that the secondary sort is ascending as shown in Figure 4.30.

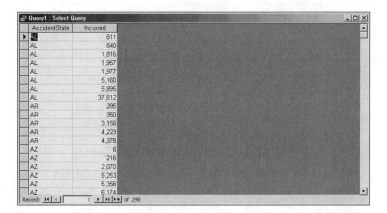

Figure 4.30: *You can change your sort results even after the query is run with the Sort Ascending or Sort Descending buttons on the toolbar.*

Both methods sorted two columns, but the second method sorted both columns in ascending order. If your table had 10 fields, and the first field to be sorted was in the first column, but the second field to be sorted was in the last column, it makes sense to create the sort in design view because the columns are not *adjacent*. Even though you can move fields around in both views, it's easier to use design view, especially if the sort orders are different.

Another important point is that in both views, the column farthest left is the primary sort field. This means that the fields must be arranged so that the fields that you want to sort are arranged from right to left in the design grid as well as in the query datasheet.

Understanding Dynasets and Their Underlying Tables

As already mentioned, a select query retrieves records according to the description you provide in the query design grid. These records are called a *dynaset*. The resulting datasheet result looks like a table, but it has different characteristics.

A dynaset is dynamic and temporary. In contrast, a table is static and permanent. A *dynaset* reflects what is in the underlying table when the query is run. When the query is closed, the dynaset goes away. Dynamic, according to the dictionary, refers to a tendency to change. If the table data changes, when the query executes, the dynaset generates the current picture of what is there. The important thing to remember is that when you save the query, you are saving the query design that generated the dynaset rather than the dynaset itself.

By saving the design rather than the records, you conserve disk space. And what's more, the dynamic nature of the query ensures that the underlying records are always up to date. These records can be updated, but that feature comes with a price. The dynaset is not the fastest record type.

Dynasets Versus Snapshots for Query Optimization

Although the dynaset is the default record type in the query, the snapshot is faster. For example, if you are creating records to populate a control for a combo box you use a snapshot record type, provided that the read-only (non-updateable) attribute of this record type is acceptable. Another example is querying a huge table just to send the results to a report. You might consider using the snapshot record type. Just be sure that you don't need to edit the results.

> ✔ For more information about creating records to populate a control for a combo box, see "The Power of Controls Revisited" in Chapter 7, "Exploring Objects."

To change a query design's record type, open the query in Design view, right-click the background above the grid, and choose Properties. Click the down arrow in the Recordset type box and change it to Snapshot.

What's Next

Now that you have been introduced to the power of queries, you have the chance to explore the power of a control, which can take advantage of a query's power. Controls are integral parts of a form. Forms can use dynasets from queries to do lookups and calculations. They are primarily used for input. All of this and more can be found in the next chapter.

Form primary for input

Part II

Forms for Input and Reports for Output

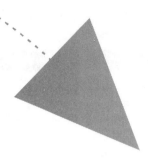

Exploring Forms and Controls

In Chapter 4, "Unleashing the Power of Queries," you learned how to create and use different types of queries. Now it's time to learn how to create a mechanism for user input that can use queries in many ways. This mechanism is called a form.

This chapter focuses on forms, controls, and events. In particular, you explore

- the differences between forms and reports
- what events are and how to use them
- how to use wizards to help you create forms
- how to examine and use your form's properties
- what a control is and how to use various types of controls effectively
- how to use queries in forms and controls

Forms Versus Reports

Generally, forms are for input and reports are for output. That doesn't mean that you can't print using a form. There's almost no end to its versatility. You can use it as a Grand Central Station of your application. A form can provide menus, open other objects such as other forms and tables, print reports, and a whole host of other things. As mentioned previously, you can pull multiple tables together using a query that feeds into a form.

The form gives you the functionality to view information from a broad range of perspectives. If that isn't enough, you can easily program various objects to perform repetitive tasks. For example, with a simple mouse click, you can filter the form, look up multiple values, calculate on multiple fields, print the current record, select items from a menu, and the list goes on.

The Datasheet view (or Table view) displays a spreadsheet-like look at the data. This is a great way to view the data from an overall perspective, but what if you want to see the details of a record with a large number of fields? In Datasheet view, you must scroll right for a while until you see the fields for which you are searching. In the meantime, the fields on the left disappear. You can move fields around, but this can quickly become more trouble than it's worth.

In contrast, a rolodex-style columnar form displays all the fields at once, one record at a time, unless you have so many fields that you have to go to a second page. In that case, you might need to normalize anyway. In certain cases a form can resemble a report, but there are distinct differences.

The beauty of a form is its capability to maneuver, control, create, and modify virtually every object in the database. The beauty of the report is its capability to dynamically present data linked to queries and tables. The primary function of the form is inputting data. The primary function of the report is outputting data. They both rely heavily on the *control*, which can be defined as any object such as a text box, list box, rectangle, or command button that you place on a form. They can both look like a spreadsheet or a page of a report in a file. They both link to tables and queries through their record source property. They both can sort and filter data, handle multiple tables, perform calculations, and execute programs.

So, what makes a form unique? Whereas a report is associated with printing, a form is associated with typing. A form can minimize mistakes made while inputting data. It can guide the user along the way with help menus, hints, and push buttons. For example, there is a sometimes-overlooked feature called *control tip text.* For more information about a control (or perhaps a button), place your cursor near the object; more help that involves a more definitive explanation of what the control does or how it is activated pops up onscreen. When you take the cursor away from the object, the help disappears.

The form usually is the place where a good deal of the programming of the database takes place. These programs are event driven. This means that object-oriented programming activates when a certain event occurs. For example, the On_Click event occurs when you click a control. This executes whatever program is attached to the event.

Defining Events

If you have worked with Access forms or reports, you have activated events. Every time you open or close a form and report, you activate the On_Open and On_Close events. The On Activate event occurs when the form becomes the active window. In contrast with many other object properties, event properties are initially left blank with no default values. If you set the event property to a macro, the macro runs when the event occurs. Let's say you have a button on a form labeled Print Record. If you click this button when the form is open (not in Design view), the On Click event activates and runs the macro or procedure attached to the event. This procedure prints the current record of your form. If you want to issue a list of Visual Basic statements when a certain event occurs, you write a procedure to attach to the event. It should be no surprise that this is called an *event procedure*.

Controlling Events

Events also occur on controls in forms. This can be very useful for lookups and pick lists. For example, suppose you have a lookup value that you have just changed. You might have another field that needs to update to correspond to the updated field. For example, if the customer decides to buy two items instead of one, the Extension field (which is computed by multiplying the quantity times the price) must change to reflect the new value.

If you want to go to a certain record or field when the form opens, use the form's On Open event. You can use this event to show or hide a toolbar when the form opens. Remember that the On Open event doesn't occur just by activating a form that's already open. The Activate event occurs in this situation. If you have records that you want to highlight by changing the color of every text box on the form that has a certain field value, use the On Current event. For example, let's say you are tracking medical students that have an active or inactive status. You can use this event to color the controls on the records of every inactive student differently than the records of the rest of the students. These are just a few examples of the things you can do with form events.

Using a Wizard to Help Design Your Form

You have discovered that Access wizards can be your friends. They effortlessly guide you through otherwise difficult procedures while saving you a great deal of time and effort. That doesn't mean that wizards are always the best way to go. But it does mean that it is a good idea to become familiar with wizards to fully utilize the functionality of your database.

The bottom line is that wizards can save you time creating forms, especially if they are relational forms. For example, a wizard can take care of the housekeeping involved in setting up a relational form, such as automatically placing the subform in the main form and automatically placing the chosen fields in the proper place. In addition, you can choose an aesthetically pleasing form style from a list of set formats.

To use the Form Wizard, follow these steps:

1. Open the Music Store database from the AccessByExample folder on your hard drive.

2. In the Database window under Objects, choose Forms, as shown in Figure 5.1.

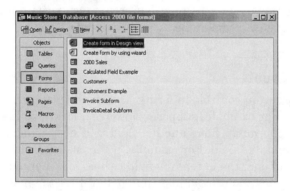

Figure 5.1: *By clicking on Forms, you see a list of forms in the Database window.*

3. Double-click Create Form by Using Wizard to open the wizard.

4. On page 1 of the wizard, under Tables/Queries click the down arrow and choose Customers, as shown in Figure 5.2.

5. Click the >> button to bring all the fields from the Available Fields box over to the Selected Fields box.

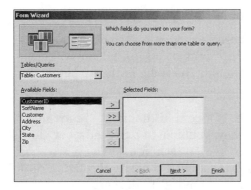

Figure 5.2: *You choose your table or query and the field names from the table or query on the first page of the Form Wizard.*

NOTE

There are four buttons between the Available Fields box and the Selected Fields box that Microsoft hasn't officially named. These buttons are explained by the following:

> Add the selected field

>> Add all fields

< Remove selected field

<< Remove all fields

---

6. Click Next to open the next page of the wizard.

7. Choose Columnar as shown in Figure 5.3, and then click Next to open page 3 of the wizard.

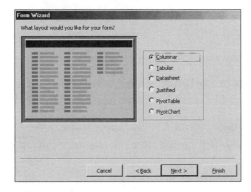

Figure 5.3: *The Columnar layout type displays each record as a page in the form.*

8. On page 3, accept the default Standard by clicking Next.

9. Type Form Customers Example in the box under "What title do you want for your form?" and click Finish. This will open the form to view or enter information as the radio button explains. Leave the form open for the next example.

That's all there is to it. Notice that the fields are arranged vertically rather than horizontally as they would be in a Spreadsheet view. While you're here, let's try a few navigation techniques. These are shortcut key combinations that provide an easy way to navigate through a record set. The following steps introduce you to some of these shortcuts, as shown in Figure 5.4.

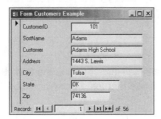

Figure 5.4: *You can use shortcut keys to navigate in the form created by the Form Wizard.*

1. In the form left open from the last exercise, press Ctrl+End. Notice the white record number box at the bottom of the form. It indicates that you are at the last record. Notice also that you are on the last field.

2. Press Ctrl+Home. This immediately takes you to the first record, and the first field of the table.

3. Press End. Notice that you are in the first record, and the last field in the record.

4. Press F5. This takes you to the record number box.

5. Type 55 and then press Enter. This should take you to record 55, as shown in Figure 5.5. Leave the form open for the next example.

You also can use the Page Up and Page Down keys to navigate from record to record, or you can use the mouse to click the navigation buttons at the bottom of the form.

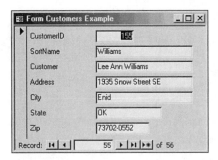

Figure 5.5: *After pressing F5 to enter the record number box, you can type the number of the record you want to see. After pressing Enter, it will be retrieved.*

Examining Your Form's Properties

Every object in Access, including the database itself, has properties. Your form is no exception. There are different categories of properties of a form. They are represented by tabs in the properties window. Some properties pertain to data; others pertain to the formatting of the form; still others pertain to events.

Table 5.1 shows what the property categories, which can be accessed by clicking tabs in the properties sheet, represent.

Table 5.1: Explanation of Property Categories

Category	Description
Format	Properties that pertain to the way an object is displayed.
Data	Properties that pertain to an object's data, whether it is how data is displayed or how data is obtained.
Event	Properties that pertain to events and the procedures that are tied to them.
Other	Properties that pertain to an object's characteristics or miscellaneous attributes.
All	All categories or all the properties of the object.

You might not fully understand what certain properties mean, but all you have to do is click a property and press F1 to get instant help on that property. Let's examine the form's property window.

1. Click View to switch to Design view while in the Form Customers Example. Right-click the title bar of the form to open the shortcut menu, and click Properties as shown in Figure 5.6.

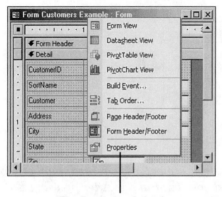

The Properties option from
the shortcut menu opens
the Properties sheet

Figure 5.6: *You can right-click the title bar of the form while in Design view to examine its properties.*

2. Click the Data tab of the properties sheet to list the properties in that category.

3. Click the drop-down box of the Record Source property, as shown in Figure 5.7. Notice that every table and query in the database is listed.

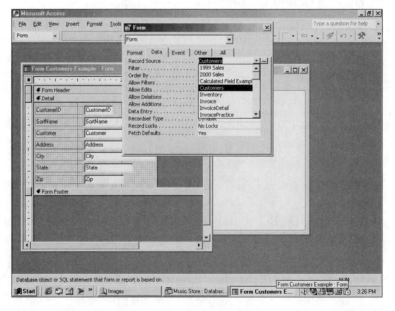

Figure 5.7: *Every available table and query is listed in the Record Source drop-down list.*

4. Close the Property sheet and the form.

NOTE

If you are having a difficult time viewing the table names, the properties sheet can be resized wider so that the table/query names in the field are wider.

Working with the Record Source Property

The record source property can easily be changed by programming a button to activate a different table or query to be the record source. For the most part, that table or query should have the same structure as the current record source. For example, imagine that you have a sales table for 1999. The 2000 table probably has the same fields as the 1999 table except they would be filled with different data.

BUILDING A COMMAND BUTTON

To see the previous year's records at the click of a mouse button, program the form to set the record source to last year's table. Assuming that the 2000 table was called 2000 Sales and the 1999 table was called 1999 Sales and you wanted to change the record source to the 1999 table, you would simply enter the On Click event on a button and enter

```
Me.RecordSource = "1999 Sales"
```

After configuring the button, last year's table data is just a mouse click away. This can be very useful.

NOTE

After the new record source is set, subsequent clicks on the same button for last year's table will not change anything because the record source is already set.

To configure the command button, perform the following steps:

1. Under Objects, click Forms to see a list of forms.

2. Click 2000 Sales and click Design on the Database window toolbar to open the form in Design view.

3. From the toolbar in Design view, click the Toolbox tool.

4. Be sure that the Control Wizard's wand at the top of the toolbox is not selected, and click the Command button as shown in Figure 5.8. Hold your cursor near the button for a few seconds to read the ScreenTip message to be sure.

Figure 5.8: Select the Command button from the Toolbox and then place the object on the form.

5. Your cursor changes to a Button cursor, shown in the lower-right corner of the Command button in Figure 5.9. To the right of the address text box, click and hold the left mouse button and form a box by dragging it from upper-left to lower-right (see Figure 5.9).

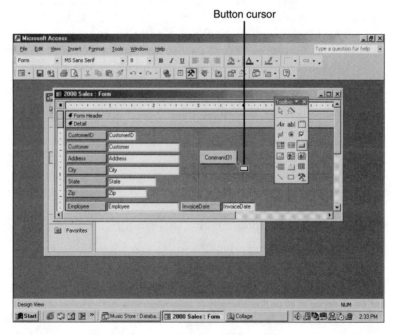

Figure 5.9: The label (Command31) that was generated when the button was created can be changed by typing over the label directly or by typing a new label in the Caption property of the Property sheet.

NOTE

When your cursor changes to a Button cursor, you can click on an area to the right of
the address field, and the button should appear. This is a shortcut, but it's also good to
know how to shape the box because you never know how much room you will have.

6. With the Command button selected, press F4. Click the All tab. In the
   Name property, type cmdChangeYear.

7. Type 1999 Sales in the Caption property box to replace the label automatically generated for the button.

8. Click the Event tab from the properties sheet, and then choose On
   Click.

9. Click the drop-down box, and choose [Event Procedure]. Click the
   Build button, and type the following code as referenced previously:

   ```
   Me.RecordSource = "1999 Sales"
   ```

10. Click the Close button. Close the properties sheet, and then close and
    save the form.

11. Double-click the 2000 Sales form that you just modified.

    Click the 1999 Sales button and watch the number after the "of" to
    the right of the navigation buttons at the bottom of the form. It should
    change to 32, because the form's record source has changed. Notice
    that the current record is also different.

12. Close the form.

Choosing a table for a record source is not the only option available for a
record source. You also can select an existing query or create a query "on
the fly" while you are in the record source property box. Follow these steps
to explore other record source options:

1. Click the Customers Example form and click Design on the Database
   toolbar.

2. Right-click on the black box left of the horizontal ruler and choose
   Properties. This produces the same result as right-clicking the title
   bar of the form.

NOTE

There are many ways to access the Properties sheet of a form. In addition to the two
methods mentioned in step 2, you can also right-click on the large gray area on the
right side of the form in Design view. You can try these options to see which one works
best for you.

3. Click on the Data tab of the properties sheet and select Record Source.

4. Click the Build button on the right side of the box to invoke the Query Builder shown in Figure 5.10.

Figure 5.10: *Invoking the Query Builder enables you to create a query and use it as a record source on the fly.*

5. Invoke the Query Builder by clicking Yes. This opens up a whole new range of possibilities. We can create a query here or use SQL code for the record source.

   Note that if there is a table or query that is already selected when the Query Builder is invoked, it will base the query on that object if you answer Yes.

NOTE

Because this query grid design is the same view that you see when you open an existing query or create a new one, it should look familiar. The difference is that this query stays with the form. When you close the Query Builder, you have the option of saving the query.

---

6. Close the query without saving it by clicking No when asked if you want to save changes. Leave the form open for the next example.

You can link to a previously created query, or create one on the fly, by using the method you just performed. These are a few of the options available to you. You can use the same methods to change the report's record source so the form and report will match. This can all happen with the click of a mouse button.

Changing the Form's Color

There are many reasons why people change a form's colors. Some do it to make the form more aesthetically pleasing. Others use colors for emphasis. For example, they might want one section or object on the form to stand out. You can also use colors to apply conditional formatting on field data. To access the form's properties so that the color can be changed, follow these steps:

1. In the form left open from the last example, right-click the Detail section of the form and then choose Properties to open the Properties sheet of this section.

2. Click the Format tab in the Properties sheet, and then click the Build button in the Back Color box to open the color palette as shown in Figure 5.11.

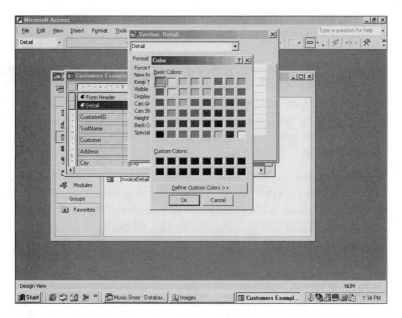

Figure 5.11: *You can choose from the color palette of the back color property to assign custom colors to your form.*

TIP

A handy shortcut for changing the color of the Detail section is to simply right-click the Detail section and then select Fill/Back Color. A drop-down list appears with a color palette for easy color selection.

---

3. From the color palette, choose the fifth box on the last row before the Custom Colors section and choose OK.

4. Close the Properties sheet.

5. Notice that the form's color is changed. Click X on the window to close the form without saving any changes (see Figure 5.12).

Figure 5.12: *You receive a message box to remind you to save the form while giving you the option to close without saving.*

✔ For information about changing object colors through VBA see "Changing Object Properties Through VBA" in Chapter 7, "Exploring Objects."

Introduction to Controls

Why are form and report objects called controls? What do controls control? Simply put, controls control data, whether it be the way data is displayed or the way data is manipulated, through expressions, queries, macros, and procedures.

It is possible to create a form from scratch by adding objects to a blank form. Objects, whether they are text boxes, list boxes, combo boxes, command buttons, option buttons, or any other objects in the form, are called *controls*. They are accessed from the form's toolbox, which has an icon for toggling on or off.

A text box can be changed into a label, a list box, or a combo box. These are just different forms of the same thing. In other words, they can all be converted to any of the aforementioned box types. This box can be bound or unbound. A *bound* box differs from an unbound box in that it has a control source, which can be a field or an expression. This expression can include functions, fields, operators, or constants. The functions can be built-in Access functions or custom functions created by the user. Other controls can also be bound, but the text box style controls are most commonly bound, because they are created with wizards.

When you use a wizard to create a form, the wizard automatically places text boxes for all fields that you have chosen and sets the record source to the table or query that you have selected. This means that all the text boxes are bound with field name labels attached.

Unbound controls, on the other hand, can be used to display text, such as a label, or they can be used as a container to hold items selected from a list. For example, if you have a list of inventory items, you might want to be able to choose from that list the items that are back ordered. This is called a *pick list*, and the unbound control is perfect for that kind of application.

Various Control Types

When you examine the various types of controls found in the toolbox, you quickly discover that there is not much that you can't do with a form. Table 5.2 lists control options available on a form.

Table 5.2: Toolbox Control Options for a Form

Control	Function
Bound object frame	Holds an OLE object or embedded picture.
Check box	Shows square with check mark if on and empty box if off.
Combo box	Drop-down list of value options for current field from another source.
Command button	Used to call a macro or procedure.
Image	Displays a bitmap picture.
Label	Displays literal text.
Line	Displays single line allowing variable thickness.
List box	Displays list of options for selection.
Unbound object frame or chart	Holds an OLE object or embedded picture not tied to a table.
Option button	Displays dot within a circle when option is on.
Option group	Holds multiple option buttons, check boxes, or toggle buttons.
Rectangle	Used aesthetically or for emphasis. Can be filled with color or blank.
Subform	Displays another form within the current form.
Tab	Can display multiple pages like a file folder for conserving space.
Text box	Used for data entry. Can be bound or unbound.
Toggle button	Used as a two-state button, up or down.

An option group allows the user to easily select field values from a group of items. Suppose you want to be able to choose between various shipping methods. Or perhaps you want to log the credit card with which your customer purchased.

OPTION GROUP

An option group combines multiple toggle buttons, option buttons, or check boxes so that they function together as a unit. The idea is to select a single item from multiple controls to store in a field or to use in a procedure for flow control. If you want to select multiple items, you can either use a list box or surround several separate buttons with a rectangle to give the effect of an option group. In the latter case, you handle each button separately from a programming standpoint.

Follow these steps to understand how an option group works:

1. Open the Northwind database. Hold the Shift key down while opening to bypass the opening screens. Under Objects, choose Forms.

2. Double-click the Orders Form to open it.

3. The Orders form shows the various shipping methods, as shown in Figure 5.13. In the Option Group section called Ship Via, you choose your shipper by clicking one of three boxes: Speedy, United, or Federal. Feel free to click the other boxes, but leave Speedy checked before closing the form.

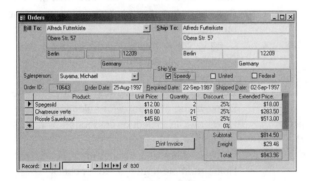

Figure 5.13: *The Option Group is a group of controls that lets you choose one option from a list of options.*

4. Close the form. Under Objects, click Tables, and then double-click the Orders table.

5. Tab to the right until you see the Ship Via field. It is important to understand that the data selected in the Ship Via option group is stored in this field. The Option Group Wizard lets you choose whether you want to store the Option Group selection in a field or just use the data programmatically.

6. Close the table, and leave the database open for the next example.

What you have just observed is a great way to give the user options for a small number of items. If you have a large number of items, using a list box or a combo drop-down box is preferable. The option group is quick and easy to set up using a wizard that automatically activates when you place the group on the form. In the preceding sample exercise, the Ship Via field was the control source for the option group called ShipVia.

COMBO BOX

The combo box is a control that gives the user a chance to select from a list of values, but instead of clicking an option button, the user chooses from a drop-down list. The Northwind database has an example of a drop-down box with just a few items to select.

While in Northwind, open the Employees form and click the Personal Info tab. This control, which resembles a file folder, is called a *tab control*; then click Title of Courtesy. This field's data source was created with what is called a *value list,* which consists of a list of titles, such as Mr. or Mrs., separated by semicolons. This can easily be converted into a much larger list by changing its row source to a table or query. Close the form.

EXPLORING EVENT PROCEDURES

Events are like launching pads for your procedures. Whenever you update an object, an event occurs, providing you an opportunity to change other objects. For example, if you want to look up a value based on another value, use the After Update event as illustrated by the following steps:

1. Open the Music Store database from the AccessByExample folder.

2. Under Forms, double-click Create Form By Using Wizard.

3. On page 1 of the wizard, under Table/Queries, choose Table:InvoicePractice.

4. Click the >> button to bring all the fields over to the Selected Fields side.

5. Click Next to open page 2 of the wizard.

6. On page 2, choose Datasheet and click Next.

7. On page 3, choose Standard and click Next.

8. On page 4, name the form InvoiceDetail Form, click Modify the Form's Design, and click Finish.

9. Right-click PartNumber in the detail section and choose Change To, and then choose Combo Box (see Figure 5.14).

10. Right-click PartNumber control again, and this time choose Properties to open the Properties sheet.

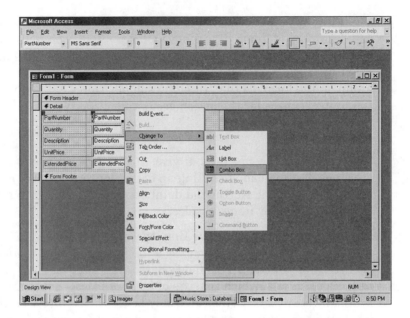

Figure 5.14: *You can change a text box to a combo box by right-clicking the text box and choosing Change To.*

11. Be sure you are on the Data tab, and click the Build button beside the Row Source property to open the Show Table dialog box.

12. From the Show Table dialog box, choose Inventory by clicking Add, and click Close.

13. Choose PartNumber, Instrument, Model, and UnitPrice from the table by double-clicking the fields in the Inventory table, as shown in Figure 5.15.

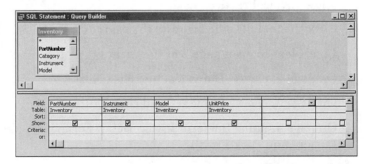

Figure 5.15: *Selecting fields by double-clicking in the Query Builder in the row source property.*

14. Click X to close the Query Builder. When a message box displays, as shown in Figure 5.16, click Yes to save the changes made to the SQL statement and update the property.

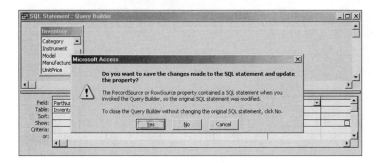

Figure 5.16: *Clicking Yes to the Query Builder message ensures that the query is saved with the form.*

15. In the Column Widths property box, which can be accessed from the Format tab, type .7;1.5;1;0 and then press Enter. Notice that the inch indicators are automatically inserted.

NOTE

This property is setting up the column widths for the fields to be viewed when the drop-down function is activated. If the first field had a zero (0) inserted (for example, 0";0.9";0.7'), you would not be able to see it. The second field would be the one that would be viewed first. However, the correct data (PartNumber) would be inserted in the underlying table. To make sure that all your field widths can be viewed, change the List Width to the sum of all the visible column widths. For example, if three columns had widths of 1.5, the List Width property should be 4.5. This will expand your viewing width to beyond the right edge of the combo box.

---

16. Set the Column Count property to 4 to match the number of columns that are in the query (see Figure 5.17) and the List Width property to 3.2.

17. Click the Event tab and then click the Build button on the After Update event.

18. Choose Code Builder and then click OK. Type the following code into this event:

```
Dim sDesc As String, dPrice As Double
sDesc = Me.PartNumber.Column(1) & " " & Me.PartNumber.Column(2)
dPrice = Me.PartNumber.Column(3)
Me.Description = sDesc
Me.UnitPrice = dPrice
```

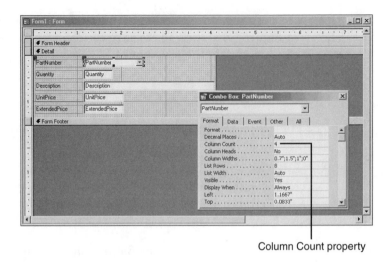

Column Count property

Figure 5.17: *You must change the Column Count property to reflect the number of columns in the table/query.*

This can be broken down as follows:

In the first line you are declaring your variables as String and Double types. The second line concatenates, or combines, three pieces of data. The first piece of data (`Me.PartNumber.Column(1)`) contains the reserved word `Me`. You can use this word in form modules to obtain a reference to the current form. In this case, you are retrieving a reference to the Column property of the PartNumber control on the form. Because you set the Column Count property to 4 and set up a query to select those fields, you can now use this property in the module to assign data to your variable.

The second piece of data is simply a space ( ). The third piece of data (`Me.Partnumber.Column(2)`) is the third column in the query. It is important to remember that the column property is zero-based, which means you start counting at zero. The first column is zero, the second column is one, and so forth. Therefore, `Me.PartNumber.Column(1)` is really the second column.

When you put all of this together, you get a value like `Flugelhorn FE747`, which is the instrument and its model number. The `Price` variable is set up much the same way, except that you have only one value to retrieve.

Next, you simply assign these variables, retrieved from another table, to fields in the underlying table. The variables act like temporary holding containers that retrieve data and quickly pass it on. As you type, you probably notice that when you type the period (.), you are able to view a list of options for whatever object you are on.

19. Select Debug, Compile, Music Store from the menu, and click the Save button.

NOTE

While compiling the module, Access checks the code for errors. Close the window.

---

20. When you are back to the Properties sheet of the PartNumber control, click the Quantity control with the sheet still open.

21. Click the After Update event and then click the Build button. Click the Code Builder.

22. Enter the following code:

```
Dim sExt As String
sExt = Me.Quantity * Me.UnitPrice
Me.ExtendedPrice = sExt
```

23. Close the property sheet, and then close the form. Click Yes when asked to save the changes.

24. Double-click the InvoiceDetail form to run the form.

25. Click the New Record button from the record selectors at the bottom of the form to add a new record. (A similar button is on the toolbar.)

26. Click the drop-down list in the PartNumber field, and select the second row as shown in Figure 5.18.

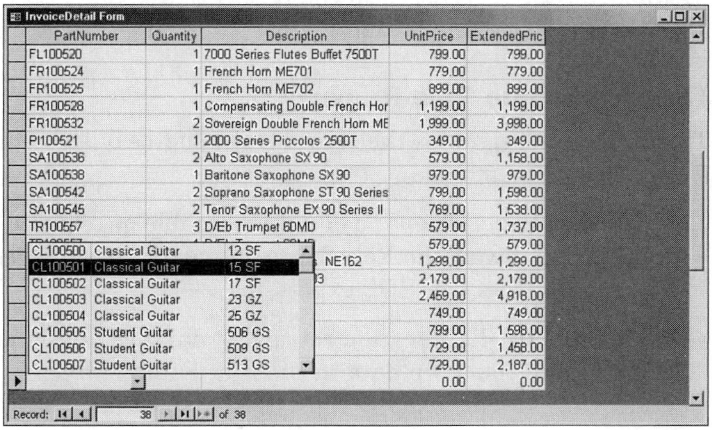

Figure 5.18: *Lookup Field values are automatically entered when a value is selected from the drop-down combo box.*

27. Notice that the `Description` field is automatically inserted along with the `UnitPrice`.

28. Tab to the `Quantity` field and type 2, and then press Enter. Notice how the correct value is automatically inserted into the `ExtendedPrice` field.

29. Close the form.

How to Control a Control

So far, you have experienced a taste of the power that's incorporated into the form. Obviously, there is much more. But before you proceed any further, there are some important control properties that need to be clearly understood. Let's first look at list and combo box properties.

The Name Property

It is easy for beginners to confuse the Control Source property with the Name property, especially because they often have the same name. The Name property is only the name by which you reference the control. This provides a way for an unbound control, with no control source, to be referenced. There is no link whatsoever with the underlying data using this property.

The Control Source Property

In contrast, the Control Source property is actually linked to the underlying data. You can link this property with a field obtained from a list generated by whatever table is chosen in the record source property of the form. You also can click the Build button to enter an expression in this property.

The Row Source Type Property

This property designates the record (row) source of the data for the control. Available options include

- **Table/Query**—The type of data is a table or a query. This works in conjunction with the Row Source property, which gives the name of the table, query, or SQL expression.

- **Value List**—Rather than retrieving data, you designate here that you are typing your own data in the Row Source property, separated by semicolons. This usually consists of a short list of values. The control displays whatever you type there.

- **Field List**—Rather than displaying records, this type indicates that you are retrieving a list of fields from the table or query specified in the Row Source property. This is an easy way to print a list of fields for whatever table structure you need.

The Row Source Property

It should be noted that you also can populate a list or combo box using code by referencing the Row Source property. When you select a table or query as the Row Source in a form's control, the combo or list box displays a list of options using the data from the table or query selected. When the user selects from the list, the control displays that value until such time as the user changes that value.

For example, if you want to let the user choose from a set of codes from an Inventory list in an Invoice form, use a combo or list box to provide a list for a lookup. The user might not remember the code, but if he or she sees a list of codes with the corresponding items, the selection becomes easy. As you have seen, the After Update event provides a way to change other fields in the form, depending on what value is selected in the control. So this is a great way to look up values to populate other fields.

The Column Count Property

Although this property can be easily overlooked, it is no less important than the others. If you have four columns to display, but leave the default setting of one, you only display one column. If you change the setting to four, you still need to properly set the Column Widths property to display all four columns. Be sure to use a numeric value.

The Column Width Property

Each value entered here sets the widths of the columns in the control and must be separated by a semicolon. Using the preceding example, let's say that you want to set all four columns to a one-inch value. You simply enter 1;1;1;1. If you type a 2 instead, the first column is set at two inches, and the rest have the one-inch default. Any time you omit a value, the program accepts the default width of one inch. If you want to hide a column, you set the width to 0. Leaving this property blank evenly spaces the columns over the width of the control.

The Bound Column Property

This property determines which column contains the value to be returned when a value is selected from a list of items. Let's say that the bound column is set to 1 and the first column is hidden, because the column width is set to 0. The displayed column would be the second field, but the returned column would be the first field. If the first field was `PartNumber` and the second field was `Part`, you would see the part displayed in the control, but the part number would be placed in the underlying table.

This method might be handy to look up values, but it's likely to be confusing, because the field would most likely be labeled `PartNumber`. However, this is easily remedied simply by changing the label to `Part`. That way, you hide the returned value of the bound column and display the lookup column. In fact, the Lookup Wizard in the table design suggests you do just that. The user never has to know, because the proper information is placed in the table. If you want to return the part, you need to set this property to 2.

Creating a Calculated Control

A bound or unbound control can easily be converted into a calculated control. Simply right-click the control and choose Properties. Click the Build button of the Control Source property to enter the expression builder. Assuming that you have a `City`, `State`, and `Zip` field in the table you are accessing, you can type an expression (or use the builder to help fill in the expression) similar to the following:

`[City] & ", " & [State] & " " & [Zip]`

This expression uses the ampersand (&) operator to concatenate (bring together) field values with literal (constant) values. The fact that `City`, `State`, and `Zip` are all enclosed in brackets indicates that they are all field values. The comma and spaces are literal values. Together, they make up a composite value that can be part of the address. If the fields were numeric values, you could just as easily create an expression that includes operators for adding, subtracting, multiplying, or dividing.

Another Way to Create Calculated Controls

You can also create a calculated control using a query. If you have the Customers table from the Music Store database in the query grid with the `Customer` and `Address` fields already in the grid, there is an empty spot to the right of the `Address` field. In the field row, type `CSZ: [City] & ", " & [State] & " " & [Zip`; then click the drop-down box of the New Object button, as shown in Figure 5.19, and choose AutoForm. The program creates a field called CSZ. A query and a form titled Calculated Field Example are in that database. Notice that the control source for that field is CSZ, as opposed to the expression in the query.

The expanded New Object button

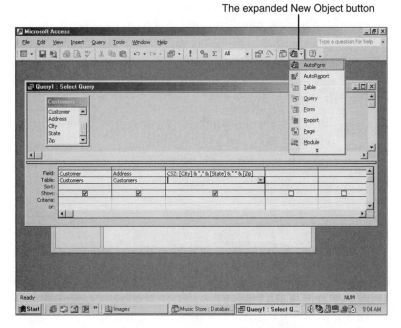

Figure 5.19: *Use the New Object button to create a calculated field in a form.*

Creating a Command Button

With the exception of the Before Update and After Update events, the command button has basically the same events as the other controls. The On Click event is probably the most commonly used event on this button. Clicking this button triggers an action, which could be in the form of a macro or a module.

Printing a Record

A common request of users is to print the current record on a form. Although Access has never added this feature, it is not difficult to produce this feature using a procedure. The following steps will guide you through the process of creating a button to print the current record:

1. Open the Music Store database from the AccessByExample folder. Under Objects, click Forms to view a list of forms.

2. Click Customers, and click Design from the database toolbar to open the Customers form in Design view.

3. In Design view, click the Toolbox icon from the toolbar.

4. Place your cursor over the control that looks like a button and watch for the Command Button ScreenTip to appear—just to be sure.

5. Be sure that the Control Wizard's wand (next to the Select Objects arrow) is not activated. Click the Command button and when the cursor changes to a Command button, move it over to the detail section of the form near the 4.5" mark.

6. Click, hold, and drag from upper-left to lower-right to form a rectangle approximately one inch in width.

7. Right-click the object and then choose Properties, as shown in Figure 5.20, to open the Properties sheet.

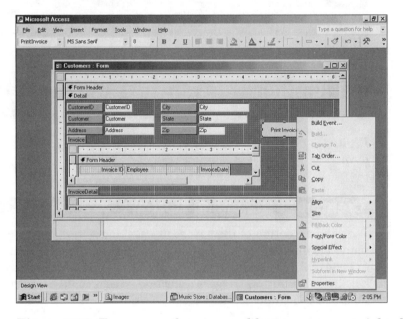

Figure 5.20: *To program the command button, you must right-click the button and choose Properties to open the Properties sheet.*

8. Click the All tab from the Properties sheet. Be sure the vertical scrollbar on the right side of the Properties sheet is at the top.

9. Change the caption to `Print Invoice`.

10. Change the name to `cmdPrintInvoice` (no space).

11. Click the Event tab from the Properties sheet.

12. Click the Build button from the right side of the On Click event box.

TIP

A shortcut that avoids the steps involved by using the Properties sheet is to simply right-click the command button and then choose Build Event, which is the first option. Although you still have to choose Code Builder at this point, this saves some steps. This is particularly handy for editing procedures, because you are not given the opportunity to select which event you want when you create a new procedure using Build Event. If you want to bypass having to choose Code Builder from the list, select Tools, Options, Forms/Reports from the Database window. Then check the Always Use Event Procedures checkbox.

---

13. Choose Code Builder, and then click OK.

14. Type the following code (excluding the first and last lines) in the Module window:

```
Private Sub PrintInvoice_Click()
On Error GoTo Exit_PrintInvoice_Click

  Dim ReportName As String, InvID As String, InvWhere As String

      'Get the invoice ID from the subform and assign it to a variable
InvID = Me.Invoice_Subform.Form.Controls![Invoice ID]
      'Set up a where expression by concatenating and assign it to a
➥variable
InvWhere = "[InvoiceID]=" & InvID
      ReportName = "Invoice"

  DoCmd.OpenReport ReportName, acViewNormal, , InvWhere
Exit_PrintInvoice_Click:
Exit Sub
End Sub
```

NOTE

Be sure you don't repeat the first and last lines (`private sub` and `end sub`) in this code. They are included in the code only for reference purposes. Therefore, you don't have to type these lines because they are inserted before and after your cursor position for you to make it easy for you to begin typing between the lines.

---

15. Click Debug, Compile Music Store, and save your changes. Close the Property sheet and the form.

16. Under Forms, double-click Customers to open the form. Press F5 to go to the Record Selector box of the form. Type 23 to retrieve Irvine Elementary.

17. Click the Print Invoice button to print the invoice for Irvine Elementary; then close the form.

How do you reference a control on a subform? The line beginning with InvID shows you how. You need the Invoice ID to be able to reference that same ID in the report. The next line sets up a where clause. Everything after the equal sign could be placed in the Filter property of a report. ReportName is simply a variable to store the report name. The OpenReport method is very powerful because you can apply a filter or a where clause to it to select records.

At this point, don't worry too much about understanding every line of this procedure. You examine code in much greater detail in subsequent chapters. This gives you an idea of what you can do with events tied to code.

Dealing with the Underlying Records

To properly explore how the underlying records relate to a form, the best place to start is the Record Source property. Both tables and queries tied to forms through the Record Source property use updateable record sets. The fields available to the form depend on the table or query that is tied to the form. This list can be expanded in a number of ways. One way is to add another table to the select query that is attached to the form. Another method is to create a lookup control that relies on another table for its fields. These fields then become available through code using the column property.

Multiple Table Queries as Record Source

If your form is tied to a select query that is based on one table, there should be no problem editing records. But when the query is based on more than one table, it gets a little more interesting. If you want to edit a join field on the one side of a one-to-many relationship, you must enforce referential integrity and cascading updates in the relationships window. This is a plus because you want to guard the integrity of your relationships.

When cascading updates is enforced, you aren't able to add or change data on a join field on the many side. And when you change data on a join field of the one side, it automatically changes the corresponding field on the many side. One exception is the Autonumber field. You aren't able to change this Join field on either side unless you temporarily delete the relationships, change the Autonumber to Number, and reestablish the relationships.

Field Names

It has been shown that the data displayed in a control does not have to be the same as the underlying data. It also should be noted that the field labels in the form do not have to be the same names as the underlying field data. For example, if you have a field named PartNum, you can go ahead and expand the name in the label to Part Number. This does not affect the underlying data but is simply a reference for the user.

Designing a Relational Form

The Form Wizard makes designing a relational form an easy task. To design a relational form from scratch, you have to create a subform for the related table. The wizard can create the subform for you and place it in the proper position on the form.

Enabling the Form Wizard to Create the Form for You

As mentioned previously, a form wizard can automatically handle house-keeping tasks for you. The next exercise shows by example how a wizard can save you time by handling tasks associated with relational forms, such as configuring a subform.

The following steps will lead you through the Form Wizard creating a relational form:

1. Open the Music Store database from the AccessByExample folder. Under Objects, choose Forms.

2. Double-click Create Form By Using Wizard to open the first page of the Form Wizard.

3. On page 1 of the wizard, under Tables/Queries, click the drop-down box and choose Table:Customers.

4. Under Available Fields: click the >> button to move all the fields over to the Selected Fields column.

5. Click the Sort Name under Selected Fields, and click the < button to bring it back to the Available Fields box.

6. Stay in page 1 of the Form Wizard dialog box. Under Tables/Queries click the drop-down box and choose Table:Invoice (see Figure 5.21).

7. Under Available Fields: click >> to move all the fields over to the Selected Fields column as shown in Figure 5.21.

8. Click the Invoice.CustomerID under Selected Fields and click < to bring it back to the Available Fields box.

9. Under Tables/Queries click the down arrow and choose Table:InvoiceDetail.

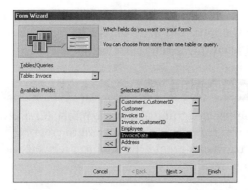

Figure 5.21: *The Form Wizard guides you through selecting objects and for-matting options for your form.*

10. Click >> to bring all the fields over to the Selected Fields column. Click InvoiceDetail.InvoiceID and click < to bring it back to the available fields box. Click Next to open page 2 of the wizard.

11. When page 2 asks, "How do you want to view your data?" click Next to select by Customers. You are also selecting Form with subform(s) from the bottom two options.

12. Page 3 of the wizard asks "What layout would you like for each sub-form?" Because Datasheet is already selected for both subforms, click Next.

13. On page 4 of the wizard, leave Standard selected and then click Next.

14. Leave the suggested names for the forms, and click Finish to open the form shown in Figure 5.22.

15. Examine the form and then close it.

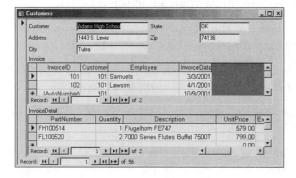

Figure 5.22: *The Form Wizard creates a relational form with subforms automatically nested within the main form.*

In a matter of minutes, you created a relational form based on three tables. The subforms are linked properly because the tables upon which they are based are linked in the Relationships window. Although this form could have been created manually, a wizard can save you time by handling subform placement, links, and other housekeeping chores for you.

What's Next

This chapter introduced you to some of the basics of form design and maintenance. You have learned about form properties and events, and control properties and events. You learned how to create a command button and a calculated control. You have also gotten a taste of attaching code to an event in a control or a form.

Chapter 6, "Exploring Reports," applies some of these same concepts to a report while introducing you to a report's versatility. Just as this chapter focuses on the way data is structured and inputted, the next chapter focuses on the way data is presented for viewing or printing. Ample space is devoted to report controls and sections.

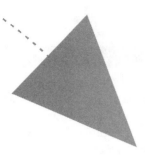

Exploring Reports

The last chapter introduced you to forms and controls. This chapter deals with the various components of reports, such as controls and sections. You learn how to group and sort controls within sections. More specifically, you learn

- the differences between spreadsheets and reports
- how to create a report from scratch
- how sections and controls work together
- how to control controls on reports
- how to set up spreadsheet-like calculations in reports
- how to take charge of grouping and sorting
- how to total within groups
- how to design a relational report using a wizard

Reports Versus Spreadsheets

Reports are about formatting data for output. You can output to any device connected to your computer, whether it be a standard device such as a screen or printer, or a more sophisticated device, such as a projector or Web server. Reports are also about flexibility. The same data can be viewed using several types of reports so that you can analyze the data from a variety of perspectives. Conversely, you also can use the same report for various data sources, such as different tables with the same structure or dynamic sources, such as queries and procedures. The record source property can be changed programmatically to accommodate a wide variety of data sources.

Reports share the same functionality as queries and forms in at least one respect: They are dynamic. This means that when the underlying data changes, the report molds itself to the new changes. In a sense, reports become living documents. In contrast to forms, they *reflect* but don't *affect* changes to the underling data. Forms can do both. However, this does not mean that you cannot perform calculations, create conditional formatting on the fly, group and sort data, and perform a whole host of other operations. But these operations only affect the way the data is displayed. If you want to make permanent changes to the underlying data, make them in an input object such as a form or a table.

This functionality gives you a major advantage over a spreadsheet. When you add data to a spreadsheet, you must also add or copy the formatting that makes it consistent with the related data. After the report has been created and refined to your specifications in Access, you can use it over and over again, feeling assured that you can expect consistent results time after time.

Although updating field data in the report's underlying table is no problem, changing table structure is another matter. In Access 97, if you renamed a field in the underlying table, the report that was based on the table with the renamed field would no longer recognize the field. With Access 2002, when you rename the field in the underlying table, that change is reflected in the report. This functionality was added in Access 2000. However, if you delete the field in the underlying table, the field in the report is still there, but it's not recognized.

Report Basics

If you look at the building blocks of a report, the main components are sections and controls. Sections organize the flow of data by processing one record at a time. So, both timing and organization must be considered. For example, the report footer section will not be processed until the last record on the report is printed. Similarly, the first group record will not be processed until the first group header (assuming there is one) is printed.

✔ For more information about controls, see Chapter 5, "Exploring Forms and Controls."

In short, sections help you view your data in whatever order and whatever format that is pleasing to you. You are not forced to use them, but they can do a lot more than just make your report aesthetically pleasing. They can summarize data for subtotals and grand totals. You also can use them to create title pages, footnotes, and the list goes on.

The text box is the most important control on the report because it is the basic building block of a report record. When you create a report using a Report Wizard, the fields you select are inserted as text boxes. When you insert page numbers, dates, or times in the report, you use text boxes. If you perform calculations, totals and subtotals, you use text boxes. Other types of controls that are used heavily in reports are labels, subforms, lines, boxes, and images.

✔ For more information on report controls, see "Taking Charge of Report Controls," later in this chapter.

The location of a control in a section determines where and how often it prints in the report. For example, if you place a text box in the group footer section of a report, you can make it a subtotal using an expression such as =Sum([UnitPrice]). This subtotal prints after each group section when you run the report. If you place a date in the page footer section, it prints once at the bottom of every page.

✔ For more information on sections, see "Understanding Sections," later in this chapter.

Events help you manage both sections and controls. Depending on the situation, your application responds to report events that Access or the user generates. You can use both report events and section events to create custom procedures that give you greater control and flexibility over virtually every object in the report. Four report events occur when the user performs an action on the report, such as opening or closing the report. The other three events, such as On No Data, are application generated. For example, if the record source produces no records, the On No Data event is triggered.

In contrast, the section events are generated before Access formats or prints each record (details section) or section (all other sections). For example, the On Format event occurs before Access formats each report record or section. This means that you can tell Access how to format each record or section before it prints. You can even use events to print conditional messages in sections. For example, you can display or hide a message congratulating a salesperson next to the salesperson's totals, depending on their sales.

✔ For more information on events, see "More on Object Events" in Chapter 7, "Exploring Objects."

The two main report types are columnar and tabular. Columnar is suited for all kinds of fill-in-the-blank style forms, such as applications or invoices. They are used to print the results after the blanks have been filled in. Tabular reports look more like spreadsheets because they typically have a design structure of rows and columns. Figure 6.1 shows both report types side by side.

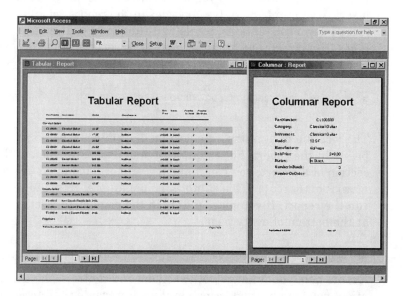

Figure 6.1: *When Columnar and Tabular are placed side by side, you can see the contrast in the two styles.*

Creating a Report from Scratch

You can create a report in a number of ways, one of which is a report wizard that functions in much the same way as the form wizard. However, if you have a report design idea that is unlike most of the standard report design formats, you might consider building the report from scratch. Using this method, you start with a blank screen and add the various components, such as sections and controls, manually. Although this method is more difficult, there is much you can learn in the process.

To get you started while equipping you with a few practical tools, allow the following exercise to guide you by example through creating a columnar report:

1. Open the Music Store database from the AccessByExample folder.

2. Under Objects, click on Reports to view a list of reports, and then double-click the Create Report in Design View option to open a blank report as shown in Figure 6.2.

The report selector

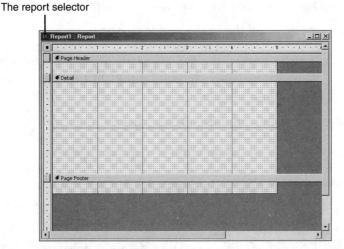

Figure 6.2: *Notice the toolbar and the grouping and sorting button in the blank report design window.*

The toolbar in Figure 6.2 is similar to the toolbar in the form design window. However, next to the Toolbox button is a button that you will not find on the form toolbar. It is the Grouping and Sorting button. You will also notice a Page Header and Page Footer section in the Design view. You can turn these on and off, but if they are on, whatever is in them will print once per page. To the left of the toolbox is the Field List button. Notice that it is grayed out, which means that it is not active.

It is important for you to remember that whether you are in a form or report, unless you have a record source, the Field List button is not activated, which is indicated by the button being grayed out.

TIP

A shortcut to right-clicking the report is to simply click the Properties button. Keep in mind that using this method, you open the Properties page of whatever object your cursor is on. For example, if you click the Report Selector, and then click the Properties button, this precludes you from having to right-click before choosing properties. Clicking either the Title bar, the Report Selector, (see Figure 6.2) or the gray area to the right of the report selects the report.

3. Click the Report Selector; then click the Properties button, and click the Data tab of the Property sheet.

4. In the record source box, type SELECT * FROM Inventory WHERE Inventory.NumberInStock>4; and press Enter. The Field List box opens, activating the Field List button. You can now turn the Field List box off and on using the Field List button.

5. After closing the Property sheet, resize the Field List box (if necessary) by placing your cursor over one of the four edges and watching for the double arrow. Then click, hold, and drag it until you can see all the items. You also can move the Field List box by dragging its title bar to a new location.

6. Click the PartNumber (first) field. While holding the Shift key down, click the Manufacturer field, as shown in Figure 6.3, to select the first five items in the Field List.

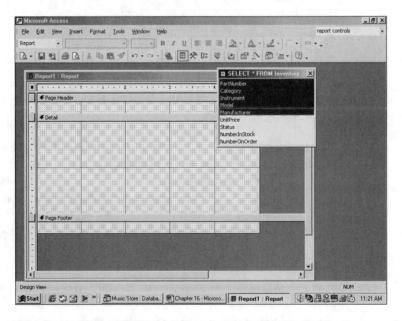

Figure 6.3: *Use the Field List to select multiple fields that can be inserted into the detail section.*

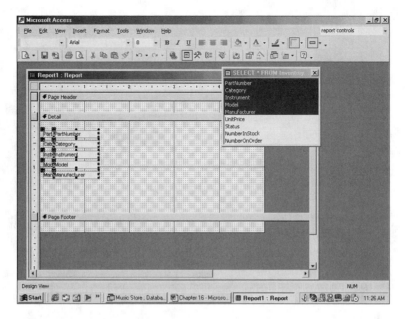

Figure 6.4: *The text boxes inserted into the detail section are fields from the underlying query.*

7. Place your cursor over the highlighted fields; then drag them down to the left side of the Detail section, as shown in Figure 6.4.

8. Click the Unit Price field and Shift-click the NumberOnOrder field to select these items and all items in between.

9. Place your cursor over the highlighted fields and click, hold and drag them down to the right side of the Detail section as shown in Figure 6.5.

10. Click on the PartNumber text box, and then place your cursor as close to the upper-left part of the letter "P" until the cursor turns into a hand with a pointing finger.

11. Click, hold, and drag the PartNumber text box to the right until the PartNumber label is completely showing.

12. Repeat step 11 for the Category, Instrument, Model, and Manufacturer text boxes. Your screen should look like Figure 6.6. Leave this database open.

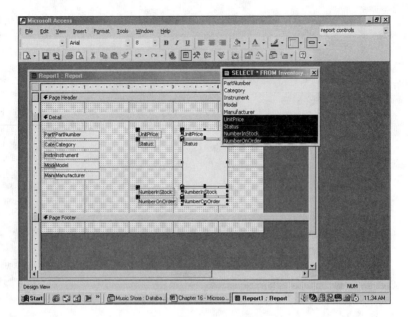

Figure 6.5: *The Detail section is populated with the second group of fields from the Field List.*

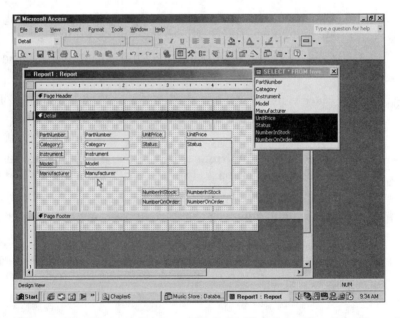

Figure 6.6: *The text boxes on the left side of the Detail section after separating them from their labels.*

13. Close the Field List box.

Controls for the Page Header and Page Footer Section

You can use the page header and page footer sections to insert controls that repeat every page. For example, if you want to repeat the report title and date at the top of every report page and the time and page number at the bottom of every report page, follow these steps:

1. Click Insert, Date and Time to open the Date and Time dialog box.

2. Uncheck the Include Time option. This ensures that you will only get a date. Click OK. The date will appear in the Detail section. Drag it to the right side of the Page Header section.

CAUTION

If you use the up-arrow key to cursor the text box up, it will enlarge the Page Header section, but if you drag it up with the mouse, the section remains the same size. Use the hand cursor instead of the pointing finger to move across sections using the mouse.

TIP

You also can type =Date() in a text box to get the same results.

3. Click the Toolbox button, and then select the Label tool (looks like upper- and lowercase italicized "a").

4. To draw the label on the left side of the Page Header section, click, hold, and drag it from upper-left to lower-right, forming a small rectangle.

5. Type Inventory Status Report in the label box. Leave the box selected for the next step.

6. From the formatting toolbar, select 14 from the Font Size drop-down box. Select Format, Size, To Fit from the toolbar. Your screen should look like Figure 6.7.

7. Click Insert, Page Numbers from the toolbar. Select Page N of M, Bottom of Page, Right alignment, and Show Number on First Page from the dialog box, as shown in Figure 6.8. Click OK.

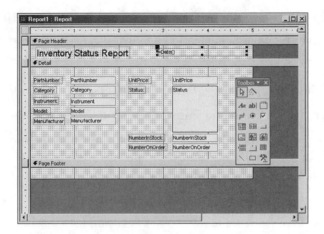

Figure 6.7: *Use the Page Header section to insert and format a report title and current date.*

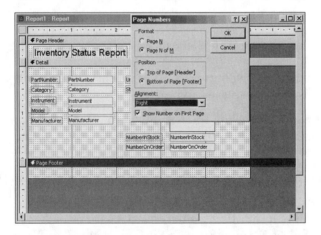

Figure 6.8: *The Page Numbers dialog box helps you position and align the page number in the report footer section.*

8. Select the Text Box tool from the Toolbox and draw the text box on the left side of the Page footer section. Click the label attached to the text box and press the Delete key to remove it.

9. Type ="Report printed at: " & Time() in the text box, (don't forget both quotes) as shown in Figure 6.9.

10. With the text box selected, press F4 and type txtTime in the Name property. Close the Property sheet, but stay in the report.

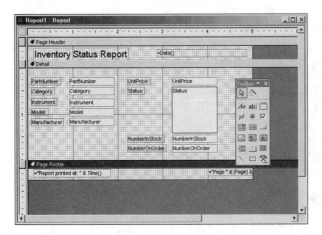

Figure 6.9: *The Page Footer section is a good place for page numbers and date or time controls.*

What to Do When No Records Are Retrieved

A common problem facing users is dealing with reports that retrieve no records. Fortunately, the On No Data event gives you a mechanism to handle such dilemmas.

1. Click the Print Preview button. Notice that no data prints. Close the preview screen.

2. Right-click in a gray area to the right of the report and choose Properties to open the Property sheet.

3. Click the Event tab and select the On No Data event. From the dropdown menu, choose [Event Procedure] and click the Build button.

4. Insert the following code between the Private Sub and End Sub lines:

```
MsgBox "No records were retrieved.", vbOKOnly
Cancel = True
```

Close the Module window and the Property sheet.

5. Click the Print Preview button again. You should now see the message in Figure 6.10. Click OK, and then close the preview screen.

6. Right-click the Report Selector, choose Properties, and click the Data tab.

7. Click the Record Source property and click the Build button. Notice that you are in Query Design view.

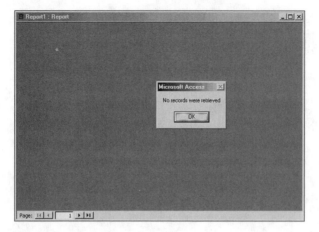

Figure 6.10: *The procedure attached to the* On No Data *event created this message.*

8. In the Criteria row, change >4 to >2. Close the Query Builder and click Yes to close and save the query; then, close the Properties sheet.

9. Click the Print Preview button again. This time you should see data. Notice that the Status field is a list box. Close the preview screen.

10. Right-click the Status text box and then choose Change To, Text Box. Choose Print Preview one last time and close the Preview screen.

11. Click the NumberInStock field, and then Shift-click the NumberOnOrder field.

12. Place the cursor over the fields. When the cursor changes to a hand, move the NumberInStock and NumberOnOrder fields up to a position just underneath the Status field.

13. Place the cursor over the top edge of the Page Footer section. When the cursor changes to a double-headed arrow, click, hold, and drag the section just under the Manufacturer field.

14. Close and save the Report as Inventory Status Report.

Taking Charge of Report Controls

In contrast to form controls, you cannot enter data into report controls. Therefore, its controls are used for display purposes. Even when you use a report control to calculate or manipulate information, it is still with a view toward displaying the data. Typically, the text box and label are the most heavily used controls in a report. Display-oriented controls, such as boxes, lines, and graphical controls are also helpful when you are endeavoring to make your report aesthetically pleasing. This chapter explains, by example, various methods for unleashing the power of the text box.

The toolbox for forms and reports is basically the same. This means that you use the same controls for reports that you use for forms, although there are differences, both in design and in function. One of the main differences you will notice when comparing report controls to form controls is the absence of events (although there is an event tab). There are other ways to program and refer to controls on the report. For example, when you right-click the various sections of the report, you can access the event tab to refer to controls in that section. You also can use the conditional formatting functionality, detailed later in this chapter, to format controls. And if that's not enough, you can use the events in the properties of the report to address and program the report's controls.

There is yet another way to control controls on the report. You can address the Control Source or the Control Name through another control. This is an easy way to set up spreadsheet-like calculations in reports. Let's try this technique by example.

Setting Up Spreadsheet-like Calculations in Report Controls

There are different ways to type expressions in report controls. You can right-click a control to access its Control Source property in the Property sheet, or you can click directly on the text box and start typing. You might be wondering, "Why not just type the formula in the box directly every time?" This method would work, except for the fact that you might need to right-click the controls anyway to check the other properties. What's more, right-clicking the control offers options for better views of your expressions.

There are two ways to refer to controls in a report. You can refer to them by their control name or by their control source, which is most commonly the field name. If the control source happens to be an expression, then you should use the control name to refer to the control. This works to your advantage by giving you a mechanism to set up spreadsheet-like calculations. The next steps show you how to accomplish this:

1. Be sure the Music Store database is open from a previous example.

2. Under Objects, choose Reports. Under Reports, click the Invoice Practice report, and then choose Design from the database toolbar.

3. Maximize the report and use the vertical scrollbar at the bottom of the report to scroll down. Notice the three labels named Sub Total, Tax, and Total, respectively.

4. Right-click the text box next to the Sub Total label and select Properties to open the Property sheet.

5. Type =sum(ExtendedPrice) in the Control Source property. Cursor down and notice how the brackets are inserted automatically as shown in Figure 6.11 to read =sum([ExtendedPrice]).

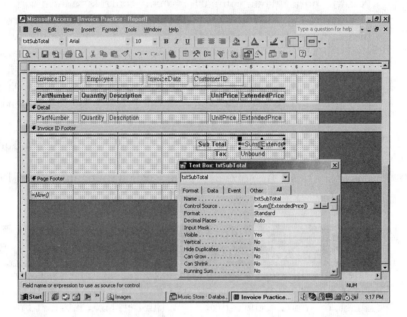

Figure 6.11: *You can type an expression directly into the Control Source property, which references the control source of another field.*

You are addressing the ExtendedPrice field by referencing its control source. The name of the control is txtExtension, *not* ExtendedPrice. The expression =sum([ExtendedPrice]) is used to generate a total for the ExtendedPrice field.

TIP

The Hungarian naming convention places a txt prefix in front of the control name to distinguish it as a text box. A combo box uses a cbo prefix, and so forth. When you see txt before the control name, you immediately know what type of control it is. You also know that it is not a field name. Access doesn't force you to use naming conventions, but using them for these kinds of situations makes good sense. Keep in mind that when you create a form or report using a wizard, the controls created by the wizard have to be changed to this naming convention manually.

6. While on the Control Source box, click the box next to the Tax label. (You might have to move the Property sheet you are in to view the text

box). This time, type =txtExtension * .08 in the Control Source property and press the down arrow (see Figure 6.12).

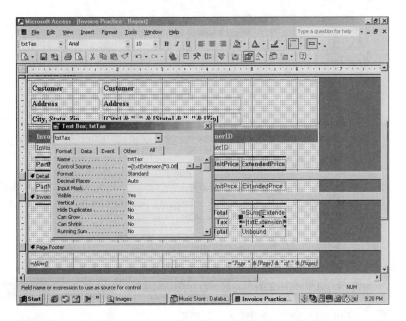

Figure 6.12: *You can use the Control Name to reference another control for an expression.*

7. Close the Property sheet of the control.

8. This time, click directly in the box. (After you slowly click twice on the text box, "Unbound" should disappear.) Type =txtSubTotal + txtTax in the box.

TIP

You also can use the Build button on the Control Source property to build your expressions. You do this by clicking an unbound control. Next, click the Properties button. Then click the Build button next to the Control Source box. The Expression Builder will open as shown in Figure 6.13.

In this exercise, you have discovered two ways to reference controls. The second method, referencing the Control Name rather than the Control Source, is similar to addressing a cell in a spreadsheet. Typing =txtSubTotal + txtTax is easier than typing =sum([ExtendedPrice]) + sum([ExtendedPrice]) * .08 for the txtTotal control. If the formula were more complicated, you would realize even more benefit.

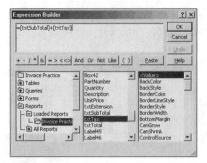

Figure 6.13: *You can use the Expression Builder to build your expressions for you.*

9. Be sure you have canceled any control operations, and click the Print Preview icon to view the report. Click the areas containing the totals to zoom closer. Close print preview.

10. Close and save the report.

Taking Charge of Grouping and Sorting

The most common need for totals in the report is for groups of like values. For example, if you were in the insurance business, you might want to see all the claims for a particular year. If you were in sales, you might want to see the sales totals per region. Grouping gives you this capability. If you group by state, you might want to sort those groups. Within each state group you might want to sort the ZIP codes. This is a multi-level sort, which you can look at as a sort within a sort.

If you wanted to group all the values for a particular year in a query, you obviously have a problem if your date field is the value to group by. You will not have like values in that field because the dates will be distributed throughout the year. There is an easy remedy for this dilemma. You can create a calculated field in a query that would look something like this: SalesYear: Year([DateField]); then group on that field and tie the query to a report. It's that simple! The same principle would also work on the month; just use the month function instead of the year function.

But there's more good news. You don't have to create a query with a calculated field to group on a date field in a report. When you group on any date field in a report, Access has the capability of grouping on month, quarter, year, and so forth.

✔ For more information about groups, see "Creating Groups in Reports," later in this chapter.

✔ To learn more about grouping on date ranges, see "Using Query By Table Example For 'If Then' Scenarios" in Chapter 16, "Overcoming the Limitations of Queries."

Creating Groups in Reports

Before you try creating groups by example, take a look at the options available from the Sorting and Grouping dialog box, as shown in Figure 6.14. The following four tables offer an overview of the Sorting and Grouping dialog box functionality, which you can use later for reference purposes. Table 6.1 explains the Group Properties section of the Sorting and Grouping dialog box by explaining the options for the various properties; Table 6.2 explains the Group On property; Table 6.3 details the Group Interval option and how it works with the Group On property; and Table 6.4 shows what various Keep Together property options mean.

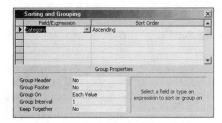

Figure 6.14: *You can set sorting and grouping options using the Sorting and Grouping dialog box.*

Table 6.1: Sorting and Grouping Dialog Box Properties

Property	Function	Options
Group Header	Turns group header on or off	Yes, No
Group Footer	Turns group footer on or off	Yes, No
Group On	Determines grouping value	See Table 6.2
Group Interval	Works with Group On	See Table 6.3
Keep Together	Keeps parts of the group (including sections) on the same page.	See Table 6.4

Table 6.2: Group On Property

Data Type	Setting	Groups Records With
Text	Each Value	Same value in field or expression
	Prefix Characters	Same n (number) of characters in field or expression

Table 6.2: continued

Data Type	Setting	Groups Records With
Date/Time	Each Value	Same value in field or expression
	Year	Dates in the same year
	Qtr	Dates in the same qtr
	Month	Dates in the same month
	Week	Dates in the same week
	Day	Dates in the same day
	Hour	Times in the same hour
	Minute	Times in the same minute
AutoNumber, Currency, Number	Each value	Same value in field or expression
	Interval	Values within specified interval

Table 6.3: Group Interval Property

Field Data Type	Group On Setting	Group Interval Setting
All	Each value	Set to 1
Text	Prefix characters	Set to 3 to group by first three characters (for example, Manchester, Manford, and Mansfield would be grouped together)
Date/Time	Week	Set to 2 to group data biweekly
Date/Time	Hour	Set to 12 for 12-hour (half day) groups

Table 6.4: Keep Together Property Groups

Setting	Description
No	Prints the group without keeping the group header, detail section, and group footer on the same page.
Whole Group	Prints the group header, detail section, and group footer on the same page.
With First Detail	Only prints the group header on a page if it can also print the first detail record.

Let's say that the Enterprise Music Store management wanted to add totals to the Inventory report. Now that you have had a chance to study the Sorting and Grouping dialog box, you can explore how to use it by example. The following example walks you through creating groups in reports teaching how to sort and place controls within the group in the process:

1. Be sure the Music Store database is open.

2. Under Reports, click the Inventory Practice Report and then click Design to open the Report in Design view.

3. Right-click the Page Header section of the report, and choose Sorting and Grouping from the shortcut menu, or click the Sorting and Grouping button from the toolbar to open the Sorting and Grouping dialog box.

4. Click the drop-down box on the right side of the Field/Expression box, and choose the Category field to open the Group Properties section.

   Notice the ascending value is automatically inserted in the Sort Order column.

5. Click the drop-down box of the Group Header box in the Group Properties section, and then choose Yes. You also can double-click the Group Header box to choose Yes.

   Notice that the Category section header is inserted into your report, as shown in Figure 6.15. Do the same for the Group Footer box. This places a group section into your report in which you can place controls, depending on what section you are in. For example, if you are in the header section, you might want to place an identifier, such as a text box, to separate and identify the groups. If you are in the footer section, you can place labels, text boxes, or calculated fields such as subtotals. Of course, you can place lines, boxes, or graphics objects in any section you like.

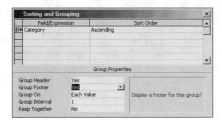

Figure 6.15: *When you choose Yes on the Group Header property, a new section is inserted into your report.*

6. Click the drop-down box in the second row Field/Expression column, and choose Status.

7. Click the drop-down box in the Sort Order column of the Status row, and choose Descending.

   Status is sorted in descending order because it makes sense to see the on-order items first in each group; but because "i" for "in stock" comes before "o" for "on order," the appropriate sort order would be reversed or ascending.

8. Close the Grouping and Sorting dialog box.

9. Click the Category Header section.

10. Click the Toolbox to activate it, and then choose the Text Box tool. Your cursor will change to text box with "ab" inside and a plus sign, as shown in Figure 6.16.

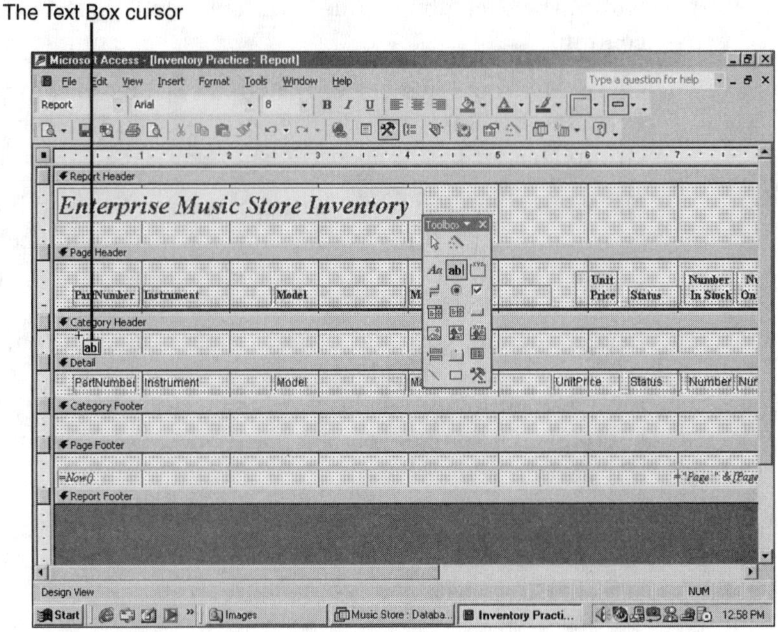

The Text Box cursor

Figure 6.16: *The cursor changes to a text box when you select the Text Box tool from the Toolbox.*

11. Click in the upper-left corner of the Category Header section. You also can click, hold, and drag it to draw the box, but in this case, it is easier to just click the area and let Access draw it.

12. Click the label attached to the text box and press Delete to remove it. (If the label is not visible, move the text box to the right.)

13. Right-click the unbound text box, and choose Properties from the shortcut menu. Click the All tab.

14. Click the drop-down box in the Control Source box, and then choose the Category field.

15. Type txtCategory in the Name property box. Close the Property sheet.

16. Making sure the text box is still selected, choose Format, Size, To Fit from the menu. Your text box should fit the text perfectly now. Also click the Bold button.

17. Close the Toolbox.

18. Move the Category text box by holding down the Ctrl key and pressing the left arrow repeatedly until the box is to the left of the part number text box in the Detail section, and even with the line that separates the labels from the fields in the Page Header section, as shown in Figure 6.17.

Figure 6.17: *The correct position for the* Category *field after formatting and moving.*

19. Click the Print Preview button. You can now easily zoom to any area of the report by clicking that area as shown in Figure 6.18.

20. Click the Close button of the Print Preview window but stay in the report.

Providing Totals for Groups

A common request from users is to provide totals for groups. For example, if you want to group inventory items by category, you need a group section in which to place controls that sum each category. The following example walks you through the process of creating the totals:

1. Click the report's horizontal scrollbar near the bottom of the design window until you can see the Extended Price label, as shown in Figure 6.19.

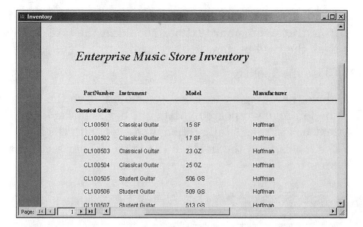

Figure 6.18: *Print preview shows how the Category field separates the groups.*

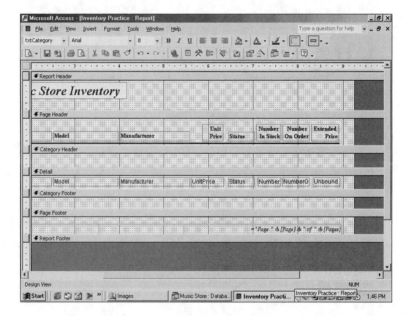

Figure 6.19: *Scroll horizontally to view the Extended Price label.*

2. Click the unbound text box in the Detail section beneath the label. Be sure the control handles are showing. Click the box again. (It might take a little practice, but the word "Unbound" should disappear, allowing you to start typing at the leftmost position.)

3. Type = UnitPrice* NumberInStock and press Enter. You don't have to type the brackets because they are filled in automatically as long as

the field names are correct. You are multiplying the UnitPrice field by the NumberInStock field by referencing the control source of both text boxes.

4. Right-click the calculated field from step 3, and then choose Properties. Click the Format tab and then click the Format property box, click the drop-down box, and choose Standard.

5. Close the Property sheet.

6. Click Print Preview again. Notice how the extended price is included.

7. Click Close to close Print Preview.

8. If not already selected, click the text box in the detail section under the ExtendedPrice label.

9. Press Ctrl+C and Ctrl+V to copy and paste the text box. The section should expand to accommodate the new control, as shown in Figure 6.20.

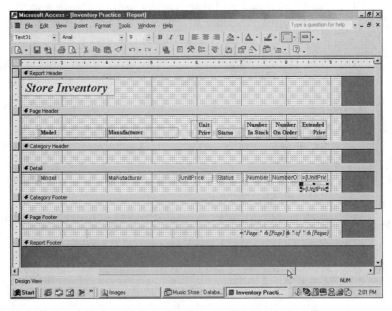

Figure 6.20: *A faster way to create a control is to copy and paste a previously created control.*

10. Move your cursor around on the bottom of the copied text box until the cursor turns into an open hand.

11. Click, hold, and drag the box down to the Category Footer section directly under the original text box.

You can also right-click the box, choose Copy from the shortcut menu, right-click the Category Footer section, and choose Paste. Keep in mind that the control will end up in the upper-left corner of the destination section using this method.

12. Click, hold, and drag the top part of Category Footer section to its original position.

13. Click the copied box, and click into the box. Type `=Sum([UnitPrice]*[NumberInStock])`. You are adding the `Sum` function to the previous formula. Press Enter to accept the new formula.

NOTE

While in the Properties page (you can just click the Properties button while on the control), if you want to view more text in a calculated field without clicking the build button, you can also right-click the Control Source property and select Zoom. This option has more viewing space than the build button. In addition, this works on some properties that don't have a build button.

---

14. Click the Label tool from the toolbox to create a label in the Category Footer under the Manufacturer text box. Draw the label directly under the text box. Type `Totals` in the box and press Enter.

15. Click the Manufacturer text box, and then click the format painter brush on the toolbar. Click the Totals label to copy the format.

NOTE

When you have more than one object to format, double-click the Format Painter button and format as many objects as you like. Click it again when you want to turn it off.

---

16. While the Totals label is selected, click the Bold button to add bolding to the label.

17. Click the text box in the detail section under the UnitPrice label.

18. Press Ctrl+C and Ctrl+V to copy and paste the text box.

19. Move your cursor around on the bottom of the copied text box until the cursor turns into an open hand.

20. Click, hold, and drag the box down to the Category Footer section directly under the original text box.

21. Click, hold, and drag the top part of the Category Footer section to its original position.

22. Type `=Sum([UnitPrice])` in the text box. Press Enter to accept the new formula.

23. With the text box containing the expression selected, hold down the Shift key and click the UnitPrice text box. With both boxes selected, one right under the other, click Format, Align, Right from the menu as shown in Figure 6.21.

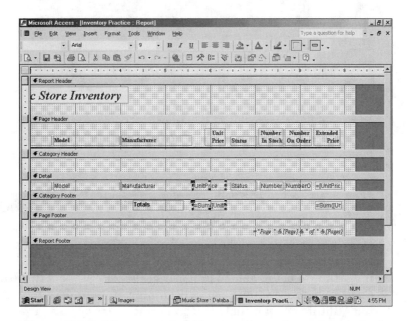

Figure 6.21: *You can right-align text boxes in reports to make sure the numbers line up.*

24. Select by Shift-clicking both text boxes under the Extended Price label and click Format, Align, Right from the menu.

TIP

You can also select boxes by clicking on the ruler directly above the boxes (look for a black arrow) to be selected for vertical selections and directly to the left of the boxes to be selected for horizontal selections. Another option is to simply click, hold, and drag with the Select Objects cursor from a blank area slightly higher and left of the objects to be selected to an area slightly lower and right of the objects to be selected. Notice the box around the text boxes in Figure 6.22. When you release the mouse, the objects will be selected.

---

25. Click the Print Preview button to view the report. Close Print Preview, save the report as Grouping Example; then close the report.

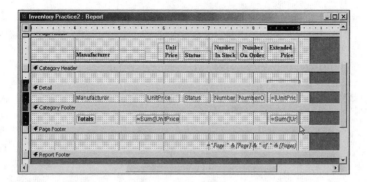

Figure 6.22: *Drawing a box around the text boxes with the Select Objects cursor (arrow pointer) selects the objects that the box encloses before the mouse releases.*

Understanding Sections

One thing to remember is that you don't have to use every section type on every report. Some might even wonder, "Why use sections at all?" It's important to recognize that a proper understanding of sections is critically important to being able to properly organize your report. If you want a cover page to print *only* at the beginning of the report, use the report section. But if you want field titles to print on every page, use the page header section. Groups enable you to separate each group of common values with some space between groups that can be used for totals or other aggregate calculations.

Table 6.5 shows an example of what you can do with sections.

Table 6.5: Controlling Sections

Section	When It Prints	Examples Of Usage
Report Header	Once at the beginning of report	Report title, company logos, cover page, date
Page Header	Once per page	Page header, field titles, report title, page number, date
Group Header	Once per group	Group title
Detail	Every record	Selected fields
Group Footer	Once per group	Subtotals, counts, averages, and so forth
Page Footer	Once per page	Page number, report name, date
Report Footer	Once at the end of the report	Grand total, notes

Some important properties are common to every section except the page section. The following discussion sheds some light on this topic.

Keep Together Property

Let's say that the records in a certain group start printing toward the bottom of the current page, making it impossible to fit the group on that page. When this property is properly set, it ensures that the records in the group are not split across two pages. The group section has two places to set the Keep Together property. Because the default is Yes for the Keep Together property in the group section, you must be sure to set the Sorting and Grouping Keep Together property to Whole Group. Otherwise, the group will still span across two pages.

Can Grow, Can Shrink Properties

Controls also have this property setting. If a control was set to Yes for Can Grow, the section in which it resides can grow to accommodate a large field, such as a memo field, that has a considerable amount of data. The subreport provides another good example of the functionality of the Can Grow property. It's difficult to determine how much vertical space you need in the subreport because the number of records can vary. However, setting the Can Grow property to Yes causes the control and the section to conform to whatever space is required.

You can set the Can Shrink property to Yes if you want the section size to reduce to accommodate less text. You also can use this property to get rid of those pesky empty address lines on controls.

Understanding the Details Section

Imagine what would happen if you took away the controls in this section. You'd be left with only subtotals and grand totals for a summary. There might be times when this is desirable. In those cases, you probably would be better off summarizing in a query to send the results to a report, which would still use the Details section. The only difference between the two scenarios is where the controls reside. In the first case, they reside in the Group Section footer. In the second case, they reside in the Details section because the totals are already calculated.

The Details section is primarily concerned with records. In columnar (rolodex-style) view, you would most likely have the field controls for records with their corresponding labels. But in tabular view, you would most like place the header labels in the page section and place the field controls in the details section.

✔ For information on how to program the Details section, see "Adding Alternating Gray and White Bars To a Report" in Chapter 7, "Exploring Objects."

The On Open Event

In reports, this event occurs before a report is previewed or printed. It is the first event to be activated, giving you an opportunity to set up some housekeeping. For example, you can use this event to change the record source to match whatever record source is selected in a form. Let's say that you changed the record source in the form from the 2001 year records to the 2000 year records. Obviously, you would want the record source in the report to match your form. You could create another report, but as long as the table or query structures match, that's not necessary.

You can click the Properties button while in Design mode of a report. After the report's properties are open, you can access this event. You also can access the report's properties just by right-clicking the gray area to the right of the report.

Working with the Record Source Property

You could also set the record source to an SQL query through this property. This gives you the ability to use variables to change table names. This makes the query a dynamic record source for the report.

There is another benefit from using a dynamic record source, and this applies to either a form or a report. If you are working with huge databases, involving hundreds of thousands of records, you can avoid the slower performance associated with opening a form or report tied to a single huge table. Break the table into smaller tables and access the tables dynamically. That way the user accesses one group of records at a time.

Designing a Relational Report Using a Wizard

Just as you designed a relational form using a wizard in the last chapter, you can use a wizard to design a report in much the same way. You can design the report from scratch or just base the report on a relational query, but for most purposes, you might as well take advantage of a Report Wizard. The following steps show you how to design a relational report using a report wizard:

1. Be sure the Music Store database is open.

2. Under Objects, click Reports to view a list of reports and report options.

3. Click Create Report by Using Wizard to open the wizard.

4. Under Tables/Queries, click the drop-down box, and then choose Table:Customers.

5. Under Available Fields, click >> to move all the fields over to the Selected Fields box.

6. Click the Sort Name field under Selected Fields and click < to bring it back to the Available Fields box.

7. Stay in the dialog box. Under Tables/Queries click the down arrow and choose Table:Invoice.

8. Under Available Fields click >> to move all the fields over to the Selected Fields box.

9. Click Invoice.CustomerID under Selected Fields and click < to bring it back to the Available Fields box.

10. Repeat steps 7 and 8 for Table:InvoiceDetail.

11. Click the InvoiceDetail.InvoiceID field and click < to bring it back to the Available Fields box. Click Next.

12. On page 2 of the wizard, which asks, "How do you want to view your data?" click Next to accept the selection "by Customers."

13. On page 3, which is the grouping levels page, click Next to accept the default grouping levels.

14. On page 4, which is the sort order page, click Next to use no sorting in this report.

15. On page 5, which is the layout page, choose Align Left 1 (leave the default of Portrait for Orientation as shown in Figure 6.23) and choose Next.

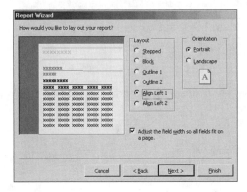

Figure 6.23: *Choosing a layout for your report using a Report wizard.*

16. On the style screen, after cycling through the various styles, leave Corporate and choose Next.

17. On the next screen, title the report Customer Invoices and click Finish.

18. Click Close to look at the design screen. Close the report.

Conditional Formatting

Conditional formatting enables you to change the format of a control in a form or report based on the value of the control. If you want to change a control's color to red when its value exceeds 2,000, you can do that using conditional formatting. In the old days, before the conditional formatting function was added to Access, it was handled through code. You no longer have to be a programmer to take advantage of this feature. The following steps guide you through adding conditional formatting to a report:

1. While in the Music Store database, open the Inventory Practice report in Design view.

2. Click the UnitPrice text box.

3. Click Format, Conditional Formatting from the menu, or right-click and choose Conditional Formatting from the shortcut menu.

4. Click the box to the right of the between box under Condition 1.

5. Type 1000 and press Tab. Type 1999 in the box after the word "and."

6. Click the B for boldface and watch the text on the large white box below the Condition 1 boxes change to boldface.

7. Click the Add button next to add the next condition. In the Condition 2 section, click the drop-down box of the between box.

8. Choose greater than and press Tab. Type 2000.

9. Click the drop-down box next to the A for alpha button as shown in Figure 6.24.

10. Choose red (the third box down from black). Click OK to set the format.

11. Click Print Preview to view the report, as shown in Figure 6.25.

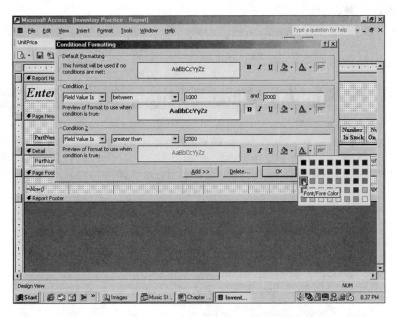

Figure 6.24: *You can use conditional formatting options in a report without programming.*

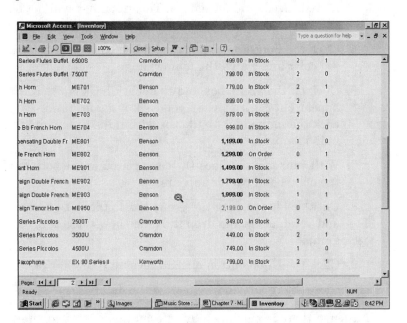

Figure 6.25: *Use the Print Preview option to check the conditional formatting results.*

12. Click the next record indicator to view subsequent pages while check-ing the Unit Price text box to confirm the conditional formatting. Close Print Preview as well as the report.

Creating a Group of Controls

Access 2002 has the capability to group controls. This is handy for several reasons. You don't have to continue to select and reselect groups of controls. Now you can group them so that they can be moved, sized, and formatted as a group. They remain grouped even after you exit (providing that you save the report) and reopen the report.

1. While in the Music Store database, open the Invoice Practice report in Design view. Cursor or mouse-click down until you see the Sub Total, Tax, and Total labels.

2. Click the Sub Total text box to the right of the Sub Total label. Hold the Shift key down, and click the Tax and Total text boxes.

3. Choose Format, Group.

4. Notice that the labels are surrounded by a box. This box can be moved, sized, and formatted. The group box will not be printed from your printer or in Print Preview mode.

5. Click the Font/Fore Color drop-down box on the toolbar. Choose the red color and watch the fonts change.

6. Click off the group box and then click back on it. The box seems to dis-appear but returns when you click it again. However, you can still click the individual text boxes within the group and format them individually.

7. With your mouse, place the cursor around the bottom of the box until the open hand cursor appears.

8. Click, hold, and drag the group box to the left of the Sub Total, Tax, and Total labels and drop it. Notice how three text boxes move as a group.

9. Click the Undo button once to reverse your changes.

10. Close the report and then close the database.

Although there is much helpful information in this chapter, it is not neces-sarily comprehensive regarding report basics. For more information about the topics covered in this chapter, see Que's *Special Edition Using Access 2002* by Roger Jennings, ISBN 0-7897-2510-X.

What's Next

In this chapter, you learned the advantages of a report over a spreadsheet. You learned how to group, sort, and work with sections. You have gotten a taste of conditional formatting and the grouping of controls. Both of these features can be used on a form, as well. The next chapter delves further into the matter of objects. This includes a further discussion of using events and Visual Basic to automate your database.

Part III

Automate Your Access Database Using Code

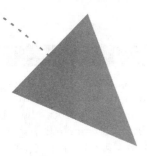

Exploring Objects

In the last two chapters, you learned about forms and reports, which are both objects that rely heavily on controls, which are also objects. This chapter delves into what objects are and what they can do for you. More specifically, you learn

- what objects are
- what objects are in Access
- how methods, properties, and events pertain to objects
- how to name objects
- how to refer to objects
- how to change object properties manually and through VBA
- how to manage object events
- how to work with object events by example
- how to program using object models
- how to program controls

Defining Objects

A search for a definition of *object* can yield anything from "data with an attitude" to "something someone at Microsoft thought up to sell more programming languages." Objects are compared to everything from black boxes to animals. You can't say that objects are anything you can click, because objects are not always visible. But you can generally say that an object is any autonomous (self-contained) program component that can be selected and modified either directly by the user or indirectly through programming. In Access, an object represents an element of an application, such as a table, query, form, report, macro, module, or control.

Access uses hundreds of objects of various types. Some types (such as forms, reports, controls, and modules) can be clicked and modified. These objects display the data available in the database. Others are used to retrieve, store, and modify the data itself. Still others facilitate writing code in VBA, which is a subset of Visual Basic. You can even create custom objects that represent real-life people, places, and things.

Objects encapsulate their own data, methods (procedures), or both data and methods. Like real-life objects, they have form and content. The *form* is how the content is presented. Part of their content is about their form. For example, object properties pertain to how the object is presented or how it behaves. What font size or color should the object use? Will it be visible or invisible? Will it output all fields? Will it set a default value? The other part of their content is the actual user data or procedures they contain.

An object has state, behavior, and identity.

- The *state* pertains to the data that the object encapsulates or the object itself. For example, the length and width of a box represents state.

- The *behavior* pertains to the object's methods, which in Access refer to sub procedures and function procedures. Behavior allows objects to interact with each other.

- The *identity* refers to a unique way to refer to the object, most commonly by a name. Suppose you had many boxes on a form. How could you distinguish between them?

Objects respond to events. However, objects can be active or passive; they can initiate or react to events. For example, opening a form object initiates the form's On Open event. When a button is clicked on a form, triggering the On Click event, a report object can react by printing the form's current record. Activation of events give objects a mechanism to relate to other objects. Objects can change or be changed. They can even allow the user to destroy other objects.

The capability to contain and hide information about an object, such as internal data and code, is called *encapsulation*. Access form and report objects generally encapsulate properties, methods, and events. These can be defined as

- **Properties**—Refers to a defined attribute (characteristic) of an object. This can be a graphical attribute, such as size or color, or a behavioral attribute, such as hidden.

- **Methods**—Refers to services (procedures) that an object provides. For example, the DoCmd object has methods that correspond to most macro actions, such as DoCmd.OpenForm.

- **Events**—Refers to behavior to which objects respond or behavior that objects create. For example, the After Update event occurs after a control's data is updated.

Defining Object Properties

Object properties are individual characteristics or attributes of the object. These properties can be changed manually or programmatically. Now it's time to take a closer look at how to name and reference objects as well as how to inspect and change object properties.

✔ For more information about changing object properties, see "Changing Object Properties" later in this chapter.

Naming Objects

If there was such a thing as an Objects 101 class, you wouldn't get very far without learning about object names. Therefore, before proceeding with object properties, we must take a temporary detour (which, in a way, is not a detour at all) to make sure you understand how to reference objects.

You have already seen that brackets are automatically inserted with object names without spaces in queries. You must manually insert brackets if your object has spaces in its name. But what if your query or form has more than one table with the same field name? How do you reference it? If you have Customer and Order tables that both have CustID fields, you can reference it this way:

```
[Customer]![CustID]
```

But if you have a form called CustForm and another form called CustOrder that have the same field names, you would reference it with the forms reserved word this way:

```
Forms![CustForm]![CustID]
```

Bang Operator Versus Dot Operator

If you want to be able to properly identify objects, you must use the correct syntax. When do you use the Bang (!) operator and when do you use the Dot (.) operator? The novice user can easily get them confused. They are both identifier operators. They both describe relationships between objects and collections, to name a few. So what is the difference?

Generally speaking, you should use the Bang operator to reference the relationship between created objects, such as tables, forms, reports, or controls, which become part of collections. The Dot operator, on the other hand, references the relationship between an object and its property, method, or collection. The following piece of code illustrates:

```
With rs 'Put them in the tables table
     .AddNew
     ![TableName] = td.NAME
     .Update
     .Bookmark = .LastModified
End With
```

The With Construct

The With construct gives you an efficient way to reference multiple properties of objects. Notice that, instead of repeating the rs variable for each object reference, you just use the dot or bang at the beginning of each enclosed line. Therefore, the With construct makes writing code faster. After the code is written, it is also easier to read and maintain.

The rs variable is referencing a recordset from a table of table names. The Bang operator in ![TableName] is referencing a field in the table, but the Dot operator in td.Name is referencing the names of all tables in the TableDef collection. Although both references created objects, the former is being used to reference and add data to a field, and the latter is being used to reference and copy data from a collection's property. The Dot operator on .Update is being used to reference a method.

Changing Object Properties

You can inspect and change object properties in two ways. You can change an object's properties manually by right-clicking on it and choosing Properties, or you can change an object's properties through code. For example, you can right-click a control and enter text into the Control Tip Text property box. You can change the same property through code. This method gives you the opportunity to make the message change depending on conditions or to delete the message altogether if need be. In other words, you have increased flexibility with code. These processes can happen on the fly, as the procedure runs, as opposed to stopping everything and opening up the form or report in Design view to change the control or whatever object you are trying to modify.

Changing Object Properties Through VBA

Although you have already been introduced to using code to change object properties, something needs to be clarified. There are several ways to reference object properties through code. You can reference an object through the Me keyword. You also can reference object properties through their object hierarchy. Assuming the form is open, the following example shows two ways you might refer to a control called ctlPhone on a form called frmCustomer:

```
'Implicit reference
Forms!frmCustomer!ctlPhone.name
'Explicit reference
Forms!frmCustomer.Controls!ctlPhone.name
```

Notice in the implicit reference that the forms collection was referenced first, followed by the form name, followed by the control name, followed by the property. Another way to reference objects and their properties is through object variables. The following example shows how to declare and set object variables:

```
Dim frm as Form
Dim ctl as Control

Set frm = Forms!frmCustomers
Set ctl = frm.Controls!strCompanyName
```

The object variables didn't refer to any objects until they were set. The Set keyword "points" to the object being referenced. Once this is done, you can refer to the objects and their properties this way:

```
VarProperty = ctl.name
```

Suppose there is a field called State on your form. If you want to assign a value to it, you can simply add a line like the following to your code:

```
[State] = "CO"
```

However, you can also reference the field using the Me keyword as follows:

```
Me.[State] = "CO"
```

This keyword is particularly handy if you don't remember the exact name of the field or other object being referenced. As previously stated, after typing Me. in a module, a list appears. It doesn't matter if the field name and control name are different, because you see both choices using the Me keyword.

You can reference this same object using an object variable. The advantage of this method is that you can reference and change every control on the form at the same time, if so desired, by using a variable. All you need to do is declare a variable as a control variable. The With statement can then be used to access the object that the variable references, as follows:

```
Dim MyControl as Control
With MyControl
.ForeColor = 255
End With
```

The With statement is covered in more depth in Chapter 5, "Exploring Forms and Controls," but remember that these various methods of referencing objects are available to you. After you get used to these methods, you're likely to use them over and over again.

More On Object Events

You have been introduced to events in this chapter in theory, as well as by example. At first, events can seem somewhat mysterious. What triggers them? How do you use them? Some events are self-evident from their name. For example, On Click occurs when you click and release the left mouse button on the object. But what about On Focus? What triggers it? Tables 7.1 and 7.2 should be helpful.

Table 7.1: When Events Occur

Event Property	Applies To	How It Is Triggered
	Data Events	
AfterDelConfirm	Forms	After record deletion confirmation or cancellation
AfterInsert	Forms	After a new record is added to the database
AfterUpdate	Forms, controls	After a control or record is updated with changed data
BeforeDelConfirm	Forms	After one or more records are deleted, but before a dialog box is displayed and after the Delete event
BeforeInsert	Forms	When you type the first character in a new record, but before the record is added to the table

Table 7.1: continued

Event Property	Applies To	How It Is Triggered
	Data Events	
BeforeUpdate	Forms, controls	Before a control or record is updated with changed data
OnChange	Controls	When the contents of a text box or the text box portion of a combo box changes
OnCurrent	Forms	When the focus moves to a record, making it the current record, or when you requery a form
OnDelete	Forms	When a record is deleted, but before the deletion is confirmed and performed
OnDirty	Forms	When the contents of a form or the text portion of a combo box changes
OnNotInList	Controls	When a value that isn't in the combo box list is entered in a combo box
OnUpdated	Controls	When an OLE object's data has been modified
	Error and Timing Events	
OnError	Forms, reports	When a Jet runtime error is produced while you are in the form or report
OnTimer	Forms	When a specified time interval passes, as specified
	Filter Events	
OnApplyFilter	Forms	When you click Apply Filter on Forms
OnFilter	Forms	When you click Filter by Forms
	Focus Events	
OnActivate	Forms, reports	When a form or report becomes the active window
OnDeactivate	Forms, reports	When a different window becomes active, but before it loses focus
OnEnter	Controls	Before a control actually receives the focus and before the GotFocus event
OnExit	Controls	Just before a control loses the focus to another control and before the LostFocus event
OnGotFocus	Forms, controls	When a control, or a form with no active or enabled controls, receives the focus
OnLostFocus	Forms, controls	When a form or control loses the focus

Table 7.1: continued

Event Property	Applies To	How It Is Triggered
Keyboard Events		
OnKeyDown	Forms, controls	When you press any key on the keyboard while a control or form has the focus
OnKeyPress	Forms, controls	When you press and release a key or key combination while a control or form has the focus
OnKeyUp	Forms, controls	When you release a pressed key while a control or form has the focus
Mouse Events		
OnClick	Forms, controls	When you press and then release (click) the left mouse button on a control
OnDblClick	Forms, controls	When you press and release (click) the left mouse button twice on a control or its label
OnMouseDown	Forms, controls	When you press a mouse button while the pointer is on a form or control
OnMouseMove	Forms, controls	When you move the mouse pointer over a form, form section, or control
OnMouseUp	Forms, controls	When you release a pressed mouse button while the pointer is on a form or control
Window Events		
OnClose	Forms, reports	When a form or report is closed and is removed from the screen
OnLoad	Forms	When a form is opened and its records are displayed before the Current event, but after the Open event
OnOpen	Forms, reports	When a form is opened but before the first record is displayed; after a report is open, but before it prints
OnResize	Forms	When the size of a form changes; also occurs when a form is first displayed
OnUnload	Forms	When a form is closed and its records are unloaded, but before the Close event
BeforeScreenTip	Forms	Before a ScreenTip is displayed for an element in a Pivot Chart view or PivotTable view

Table 7.2: New Pivot Table and Pivot Chart Events

Event	Available in PivotTable view	Available in PivotChart view
OnConnect, OnDisconnect	Yes	No
BeforeQuery, Query	Yes	No

Table 7.2: continued

Event	Available in PivotTable view	Available in PivotChart view
`AfterLayout, BeforeRender, AfterRender, AfterFinalRender`	No	Yes
`DataChange`	Yes	No
`DataSetChange`	No	Yes
`PivotTableChange`	Yes	No
`SelectionChange, ViewChange`	Yes	Yes
`CommandEnabled, CommandChecked, CommandBeforeExecute,CommandExecute`	Yes	Yes
`KeyDown, KeyPress, KeyUp, MouseDown, MouseMove, MouseUp, MouseWheel, Click, DblClick`	Yes	Yes

Only one item at a time can have the focus. If you enter data in a text box, the string of data appears only if the text box has the focus. On controls, the `Enter` and `GotFocus` events occur in this order: `Enter`, then `GotFocus`.

The `On Click` event is likely to be the preferred event for a command button. It's not a good idea to attach different procedures to the `On Click` and `On Dbl Click` events on the same button; Access is likely to interpret a double-click as a click, thus triggering the `Click` event.

It should be noted that when you find a particular event in the Property Sheet, it will contain spaces to make the property name more readable. For example, the `OnOpen` property in VBA is labeled `On Open` in the Property sheet.

Adding Alternating Gray and White Bars to a Report

Events only make sense in relation to the behavior of the object in which they are encapsulated. You don't open a combo box, so there is no need for a COMBO BOX to have an `On Open` event. You do format the detail section in a report. Consequently, because the detail section is an object, it has an `On Format` event. This event allows you to format each record differently, if this is what you want to do.

The following exercise, which uses a simple procedure, is useful from three perspectives. First, it gives you a taste of the power of Visual Basic for Applications (VBA). Second, it stimulates your thought processes by making you aware of what the details section actually does. Third, it gives you a feel for how to work with events.

1. Open the Inventory Practice Report in the Music Store database, and then click Design view.

2. Right-click the details section and choose Properties from the shortcut menu. The Properties sheet opens.

3. Click the Event tab. After selecting [Event Procedure] from the drop-down box of the On Format event, click the Build button to open the module window shown in Figure 7.1.

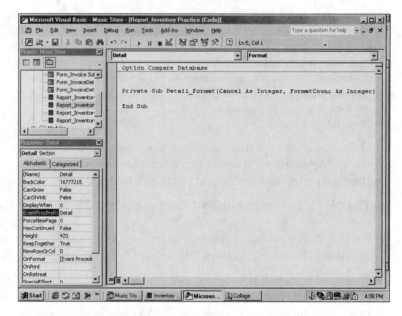

Figure 7.1: *Click the Build button to open the module window in which you can type Visual Basic code.*

4. Enter the following code in the window from the insertion point above the End Sub line. Stay in the module.

```
'Set Constants
Const White = 16777215
Const Gray = 12632256

'Tell the procedure what color to set
'depending on the state of BackForth
Select Case BackForth
  Case True
    Me.Detail.BackColor = White
  Case False
    Me.Detail.BackColor = Gray
End Select
```

```
'Alternate the state of BackForth from True to False and back
'every time the procedure runs (every record)
BackForth = Not BackForth
```

Using an Event to Apply Color to the Details Section

You can use the QBColor function or the RGB function to assign colors to the White and Gray constants, but they do not have a broad enough range of colors. However, if you just need one of the basic colors, these functions work. A typical QBColor statement is Blue = QBColor(2). A typical RGB statement is Red = RGB(255, 0, 0). Tables 7.3 and 7.4 give you the values for the arguments that need to be supplied for standard colors.

Table 7.3: **QBColor** *Function Color Table*

Number	Color
0	Black
1	Blue
2	Green
3	Cyan
4	Red
5	Magenta
6	Yellow
7	White
8	Gray
9	Light Blue
10	Light Green
11	Light Cyan
12	Light Red
13	Light Magenta
14	Light Yellow
15	Bright White

Table 7.4: RGB Function Color Table

Color	Red Value	Green Value	Blue Value
Black	0	0	0
Blue	0	0	255
Green	0	255	0
Cyan	0	255	255
Red	255	0	0
Magenta	255	0	255
Yellow	255	255	0
White	255	255	255

Whenever you have numbers that will not change, you might as well assign them to constants (Const) to save memory. A constant represents a constant or unchanging value, such as a string or numeric literal. You might ask, "Why not just type in the value directly into the code?" If you had a long string or large numeric value that you did not want to repeat over and over in your code, you should use a constant to represent the value. Another reason to use constants is that they make your code more understandable. "Gray" is easier to understand in your code than "12632256."

There are built-in constants representing colors that you can use in your procedures. Suppose you want to have green and white bars instead of gray and white bars. You can use the vbWhite and vbGreen built-in constants for these colors. You also can use vbBlack, vbRed, vbYellow, vbBlue, vbMagenta, and vbCyan for their respective colors. The reason they were not used in the last procedure is that the vbGreen constant produces a green color that is too dark for the purpose of the procedure.

Declaring Public Variables

At first glance, there seem to be no variables in this code. However, the key to the whole procedure is the BackForth variable. It does the alternating by changing back and forth from True to False. It is declared elsewhere as a global (public) variable. This provides the select case statement with an easy way to alternate colors.

Because procedures in the detail section run over and over each time a record is processed, you have to take special care when writing them. For example, if you wrote a one-line procedure that incremented a variable such as "x = x + 1", it would evaluate to "1" for each record instead of incrementing sequentially (for example, 1, 2, 3). That's why you have to declare public (sometimes called global) variables outside the procedure in a standard module. Public variables can be used in any module in Access.

✔ For more information about public variables, refer to the section titled "What Is Scope?" in Chapter 10, "Customizing Your Access Database Using the Power of Functions."

For the reasons just examined, you have to initialize (set for the first time) the BackForth variable somewhere other than in the Details section. If you set it to False in the Details section, it stays set to False with every record, every time the procedure runs. The Not operator changes the variable to the opposite of its current state. If it is True, it changes to False, and vice versa.

The sub procedure you started is not quite finished. You have two more items to take care of. You need to declare a public variable and declare it as False in the page header section.

Follow these steps to guide you to the finishing touches of the procedure:

1. From the Module menu, click Debug, Compile Music Store, as shown in Figure 7.2, and click Save.

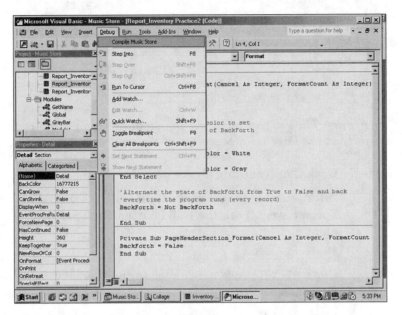

Figure 7.2: *Choose Debug, Compile Music Store to test your code.*

2. Click Insert Module to open a new standard module that is not listed in the report's modules. Because you didn't choose Class Module from the Insert menu, you inserted a standard module.

3. Enter the following statement under the Option Compare Database line at the top of the module:

```
Public BackForth As Boolean
```

4. Click the Save button. When the message asks, "Save changes to the following objects?" click Yes. Save the module as basGlobal. Declaring the variable to be Public opens it up to other modules. Boolean variable types have only two states: True and False.

5. Minimize the Module window and click the Page Header section of the Report.

6. You should see the Property sheet shown in Figure 7.3. If not, press F4.

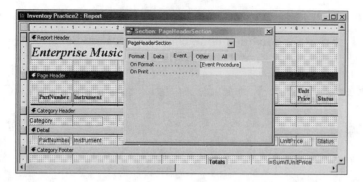

Figure 7.3: *You can minimize the Module window and create another procedure in the Page Header section of the report.*

7. Click the Event tab, if necessary.

8. After selecting [Event Procedure] from the drop-down box of the On Format event, click the Build button and enter the following statement:

```
BackForth = False
```

9. Close the VBA code window, close the Property sheet, and go back to the report.

10. Click Print Preview to view the results of all the code that you inserted. You should see gray and white bands on the report as shown in Figure 7.4.

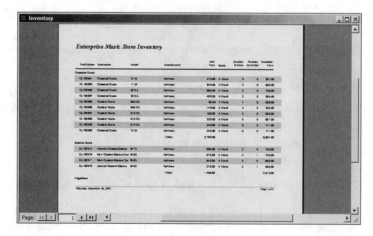

Figure 7.4: *Print preview the alternate report color bar report to test the procedure.*

11. Close Print Preview, save and close the report.

At this point, you might be wondering, "Where do you get those numbers for the colors?" That's a good question. You don't have to fumble through help screens, manuals, or the Internet to get them. If you want light blue instead of gray to be the alternating color, for example, there is an easy way to get the number for it.

All you have to do is right-click any control in Design view, choose Properties, and click the Build button of the Back Color property to choose your color. Clicking Define Custom Colors gives you the opportunity to lighten or darken your color. You can then select by highlighting the resulting number (after clicking OK) with your mouse and press Ctrl+C to copy the number as shown in Figure 7.5. Then simply paste the number into your code using the paste icon or Ctrl+V. You also can just right-click the control and choose Fill/Back Color, but the palette is a little different.

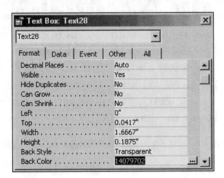

Figure 7.5: *You can copy the color number from the Back Color of a control and use it in your procedure.*

Object Methods

A *method* is a procedure that performs on an object. Access has its own built-in methods, or you can create your own procedures through VBA. You can examine an object's methods through the object browser or by referencing it with any of the previously mentioned methods.

Object Models

An object model provides the structure to access and modify objects. Microsoft Access 97 used an object model called DAO (Data Access Objects). Starting with Access 2000, ADO (ActiveX Data Objects) became the new standard for Access, though DAO libraries are still available. Although ADO is powerful and more flexible than DAO, DAO still has the overall edge in terms of performance, especially when working with Microsoft Jet.

However, if you plan to access SQL server or Oracle databases, ADO is the preferred choice. Also, because Microsoft considers ADO to be the future of data access technology, it is wise for those wanting to stay on the cutting edge to take advantage of it.

Because the ADO object model is based on the DAO object model, the two have many similarities. Those who are already acquainted with DAO should not have a difficult time learning ADO. This book presents programming examples of both models. It is a good idea to activate only the library you need.

✔ To learn more about object models, see Chapter 8, "Writing Your Own Visual Basic for Applications Code."

Setting a Reference in the Reference Library

If your Visual Basic code has references to objects in other applications, you need to create or activate a reference to the object libraries of those applications. The reference libraries show all the libraries registered with the operating system. This also gives you an opportunity to see the DAO and ADO listings. If you plan to use DAO, you must set a reference to it because it is not set by default in Access 2002.

The following exercise walks you through setting library references:

1. While in the Access Database window, choose Insert, Module to open a Module window.

2. While in the module, choose Tools, References to open the Reference dialog box, as shown in Figure 7.6.

3. The fourth option down should be the ADO reference library.

4. On the vertical scrollbar, scroll down to Microsoft DAO 3.6 Object Library.

5. To set a reference, simply click any box next to the desired reference.

6. Click Cancel to close the References dialog box, and press F2 to view the objects for the selected reference, as shown in Figure 7.7.

Setting a Reference for Another Application

If an application that you want to reference is not listed, you can use the Browse button to search for object libraries (*.olb and *.tlb). Keep in mind that references that are not checked are not used by your project but can be added at any time.

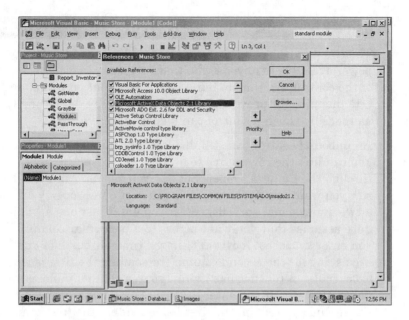

Figure 7.6: *You can use the reference library to set the proper reference to your object model.*

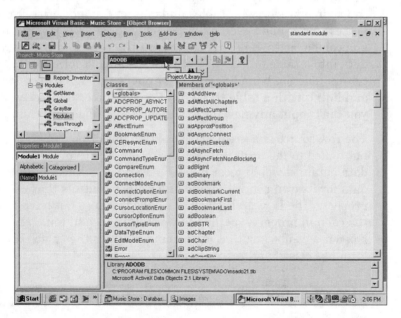

Figure 7.7: *Pressing F2 while in the Module window lets you view the objects for the libraries that are set.*

The Power of Controls Revisited

The two previous chapters presented a glimpse of the functionality and power available to anyone who takes the time to explore the inner workings of the control. It's time to build on that foundation by delving a little deeper into this thought-provoking topic. Let's start by discussing the various methods by which a control can display data.

An unbound control can still display data through its row source property. You can link the row source to a table and maintain access to its fields through the Column property of the control. You can even designate which row you want to reference because the column property can be accessed like a two-dimensional spreadsheet. If you enter just one argument, the procedure assumes that you want access to a particular column. For example, if you enter MyControl.column(1) in the control source of another control, you are asking for the second column (remember, the first is zero) from the MyControl control that has its row source set to a table with at least two fields. However, if you enter MyControl.column(0, 1), you are asking for the second row (again, the first being zero) in the first column of the same control. Always be aware that this property is zero based.

The question, "Why not just use the row source property instead of the control source property for tables and queries?" might arise. First of all, regular text boxes don't even have the row source property. But even with list and combo boxes, unless there is a control source, the user cannot input data into a table or query. If you create a blank form, place an unbound control (one not bound to a table or query through its control source) on it, and link it with a table through the row source, you can view the data, but you can't input any new data without doing some programming.

The row source is a great way to obtain data from tables or queries that are not linked to the form through the record source property. However, the data obtained would most likely be used for lookups. A control can look up data for its own control source or for other controls that use its Column property. The Lookup list box or combo box does not have to be bound for the column property method to work. But keep in mind that neither a list box nor a combo box that is unbound displays the choice you made after the form has closed and reopened.

Three Sources

Three properties on a form or report can become sources of table or query data. These three sources can all work together. For example, the form's record source property can be linked to a table or query. The moment you set the record source of a form or report to a table or query, the fields become available to the form or report through the control source of any text, list, or combo box you place on the form, for example. The row source can become a source of data for the control source of the same control.

Another way to look at it is that you can use the control source to both display data from and insert data into the underlying table. The row source, on the other hand, only displays and retrieves data, unless you program around this. The record source property is available on all forms and reports, but the control source and row source properties are only available on certain types of controls. Table 7.5 explains the differences between the three properties and shows on which objects they are available.

Table 7.5: Properties Used for Data Source

Property	Obtained From	Property Of	Available On
Record Source	Table or query	Form or report	Form or report
Control Source	Field or expression	Control	Text box, list box, combo box*
Row Source	Table or query	Control	List box and combo box, but not text box*

*And other controls

Figure 7.8 is an example of the Row Source property being populated with a value list separated by semicolons. Notice that the Row Source Type property is set to Value List.

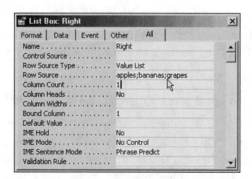

Figure 7.8: *Use the row source property as a value list by either typing the list separated by semicolons or creating them through code.*

Pick List

A pick list, shown in Figure 7.9, is an excellent example of the functionality of controls. The list box provides a great way to choose items from a list in a form. For what purpose can you use this? Use your imagination. You can choose reports to print. You can select key sales regions upon which to focus. You can single out top employees to be honored.

The interesting thing about this form is that all four list boxes are unbound. There is no control source set anywhere, neither is there any record source set for the form. Yet you can either retrieve data from or add data to three tables called Fruit, Vegetables, and Grocery. You accomplish this simply by picking (clicking) the items you want and moving them from one list box to another.

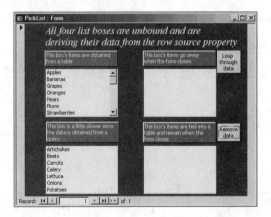

Figure 7.9: *Use the pick list form to transfer items from one list box to another.*

For a simple demonstration, let's examine a grocery list of fruits and vegetables. It demonstrates the function of the row source.

1. In the AccessByExample folder, open the FormsAndControls database.

2. Under Objects, choose Forms. Open the form PickList by double-clicking.

3. In the box labeled "This box's items are obtained from a table," choose any three fruits by clicking the first two and double-clicking the last selection. Notice that double-clicking moves the items to the box on the right.

4. Click the Loop Through Data button. Notice that you can view each item sequentially.

5. Close the form and reopen it. Notice that the items on the upper-right box are gone.

In the exercise you just performed, you chose items to be added to the ItemsSelected property of the control. Through programming that you can examine, the double-click event triggers a procedure that looped through the selected items and copied them to the Row Source property of the list box on the right. The Row Source Type of that box had to be set to Value List. Though it was input by the procedure to the Row Source as a Value List, it was retrieved by the procedure by referencing the column property of the control.

It is not very useful to add items to a list box that can't be retrieved. If your pick list was reports, you would want to be able to retrieve the list to be printed. Because the value list has a limited size, and because the values are only kept in memory as long as the form is open, this method is more appropriate for short lists that are quick and easy. Figure 7.10 shows the code that drives the list box on the first pick list to be tested.

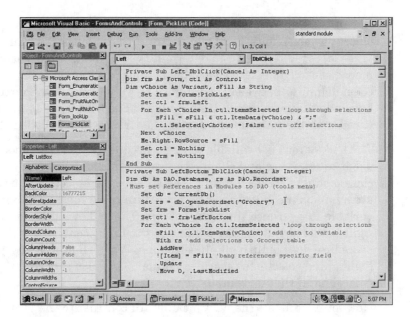

Figure 7.10: *You can examine the list box code to determine what's going on behind the scenes.*

Before you test the next pick list, let's take a peek at the code behind the scenes. The code is analyzed line by line in the paragraphs that follow it.

1. While in the FormsAndControls database, under objects, click PickList and choose Design.

2. Click the top-left list box and press F4 to open the Property sheet.

3. Click the Event tab (if it's not already selected) and then click the Build button of the On Dbl Click event with [Event Procedure] selected.

You should see the following code:

```
Private Sub Left_DblClick(Cancel As Integer)
Dim frm As Form, ctl As Control
Dim vChoice As Variant, sFill As String
    Set frm = Forms!PickList
    Set ctl = frm.Left
    For Each vChoice In ctl.ItemsSelected 'loop through selections
        sFill = sFill & ctl.ItemData(vChoice) & ";"
        ctl.Selected(vChoice) = False 'turn off selections
    Next vChoice
Me.Right.RowSource = sFill
    Set ctl = Nothing
    Set frm = Nothing
End Sub
```

In this code, the procedure first uses the Set keyword to set pointers to object variables for a form and control. It next loops through the ItemsSelected collection to determine which fruits were selected by a mouse click. The fillCtl variable is filled, an item at a time, with the semicolon delimiter between each item. The Value List Row Source Type has to have a list like so: Item1; Item2; Item3. The RowSource property is referenced with the name of the box on the right, which is called Right.

The Me keyword is available to every procedure in a class module. You can use it to reference and change controls. Type Me, followed by a period, in a class module such as a form to see a list of the objects and procedures that are available in that form. The procedure could have used another control variable to reference the right list box. The Me keyword is used to fill the right list box by assigning a value to the Right control. The last thing the procedure does is turn off all selections. When that happens, you see all the highlighted selections return to normal. This also sets the stage for another go around, if that is desired.

Now let's check out the next pick list. In contrast to the previous list, this list produces a permanent pick list. Keep in mind that permanent, when it comes to computer jargon, means permanent until you change it, or "stored." This program also handles the selections a bit differently. It waits until you delete the pick list to turn off the selections from the box on the lower left.

The next set of steps walks you through selecting items from the second pick list:

1. Close the Module window and Property sheet from the preceding example. Close and reopen the form or click the View button from design mode for a shortcut.

2. Click three vegetables from the lower-left box, double-clicking the last selection (see Figure 7.11). So far it works about the same as the previous pick list, except for the fact that the double-click doesn't turn the selections off.

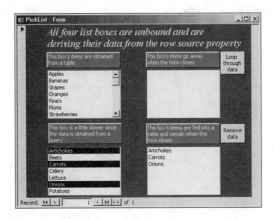

Figure 7.11: You can use the row source of a list box to save selected data when the form closes.

3. Click the Remove Data button. Notice that the selections in the lower-left text box are removed so that you can reselect.

4. Choose three different items, double-clicking the last selection as before. Close and reopen the form. Notice that the data remains in the lower-right text box.

5. Click the Remove Data button.

This last example demonstrates a method of saving the pick list data for later use. The data is stored in a table called Grocery. You might want to make your grocery list now to use later. You can also use a pick list as criteria for a query or a report. Now let's take a peek at the code behind the scenes:

1. Click the View button to switch to Design view while in the PickList form. Right-click the lower-left text box and choose Properties.

2. Be sure you are in the Event tab and click the Build button of the double-click event. Notice that the comments point out that a reference should be set to DAO. Also notice the database and recordset variables.

Let's break down the following code:

```
Private Sub LeftBottom_DblClick(Cancel As Integer)
Dim db As DAO.Database, rs As DAO.Recordset
```

```
'Must set References in Modules to DAO (tools menu)
    Set db = CurrentDb()
    Set rs = db.OpenRecordset("Grocery")
    Set frm = Forms!PickList
    Set ctl = frm!LeftBottom
    For Each vChoice In ctl.ItemsSelected 'loop through selections
        sFill = ctl.ItemData(vChoice) 'add data to variable
        With rs 'add selections to Grocery table
        .AddNew
        ![Item] = sFill 'bang references specific field
        .Update
        .Move 0, .LastModified
        End With
    Next vChoice
Set ctl = Nothing
Set frm = Nothing
rs.Close
db.Close
Set rs = Nothing
Set db = Nothing
Me.Refresh
End Sub
```

The first two lines after the variables are defined (not counting the comment) set pointers to object variables to access table data using the Set keyword. Just supply whatever table name you need or set up a variable for user input. The CurrentDb function is an easy way to refer to the current user database. Another way to refer to the current database is with DBEngine(0)(0). This method requires refreshing before you can use any collection associated with it.

A table is not the only type of recordset that you can open. You can use an SQL statement with the OpenRecordset method to open a query recordset just as easily, but in this case you just need to access table data.

The next two lines use the Set keyword to point the object variables to the current form and a list box. After the procedure retrieves the control's selections, it adds the data to the underlying table in the list box on the lower right. The syntax after the With statement can also be used again and again to add and update table data. It is nested within the For Each loop. The refresh statement refreshes the screen so that you can see the updates.

It should be noted that the Row Source Type property of the lower-right list box is set to Table/Query as opposed to Value List, as it was in the previous example. It doesn't matter that the control is unbound because you are not referencing its Control Source property. If you press the Remove Data button, an SQL routine takes care of deleting the data. You can examine the

following code by right-clicking the lower-right list box and inspecting the
On Click event of the box:

```
DoCmd.SetWarnings False
DoCmd.RunSQL "Delete * from Grocery" 'clear all records in table
DoCmd.SetWarnings True
    Set frm = Forms!PickList
    Set ctl = frm!LeftBottom
    For Each vChoice In ctl.ItemsSelected
        ctl.Selected(vChoice) = False 'turn off selections
    Next strChoice
Set ctl = Nothing
Set frm = Nothing
Me.Refresh
```

Lookup List

A common database convention is lookups. You might want to look up a customer address, or you might not remember the product code for an inventory item. Therefore, you need to see a list of products. You also might want
to see the item itself, along with its code. Lookups can fill other controls
with synchronized data.

Let's take a look at a few techniques that use controls for table lookups.
The first method uses a query to look up data. The second method uses calculated fields to obtain the lookup data. The third method combines
lookups and calculations. The first two methods have a control source in
the Lookup field. This ensures that the data remains when the form closes.

The next steps take you through the various techniques:

1. While in the FormsAndControls database, double-click the
   LookUpList form to open it.

2. Click the New Record button to add a new record to the underlying
   table.

3. Click the top Zip control drop-down box and then choose 49344. Notice
   that Shelbyville, Michigan appears in the first two lookup groups (see
   Figure 7.12).

Now let's look at the query that is behind the first lookup. This JoinZip
query is the record source for the form.

1. Under Objects, click Queries.

2. Click JoinZip and then click Design. Notice that there is a one-to-
   many relationship between the two tables.

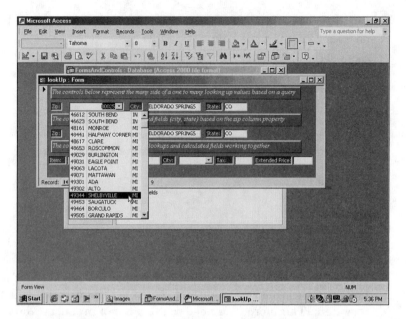

Figure 7.12: *Selecting an item from a lookup list that automatically inserts the correct information into corresponding fields.*

3. Click the run icon (!) to run the query.

4. Type 46526 in the Zip field of a new record (*) and press Tab (see Figure 7.13). Notice how the corresponding information is automatically entered.

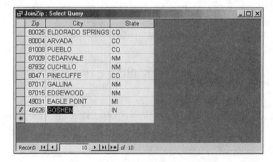

Figure 7.13: *Testing the relational lookup query that feeds into the form.*

This technique is both useful and interesting. When you enter information on the many side of the relationship, corresponding information from the one side of the relationship appears. What is interesting is the way this method works. The zip information is actually added to the underlying

LookZip table, which represents the many side of the relationship. However, there is nothing being added to the one side of the relationship. This side is simply *reflected* dynamically.

The reason that this is significant is that this is the whole point behind the relational model. As much as possible, data should not be entered in more than one place. You have to repeat data in the joining fields to link the data. But other than that, you are simply displaying data that is already there. If you want to bring in data from 30 or 40 fields in the linking table, go right ahead. You don't have to worry about repeating anything but the field data that's already there.

Some database users retrieve data from another table using the Dlookup function. There is a place for this function, but there is usually a better way to look up data. Copying field data from one table to another using a lookup enters data in more than one place. A better technique is to reflect the data dynamically, especially if there is a substantial amount of field data to be inserted.

Certain circumstances preclude the query lookup method. Suppose you already have a different query as the record source for the form. Suppose again that this query is not a Lookup query or contained the wrong field data for your lookup. Even if you access a Lookup query through the Row Source property, you still need a method to access the columns of the query. Fortunately, there is another method that can look up data dynamically that is relatively simple. Even though the next lookup group of controls are unnecessary (because the first group can also look up values), this group illustrates a completely different lookup method even though it looks and feels the same.

1. From the FormsAndControls database under Forms, double-click the LookUpList form to open it.

2. Click the New Record button. Notice that all the boxes on the form are blank, indicating that you are ready to enter a new record.

3. Click the second Zip control down arrow and choose 49031 as shown in Figure 7.14. Notice that Eagle Point, Michigan appears in both groups.

At this point, it is impossible to notice any difference between the two methods. It's time to examine the differences in Design view.

1. Click the View button to switch to Design view.

2. Right-click the top Zip combo box, and then choose Properties.

3. Click the All tab. Be sure the vertical scrollbar is at the top.

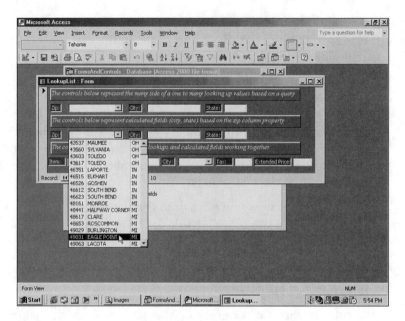

Figure 7.14: *You can select a lookup item and use the column property of another control to retrieve the item.*

4. Notice that there is a Column Count of 3. Also notice that the Row Source is the Zipcodes table.

5. The Control Source is the Zip table.

6. While you are still in the Property sheet, click the Zip Combo Box in the second lookup group. You might have to move the Property sheet box by dragging the title bar until the Form design is visible.

7. Making sure that you are at the top of the sheet, notice that the Row Source, Control Source, and Column Count properties are the same as the first combo box. So what's the difference?

8. Click the City text box in the second row of controls. Note the expression contained in this control as shown in Figure 7.15. Close the form.

The difference between the two methods lies in the expressions in the City and State text boxes in the second group. This lookup method works even if there is a completely different query linked to the form with no lookup ability. The table would have to have a Zip field to have a control bound to the field. In the expression =[PickZip].column(1), Pickzip is the name of the control, not the Control Source. Column(1) represents the second field. The State field is the same expression with the exception of the Column(2) reference.

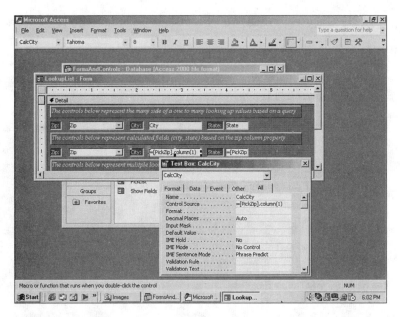

Figure 7.15: *Check the expression in the City field in the second row to understand how the second lookup works.*

In short, the first lookup group must have the JoinZip query as the Control Source, while the second lookup group can work with another query or table as Control Source as long as it has a Zip field. The first method is a relational lookup using a join; the second method can work without a join by using expressions. Both methods have their pros and cons, depending on the situation.

If you choose a table as Control Source, use the second method. If you choose a nonrelational query as Control Source, use the second method. But if you have a joined query properly configured as Control Source, even if the joins are not defined in the Relationships window, use the first method.

Combination Group

Some situations lend themselves to both lookup and calculated fields. When you purchase an item, you need to look up the price for that item, but you also need to compute the local sales tax. Let's see what the last lookup group of controls can do.

1. Under forms, double-click the LookupList form to open it.

2. From the bottom group of controls, click the drop-down box of the Item control.

3. Choose 15 inch Wall Plaque. Notice how the price is automatically inserted.

4. Choose the city named Alden from the drop-down list of the control named City. Notice how the tax and extended price are inserted as shown in Figure 7.16.

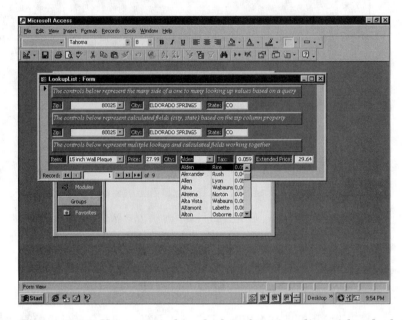

Figure 7.16: *You can combine lookup functionality with calculated fields.*

This technique works much like a spreadsheet; you can go back and enter another product, and a new extended price is computed using the same sales tax. This combination of lookup values and calculated fields illustrate how Lookup controls can work together with calculated fields.

1. Click the View button to switch to Design view.

2. Click the vertical scrollbar until you see the last group of controls.

3. Notice the pattern in the group. First the lookup control, then the column lookup. The price is looked up and then the tax is looked up.

4. The last control to the right pulls it all together. This column has the expression =[price]+([price]*[tax]). Both price and tax are control names.

What's Next

Now that you have been introduced to objects and their properties, let's move on to the next chapter, which takes you deeper into VBA programming that you will eventually apply to objects. This chapter is where you can get your feet wet by writing your first programs. You will learn all about the power of functions.

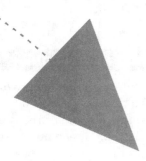

Writing Your Own Visual Basic for Applications Code

So far, you have examined code, but you haven't written any code of your own. This chapter gives you a chance to write your own code. You start with simple procedures and progress to procedures that are a bit more complex and powerful. You also learn how to test your procedures. After you understand what combining function power with query power can do for you, don't be surprised if you suddenly acquire the motivation to start writing creative procedures of your own.

In this chapter, you learn

- how to use Access built-in string functions
- how to use the immediate window to test functions
- how to create your own functions
- how to use arrays with functions
- how to combine functions with queries

Function Procedures, Sub Procedures, and Modules

Visual Basic for Applications (VBA) is the programming language provided with Office applications, such as Access 2002. The three types of programming structures used in VBA code are *sub* procedures, *function* procedures, and *property* procedures. You can think of these as your "bread and butter" for automating your database. This chapter covers the first two types.

✔ For more information about procedures, see "Functions Versus Subs" in Chapter 10, "Customizing Your Access Database."

The place to write VBA code in Access is in a *module*. A *module* is a set of VBA procedures that are stored together as a unit. Modules don't run; they contain procedures that run. The two types of Access modules are standard and class. Standard modules are the modules stored under objects in the database window. This is where you can place Sub and Function procedures that you want to be available to other procedures throughout your database.

A class module can contain the definition of a new object. Therefore, it is not surprising that class modules are often associated with forms and reports, which are new objects that you create. However, you can create class modules that are not associated with a form or report. This type of class module gives you the ability to create and modify your own custom objects using code.

You might be wondering what the difference between a function procedure and a sub procedure is. A *function procedure* can accept and return values, process data, and perform as part of an expression. A *sub procedure*, on the other hand, accepts values, but does not return values. It cannot be used as part of an expression. Functions can be used in queries, sub procedures, calculated controls, and macros. Sub procedures are more typically used in form and report class modules. Sub procedures that are associated with a form or report are also called event procedures.

Access String Functions

The simple reason why it is a good idea to use built-in string functions is that they are very useful to anyone who wants to have a good understanding of development using Microsoft Access. Databases are about data and how data can be manipulated. Queries can manipulate data, but queries have limitations. Suppose you want to pull the first name out of a full name in a field located in a table having 30,000 records. How can you do that in a query without using a string function? You can use an SQL string in VBA, but even there, the best way to extract the data is to use a string function. You also can benefit from using string functions in your own functions to create utilities custom made for your applications.

String functions are not the only built-in (intrinsic) Access functions that are useful, but they could very possibly be the functions that you use the most. Like other intrinsic functions, string functions have arguments separated by commas. Some arguments are optional, others are required. Each argument can have its own data type. For example, in the left function, the first argument requires a string and the second argument requires a number (long integer). Thus, the syntax is as follows:

```
Left(string, length)
```

If you type ? left("Park Place",4) in the immediate window, Park (the first four characters of the string) is returned. Park Place is the first argument and 4 is the second. Notice that the number 4 does not have to be in quotes, because it is a number. You input two values but return only one. Both arguments are required in the left function. If you try to use one argument, you get a compile error.

Arguments can be constants, variables, or expressions. A *constant* is a value that doesn't change. A *variable* is a named storage location for data that behaves like a temporary holding container. It must begin with an alpha character. Living up to its name, variable data typically varies or changes frequently. An *expression* can contain other functions, and a function can be "nested" as an argument within another function.

The Access Immediate Window

One of the easiest and most useful tools that you encounter in your quest to learn Access is the immediate window, which is a command-line window and debugging window rolled into one. It is a command-line window because commands and procedures can be typed directly as a single line into the window and they will run after you press Enter. It is a debugging window because debugging statements nested in your code will display there. You can also run your procedures from there to test them. Whether you want to test a variable, an expression, or an entire procedure, the immediate window can handle it. After you use it and become familiar with it, it becomes almost indispensable.

Let's get started by counting the letters of your first name.

1. Open the Music Store data base from the AccessByExample folder, and press Ctrl+G to open the Access immediate window.

2. Type ? left(*First&LastName*, *NumberOfLettersInFirstName*) and press Enter. For example, John Smith would type ? left("John Smith", 4). Be sure to enclose your name in quotes. You should see your first name only (see Figure 8.1).

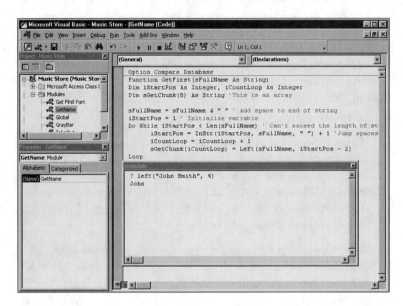

Figure 8.1: *You can test the left string function in the immediate window.*

This is great when you need to find only your name, because you know how many characters your first name has. But suppose you have a list of names. The number of characters in the first name is obviously going to vary. You need a mechanism to find the position of the space and then back up one position to the last character of the first name. This gives you the number that you need. The Access InStr function provides just such a mechanism to find the space position.

If you type InStr("John Smith", " "), you are saying in effect, find the position of the space in the string "John Smith". The first argument is the string you want to search. The second argument is the character or string of characters you want to search for. If you tried this in the immediate window, the function would return "5," which is the position of the space. However, the position of the "n" in John, which is the number of letters in the name, is one position to the left, or "4."

Suppose you nested the two functions together. It would look like the following:

```
Left("John Smith", InStr("John Smith", " ") -1)
```

Although this expression requires a little more typing, the benefit is worth it. Now it doesn't matter how many characters the first name has. It works with "Elizabeth Williams" just as well as it works with "John Smith" (see Figure 8.2). The InStr function becomes the second argument that supplies the number, which can vary, according to how many letters the first name has. Notice the minus one (-1). This subtracts one character, thus moving back one position to the "n" in "John."

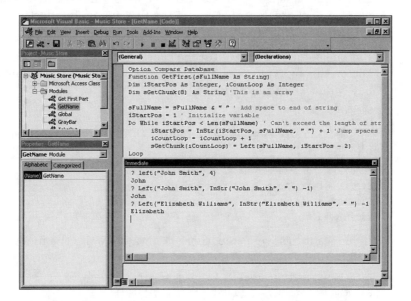

Figure 8.2: *The nested functions work regardless of the size of the first and last names.*

Try substituting your name for "John Smith" in the previous expression in the immediate window. Don't forget to start with a question mark (?) and end by pressing Enter. Rather than having to type all this every time you use this combination of functions, why not try to incorporate everything into a custom function?

The next example shows you how to write your own procedure that you can use whenever you need it:

1. From the Database window of the Music Store database, click Insert Module.

2. In the module window after the declaration, type the following code:

```
Function ShowName(StrVal As String) as String
```

After you press Enter, End Function is inserted automatically. So far, you have declared your procedure to be a function. You also have declared your input variable, which is the only argument, to be a string. For this simple procedure, it is the only variable you need. On the next line, type the following code:

```
StrVal = Left(StrVal, InStr(StrVal, " ") -1)
```

Notice that you use the same technique that we used previously, except for the fact that StrVal is substituted for "John Smith". Notice that StrVal is used three times. The StrVal variable is reevaluated to become the leftmost number of characters that are in the first name. In effect, the procedure is extracting out the first name.

But one stone remains unturned. The function has yet to return a value. You do this by typing the function name followed by an equal sign and the new value. Observe the following:

```
ShowName = StrVal
```

That's it! Pretty easy, huh? If you put it all together, your code should look like this:

```
Function ShowName(StrVal As String) as String
StrVal = Left(StrVal, InStr(StrVal, " ") -1)
ShowName = StrVal
End Function
```

If you want to save a step, there is a way to write the function that is easier still:

```
Function ShowName(StrVal As String) as String
ShowName = Left(StrVal, InStr(StrVal, " ") -1)
End Function
```

This method cuts right to the chase and returns the value with the first line of code between the Function and End Function lines. The only difference is that you are assigning the value returned by the left function directly to the ShowName custom function, as opposed to assigning it to the StrVal variable first. Notice the results of this function in Figure 8.3.

Now let's try it out. If your immediate window isn't already open, press Ctrl+G. In this window, substituting your name for John Smith, type

```
? ShowName("John Smith")
```

After pressing Enter, you should see your first name. Now try another name, just to make sure it is working properly. If everything checks out, you have just written your first function. If it doesn't work, go back and reexamine your code, making sure that there are no typos.

This function is small but powerful. However, there is still a small problem. Suppose a person uses his or her middle name. In this situation, the function you just created would return only the first name. You need a function that knows how many words the string has and leaves off the last name.

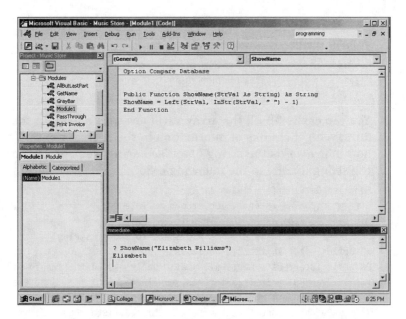

Figure 8.3: *You can use your nested function over and over again by placing it in a custom function.*

Using Arrays with String Functions

The function that you are about to examine counts the words, but it does more than that. It pieces together a string one word at a time. It uses a type of variable called an *array*. Arrays intimidate some people, but they are actually quite simple. Instead of filling variables one string at a time, arrays enable you to get a whole batch of strings and reference any of them.

Think of an array as if it were a group of cells in a spreadsheet. If you have information in cells A1 through A3, you have an array of cells. If A1 contained FirstName, A2 contained MiddleName, and A3 contained LastName, then you could reference the contents by clicking the appropriate cell. In much the same way, you could set up an array variable. If the name of the array was Fill, you could declare Fill with the statement `Dim Fill(2) as String`. The (2) simply tells the procedure to allocate three locations for storing variables. The reason that it is three instead of two is that it is zero based. In effect, you are reserving three blocks of memory for the three elements of the array. `Fill(0)` is a totally different variable from `Fill(1)`. Table 8.1 illustrates the way array variables are stored.

Table 8.1: Array Storage Example

Variable Name	Information Stored
Fill(0)	FirstName
Fill(1)	MiddleName
Fill(2)	LastName

You can easily fill all the array variables with a loop. In the following procedure, you get chunks of information in the form of words. The loops tell you how many words the string has. Each array element adds one more word to the string. Examine the following code:

```
Function GetFirst(sFullName As String)
Dim iStartPos As Integer, iCountLoop As Integer
Dim sGetChunk(8) As String 'This is an array
sFullName = sFullName & " " ' Add space to end of string
iStartPos = 1 ' Initialize variable
Do While iStartPos < Len(sFullName) ' Can't exceed the length of string
      iStartPos = InStr(iStartPos, sFullName, " ") + 1 'Jump spaces
      iCountLoop = iCountLoop + 1
      sGetChunk(iCountLoop) = Left(sFullName, iStartPos - 2)
Loop
GetFirst = sGetChunk(iCountLoop - 1) ' Leave off last word
End Function
```

The sGetChunk variable is obviously your array. Although it has nine array elements set up, or "dimensioned," you probably don't need this many words. If your name was "John Wilkes Booth," the first array element (sGetChunk(1)) would equal "John," the second would equal "John Wilkes," and so forth. The way this procedure is set up, you skip the zero element of the array, so that the first array element you assign becomes 1. You are already familiar with the InStr function; this time the optional first argument was used first so that you could tell the InStr function the position from which to start.

The do loop syntax is

```
Do...While [Condition is True]
Loop
```

The words between the brackets represent a condition usually comprised of an expression. As long as that condition is true, the loop runs. When the condition is no longer true, the procedure exits the loop and continues on the next line after the Loop statement.

TIP

You also can stop a loop in progress using End Do.

✔ For more information on various types of VBA loops, see "Creating Procedures" in Chapter 10, "Customizing Your Access Database."

On the first loop, the procedure uses the first position to search for the space but sets the iStartPos variable to one position right of the first space (the first letter position of the next word for the search in the next loop). This way, it "jumps" words. If you want to see the procedure work, from the Music Store database, open the GetName module in Design view. Set your cursor on the line after the last Dim statement and press F9. This toggles a breakpoint.

NOTE

You also can click the vertical gray bar just left of the line on which you want to set a breakpoint (see Figure 8.4). A large dot appears on the bar, and the line is highlighted. This can also be toggled on and off with the click of a mouse button; however, don't try to set breakpoints on Dim statements using either method.

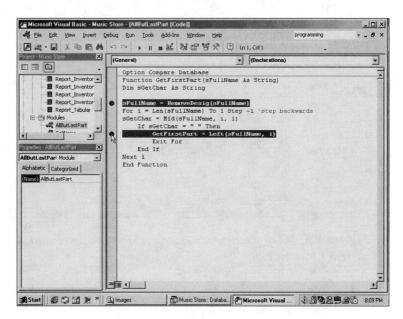

Figure 8.4: *Use your mouse to set break points by clicking the vertical bar in the module window.*

In the following example, you get to go behind the scenes of VBA programming to get a glimpse of how the procedure works. The techniques learned here can be invaluable when you debug your own programs.

1. Press Ctrl+G to enter the immediate window. Type ? GetFirst("Mary Ann Mobley") and press Enter.

   You should see the breakpoint line turn yellow (or another color, depending on your settings).

2. Place your cursor on the sFullName variable. A box that shows "Mary Ann Mobley" pops up. Press F8, which is a shortcut for "Step Into." You can step through your code using Step Into.

   Now the same variable says Mary Ann Mobley with a space at the end (see Figure 8.5).

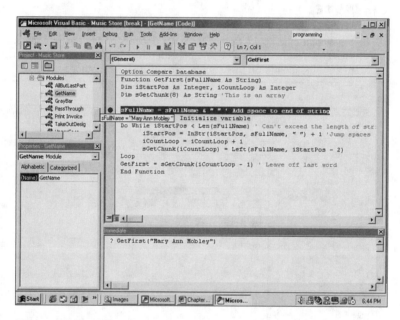

Figure 8.5: *Place your cursor over variables to watch them change as your custom function runs.*

3. Press F8 several times until you get to the line just after the Do While statement.

4. Place your cursor on the iStartPos variable. It should read 1. Press F8, leaving your cursor in the same position. It should now read 6.

5. Now place your cursor on the iCountLoop variable and notice that it reads 0. Press F8 and watch it turn to 1.

6. Finally, place your cursor on the sGetChunk variable and press F8.

Notice that the sGetChunk(iCountLoop) variable was assigned the value of the string "Mary." sGetChunk(iCountLoop) is really sGetChunk(1) because the value of iCountLoop is "1" at this point in the procedure.

The next time through the loop, sGetChunk(iCountLoop) becomes sGetChunk(2) and is assigned "Mary Ann."

The Left(sFullName, iStartPos - 2) is backed up two positions from the first letter (character) of the second word (in this case the "A" in Ann) to the last character in the previous word (in this case the "y" in Mary) so that the left function evaluates to the word "Mary."

You can continue to examine variables and how they change with each loop if so desired, but this should give you an idea of what's going on in the procedure. In this little exercise you have also acquired the knowledge of how to troubleshoot your own procedures.

You might wonder, "Why add the space to the input string?" The InStr function is used to determine words by finding spaces. The last word could not be determined without a space at the end. You also might wonder, "How does sGetChunk(iCountLoop - 1) leave off the last word?" The procedure simply reverts back to the last iteration or loop to get the array variable before the last word was added. So, if there are three words, the procedure gets two. If there are two words, the procedure gets one; and so on.

Obviously, this procedure is still not perfect. What if a guy was named John Brown III? The function would return John Brown instead of John. You can adjust the procedure to fix various anomalies such as this one, but it is not the purpose of this book to give you a solution for every possible scenario; however, it is the purpose of this book to give you the tools that provide you with a jump start toward programming solutions for yourself.

If you want to test the last word in a name to see if it is a designation such as "MD" or "III," the first thing you must do is find the last word. The GetFirst function can be written a different way. This method can easily find either the last name or the first and middle name. You also can use this method, which involves finding the last space in a string, to find the ending designation of a name. The following code can be expanded to find the last space in a string.

✔ For more information on the For..Next loop, see "Creating Procedures" in Chapter 10, "Customizing Your Access Database."

```
For i = Len(sFullName) To 1 Step -1
sGetChar = Mid(sFullName, i, 1)
Next i
```

At this point, all you have to know about this code is that it steps backward one character at a time. If you can do this, then all you have to do is use an If statement to test for a space. Once the position of the last space in the string is found, you just take that number and use it for the second argument of the left string function. Now you have the "John Wilkes" in "John Wilkes Booth" as well as the "John" in "John Booth." You can rewrite the GetFirst function this way:

```
Function GetFirstPart(sFullName As String)
Dim sGetChar As String

For i = Len(sFullName) To 1 Step -1 'step backwards
sGetChar = Mid(sFullName, i, 1)
    If sGetChar = " " Then
        GetFirstPart = Left(sFullName, i)
        Exit For
    End If
Next i
End Function
```

This procedure does the same thing that GetFirst does, but it is shorter. It exits the loop when the space is found after removing the last name. The following function will remove the ending designation, such as "Jr." or "III":

```
Function RemoveDesig(sFullName As String)
Dim i As Integer, sGetChar As String
Dim sLast As String, sFirst As String

For i = Len(sFullName) To 1 Step -1
sGetChar = Mid(sFullName, i, 1)
    If sGetChar = " " Then
        sLast = Right(sFullName, Len(sFullName) - i)
        sFirst = Left(sFullName, i - 1)
        If sLast = "Jr." Or sLast = "Sr." Or sLast = "III" _
            Or sLast = "M.D." Or sLast = "R.N." Then
            RemoveDesig = sFirst
        Exit For
        Else
            RemoveDesig = sFullName
        Exit For
        End If
    End If
Next i
End Function
```

You can string as many "ors" as necessary to accommodate the designations that you need. Some of the most common designations are used. You can add your own.

✔ If your list of "ors" is too long, try employing a technique to handle these "ors" using a query. See "Using Query By Table Example For If Then Scenarios" in Chapter 16, "Overcoming the Limitations of Queries."

One line needs to be added to the GetFirstPart function:

```
sFullName = RemoveDesig(sFullName)
```

Now the function looks like this:

```
Function GetFirstPart(sFullName As String)
Dim sGetChar As String

sFullName = RemoveDesig(sFullName)
For i = Len(sFullName) To 1 Step -1 'step backwards
sGetChar = Mid(sFullName, i, 1)
    If sGetChar = " " Then
        GetFirstPart = Left(sFullName, i)
        Exit For
    End If
Next i
End Function
```

Now the two procedures have been combined because GetFirstPart calls RemoveDesig. The first thing the procedure does is remove the designation at the end of the string. Then it finds the first part of the name without the designation. As stated previously, this does not necessarily cover every possible scenario when it comes to names. It does give you an understanding of how to handle them.

As you did with the GetFirst function, you can test these procedures using the tools provided in the module window. You also can return to these procedures after gaining additional programming knowledge in the chapters ahead.

Combining Function Power with Query Power

Obviously, you want to be able to do more than just experiment with the GetFirstPart function in the immediate window. The following steps will guide you through combining this function with a query:

1. In the Music Store database, under Queries, click Create query in Design view to open the Show Table dialog box. Double-click Employees and click Close.

2. Double-click the Employee field in the Employees table, and then right-click in the Field row in the blank column on the right side of the Employee field. Choose Zoom.

3. Type `Fname:GetFirstPart(Employee)` and then click OK. Brackets will be inserted.

4. Double-click the right edge of the field to view the entire expression (best fit).

5. Click the Run button to run the query (see Figure 8.6).

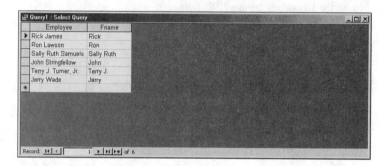

Figure 8.6: *The results of combining a query and a function show increased functionality.*

Notice "Terry J. Turner, Jr." The function evaluates this name to "Terry J." just as it should.

6. Close the query without saving it.

You have written your first code. You have learned how to use the immediate window to test your procedures. You have been introduced to variables and arrays, and you have learned how much fun it is to see what procedures do by seeing them in action. The more you work with procedures, the easier they become. And the easier they become, the more fun you have working with them.

What's Next

In the next chapter you learn the differences between macros and VBA, and how to convert a macro to VBA. You can look at converting macros as a practical assistant to learning VBA. You also learn various methods of sending messages to users.

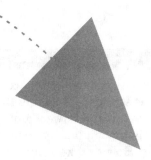

Macros, Modules, and Messages

In Chapter 7, "Exploring Objects," you learned about objects. In Chapter 8, "Writing Your Own Visual Basic for Applications Code," you were introduced to writing VBA code using functions. This chapter combines VBA and objects to show how they interact. A common database task is opening database objects such as tables, forms, and reports. These repetitive tasks can be automated using code.

Macros can also automate repetitive tasks, such as opening forms and printing reports, and creating them is easier than writing code. Because you usually set arguments for macros from a list of selections in the Macro window, you don't have to rely on remembering a complex syntax. In this chapter, you discover how to use macros to create VBA code. You also learn how to effectively use Access messages. Specifically, you learn

- the differences between macros and modules
- when to use macros and when to use modules
- how to use special macros
- how to learn VBA by converting macros to VBA
- how to use the MsgBox function
- how to use the InputBox function
- how to convert the macro to VBA by example
- how to print the current record using a macro

Visual Basic Versus Macros

In the early versions of Access, the programming environment was Access Basic; however, in recent years VBA replaced Access Basic, becoming the standard for Office applications such as Access, Excel, and PowerPoint. This uniformity provides the added benefit of only having to learn one programming language across multiple applications. However, keep in mind that you need to include the library references for the various applications that need to be incorporated into the program.

Both Visual Basic and macros are powerful tools to help you automate your Microsoft Access applications, but which one should you use? Both macros and modules can automate repetitive tasks. They both can access forms and reports and be attached to their events.

Beginners usually find it easier to write macros than to write VBA programs. With macros, you simply select from a list of commands to create a series of user-defined actions. These actions are executed sequentially to produce a program. However, shortly after you begin using macros, their limitations become apparent.

When to Use VBA and When to Use Macros

Although macros are very powerful, there are circumstances in which a macro just won't do. Suppose you want to create and manipulate objects. Macros don't have the power to do this effectively; neither can they manipulate record sets on a record-by-record basis. You can move to or find a particular record in a set using a macro, but you can't manipulate the records the way you can in VBA without calling on a function or a query to do the work. Because modules are compiled, they execute faster than macros, which makes them better for optimization purposes. You also can pass arguments, return values, and use variables for arguments using VBA.

Macros are useful for simple tasks, such as opening and closing forms, or for small applications that don't require much automation. You also can use a macro to create an application that is easy to take over and modify by people who don't know how to program. Using macros to set up a prototype program that could later be expanded into a full-blown application using VBA code is another example of good macro use. Although macros are usually less time consuming to create than VBA, the down side is that they are not as powerful as VBA. Because the debugging tools are limited when compared to the tools available with modules, macros can also be somewhat more difficult to troubleshoot and maintain.

Special Access Macros

Two types of macros are used for special purposes—the AutoKeys macro and the AutoExec macro.

If you want to perform some action when a keystroke (or keystroke combination) is pressed, a macro is the way to go. What's more, you also can attach code to keystrokes using the RunCode macro action. You can set up one macro with all the keystroke actions you need for the database, but keep in mind that you need to call the special macro AutoKeys, as shown in Figure 9.1. Also remember to use the Macro Name column (which can be inserted by the Macro Names icon) to place the keystrokes.

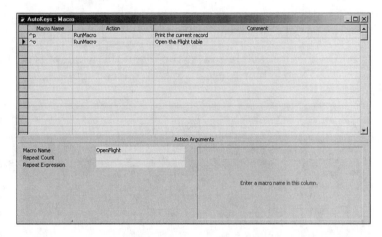

Figure 9.1: *The special AutoKeys macro group enables you to set up a group of actions that are carried out individually when a keystroke or keystroke combination is pressed.*

Another special kind of macro called AutoExec initiates an action or a series of actions, such as displaying a menu or opening a form, when the database first opens. After opening the database, Microsoft Access looks for the AutoExec macro and runs it automatically if it finds it.

Visual Basic for Applications definitely is superior to macros when it comes to error handling. You can use variables and create looping constructs within VBA. You can run SQL statements from VBA interspersing variables within the string. You can use VBA to work with all kinds of object collections. For example, you can examine and modify object properties using code. If you wanted to add a record to a table, manipulate controls on forms and reports, or create custom-made functions to customize your database, VBA is definitely your answer. In short, VBA has greater power, control, and flexibility than macros can offer. Although the learning curve is also greater, the benefits are worth it.

Learn VBA By Converting Macros to VBA Code

Converting macros to VBA code is very easy. This is very helpful in the learning process, and helps you get your feet wet in programming. This method only takes you so far, because there are many things that macros just can't do. Nevertheless, it is still a good way to get you on your way to writing procedures.

The following example shows you how to create a macro that opens a form. Next, you learn how to convert the macro to VBA code.

1. Open the Convention database from the AccessByExample folder on your hard drive.

2. Under Objects, click Macros, and then click New to open the Macro window in which you can create and modify macros.

3. On the first action row at the top of the window, type ms and press Tab. Notice how MsgBox is inserted (see Figure 9.2).

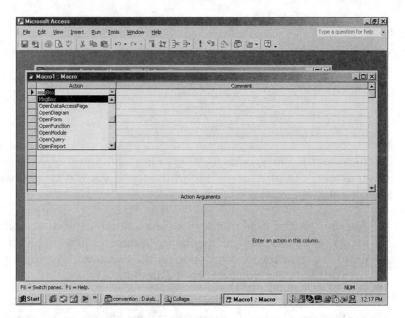

Figure 9.2: *Rather than scrolling the option list, you can simply type the first few letters to retrieve the option.*

4. Press F6 and then type Open the Flight table.

5. Click the second action row in the upper section of the macro.

6. On the Window menu, click Tile Horizontally. Make any necessary adjustments to be sure you can see enough of both windows.

7. In the Database window under Objects, click Tables.

8. Click, hold, and drag the Flight table to the second object row in the macro. Notice how everything is inserted properly in the lower section (see Figure 9.3).

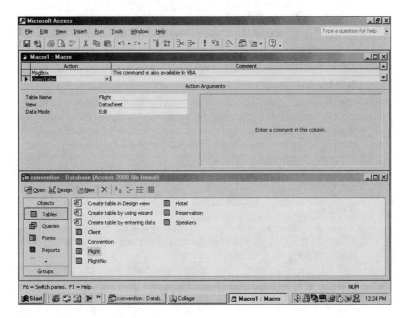

Figure 9.3: *You can drag and drop your table to create an OpenTable action.*

9. Click Window, Cascade to resize your database window so that it won't extend too far across the screen after the Macro window is closed.

10. Click the Save (diskette) icon. Save as macOpenFlight and then close the macro.

11. Under Objects, click Forms; then click Client and then Design.

12. If the Toolbox is not open, click the Toolbox icon.

13. Be sure the Control Wizards wand is not selected, and then click the Command button to make the cursor change to a plus with a rectangle.

NOTE

The Wand button that usually is in the top part of the Toolbox, depending on how you have the Toolbox configured, is called Control Wizards. When it is activated, it walks you through the control creation process by asking a series of questions. When this process is finished, your control is configured based on the answers you furnished. The wizards will help you with combo boxes, list boxes, option groups, command buttons, subforms, and more. If you prefer to create the control manually (as you are doing here), just deactivate the wand.

14. To the right of the Ccity textbox, draw a box about the size of the Ccity textbox.

NOTE

The Command button is one of those controls that allows a shortcut. Rather than drawing the box, you can just click the area in the detail section where you want the button to appear and a default sized command button will be placed on your form. Other controls, such as the toggle button, also have this functionality.

15. Type `Open Flight Table` over the text on the button.

NOTE

If your text is too large for the button, this is a good place to use the Format, Size, To Fit option from the menu. This option is also available by right-clicking the button and then choosing Size, To Fit.

16. Right-click the Command button and click Properties from the short-cut menu to access the Property sheet.

NOTE

To bypass the shortcut menu, you can click the button and press F4 to access its Property sheet.

17. Click the Other tab, and then type `cmdOpenFlight` in the Name property.

18. Click the Event tab, and then choose On Click.

19. Click the drop-down box of the On Click event and choose macOpenFlight.

20. Close the Property sheet. Close and save the form.

21. Test the macro by reopening the form and then clicking the button you just created.

22. You should see the message box with the message "Open the Flight table" (see Figure 9.4). Click OK to open the Flight table.

Figure 9.4: *When you test your macro, a message box appears prior to opening the table.*

THE MsgBox FUNCTION

Whether you know it or not, you took advantage of one of the many built-in functions available in Access. The MsgBox function is a useful tool for sending messages to the user. Another similar function is InputBox, which provides the added functionality of letting the user input information based on the message. When MsgBox is running, the user is prevented from clicking on anything in the Access application but the OK button. For example, the user cannot select from the menu bar while the message box is running. However, the user still has access to the operating system through the Start button, which opens the door to other applications.

The syntax for MsgBox usage (bracketed items represent optional arguments) is

```
MsgBox(prompt,[ buttons], [ title], [ helpfile, context])
```

Table 9.1 explains the requirements for each argument. You can use the MsgBox function with a text string to relay a message, or you can use it to show what value a variable has at a particular time.

Table 9.1: **MsgBox** *Arguments*

Argument	Inclusion	Description	Example
Prompt	Required	String expression	"Open Form"
Buttons	Optional	Numeric expression	1
Title	Optional	String expression	"Warning"
Helpfile	Optional	String expression	"acmain9.chm"
Context	Optional	Numeric expression	5003042

The following procedure gives the user an option to use Access help:

```
Private Sub cmdMsgBox_Click()
Dim Path As String, Button As Integer
Dim Title As String, HelpFile As String

Path = "C:\Program Files\Microsoft Office\Office\1033\"
Button = 64
Title = "System Message"
```

```
HelpFile = "acmain9.chm"
MsgBox "Click help to search Access help", _
Button + vbMsgBoxHelpButton, Title, Path & HelpFile, 0
End Sub
```

This sub procedure uses all the available MsgBox arguments. Notice the use of the vbMsgboxHelpButton to create a button that accesses the help file. The Context argument specifies the help topic to be accessed in the HelpFile argument. Thus, the two arguments work together.

The variables were created to simplify typing the arguments and to make the program easier to read. The path was concatenated to the filename using the ampersand (&) operator. If you want to provide help for an error of a table that cannot be found, change the path to c:\windows\system (depending on your system), the helpfile to Jeterr40.chm, and the context (0) to 5003024.

Table 9.2 outlines the possible values for the *buttons* argument.

Table 9.2: Button Settings

Button Type (Constant)	Value	Function
VbOKOnly	0	Displays OK button only.
VbOKCancel	1	Displays OK and Cancel buttons.
VbAbortRetryIgnore	2	Displays Abort, Retry, and Ignore buttons.
VbYesNoCancel	3	Displays Yes, No, and Cancel buttons.
VbYesNo	4	Displays Yes and No buttons.
VbRetryCancel	5	Displays Retry and Cancel buttons.
Icon Style		
VbCritical	16	Displays Critical Message icon.
VbQuestion	32	Displays Warning Query icon.
VbExclamation	48	Displays Warning Message icon.
VbInformation	64	Displays Information Message icon.
Default Choice		
vbDefaultButton1	0	First button is default.
vbDefaultButton2	256	Second button is default.
vbDefaultButton3	512	Third button is default.
vbDefaultButton4	768	Fourth button is default.
Modality		
VbApplicationModal	0	The user must respond to the message box before continuing work in the current application.
VbSystemModal	4096	All applications are suspended until the user responds to the message box.

Table 9.2: continued

Button Type (Constant)	Value	Function
	Special	
VbMsgBoxHelpButton	16384	Adds the Help button to the message box.
VbMsgBoxSetForeground	65536	Specifies the message box window as the foreground window.
VbMsgBoxRight	524288	Text is right aligned.
VbMsgBoxRtlReading	1048576	Specifies text should appear as right-to-left reading on Hebrew and Arabic systems.

The message box returns a value, depending on your choice. This is a handy technique for programming, as you shall see. For example, if you want to continue your program based on the user's response, you can create a message box with the following code:

```
Msgbox("Do you want to continue?", 4 + 32 + 256)
```

If you add the three numbers together in the function, you get the same message box. Assuming that you prefer a certain number combination, you can add the numbers together, write down the total number and what it represents, and use it over and over. Typing one number is faster than typing three constants. Notice that 4 + 32 + 256 are added together in the following code:

```
Msgbox("Do you want to continue?", 292)
```

Even if you remove the questions mark at the end of the sentence, it is still obvious that you are posing a question. The question mark is supplied by the box because 32 is used. Notice Figure 9.5. Combining the numbers yields three box options. You could just as easily substitute the equivalent constant for each option value to make the code more understandable. As you type your code in the Module window, VBA presents you with a list of MsgBox constants from which to choose. Had you used the built-in constants instead of the values, the code would have looked similar to the following code.

```
Msgbox("Do you want to continue?", vbYesNo + vbQuestion + vbDefaultButton2)
```

NOTE

Access provides constants (all starting with the letters "vb") for Msgbox arguments that make your code more understandable. You can use values or constants or mix both values and constants.

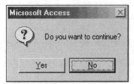

Figure 9.5: *The message box with a question is an option that can be selected by using the proper* MsgBox *argument.*

Try the first form in the immediate window by pressing Ctrl+G and typing ? Msgbox("Do you want to continue?", 4 + 32 + 256). If you click Yes, 6 is returned. If you click No, 7 is returned. You can use this technique in your program, which the following example illustrates:

```
If MsgBox("Do you want to continue?", 4 + 32 + 256) = 6 Then
MsgBox ("yes")
Else
MsgBox ("no")
End If
```

Of course, this example only serves to test the procedure. After you deter-mine that it works, you could substitute whatever code you wanted to replace MsgBox ("Yes") and MsgBox ("No"). Table 9.3 shows the returned values for each button type.

Table 9.3: Returned Values

Constant	Value	Description
vbOK	1	OK
vbCancel	2	Cancel
vbAbort	3	Abort
vbRetry	4	Retry
vbIgnore	5	Ignore
vbYes	6	Yes
vbNo	7	No

THE InputBox FUNCTION

Aside from the input area, the InputBox function seems almost identical to the MsgBox function at first glance. However, it allows the prompting of the user for information that can be stored in a variable. The syntax of the InputBox is similar to the MsgBox.

InputBox ([prompt], [title], [default], [xpos], [ypos], [helpfile, context])

The common arguments between the two functions (prompt, title, helpfile, and context) work identically. The default argument is an optional string or expression that is placed in the text box when it appears. The optional xpos and ypos arguments give coordinates to position the box on the screen. The following line of code is a typical use of this function:

```
SSN = InputBox("Please enter your social security number", ,"000-00-0000")
```

Notice that what is returned from the user response is assigned to the variable SSN. This capability makes the InputBox function very useful. Also notice that the extra comma between the prompt and the default string omits the title. This code produces the screen shown in Figure 9.6.

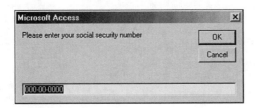

Figure 9.6: *You can use the* InputBox *function to assign a value to a variable.*

CONVERTING THE MACRO

Now you know a bit about the message boxes available to macros. Let's next cover converting a macro to VBA. The good news is that you can convert any macro you have into VBA code. A further benefit of doing this is that an error-handling routine is automatically generated. Examining this routine can teach you as you go.

✔ To learn more about error handling, see "Determining which Errors Occur" in Chapter 11, "Handling Access Error Codes."

1. Under Macros, select the macro to be converted in the Database window.

2. From the menu bar, click Tools, Macro, Convert Macros to Visual Basic.

3. Be sure to accept error handling and macro comments.

That's it! Notice that a new module appears under Modules, as shown in Figure 9.7.

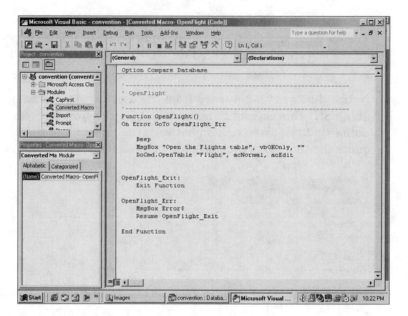

Figure 9.7: *When Access converts a macro to a VBA procedure, it adds error routines.*

Printing the Current Record Using a Macro

The RunCommand action can run built-in Access commands from the Access menu bar, toolbar, or shortcut menu. This action replaced the DoMenuItem action from Access 97. The one required argument, which can be selected from a drop-down list, is required.

You can use a macro to print the current record on a form. This macro can be easily converted to VBA code. You use the RunCommand action to select the current record and then print the selection.

The following steps guide you through the process of creating the macro:

1. Under Macros, click New from the Database toolbar to open the Macro window.

2. Click the drop-down box in the first row of the Action column and choose RunCommand. You can type r in the column to speed up your search for the action.

3. Press F6 to enter the Action Arguments section of the RunCommand action. From the drop-down box of the Command argument, choose SelectRecord.

4. Choose PrintOut from the drop-down box of the second row of the Action column. Typing a p retrieves the action.

5. Press F6 to enter the Action Arguments section of the PrintOut action. In the Print Range argument, choose Selection from the drop-down box as shown in Figure 9.8.

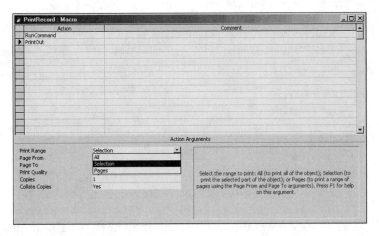

Figure 9.8: *Only two actions in the Macro window print the current record of a form.*

6. Click the Save button from the toolbar and name the macro macPrintRecord. Close the macro.

7. Open the Client Form in Design view. Create a Command button under the Open Flight Table button and label it Print Record.

8. Click the Command button and press F4 to access the Property sheet of the button.

9. Click the Event tab, and then choose On Click. Click the drop-down box of the On Click event and choose macPrintRecord.

10. Close the Property sheet. Close and save the form. Test the macro by reopening the form and then clicking the button you just created.

11. Close the form.

You might recall that you learned how to print the current record from a form in Chapter 5; however, this technique is unique from several perspectives. First, it doesn't print to a report as does the example in Chapter 5. Instead, it prints the current record of the form using the form design that you created. Second, it uses the PrintOut action instead of the OpenReport action to print the record. Third, it introduces you to the RunCommand and PrintOut actions that open up more database functionality to you.

If you save the macPrintRecord macro as a module, your code looks like the following:

```
Function macPrintRecord()
On Error GoTo PrintRecord_Err

    DoCmd.RunCommand acCmdSelectRecord
    DoCmd.PrintOut acSelection, , , acHigh, 1, True


PrintRecord_Exit:
    Exit Function

PrintRecord_Err:
    MsgBox Error$
    Resume PrintRecord_Exit

End Function
```

Macros are easy and fun. Although they have their limitations, they also have their place. Perhaps their best benefit is helping you learn how to write code.

What's Next

In the next chapter you learn how to customize your application using code. VBA can give you so much flexibility that your imagination is perhaps your only limitation. Functions, subs, scope, flow control, and loops are some of the topics that are covered. If you can't find a built-in Access function that meets your needs, you can create your own.

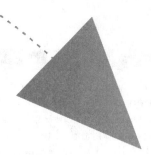

10

Using Procedures to Customize Your Database

In the last chapter, you not only learned about macros and modules, but about how to send messages to users. This chapter will take you deeper into programming by teaching you how to use various flow control statements that are part of VBA.

You have already been introduced to the power of functions. This chapter gives you a chance to get your feet wet with some hands-on examples using functions. The examples near the end of the chapter use many Access intrinsic functions. Specifically, you learn

- how to use Access's built-in string functions
- the differences between function procedures and sub procedures
- what is scope and how to use it
- how to create procedures
- how to use programming loops
- how to use conditional constructs
- how to use functions to customize your database
- how to use functions to overcome the limitations of wildcards

Exploring Procedures

One of the advantages of an Access database is that you can tailor applications to suit your specific needs. Subs and functions can give you the flexibility to do almost anything that you want to do in terms of customizing and optimizing your database for maximum efficiency. The dividends of increased productivity more than make up for the time you spend learning how to properly implement an automated customization of your application.

Instead of paying a programmer to write a custom application from scratch, you can use the Access database model as a base for your programs. A likely reason that more people don't do just that is intimidation. They feel that it would take them too much time to develop the skills necessary to accomplish the task.

In view of the help screens and user-friendly options that have been added in recent years, it has become more difficult to make a convincing argument that Access is too difficult. But there are lingering educational gaps that prevent people from putting the pieces together. This chapter attempts to bridge the gaps that the Access help menus and the Web tutorials open. This is not to minimize the value of these methods; it's just that there are some important questions for which it is difficult to find answers.

The educational gap usually surfaces with a challenge. You know exactly what you want to do, but you don't know how to do it in Access. For example, suppose you want to capitalize the first letter of each word in a field while leaving the rest of the letters in the word lowercase. Try searching for a built-in Access function that can accomplish this. This function is nonexistent, but at this point, you don't know this. Even if the function did exist, if you don't know which keywords to use in your search, chances are you can't find the function. Rather than searching for hours through help screens and Web sites for a built-in Access feature that might not even exist, you just write your own code to perform the operation you desired.

What you need to do is develop a custom function that enables you to accomplish your task. This means that you can customize your database by using your own procedures that Access either forgot or didn't think were important enough to include. Even if there is an Access utility that does exactly what you want to do, it is not always easy to find it. You learn how to write custom code later in this chapter.

When you realize the power that is available to you through code, you begin to see that there are almost no limitations to what you can do. Access built-in string functions can make your life easier along the way. Two intrinsic string functions that are used heavily are Mid and Instr. The Mid string function has three arguments, as the following line shows:

```
Mid(string, start, [length])
```

The first argument is the string, which can be represented by a variable, constant, or expression. The second argument (start) is the starting position in the string that you want to retrieve. The third argument (length) is the number of characters you want to retrieve. This argument is optional. If you leave it out, you simply retrieve the remainder of the string from the starting position. Table 10.1 describes the arguments for the Mid string function.

Table 10.1: **Mid** *Function Arguments*

Argument	Inclusion	Data Type	Description
String	Required	String	String expression from which characters are returned.
Start	Required	Long	Starting character position in the string of the piece to be taken. If start is greater than the number of characters in the string, Mid returns a zero-length string (" ").
Length	Optional	Variant(long)	Number of characters to return. If omitted or if there are fewer than length characters in the text (including the character at start), all characters from the start position to the end of the string are returned.

The InStr function has four arguments but often is used without the first and last arguments. The first argument is the starting position of your search. The second argument is the string in which to search. The third argument is the string for which to search. The last argument is the type of string comparison. It returns the numeric position of the string that is sought within the string that is searched. The syntax looks like the following:

```
InStr([start], string being searched, string searched for, [comparison type])
```

The brackets indicate optional arguments. Table 10.2 is more descriptive than the prototype just presented with brackets.

Table 10.2: **InStr** *Function Arguments*

Argument	Inclusion	Data Type	Description
Starting position	Optional	Numeric expression	Sets the starting position for the search. If omitted, the search begins at the first character position.

Table 10.2: continued

Argument	Inclusion	Data Type	Description
String to be searched	Required	String expression	Can be a string, field, or expression, which can include another function. The search is performed within the bounds of whatever is entered here.
String to search for	Required	String expression	The string or expression that is sought.
Comparison	Optional	Constant or value	Optional. Specifies type of string comparison.

Table 10.3 describes other useful string functions.

Table 10.3: Other Useful String Functions with Examples

Function	Argument 1	Argument 2	Result	Example	Returns
Lcase	String or expression		Converts to lowercase	Lcase("KID")	kid
Left	String or expression	Number of leftmost characters to include in the results.	Returns x number of characters on the left side of the string	left ("Bobby",3)	Bob
Len	String or expression		Returns the number of characters in the string.	len("Karen")	5
Ltrim	String or expression		Removes spaces on the left of the string.	Ltrim (" Street")	Street
Right	String or expression	Number of rightmost characters to include in the results.	Returns x number of characters on the right side of the string	Right("my way",3)	way
Rtrim	String or expression		Removes spaces on the right of the string.	Rtrim ("Street ")	Street

Table 10.3: continued

Function	Argument 1	Argument 2	Result	Example	Returns
Str	Numeric value or expression		Converts a numeric value to a string. (variant)	Str(224)	"224"
Trim	String or expression		Removes spaces on both sides of the string.	Trim (" Street ")	Street
Ucase	String or expression		Converts to uppercase	Ucase("cia")	"CIA"
Val	String or expression		Converts a string value to a numeric value.	Val("1618")	1618

Functions Versus Subs

You have already examined some of the differences between functions and subs. Functions return values; subs don't return anything. Functions can be called from almost any place in Access, but because sub procedures are not used in expressions, you typically call sub procedures from an event (on a form or report), a function, or another sub procedure. For example, because sub procedures do not return a value, they cannot be used on the right side of an expression the same way you use any intrinsic functions such as Left or Len. For the same reason, you cannot call a sub procedure by assigning it to a variable. Furthermore, if you tried to use a sub procedure with an argument in a place that you normally use a function, such as a query, you receive the message Undefined function (subname) in expression. On the other hand, functions can be called from queries, controls, macros, forms, reports, or other procedures because you can use expressions with all these objects. If not explicitly specified otherwise, both Sub and Function procedures are public by default.

✔ To learn more about public procedures, see "What Is Scope?," later in this chapter.

✔ To learn more about subs, see "How to Use DAO and ADO to Manipulate Data" in Chapter 12, "Access Visual Basic Tools, Tips, and Techniques."

> ✔ To learn more about functions, see "Using Functions with Queries, Revisited" in
> Chapter 16, "Overcoming the Limitations of Queries."

Both sub and function procedures can be called within other subs and functions. This makes them *modular*, which means they can be reused over and over again, making the code easier to debug while decreasing the overall amount of code that needs to be written. Rather than writing the same procedure over again when you need it, you simply call it.

Combining functions with queries can be extremely powerful. Suppose you created a function that saved you time by automatically capitalizing a string. Now think how much more time you could save if you used this function on a table with thousands of records! For example, the Proper function that is presented in this chapter capitalizes the first character of each word in a field. A query using this function saves you time with any table in your database.

Subs can powerfully handle data manipulation and housekeeping tasks in forms and reports. With the click of a mouse button, complex tasks can be handled seamlessly. If that isn't enough, both functions and macros can be called within sub procedures. Because the underlying objects of forms and reports can be easily accessed by sub procedures tied to their events, the benefits of such sub procedures become apparent.

What Is Scope?

Scope refers to the range, reach, extent, or sphere of availability of a variable, constant, or procedure to other procedures. A variable, constant, or procedure can be declared *public* or *private*. If they are declared with Public scope, they are available to all procedures in all modules in all applications unless Option Private Module is in effect; in which case, they are available only within the project in which they reside. Anything that is declared with Private scope is available only within the module in which it was declared.

NOTE

Any variable declared as private in the declarations section of the module is available to any procedure in the module. If a variable is not in the declaration section (in other words, it is declared within the procedure), it is available only to the procedure itself. The declaration section is at the top of a standard module, before any procedures have been declared. Just to be sure, select declarations from the upper-right drop-down box of the procedure to go there. The Dim statement is functionally like the Private statement, but the Private keyword makes the intentions more obvious.

Keep in mind that the default scope for all function and sub procedures is public, except for event procedures. The Private keyword is automatically inserted before the procedure declaration when VBA creates an event procedure. In any other situation, if you do not explicitly declare your procedure to be private, it becomes public. For example, if you want your function to be available to your queries, don't declare it to be private.

If a variable is declared static, it is available as long as the application is running. This is in contrast to dynamic variables that are reinitialized each time a procedure is run. When do you use it? If you wanted to know how many times an object such as a combo box or a command button was run, you could declare an incremental counter variable to count each time the program was run as follows:

```
Counter = Counter + 1
```

The only problem is that each time the object was run, it would be reinitialized to 1. On the other hand, if it was declared to be static, it would accumulate as long as the database session was open, thus giving you the correct number.

Creating Procedures

You have already created a procedure, but take a closer look at the process. Open any Access database. Under Objects, click Modules, and then click New. Click Insert, Procedure. You should see the Add Procedure window into which you enter the name of the procedure (see Figure 10.1). You can also select its type and scope, or you can elect to declare all local variables to be static. You can just as easily skip the insert procedure option and create your function or sub manually, but this saves you a little time.

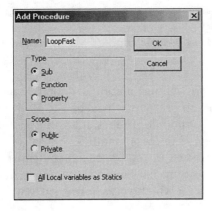

Figure 10.1: *You can use the Add Procedure dialog box to set options for your procedures.*

Your choices for the Type of procedure are Sub, Function, or Property. You should be familiar with subs and functions by now, but what about Property procedures? A Property procedure enables you to add and manipulate custom properties. After it is created, it becomes a property of the module containing the procedure.

Visual Basic for Applications (VBA), a subset of Visual Basic, is provided with your Access program. After you click New, you enter the Visual Basic window, which opens when you use the Visual Basic Editor, a program that lets you create and edit VBA code as shown in Figure 10.2.

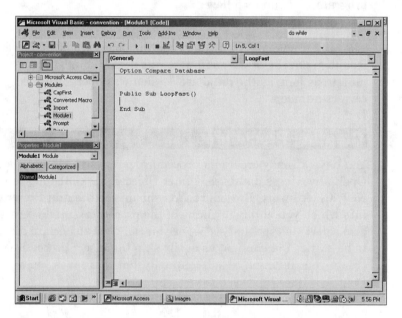

Figure 10.2: *The Visual Basic Editor enables you to create code in the Standard Module window.*

If you are creating a function, you use a standard module as you just did, but if you want to create a sub procedure attached to an event on a form or report, you would use a class module. In fact, all event procedures are sub procedures, which are collected in class modules. In the code window of a form or report, the object list box in the upper left indicates the control you are currently using; the procedure list box in the upper right indicates the name of the event procedure on which you are currently working.

In the project window to the left you can access any procedure in the database by double-clicking. It first lists any modules attached to forms or reports. Next, it lists standard modules. This means that you do not have to exit your standard module procedure to modify a class module procedure, or vice versa. Although you have the same lists whether you are in a class or standard module, the class modules usually have many more items listed.

More Than One Way to Loop

A *loop* is a repetitive programming construct that allows a statement or a series of statements to process over and over again until a condition is met. Consequently, loops provide an excellent way to cycle through code. If you are examining a string, you can cycle through one character or word at a time. If you are incrementing a number, each loop can add another value to your number. If you are looking for an object in a collection of objects, the loop is the perfect vehicle to enumerate (list) your objects.

Do..Loop

The Do..Loop statement executes code inside the Do..Loop either while a condition remains true or until a condition becomes true, depending on how the statement is constructed. There are two ways to use the While or Until keywords to check a condition in a Do..Loop statement. You can check the condition before you enter the loop or you can check it after the loop has run at least once.

Let's have some fun. Imagine that your Access professor gave you an assignment to write a program that counts from 1 to 10. That sounds simple enough, but how would you accomplish it? Perform the following steps to write just such a program in three different ways:

1. From within Access, open a new module.

2. Click Insert Procedure, and name it CountLoop. Leave all the defaults, including Sub and Public, as they are.

3. Insert the following code between the Public Sub and End Sub lines (see Figure 10.3) and press Ctrl+G to open the Immediate window.

   ```
   Dim iCounter As Integer

   Do While iCounter < 10
       iCounter = iCounter + 1
       Debug.Print iCounter
   Loop
   ```

4. Be sure the cursor is on the Public Sub line, and then click the Run button. You can also press F5 to run the procedure.

   You should see the numbers 1 through 10 in the Immediate window (see Figure 10.4). Press Ctrl+G if you missed opening the window in step 3. You can click on the top part of the Immediate window and drag it up if you need more space.

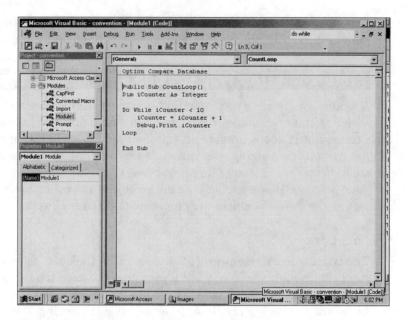

Figure 10.3: *The* CountLoop *sub procedure can be run from the Module window.*

The Run button resembles the play button on a CD player.

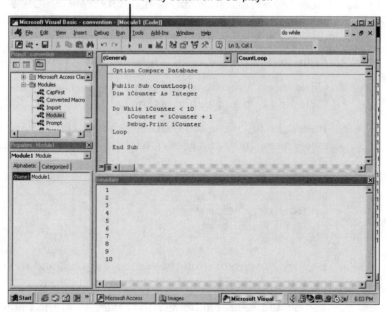

Figure 10.4: *You can view the results of the* CountLoop *procedure in the Immediate window.*

5. Change While to Until and < to =. The line should now read

   ```
   Do Until iCounter = 10
   ```

6. Click the run button again.

   The results should be the same.

7. Place the cursor in front of the U of Until. Select the words Until iCounter = 10, and then click the Cut button, or choose Edit, Cut from the menu.

8. Place the cursor one space after the Loop statement and then choose Paste. The procedure should now read

   ```
   Dim iCounter As Integer

   Do
   iCounter = iCounter + 1
   Debug.Print iCounter
   Loop Until iCounter = 10
   ```

9. Run the program again. It should produce the same results. Stay in the window for the next example.

By this time you might be thinking, "So what's the point? Why not just use one method and stick with it?" By using more than one method you have gained more flexibility. Although order is not so important in a small program like this one, it becomes very important in the larger programs. The Until part of the program gives the loop construct a way to end the procedure by breaking out of the loop when a condition becomes true. Until the iCounter variable is equal to 10, the program will run.

If you don't construct the conditional statement properly, you could create an endless loop. If this happens, just press Ctrl+Break to break out of the program. In effect, you are back in Editing mode, where you can make any adjustments you need to make. You can also break out of a loop by inserting a conditional End Do statement within the loop. Another interesting twist to illustrate loops is to change the Debug.Print statement to MsgBox. When you run the next program, you see the results of the loop in the message box.

For..Next Loop

You can use the For..Next loop to execute code within the loop a set number of times. The Step clause followed by a number allows you to increment the iCounter variable by more or less than one.

Imagine that your professor changed his mind and decided that you need to make your program count to 100 in increments of 10 starting at 20.

Although you can do this with a Do loop, the For...Next loop construct is perfectly suited for this.

1. In the Visual Basic window that you left open from the last example, replace everything from Do to 10 in the previously written program with the following code:

```
For iCounter = 20 To 100 Step 10
MsgBox iCounter
Next iCounter
```

2. Run the code and then watch the results in the MsgBox. Be sure the Immediate window is open.

3. Close the window.

Notice the line that is missing. There is no iCounter = iCounter +1 line. You don't need a variable that increments with this loop construct. The code is also smaller. If you take the Step 10 statement out, the program counts from 20 to 100 in increments of 1. In other words, you don't have to use the Step option; you simply add it if you want to increment more (or less) than the default, which is one.

If you know the number of loops (iterations) that you want, this is the perfect construct for your purposes. You don't have to worry about setting any condition to end the looping. If you want your code to count backward, simply set the step to -1. For example, the following program counts backward from 100 to 90:

```
Dim iCounter As Integer

For iCounter = 100 To 90 Step -1
Debug.Print iCounter
Next iCounter
```

For...Each Loop

The loop constructs you just learned are great for regular variables, but what about objects and object variables? Although you can use the Do and For loops with objects, VBA has a loop construct especially suited for objects.

The For...Each loop is designed specifically to work with collections of objects such as controls. Like the For...Next loop, the For...Each loop cycles through a sequence of values. The difference is that the values are, in reality, pointers to objects.

Suppose you want to enumerate every control in your form. The following program does just that. You need to create a Control variable for use in the program.

1. Open the Convention database from the AccessByExample folder.

2. Under Objects, choose Forms and the select the Client form. Click Design on the Database toolbar.

3. Copy and paste Open Flight Table button. With the new button selected, press F4 to open the Property sheet, as shown in Figure 10.5.

Figure 10.5: *You can use* For..Each *loops to enumerate controls on your form.*

If the control is selected, you also can use Edit, Duplicate from the menu to copy the control.

4. Click the All tab. Set the Name property to cmdEnumerateControls and the Caption property to Enumerate Controls.

5. Click the Event tab, and click the drop-down box of the On Click box. Choose Event Procedure, and then click the Build button to open the procedure using the For..Each loop, as shown in Figure 10.6.

6. After the Private Sub line, type the following code:

```
Dim Ctrl As Control

For Each Ctrl In Me.Controls
MsgBox Ctrl.Name
Next
```

7. Close the Module window and Property sheet.

8. Click the View button to switch to Form View, and then click the Enumerate Controls button. Notice how you can cycle through the controls, as shown in Figure 10.7.

9. Close the form.

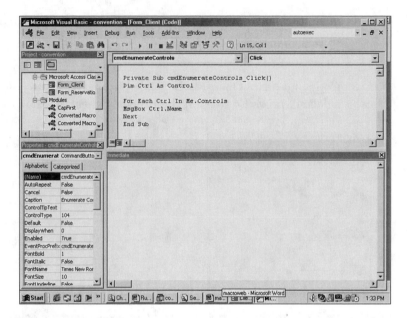

Figure 10.6: *The simple program that is attached to a command button for enumerating controls on a form.*

Figure 10.7: *When you see the code for cycling through controls, you begin to understand the power that is available to you.*

Consider the power you have at your disposal. If you can cycle through the controls, then you can change properties for each control. If you attach the following code to a button, you change the font color of every text or combo box to red:

```
Dim Ctrl As Control

For Each Ctrl In Me.Controls
  If TypeOf Ctrl Is TextBox Then
    Ctrl.ForeColor = 255
  ElseIf TypeOf Ctrl Is ComboBox Then
    Ctrl.ForeColor = 255
  End If
Next
```

This code can also be slightly modified and attached to the On Current event of the form to change every text or combo box in every record that had a field checked No (on a Yes/No field) to red (or whatever color you desire). As you check each record in your form, you see the font colors change in any record checked No in the Yes/No field.

More than One Way to Handle Conditions

Programs must be able to make decisions based on conditions. It is not unusual to be confronted with a task that involves what is called *conditional processing*, which is the ability to determine which direction to take the program based on a value or a set of conditions. If X value is true, then do Y. If it is false, then do Z. If Ralph has a grade point average of B or better, then put him in the scholarship program. If it is not equal to or better than B, then don't put him in the scholarship program. These are the kinds of real-life situations that you can encounter. In short, you need to have the ability to control your program. You have already been introduced to the following flow control structures, now you have the opportunity to evaluate them by example.

If...Then...Else Construct

The If...Then...Else construct enables you to check a condition and, based on whether that condition is true, perform an operation or a set of operations. That condition can be a single value, a range of values, or a set of values linked together with operators such as AND or OR. Table 10.4 illustrates some examples.

Table 10.4: Types Of Conditional Expressions

Condition	Example
Single Value	X = 2
Range of Values	X>=100 and X <200
Set of Values	X = 220 and Y = 480 or Z = 370

If you have properly set up a range of values in your If statement, then anything that falls within that range becomes true. If your range is between 100 and 200, then 150 or any other value in that range is also true. With a set of values, only specified values are true. However, if the AND operator is between two values, then *both* values must be present before the condition is true. On the other hand, with the OR operator, if *either* value is present, the condition evaluates to true.

Remember that the Else clause is optional. You might not need to do anything if the condition is not true. Your specific situation determines its need. The following code illustrates:

```
Sub done()
Dim i
For i = 1 To 10
    If i > 8 Then
        MsgBox "Almost done!"
    End If
Next i
End Sub
```

There is no need to use an `Else` statement because the message will activate only if the variable is greater than 8. If the condition is not true, then the program runs as usual, by simply counting.

NOTE

Whenever you declare a variable without assigning a data type, it is assigned the variant data type. Variant data types use more resources, so be discriminating with their use.

When you get into more complicated situations, you will discover that the `Else` clause can be essential. Consider this excerpt from the program that was promised earlier in the chapter:

```
For i = 1 to Len(StrInput)
    Char = Mid(StrInput, i, 1)
    If Char = " " then
        Mark = i
    ElseIf i = Mark + 1 Then
        Mid(StrInput, i, 1) = Ucase(Mid(StrInput, i ,1))
    Else
        Mid(StrInput, i, 1) = Lcase(Mid(StrInput, i ,1))
    End If
Next I
```

In this procedure, you have a specific function to accomplish if the condition is not true. If the character you are examining is one position after the space, then capitalize it. If it is not, then make it lowercase. The `ElseIf` clause provides an opportunity to add another condition without going to the `Select...Case` statement.

✔ To learn more about the custom procedure that capitalizes the first letter of each word, see "Using Functions to Customize Your Applications," later in this chapter.

Select...Case Construct

The `Select...Case` construct fills in the gaps that the `If...Then...Else` construct leaves. If you are just testing one variable with multiple conditions, then the `Select...Case` is your answer. The `If` statement can test many values at once, but when you add multiple conditions by using multiple ElseIfs, your code can get confusing. That's where the Select...Case construct comes in. It is designed for multiple conditions.

Let's start with a simple example. Suppose you want to convey a different message for each loop. The following code illustrates:

```
Dim i
For i = 1 to 3
    Select Case i
        Case 1
        MsgBox "This is the first pass."
        Case 2
        MsgBox "This is the second pass."
        Case 3
        MsgBox "This is the third pass."
    End Select
Next I
```

Notice that there is only one variable to test with multiple conditions. You can also use ranges and sets of values with each case clause, as the following illustrates:

```
Select Case i
    Case 2, 4, 10 to 20, 31, 43
    MsgBox "Number found"
    Case Is = NewNum
    MsgBox "Number found"
    Case Else
    MsgBox "Sorry, no match"
End Select
```

In this example, if the variable in the Select clause is matched with a listed number—or is part of a range of numbers (10 to 20)—or equal to the NewNum variable, the MsgBox displays Number found. Otherwise, the MsgBox displays Sorry, no match.

Think of this construct as a filter. The variable is tested against each value until a match is found, at which time the code following the Case clause is run. After the condition is matched, the subsequent conditions are ignored. If no match is found, then the code following the Case Else is run.

Another benefit of the Select...Case construct is readability. It is much easier to read a list of conditions in a Select...Case construct than an If...Then...Else construct with an almost endless list of ElseIfs. A Case Else clause is usually recommended just in case all the conditions are false.

Using Functions to Fulfill Your Wish List of Features Access Forgot

By now you're beginning to realize the power that is available to you through programming. If you are like most users, you have a wish list of features that you would like to see in a database. If you can't find these features in any help menu or tutorial, it's time to try to create them yourself. If you create a feature as a function, then you can use it practically anywhere in the database.

At the beginning of this chapter, you were promised a function that would capitalize the first letter of each word in a string. Two versions are presented for analysis. The first version "hops" words by using the InStr function to find the spaces in the string. The second version analyzes the string character by character. You get a chance for some hands-on experience with this version. Take a look at the following code:

```
Function Proper(strWord As String)
Dim GetWord As String, pos As Integer
Dim Build As String, NewString As String, Char As String

NewString = strWord & " "
Do Until NewString = ""
    pos = InStr(NewString, " ") ' find space position
    GetWord = Left(NewString, pos) 'get word
    'subtract word for next iteration
    NewString = Right(NewString, Len(NewString) - pos)
  For i = 1 To Len(GetWord)
    Char = Mid(GetWord, i, 1) 'analyze each character
    If i = 1 Then
      Char = UCase(Char) 'change to upper if first letter
    Else
      Char = LCase(Char)
    End If
  Build = Build & Char 'string rebuilt one letter at a time
  Next i
Loop
Proper = RTrim(Build) 'remove end space
End Function
```

You don't need to understand everything that is going on in this function, but many of the elements that you have studied in this chapter are presented here. The code takes the string one word at a time and analyzes each word one character at a time. The program looks for the first character of each word to capitalize. Read the comments to help you understand any difficult line. It uses Access's built-in string functions heavily. Also notice the loops and the conditional constructs.

Using Functions to Customize Your Applications

Now let's look at a function that performs exactly the same operation, but does so with much less code. This function is provided for you in the Convention database from your download. You don't have to add or remove spaces with this function because it simply checks and changes each character as it goes. Let's see how it works.

```
Function CapFirstLetter(StrInput As String)
Dim Mark As Integer, Char As String

For i = 1 To Len(StrInput)
  Char = Mid(StrInput, i, 1)
  If Char = " " Then
    Mark = i
  ElseIf i = Mark + 1 Then
    Mid(StrInput, i, 1) = UCase(Mid(StrInput, i, 1))
  Else
    Mid(StrInput, i, 1) = LCase(Mid(StrInput, i, 1))
  End If
Next i
CapFirstLetter = StrInput

End Function
```

This entire procedure uses only three variables. Notice how much shorter it is. The position or number that the space occupies in the string is assigned to the Mark variable. When the position in the string is Mark + 1 or the first character past the space, the character is capitalized. Any other character is set to lowercase.

Using the Immediate Window to Test Your Functions

Notice in the CapFirstLetter function that the mid function provides an ideal method of evaluating strings one character at a time. In this case, you are not only evaluating each character, you are changing the characters that meet the conditions.

The Immediate window gives you a quick and easy method to test your program with its command-line capability. The following steps walk you through testing the function in the Immediate window:

1. Open the Convention database, under Objects click Modules, click Proper, and then click Design to open the module in Design view.

2. Press Ctrl+G to open the Immediate window.

3. With your cursor in the Immediate window, type ?
   CapFirstLetter("pARk pLaCe") and then press Return. The program
   should return Park Place, as shown in Figure 10.8.

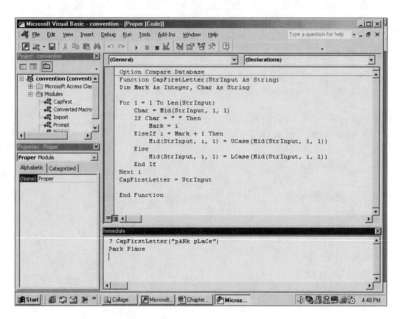

Figure 10.8: *The Immediate window shows what your function returns to
reassure you that your program is working properly.*

4. Close all windows in the module.

5. Under Objects, click Tables.

6. Under Tables, double-click Speakers.

7. Notice that everything is in uppercase. You can assume that this data
   came from an outside source. Close the table.

8. Right-click the Speakers table and choose copy. Click the Paste button
   and name it tblSpeakers.

9. Under Tables, click tblSpeakers.

10. From the toolbar, click New Object, Query to open the New Query
    dialog box.

11. Click OK to accept Design View from the New Query Dialog box.

12. Double-click the title bar of the tblSpeakers table and then click, hold,
    and drag the fields to the grid.

13. Click the drop-down box of the Query Type button, and choose Update Query.

14. In the Update To: row of the Speaker field, type `CapFirstLetter([Speaker])`.

15. In the Update To: row of the Topic field, type `CapFirstLetter([Topic])`, as shown in Figure 10.9.

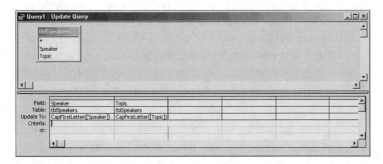

Figure 10.9: *You can combine custom functions with queries to powerfully enhance your queries.*

16. Run the query. Close the query without saving it, and then open the tblSpeakers table.

    Notice that everything has been changed (see Figure 10.10) to capitalize the first letter of each word. Just in case anything went wrong, you have the Speakers table to fall back on. If everything went fine, then delete the tblSpeakers table.

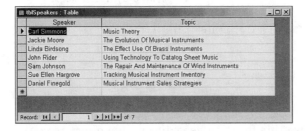

Figure 10.10: *The* `CapFirstLetter` *function changed all the data in the tblSpeakers table from uppercase to upper- and lowercase combinations.*

Can you imagine if the tblSpeakers table had several thousand records and you were given the task of changing everything from uppercase to proper capitalization? Think how daunting that task would be without a function.

Using Functions for Pattern Matching in Queries

Custom functions can do more than fulfill your wish list. They can fill in the gaps of features that Access forgot. Sometimes, problem solving requires you to seek a solution that Access doesn't offer in its standard list of features.

Suppose you had a table that you had obtained from an outside source that had a list of names that you wanted to parse into first, middle, and last name fields. First you would need to find out which records had only first and last names as opposed to first, middle, and last. You could use the Like "* *" wildcard pattern for the criterion in a query to pick up first and last names only. The only problem is that this wildcard pattern will also pick up first, middle, and last names. If you wanted three words in a list that also had four words in a field, Like "* * *" will also pick up four words.

The good news is that you can use a simple function provided with the download in the Convention database to count words for you, allowing you to selectively deal with situations of this nature. This solution gives you better accuracy in pattern matching. Examine the following code:

```
Function CountWord(FullString As String)
Dim AddWord As String, Build As String
Dim Iteration As Integer

Build = FullString & " " ' space makes sure you get the last word

  Do Until Left(Build, InStr(Build, " ")) = "" 'set the limit
    AddWord = Left(Build, InStr(Build, " ")) 'get word
      If AddWord <> " " Then
        Iteration = Iteration + 1 'count only valid words
      End If
    Build = Right(Build, Len(Build) - Len(AddWord)) 'subtract word
  Loop

CountWord = Iteration

End Function
```

You could use this function as criterion in a query to count the words, so that you could selectively parse the records that have precisely the number of words you are looking for. The function counts the words by counting the iterations necessary to accommodate all the spaces in the string. The bottom line is that custom-made procedures can give you much greater flexibility with your applications because they allow you to do what you want to do, regardless of whether there is a built-in function or other Access feature that provides a solution.

What's Next?

You have seen how VBA can open up a whole range of possibilities to enable you to do what you want to do. You can get around any perceived limitations or missing features by using your own custom procedures. The next chapter explains what to do when you encounter an error. There are several options available to you, the developer, for error handling. Error routines help make your application more professional as well as user friendly. In short, effective error handling will make you look better.

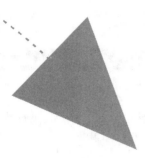

11

Handling Access Error Codes

In the last chapter, you learned about customizing your database by using many of the features available in VBA. This chapter focuses on what to do when you have an error. Adding error handling to your procedures makes your code run smoother. Specifically, in this chapter you learn

- what options are available to you when you have an error

- how to determine which errors have occurred

- how to write procedures that provide information concerning which errors have occurred

- how to fix errors after trapping them

- how to use the Resume statement

What To Do When Errors Occur

In a Utopian world, an error would never disrupt any program that you write. Anyone who is honest about the reality of real-world programming has to admit that programs, regardless of how carefully they are written, have errors from time to time. Because this is indisputable, is it not in your best interest to add error-handling routines to your procedures?

Let's examine some of the options that are open to you when an error occurs:

- Ignore it in your program by having no error handling whatsoever

- Ignore it in your program with error handling that resumes the program while bypassing the error

- Handle the error in your program by trapping the error, pausing the program, and giving the user an error message with the option to continue or seek extra help

- Handle the error by trapping the error and then calling a subroutine that fixes the problem

- Handle the error by logging the error in a table while letting the user continue

- Handle the error by coding around it

The third option is one that is commonly used. The fourth option is not always possible. For example, a particular table might not be available because it was accidentally deleted. Although a table can be created on the fly in the error subroutine, this must be anticipated in advance. You can combine the fourth and fifth options by giving the user a message with the option to fix the problem by creating a table. The last option is a good way to test your application from its launching. If you had a table that served as a log for the day-to-day errors that occurred, it would be easy to debug your program while determining whether additional error routines should be added.

The last option, though sometimes very difficult, is an excellent way to handle the error. For example, if you are looping through controls on a form while changing the forecolor of each control, you generate an error because not all controls have a forecolor property. You could totally bypass this error by using an `If..Then..Else` construct to examine each control type. Because the program selects only `TextBoxes` and `ComboBoxes`, controls without a forecolor property are effectively eliminated. The following code excerpt taken from the previous chapter illustrates:

```
If TypeOf Ctrl Is TextBox Then
   Ctrl.ForeColor = 255
ElseIf TypeOf Ctrl Is ComboBox Then
   Ctrl.ForeColor = 255
End If
```

No error routine has to be written, at least not for this particular problem. That means that the user is never confronted with the error. That also means that you have saved time writing extra code for error trapping. Unfortunately, this is not always possible. But when it is possible to code around the problem, by all means, take advantage of the opportunity.

Determining which Errors Occur

The question naturally arises, "How do you know what error has occurred?" Even though Access provides error codes and messages, they are often difficult for users to interpret. If that isn't enough, they usually don't have a clue as to what to do about the error. Error handling makes your application more user friendly while giving you more control over what the user encounters.

Suppose you have a table with error codes and their corresponding messages. The following DAO program generates just such a table:

```
Sub GenerateErrorTable()
Dim db As DAO.Database, rs As DAO.Recordset
Dim i As Integer, Msg$

Set db = CurrentDb()
Set rs = db.OpenRecordset("ErrorCodes")
For i = 1 To 32766
  Msg$ = Error$(i)
  If Msg$ <> "Application-defined or object-defined error" _
  And Msg$ <> "Reserved Error" Then
    rs.AddNew
    rs![ErrorNumber] = i
    rs![ErrorMsg] = Msg$
    rs.Update
  End If
Next i
rs.Close
db.Close
Set rs = Nothing
Set db = Nothing
End Sub
```

You don't have to worry about generating this table yourself. It has already been done for you. It is in the `ErrorHandle.mdb` database that you down-loaded, along with the code that generated it. Notice the `If` clause in the program. It eliminates every message that has `Application-defined or object-defined error` in it. The only problem is that the greater part of the records include this message. Consequently, only 87 records are left in the table rather than several thousand records.

Open up the ErrorCodes table from the ErrorHandle database shown in Figure 11.1. This is only a fragment of the messages that Access generates. The question remains, "How do you find the rest of the messages?"

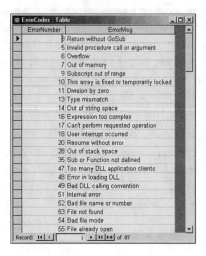

Figure 11.1: There are missing errors in the ErrorCodes table.

Before this question is answered, another question should be posed and answered. What is Microsoft Jet? It is the database engine that creates tables and runs queries. Although you have a choice of database engines beginning with Access 2000, Jet Database Engine is still adequate for appli-cations that are not too huge. What does this have to do with finding error messages?

Both DAO and ADO object models can generate errors when working with Jet. According to Microsoft, DAO makes much more efficient use of the Microsoft Jet database engine than ADO, and many operations are faster under DAO, sometimes up to 5 to 10 times faster. On the other hand, ADO is an excellent object model for "front-end" client/server style solutions that usually involve larger databases. Because they both have their advantages and disadvantages and they both generate errors, you have the opportunity to see a sampling of error handling from both object models.

Both DAO and ADO have errors collections; however, DAO errors are part of the DBEngine object, where ADO errors are part of the Connection object.

The following exercise by example gives you a better understanding of the error collections of both object models:

1. Open the ErrorHandle database again, if it is not already open.

2. Under Objects, click Forms, and then double-click the JetErrorCodes form.

3. Select by highlighting the 1 on the Record indicator at the bottom of the form (refer to Figure 11.1). Type 51 and press Enter to go to record 51.

   Error code 3024, which lists Could not find file <name>, appears onscreen, as shown in Figure 11.2.

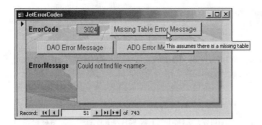

Figure 11.2: *Record 51 shows Error Code 3024, which is the missing table error along with the* Could not find file <name> *error message.*

4. Place your cursor on the command button Missing Table Error Message (don't click) for at least three seconds. You should see the ControlTip Text property of the command button that says This assumes there is a missing table. Actually, it just acts as if there is a missing table.

5. Click the Missing Table Error Message button to open the pop-up form shown in Figure 11.3.

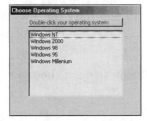

Figure 11.3: *A pop-up form allows you to select your operating system so that the correct path to the help system is supplied.*

Figure 11.3 shows the pop-up form that appears, asking you to select your operating system. The PopUp and Modal properties of this form are set to Yes. The BorderStyle property is set to Dialog and the ControlBox property is set to No. When using the OpenForm action of the DoCmd object to open the form, you must set the Window Mode argument to Dialog (see procedure in step 13) so that the procedure is suspended until the form is closed. Otherwise, the message box opens on top of the form.

6. After selecting your operating system, click the Help button on the message box that appears, shown in Figure 11.4.

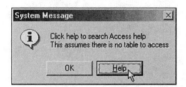

Figure 11.4: *The message box that appears when the Error Message button is clicked has a Help button.*

When you click the help button, a window with two panes appears. If you just have one pane, click the Show button at the top of the window. The Microsoft Jet Error Message Reference displays in the pane on the left, and the error that was referenced appears in the pane on the right. If you click the plus (+) to the left of the Microsoft Jet Error Message Reference and then click the Error Code Index, you will see the entire list of error codes and corresponding messages, as shown in Figure 11.5. These are in HTML format. These errors are what you see in the underlying table of the form in which you are currently working.

7. Close the Microsoft Access Help window, and then click OK in the message box that should still be open from step 6. (See Figure 11.4).

8. Place your cursor by the button labeled DAO error message for at least three seconds. Notice that the button's control tip text tells you Set reference to latest DAO library. This is already set for the database.

9. Click the DAO error message button to open the message box as shown in Figure 11.6.

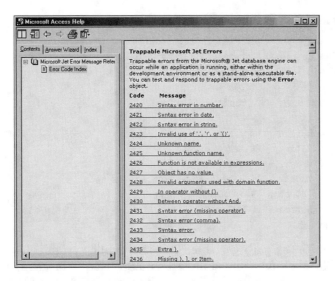

Figure 11.5: *Microsoft's Jet Error Message Reference Window contains an index of trappable Microsoft Jet errors.*

Figure 11.6: *The message box for the DAO error gives you relevant information such as the error source.*

The error number is the same as the current record (if it is still record 51). Also notice that it says Source: DAO workspace. This means that DAO generated the error. (This time it really did.) Finally, notice that it references topic 5003024 in the file jeterr40.chm. This is all helpful information; much more helpful than you would normally receive. Now let's take a peek behind the scenes to understand even more.

10. While still in the form, click OK to the message and then click the View button to go to the Design view.

11. Click the Missing Table Error Message button, and press F4 to open the button's Property sheet.

12. Click the Event tab, and then click the On Click Build button.

13. Observe the following:

```
Private Sub cmdMissingTable_Click()
Dim Button As Integer, Title as String
Dim HelpFile As String

DoCmd.OpenForm "PopUp",,,,,acDialog

    Button = 64
    Title = "System Message"
    HelpFile = "Jeterr40.chm"
    MsgBox "Click help to search Access help" & _
    vbCrLf & "This assumes there is no table to access", _
    Button + vbMsgBoxHelpButton, Title, Path & HelpFile, 5003024
End Sub
```

Notice the path variable. This is a public variable defined in the Global standard module. This might need to be changed because your operating system could place the file in another folder. However, Access should still find the Jeterr40.chm file. Besides, your operating system should be listed in the pop-up form. However, if it doesn't find the help file, search your hard drive for the file and change the path to the folder that Windows finds in the On Dbl Click event property box of the form called Popup.

Because MsgBox arguments have already been covered, there are only a few other things you should observe. Notice that the HelpFile and HelpContextID are set in the message box arguments. Instead of 3024 for the error message, the HelpContextID reads 5003024.

NOTE

The vbCrLf built-in VBA constant is very handy. The CrLf part of the constant stands for carriage return line feed. Instead of having to worry about writing a string such as "& Chr(13) & Chr(10)" to add a new line thus breaking up a long string, you can just use this constant. You also see the shortened vbCr form, which is fine for screen text.

---

14. While you are still in the module, cursor down until you see the DAO error handler. Notice the following code slightly modified from Access Help:

```
Private Sub Command5_Click()
'From Microsoft Help
'Must set latest DAO library in Tools Reference

    Dim dbsTest As Database

    On Error GoTo ErrorHandler
```

```
        ' Intentionally trigger an error.
        Set dbsTest = OpenDatabase("NoDatabase")

        Exit Sub

    ErrorHandler:
        Dim strError As String
        Dim errLoop As Error

        ' Enumerate Errors collection and display properties of
        ' each Error object.
        For Each errLoop In Errors
            With errLoop
                strError = "Error #" & .Number & vbCr
                strError = strError & _
                    " " & .Description & vbCr
                strError = strError & _
                    " (Source: " & .Source & ")" & vbCr
                strError = strError & _
                    "Press F1 to see topic " & .HelpContext & vbCr
                strError = strError & _
                    " in the file " & .HelpFile & "."
            End With
            MsgBox strError
        Next

        Resume Next

    End Sub
```

Error-Checking Sub Routines

A few things about this program need to be brought to your attention. The first thing to notice is the On Error Goto [Label] statement. This executes only if there is an error, but in this case, an error is intentionally triggered, as the comment indicates. Notice that the statement directs the program to the ErrorHandler label, where the error is handled by finding the error properties for the MsgBox. The second thing to notice is that the For..Each construct, which has been covered, loops through the Errors collection, which in this case only has one error, to find the error. The With statement, nested within the For..Each loop, is a great way to examine, read, or change object properties. The following example illustrates the dot (.) identifier operator, working in conjunction with the With statement, accessing the properties of whatever object is being referenced.

```
With MyControl
.FontSize = 12
.ForeColor = 255
End With
```

Fixing Errors After Trapping Them

The preceding example handled the error by invoking a MsgBox with additional information. That is one option, but in certain cases, it might be possible to actually fix the error that is causing the problem—especially if it is impossible to code around the problem. The following code handles the error by creating the missing table that caused the error:

```
Private Sub Command18_Click()
Dim td As TableDef, fld As Field, test As String
Dim db As Database, rs As Recordset, ws As Workspace
DoCmd.SetWarnings (False)
DoCmd.RunSQL "Delete NonCurrent.[Table Name] " & _
"FROM NonCurrent;"
DoCmd.SetWarnings (True)
' This program creates a Table of Tables in your database
  Set ws = CreateWorkspace("JetWorkspace", "admin", _
    "", dbUseJet)
  Set db = ws.OpenDatabase("l:\office\Archive.mdb")
  On Error GoTo FixIt
  test = CurrentDb.TableDefs("NonCurrent").NAME 'see if table exists
  Set rs = CurrentDb.OpenRecordset("NonCurrent") 'if it does open it
  For Each td In db.TableDefs
    If Left(td.NAME, 2) <> "MS" Then
    With rs
     .AddNew
     ![Table Name] = td.NAME
     .Update
     .Bookmark = .LastModified
    End With
    End If
  Next
Set db = Nothing
Set td = Nothing
Me.Refresh
Exit Sub
FixIt:
  Set td = CurrentDb.CreateTableDef("NonCurrent")
  Set fld = td.CreateField("Table Name", dbText, 55)
  td.Fields.Append fld
  td.Fields.Refresh
  db.TableDefs.Append td
```

```
    db.TableDefs.Refresh
    Resume Next
End Sub
```

Although this DAO program is long and perhaps somewhat advanced for you at this point, there are only a couple of things that you need to notice. The program uses an empty table (NonCurrent) to fill with table names by accessing the TableDefs collection. If the NonCurrent does not exist, the code following the FixIt label creates the table that the program needs. The On Error GoTo statement behaves as if nothing happened, because it is transparent to the user. There is no need for an error message because everything is fixed.

Resume Statements

As listed at the beginning of the chapter, one option to consider when encountering an error is to ignore it in your program with error handling that resumes the program while bypassing the error. The On Error Resume Next statement allows the program to continue without the user seeing the error, or worse yet, having access to your program. Unfortunately, it doesn't give any information about the error, much less how to fix it. In fact, the user doesn't even know that the error happened. This can be dangerous.

Although there are situations that are appropriate for this statement, its use should be minimal. One example of an appropriate use of the On Error Resume Next statement is in Chapter 18, "Working with Data from External Sources," in the section, "Using the File Dialog Method." When you want to defer an error message or control when an error message fires, use the On Error Resume Next statement.

It is a good idea to go back to the JetErrorCodes form and run that last button, which creates an ADO message. The ErrorHandle database has both DAO and ADO references set, so the button should run fine. If it doesn't, try deselecting the DAO reference and running the button again.

The **Err.Raise** Method

Two situations that can possibly arise from time to time involve creating errors and simulating errors. The thought of actually creating or simulating an error seems ludicrous to the beginning programmer. Doesn't the novice programmer already have enough errors to tackle? What situations would necessitate such decisions?

Suppose you wanted to send your user a message if a value exceeded a certain number, or suppose you wanted to test a certain error to determine the best way to handle it. In the former situation, you need to create an error.

In the latter, you need to simulate an error.

The following code creates an error message when a number exceeds a certain value. You insert a high error number so that you don't duplicate an error code that the system uses, but don't exceed 65535, which is the largest value that the Number property will accept. Notice the way the error is generated:

```
Function CheckNumber(lngNumber As Long)
On Error GoTo HandleRaisedErr
    If lngNumber > 100000 Then
            Err.Raise 65530, Application.CurrentObjectName, _
            "You have exceeded 100,000.  Try a lower number"
    End If
Exit Function


HandleRaisedErr:
MsgBox "Error Number: " & Err.Number & vbCrLf & "Error Source: " _
& Err.Source & vbCrLf & "Error Description: " & Err.Description
End Function
```

You can test this code in the from anywhere in the ErrorHandle database by pressing Ctrl+G and typing ? CheckNumber(100100). The message box in Figure 11.7 appears.

Figure 11.7: *The err.raise message box shows a custom made error suited to your needs.*

In the next situation, you simulate an error for testing purposes. A common error message is Type mismatch. If you want to write an error-handling subroutine for this error, you can simulate the error by typing

```
Err.Raise 13
```

That's all you need to generate the error between the Sub and End Sub lines in a procedure. Of course, if you want to trap the error, you need to insert an On Error Goto line before the statement and a subroutine after the statement to look something like the following:

```
Sub Test()


On Error GoTo ErrHandle
Err.Raise 13
```

```
Exit Sub

ErrHandle:
Msgbox Err.Number & vbCrLf & Err.Description

End Sub
```

If you anticipate a user error for which there is no system error, use the first method. If you anticipate an error that already has an error message, such as not finding an object, then use the second method. When you raise a system error, you cause your procedure to behave as if the error actually occurred.

What's Next

Because this is not an advanced-level book, this chapter is not comprehensive, but it gets you well on your way to understanding and handling errors, should they arise. The next chapter builds on your introduction to DAO and ADO. You are introduced to the programming of both object models.

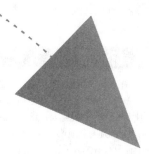

12

Access Visual Basic Tools, Tips, and Techniques

In the last chapter, you learned about how to trap and handle Access errors. In this chapter, you learn about programming with both DAO and ADO object models. The two object models are compared from a number of different standpoints. Specifically, you learn

- how to use object models to run queries

- how to determine the best method to manipulate recordsets

- how to evaluate performance criteria to determine the best object model to use

- how to use the collections of DAO and ADO

- examples of using SQL with VBA

- how to use variables with SQL

Comparing DAO and ADO

Although both DAO and ADO were discussed in the previous chapter, this chapter will take you into the particulars of programming using the two models. Along the way, you will acquire some additional tools, tips, and techniques. We are building on the foundation began in Chapter 7, "Exploring Objects," which is working with objects. Because there are many alternatives available to you, an examination of the various performance issues would be in order.

Considering the fact that computers are getting bigger and faster with each passing day, some might be tempted to assume that issues such as disk space and speed are no longer a concern. However, even with larger and faster systems, working with the larger recordsets require the best software performance possible. Saving a few seconds might not seem to be a major advantage. But those few seconds add up over the long haul while larger databases increase the need for faster searches and more efficient queries.

The other consideration is that disk space and speed are related. For example, suppose that you decided to make every numeric field a double-precision field, regardless of whether there was a need for double precision. The only problem is that you would be wasting disk space. Even if you had enormous amounts of disk space, this would not be wise. As it says in Chapter 3, "The Table—The Heart of Any Database," "Even if you have an abundance of space, it is not a good habit to be wasteful. When your databases grow too large, they take longer to compact, run queries, and perform calculations. If space limitations won't get your attention, then the slower speed will."

The bottom line is that it is always a good idea to be frugal, regardless of the system that you have. This applies to programming as well, because programming allows you to create tables, change data within tables, run queries, and access recordsets. So, maximum performance should always be in the back of your mind as you write procedures.

Using VBA to Run Queries

You can run queries from VBA in a number of different ways. You can run either SQL strings or queries that are already stored in your database in a variety of ways. Table 12.1 shows some common methods of running queries that are available to you.

Table 12.1: Ways to Run Queries from VBA

Action, Method, or Object	Object Runs From	Source	Example
runSQL action	DoCmd	SQL string	docmd.runSQL strSQL
OpenQuery action	DoCmd	Stored query	docmd.OpenQuery "qryTotals"
OpenRecordset method (DAO)	Connection or database	SQL string or stored query	db. OpenRecordset strSQL
Open method (ADO)	Connection or recordset	SQL string, stored query or stored procedure	rs.Open "SELECT * FROM Customers, cn
Execute method (DAO)	Connection or database	SQL string	db.execute strSQL
Execute method (ADO)	Connection or command	SQL string	cnn. execute strSQL
QueryDef (DAO stored query)	Connection or database	Stored query	db.QueryDefs ("qryTotals")

Manipulating Recordsets Using Collections Versus Manipulating Recordsets Using Queries

The normal methods for retrieving and manipulating recordsets using Access VBA are queries and recordset loops. Yet, while there is plenty of documentation for both methods, a beginning developer may be hard-pressed to find instructions that detail when or why to use one method as opposed to another. Although some sources might explain that recordset loops should be used to modify recordset properties while queries should be used to modify recordset data, this raises more questions than it answers. For example, you can modify recordset properties using DDL (data definition language) queries and you can modify data using loops.

In a nutshell, there is an overlap between the two methods. If that's not enough to make your head spin, you have two different object models (ADO and DAO) that can be used to manipulate recordsets. So, which method do you use for a given situation?

Performance Criterion

If you know for certain that the task that is set before you can be accomplished either by a query or by recordset loops, then performance is probably the first measuring stick that should be applied. Generally speaking, queries are faster than recordset loops. That's because the query optimizer stores the best query execution plan the first time Jet runs the query.

Subsequent query runs use this stored schema for optimization. Because recordset loops don't have an optimization plan, they are effectively run "for the first time" each time they are run. The following examples that perform the same calculation on a rather large table with results following will prove this assertion:

```
Sub ADOElapsed()
Dim Cnn As New ADODB.Connection
Dim rsADO As New ADODB.Recordset

BegTime = Time
Set Cnn = New ADODB.Connection
Set rsADO = New ADODB.Recordset
'Set the Data Source to the proper drive and folder designation
Cnn.Open "Provider= Microsoft.jet.oledb.4.0;" & _
 "Data Source =D:\Database\Access\Timing.mdb;"
rsADO.Open "tblAccount", Cnn, adOpenKeyset, adLockOptimistic
Do While Not rsADO.EOF
 rsADO![Commission] = rsADO![SellingPrice] * 0.07
 rsADO.Update
 rsADO.MoveNext
Loop
EndTime = Time
Interval = DateDiff("s", BegTime, EndTime)
MsgBox (Interval)
Set rsADO = Nothing
Set Cnn = Nothing
RsADO.Close
Cnn.Close
End Sub
```

Establishing an ADO Connection

What does `Set Cnn = New ADODB.Connection` mean? You are simply setting up a connection to a data source. This demonstrates the flexibility advantage of ADO over DAO. ADO is an interface for OLE DB, Microsoft's latest data access technology, which allows access to a much broader range of data providers. That means that if you want to connect *to* and access data *from* larger database systems, such as SQL Server or Oracle, ADO is your answer. If you want Internet/intranet data access, ADO is the right tool for the job. Even non-relational data, e-mail data, and CAD/CAM data stores are now open to you through ADO.

You can also use the IN clause of SQL to make connections to external sources. For more information about this technique, see "Importing and Exporting Data" in Chapter 18, "Working with Data from External Sources."

As promised, you can examine two sub routines performing the same task using both ADO and DAO for comparison purposes. All three examples use the DateDiff function to time the execution of the code. The s argument represents seconds. The BegTime and EndTime arguments were subtracted to determine the interval between the two times as if we were using a stopwatch. Where were these variables declared? At the top of the module in the declaration section. (You will see.) The EOF function was used to test for the end of a table containing 68,586 records. It returns False until it reaches the last record, at which time it returns True.

What was the result? Using a fairly slow machine, the procedure executed in 119 seconds.

The next code sampling is written using DAO:

```
Sub DAOElapsed()
Dim db As Database
Dim rs As Recordset

BegTime = Time
Set db = CurrentDb
Set rs = db.OpenRecordset("tblAccount")
Do While Not rs.EOF
 rs.Edit
 rs![Commission] = rs![SellingPrice] * 0.07
 rs.Update
 rs.MoveNext
Loop
EndTime = Time
Interval = DateDiff("s", BegTime, EndTime)
MsgBox (Interval)
Set rs = Nothing
Set db = Nothing
End Sub
```

This code is similar because, as previously mentioned, the ADO object model is based on the DAO object model. Although the recordset loops of the two procedures are almost identical, the method of opening the recordset is quite different. This procedure completed in 30 seconds. That's almost four times faster than the ADO routine.

The following code uses a query for the same task the previous procedures tackled:

```
Option Compare Database
Dim BegTime As Date
Dim EndTime As Date
Dim Interval As Integer
```

```
Sub QryElapsed()
Dim db As Database
Set db = CurrentDb()
DoCmd.SetWarnings False
BegTime = Time
db.Execute "UPDATE tblAccount " _
& "SET tblAccount.Commission = [SellingPrice]*0.07;"
EndTime = Time
Interval = DateDiff("s", BegTime, EndTime)
MsgBox (Interval)
DoCmd.SetWarnings True
End Sub
```

Notice that the first four lines before the sub procedure starts are declaring variables. Because these variables are in the declaration section, they are available to the other procedures in the module, which include all the procedures reviewed so far. There are different ways to run queries using VBA. For example, a DoCmd.RunSQL action could have been used instead of the db.Execute statement. Had this action been used, the rest of the procedure would have remained unchanged and the procedure would have executed in 10 seconds; three times faster than the DAO procedure. However, the procedure as written runs in just 7 seconds.

SetWarnings Action

To properly evaluate the query in the example, the warnings had to be turned off because they would add a few seconds to respond to the warnings. As previously mentioned, action queries warn the user before making changes to table data. Not to be confused with action queries, actions in Access are macro commands. Most macro actions can be accessed through the DoCmd object. If you type DoCmd followed by a dot identifier while in a module, you can see the list of actions available. The DoCmd.SetWarnings True line turned the warnings on again.

As you can see, there is a huge performance difference between queries and recordset loops. But performance isn't the only criterion that should be used. You can't set controls using queries. There are properties of certain objects that cannot be changed even with a DDL (Data Definition Language) query.

A DDL query will let you create a table or alter its structure. Even though these queries have limitations, they can come in handy when you need them. For example, the following DDL code will change the LastName field size from 50 to 55 characters:

```
Sub ModField()
Dim db As DAO.Database
```

```
Set db = CurrentDb()
db.Execute "ALTER TABLE tblCustomer " _
& "ALTER COLUMN LastName TEXT(55)"

End Sub
```

✔ See "Data Definition Queries" in Chapter 17, "Getting the Most from Your Queries," for more information on DDL queries.

Even though you can change a table's properties using this method, you can't change a control's properties on a form using this type, or any other type of query. Other tasks preclude using a query for manipulating recordsets, as you shall discover. Although performance is a good place to start, there are other considerations to determine the appropriate method for the task. For most purposes, if you can use a query, use it. It will most likely be faster.

Although DAO outperformed ADO in the examples just analyzed, ADO outperforms DAO when used with non-Jet databases. It boils down to what you want to do. Let's take a closer look at programming using the two models.

DAO Collections and Objects

When DAO appeared in 1992, it worked exclusively with the Jet database engine. Starting with Access 97, DAO (3.5) supported ODBCDirect in addition to Jet, opening up access to enterprise servers such as SQL Server. DAO is organized into a hierarchy of collections and objects. This means that all tables, fields, queries, and so forth, are represented by objects arranged into collections. For example, the reports collection of the Application object contains all the reports that are currently open in the Access database. The Application object refers to the active Access application.

Think of objects as storehouses for collections, which in turn store other objects, and down the hierarchy it goes. For example, you can access a field object through the Fields collection in both object models.

The DBEngine Object and Workspaces Collection

Because the DBEngine object contains and controls all the objects in the hierarchy, it represents the top-level object. Within Access, you should use the CurrentDb function to access objects in the current database. Instead of working your way down the hierarchy to find the object you want, much like drilling down to subfolders, you can take a shortcut and use this function to reference the database in which you are working. When working outside Access using an ODBC connection (in which case, you might consider ADO because it can also access ODBC data sources), you should use the DBEngine object.

The Workspaces collection of the DBEngine object contains the Databases, Users, and Groups collections. If you wanted to refer to noncurrent databases (not currently open) you can use this collection. A workspace object supplies a connection object when working with ODBCDirect. The Users and Groups collections are used for security purposes.

The Database Object

In DAO, a database object references a database currently open. Actually, you are allowed to have multiple databases open at the same time, even if they are of different types. Whereas the databases collection contains all database objects for a particular workspace, the database object contains five collections of objects in the current database. Table 12.2 describes the collections.

Table 12.2: Five Database Object Collections

Collection	Description
TableDefs	References the tables in the database but does not contain table data.
QueryDefs	References the queries in the database but does not contain query data.
Containers	The collection of Container objects, which reference a Documents collection that relates to database security.
Relations	References the relationships between tables in the database.
Recordsets	References recordsets from tables or queries in the database. These recordsets contain the field structure of each table or query. Each field's data can be referenced through its value property.

There are four ways to reference objects in a collection, as shown in Table 12.3.

Table 12.3: Methods to Reference Objects In a Collection

Syntax	Example
Collection(0)	Fields(3)
Collection(expression or variable)	TableDefs(strTable)
Collection("name")	QueryDefs("PaidCustomers")
Collection![name]	Fields![Last Name]

The first method is using the ordinal position (also called index) to reference the object. Each object in all collections in DAO has a built-in number beginning with 0. This is handy for enumerating objects in a collection. However, if you know the name of the object, you can also make specific reference the object this way, as shown in the third and fourth examples.

Using the second form, the *Collection(expression or variable)* syntax, you can refer to an object using a variable:

```
Dim strName As String
strName = "Customers"
TableDefs(strName)
```

You don't have to use brackets (last form) to reference objects unless there is a non-standard character such as a space in the object name. If you want to access a collection property by number you can do that, as the following example illustrates:

```
Debug.Print CurrentDb.TableDefs(0).Name
```

Each object has both properties and methods. DAO provides access to these properties, which define the object's characteristics (attributes), but they must be referred to with the correct syntax. You can use object variables to represent objects in your syntax. For example, if you want to refer to a querydef (represented by the qd variable) object's name property, you could use the following syntax:

```
strQueryName = qd.Name
```

Notice that the last example does not have parentheses. This is because it is an object rather than a collection. In a collection, you use parentheses to refer to specific objects within its collection followed by the dot identifier if you want to reference a property of that object. If it is an object or object variable, just use the dot by itself to reference a property of the object.

Methods are procedures that perform operations on objects. These procedures are distinguished from user-defined procedures in that they are tied to objects and cannot be called independently. Methods can do things like open or close a table or find a record within a table. If you wanted to open a table in a database, you might use the OpenRecordset method, as the following code illustrates:

```
Dim db as DAO.Database, rs as DAO.Recordset

Set db = CurrentDb()
Set rs = db.OpenRecordset("tblCustomers")
```

Unlike other variables, object variables in Access must use the set keyword to refer to a real object or a new object created by the new keyword. Once this is done, all the properties and methods of the object that is referenced becomes available through the variable as the db.OpenRecordset("tblCustomers") example demonstrates. If you wanted to move to the next record in a recordset represented by the rs variable, you would use the following code:

```
rs.MoveNext
```

ADO Collections and Objects

The ADO object model is structurally simpler than either DAO or Visual Basic's RDO object model. The Connection object is the top object in the hierarchy and represents a connection to a data source. This object contains the Command and Recordset objects as well as the Errors collection. Table 12.4 defines the functions of the main ADO object model components.

Table 12.4: ADO Object Model Functions

Object or Collection	Function	DAO Nearest Equivalent
Connection	Create a connection to a data provider	Database Object
Recordset	Create a recordset using a query	Recordset Object
Command	Execute SQL strings, action queries, or stored procedures	QueryDef Object
Errors	In the event of an error, one or more errors is inserted into this collection	Errors Collection

The Connection Object

A Connection object in ADO represents a physical connection to a data store. If you want to create a Connection object, you simply supply the name of either an ODBC data store or an OLE DB data provider. Opening the Connection object is attempting to connect to the desired data store. You can determine whether your attempt was successful by referencing the State property of the Connection object. A successful attempt returns the intrinsic (built-in) constant adStateOpen as the following example, which uses the cnn variable as a connection object, demonstrates:

```
If cnn.State = adStateOpen Then
 MsgBox "You were successful"
Else
 MsgBox "Please try again"
End If
```

The Recordset Object

The ADO Recordset object represents a set of records retrieved from a query with a cursor into those records. If you want to open a Recordset object without explicitly opening a Connection object you can pass a connection string to the Recordset object's Open method. However, by creating and opening a Connection object, you can open multiple Recordset objects using the same connection. Although the Recordset object represents an entire set of records, at any given time the object refers to only a single current record within the set.

Because the Recordset object has the most properties and methods, and because ADO uses Recordset objects almost entirely to manipulate data, you could say that it is the heart and soul of ADO. Each Recordset object consists of records (rows) and fields (columns). The Recordset methods and properties that are available depend on the provider.

Cursors and Cursor Types

An ADO cursor maintains the query result recordset for browsing. In fact, a cursor is sometimes called a recordset. The current position in the recordset is provided for forward and backward scrolling.

Cursors have three purposes in ADO. First, the cursor determines movement within the recordset and whether the recordset will reflect user changes. Second, the cursor determines the storage location of the recordset while the cursor is open. Third, the cursor's locking type determines how the ADO datastore will lock the records when they are changed.

ADO provides four cursor types, as shown in Table 12.5.

Table 12.5: ADO Cursor Types

Type	Function
Static cursor	Provides a static copy of a set of records that allows all types of movement through the recordset. Does not allow viewing of additions, changes, and deletions by other users.
Dynamic cursor	Allows all types of movement through the recordset that does not rely on bookmarks but does allow bookmarks if supported by the provider. Allows viewing of additions, changes, and deletions by other users. Microsoft Jet OLE DB does not support this type, but other providers may support it.
Keyset cursor	Behaves like a dynamic cursor except that additions and deletions made by others are not visible. However, changes to data made by others will be visible.
Forward-Only cursor	This type is the default. You can only scroll forward through the recordset. Additions, changes, and deletions by other users will not be visible. This improves performance when you only need to make a single pass through the recordset.

There are three ways to open a Recordset object using ADO:

- By opening the recordset using the Connection.Execute() method.

- By opening the recordset using the Command.Execute() method.

- By opening the recordset object without a Connection or Command object, and passing a valid Connect string to the second argument of the Recordset.Open() method.

As you can see, you have some flexibility when it comes to ways to open a recordset. Consider the following example that populates a form when it opens:

```
Sub Form_Open(Cancel As Integer)
 Dim cn As ADODB.Connection
 Dim rs As ADODB.Recordset

  'Easy way to use Microsoft Access's OLEDB connection
  'to the Jet database
  Set cn = CurrentProject.Connection
  Set rs = New ADODB.Recordset
  With rs
  .Source = "SELECT * FROM Customers"
  .ActiveConnection = cn
  .CursorType = adOpenKeyset
  .LockType = adLockOptimistic
  .Open
  End With
  Set Me.Recordset = rs
End Sub
```

This procedure is unique, at least in one aspect. Normally, toward the end of the procedure, you close the recordset with statements such as rs.Close and set rs = Nothing, but in this case, the form's close event takes care of these kinds of housekeeping tasks to free up memory. This is because the procedure sets the form's recordset to the ADO recordset. What's more, had you closed the recordset and connection, the form would not have a connection to ensure that changes to the form are reflected in the underlying table.

Command Object

The ADO Command object can be used to query a database and return records by pointing to action queries, SQL strings, or stored procedures. The objective is to create a specific command to execute upon a data source. The DAO QueryDef object is similar to the Command object. The syntax to return recordsets would be as following:

```
Set recordset = command.Execute(RecordsAffected, Parameters, Options)
```

How to Use DAO and ADO to Manipulate Data

Although this chapter has presented many programming examples, no "by example" hands-on tips and techniques have been offered so far. This was intentional, because you must understand the fundamentals before you can apply them. The following "by example" will accomplish two purposes at the same time. First, it will give you first-hand knowledge of how to manipulate recordsets using both object models. Second, it will give you a valuable technique that you can easily adapt to your business needs.

It must be reemphasized that there is a need to set references to the proper libraries in the module window, as explained in Chapter 7. In this case, because you work with both DAO and ADO in the following exercises, references to both libraries should be set. If both libraries are set, be sure to reference the proper object model in your dim statements. For example, you declare a recordset object with the statement

```
Dim rs As DAO.Recordset
```

Suppose you had a business that sold fruits and nuts. You give price breaks for larger quantities. You want an Excel-style lookup table that can pinpoint the coordinate to determine the proper price. At first you think of setting up your price table similar to Table 12.6.

Table 12.6: Lookup Table Example

Product	Pounds	Price
Peanuts	1–10	$1.95
Peanuts	11–50	$1.60
Peanuts	50+	$1.20
Cashews	1–10	$4.30
Cashews	11–50	$3.50
Cashews	50+	$2.63

But then you realize that this approach creates too much redundancy. Notice how the nuts repeat for each price break. Then you get the idea to crosstab the table so that the pounds are column headings, thus eliminating the redundancy. However, now you have another problem. How is the procedure going to select the proper column for the price break? A technique using a lookup is the only answer.

1. Open up the FormsAndControls database from the AccessByExample folder.

2. Double-click the LookNuts table to open the datasheet.

3. Notice the table shown in Figure 12.1. Click, hold, and drag the title bar of the table to as far left as possible on the screen; then best fit the columns, and shrink the window so that it fits on approximately the left half of the screen.

4. If you can click on the Database window, do so. If not, press F11 to move the focus to the Database window.

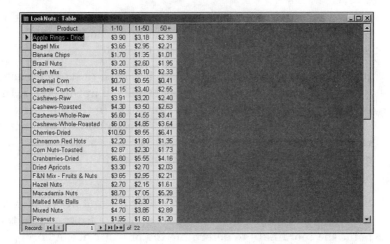

Figure 12.1: *The LookNuts table is used in the procedures to lookup values.*

TIP

The F11 key works fine in most places in Access to show the Database window. One exception is the Module window. In that case, Alt+F11 does the job. In contrast to F11, Alt+F11 works as a toggle so that you can switch back and forth.

---

5. Under Forms, click on the FruitNutOrder form. You should see three windows. Figure 12.2 shows the windows arranged.

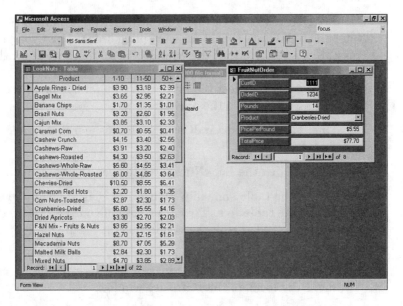

Figure 12.2: *The three windows are arranged so that you can view the lookup table while the form accesses it.*

6. Click on the table window; then, click on the form window. Move the form window to the right to look like Figure 12.2. Now you are in a position to check your results.

7. Click on the add record selector (with the asterisk) at the bottom of the form, as shown in Figure 12.3, to open a new record.

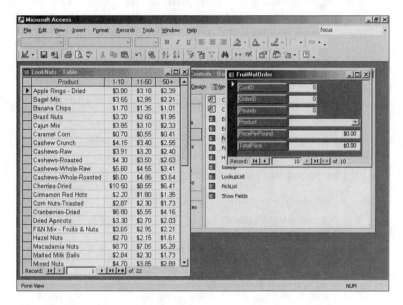

Figure 12.3: *The three windows are arranged so that you can view the lookup table while the form accesses it.*

8. Type 1119 in the CUSTID field. Type 2742 in the OrderID field.

9. Type 50 in the Pounds field, and then choose Banana Chips from the drop-down list of the Product field.

It should automatically enter $1.35 for the price per pound, as shown in the LookNuts table on the left. Notice in the table that $1.35 is the correct price break for 50 pounds. Also notice that a total price of $67.50 is computed.

10. Try a few other products using various amounts and products.

11. Stay in the database.

12. Close the LookNuts table and the FruitNutOrder form.

You might have noticed that the table is arranged like a crosstab query result. This DAO technique is perfect for lookups. What is your application? If you are an insurance broker, you could use this technique for looking up workers' compensation rates. If you are a banker, you could use this technique for looking up interest rates. You get the idea.

Using SQL Within VBA

In case you are thinking that such a lookup technique would be too difficult to write, let's look at the code behind the scenes. The following example brings together many of the programming operations that you have already learned with a relatively simple procedure:

1. Under Forms, click on the FruitNutOrder, and then click Design to open the form in Design view.

2. Click the Product combo box and press F4 to open the Property sheet of the control.

3. Click the Event tab. Click the After Update box, and then click the Build button to open the module window containing the procedure attached to the event.

   You should see the following code:

```
Dim db As DAO.Database
Dim rs As DAO.Recordset
Dim sQuote As String, dPPP As Double
Dim sFld As String, sCrit As String

sCrit = Me.Product 'Assign selected value to variable
sQuote = Chr$(34)

Select Case Me.Pounds 'Find the correct field for lookup
  Case 1 To 10
      sFld = "[1-10]"
  Case 11 To 50
      sFld = "[11-50]"
  Case Is > 50
      sFld = "[50+]"
  Case Else
      MsgBox ("Please reenter pounds")
End Select

Set db = CurrentDb()
'Perform the lookup using the correct poundage rate
Set rs = db.OpenRecordset("SELECT LookNuts.Product, " _
& "LookNuts." & sFld _
& "FROM LookNuts " _
& "WHERE LookNuts.Product = " & sQuote & sCrit & sQuote & ";")
```

```
dPPP = rs.Fields(sFld)
Me.PricePerPound = dPPP
rs.Close
Set rs = Nothing
Set db = Nothing
End Sub
```

4. Stay in the database and leave the Module window with the procedure open until you read the next section. Close the Module, Property sheet, and form.

Using Variables with SQL

The procedure you just examined has some interesting aspects. For example, notice how the OpenRecordset method used and SQL string to run the query. Because the field name can vary, a variable is substituted in the SQL statement using the ampersand (&) concatenation operator. The query uses the sFld variable in the SQL string to ensure that the proper field name is chosen for the lookup. The selected column, in turn, gives the correct price break corresponding to the number of pounds that the customer ordered.

Another thing to notice is the Select..Case statement, which is an important part of the lookup because it makes sure that the correct field name is assigned to the sFld variable. The sCrit variable handles the criterion for the Product field to ensure that the query chooses the correct product.

The query only returns one record, based on the correct product for the lookup. Then it is simply a matter of selecting the correct field (out of two) in the record, which the dPPP = rs.Fields(sFld) assignment does beautifully. There are three variables in the assignment. The first is dPPP (price per pound), which is assigned the value for the field represented by the sFld variable in the rs (recordset) variable object reference. Finally, the value is assigned to the PricePerPound field in the form with the Me.PricePerPound = dPPP statement.

In short, the DAO procedure implements a coordinate lookup that selects the coordinate (or "cell," for you spreadsheet users) where the product row and poundage column intersect. Remember that you can just as easily use a variable to represent a table name as you can to represent a field name in an SQL string. This can be a powerful tool at your disposal. There are so many ways to implement SQL in both DAO and ADO.

Same Result, Different Object Model

The following code is the same procedure adjusted for ADO. The major difference is the way the recordset is accessed. The programming logic, however, remains the same.

```vba
Private Sub Product_AfterUpdate()
Dim cn As ADODB.Connection
Dim rs As ADODB.Recordset
Dim sQuote As String, dPPP As Double
Dim sFld As String, sCrit As String

sCrit = Me.Product 'Assign selected value to variable
sQuote = Chr$(34)
Select Case Me.Pounds 'Find the right field for lookup
 Case 1 To 10
 sFld = "[1-10]"
 Case 11 To 50
 sFld = "[11-50]"
 Case Is > 50
 sFld = "[50+]"
 Case Else
 MsgBox ("Please reenter pounds")
End Select
Set cn = CurrentProject.Connection
Set rs = New ADODB.Recordset
 With rs
 .Source = "SELECT LookNuts.Product, " _
 & "LookNuts." & sFld _
 & "FROM LookNuts " _
 & "WHERE LookNuts.Product = " & sQuote & sCrit & sQuote & ";"
 .ActiveConnection = cn
 .CursorType = adOpenKeyset
 .LockType = adLockOptimistic
 .Open
 End With

dPPP = rs.Fields(1)
Me.PricePerPound = dPPP
rs.Close
cn.close
Set rs = Nothing
Set cn = Nothing
End Sub
```

Notice that the SQL statement is used with the Source property of the recordset to produce the same result. The With construct is used to set the record source, open the recordset, and set other options, such as CursorType. You can test this program by simply opening the FruitNutOrder ADO form and using the same testing procedures as applied to the FruitNutOrder form.

How to Use DAO and ADO to Enumerate Objects

There might be times when you need to enumerate objects. Why is this important? Suppose you wanted to show the users a dynamic list of reports from which he or she could select for printing. Or suppose that you wanted the user to select from a list of tables for exporting or importing. You could combine the code presented in this chapter with the "pick-list" techniques you have learned to design creative applications for users. In fact, Chapter 18, "Working with Data from External Sources," explains how to do just that.

There are many ways to enumerate Access objects. One method requires no programming at all. You simply construct a query. Actually, it has already been done for you. The query makes more sense when you understand which objects are being accessed by the query. You can see a system table named MSysObjects in the Database window simply by clicking Tools, Options, View from the Access menu bar and clicking both Hidden objects and System objects. Figure 12.4 shows the View menu.

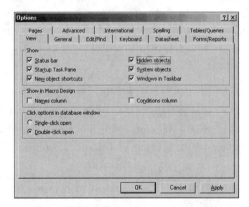

Figure 12.4: *Select Tools, Options, View to check the Hidden Objects and System Objects options so that they can be viewed.*

When those two options are checked, you can see tables in the Database window that are not normally visible. When the boxes are checked, click Apply and click OK. Double-click the MSysObjects table and scroll right until you see the Name and Type fields. The name field lists all the user objects in the Database window. The type field refers to the type of object in the Name column.

Figure 12.5 is a QBE design grid that accesses the MSysObjects table.

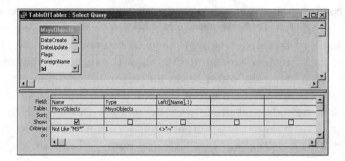

Figure 12.5: Setting the Type field in the MSysObjects table to 1 retrieves all the tables in the database.

Creating a List of Objects

The Name and Type fields are accessed by the TableOfTables query. They are the keys to setting up a query accessing database objects. The type of object list you want is determined by the Type field and, of course, the object you want is determined by the Name field. The Name field is also where the system objects are excluded by using a wildcard in the criterion. Reverse the changes you just made in Tools, Options, View and take the following steps to examine and run the query:

1. Open the TableOfTables query in Design view.

2. Click the drop-down box of the View button and switch to Design view. Notice the Name column criterion excludes the system tables by using Not Like MS* for criterion. Notice also that the object type is "1" for table.

3. While in QBE view, click the Run button to retrieve the database tables as shown in Figure 12.6.

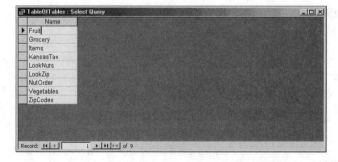

Figure 12.6: You can create a query that accesses the system objects, such as tables and queries, for enumeration.

Notice that all the tables are reflected dynamically, making the query continually current. This means that if you add a table and rerun the query, the new table will appear along with the others.

4. Go back to QBE and change the 1 in the Criterion row of the Type column to 5. Rerun the query and notice that all queries in the database are listed.

5. Perform step 4 using -32768 under Type for forms and -32764 for reports, and then change the Type back to 1.

6. Choose View, SQL to open SQL view. Select by highlighting (if not already highlighted) the entire SQL code and press Ctrl+C to copy the code.

7. Close the query without saving. You can now paste the copied SQL string into a form.

8. Under Forms, double-click the EnumerationForm to open it.

9. Click on the Enumerate Tables button, and cycle through the tables in the database. Click on the Enumerate Queries button as well. This is one way to enumerate objects. You will examine the code behind the buttons shortly.

10. Click the View button to enter Design view; then right-click the top list box and choose Properties.

11. Click on the Data tab, which contains the Row Source property.

12. Click on the Row Source property box and press Ctrl+V to paste the code copied in step 6 (see Figure 12.7).

Don't worry about the carriage returns in the SQL string. You see only one line of code at a time in the box, but you can simply click anywhere in the box and press the down arrow to see the rest of the string; or you right-click the box and choose zoom to see the entire string.

13. Click on the second list box labeled Dynamic List of Queries.

14. Paste the same data that was pasted in step 12 into the Row Source box, and then click on the Build button.

15. Change the 1 under Type to 5 in the QBE Design view to make the query retrieve query objects. Click Close and click Yes to save changes to the SQL statement. Close the Property sheet.

16. Click the View button to save and open the form.

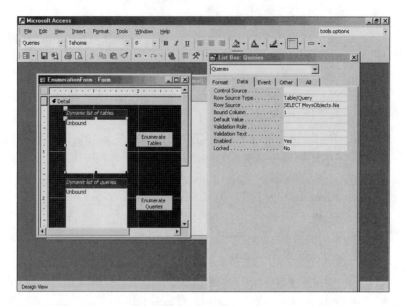

Figure 12.7: *Pasting the SQL string in the Row Source property box creates a dynamic reflection of objects in your database.*

Notice that the two queries that are the row sources for two list boxes are identical except for the criterion of the Type field. As mentioned earlier, those list boxes will always reflect the current state of the databases. The following steps explain by example how the list boxes work:

1. Look at both list boxes in the form and notice that all tables and queries in the database are listed.

2. Click on Design view again to open the form in Design view. Right-click the Enumerate Tables button, and then choose Build Event to open the Procedure. You should see the following code:

```
Option Compare Database
Dim db As Database

Private Sub Command4_Click()
Dim td As TableDef

Set db = CurrentDb
 For Each td In db.TableDefs
 If Left(td.Name, 2) <> "MS" And _
 Left(td.Name, 1) <> "~" Then 'Exclude system objects
 MsgBox td.Name
 End If
 Next
```

```
Set db = Nothing
Set td = Nothing
End Sub


Private Sub Command5_Click()
Dim qd As QueryDef

Set db = CurrentDb
 For Each qd In db.QueryDefs
 If Left(qd.Name, 2) <> "MS" And _
 Left(qd.Name, 1) <> "~" Then 'Exclude system objects
 MsgBox qd.Name
 End If
 Next
Set db = Nothing
Set qd = Nothing

End Sub
```

Because both procedures needed the db object variable, it was declared in the declaration section of the module containing the procedures. Notice that the second procedure doesn't declare the db variable. Just as the query eliminated any objects that began with "MS" or "~", both procedures do the same using an If statement. Both procedures are fairly simple and straightforward. You could have just enumerated the items in the list box, but then you wouldn't have the knowledge of how to do what the query did in DAO. The only difference between the two procedures is the use of either TableDef or QueryDef objects.

1. Close the first enumeration form. Double-click the EnumerationForm ADO form to open it in Form view.

2. Paste the SQL code from the TableOfTables into the Row Source of both list boxes without referring to instructions. Be sure to change the Type field in the second box to 5 after you paste it.

3. Click the Enumerate Tables and Enumerate Queries buttons to sequence through the tables and the queries in the database using ADO.

4. Access the code behind the buttons without referring to instructions. You should see the following code:

```
Private Sub EnumQueries_Click()
Dim obj As AccessObject, dbs As Object
Set dbs = Application.CurrentData 'Modified from Microsoft help
```

```
'Search for AccessObject queries in AllQueries collection.
For Each obj In dbs.AllQueries
'Print name of obj.
MsgBox obj.Name
Next obj

End Sub


Private Sub EnumTables_Click()
Dim cn As ADODB.Connection
Dim cat As New ADOX.Catalog 'Must set ADO Ext. 2.5 for DDL
Dim tbl As Table

Set cn = CurrentProject.Connection
Set cat.ActiveConnection = cn
For Each tbl In cat.Tables
 If Left(tbl.Name, 2) <> "MS" And _
 Left(tbl.Name, 1) <> "~" And _
 tbl.Type = "TABLE" Then 'Exclude view objects
 MsgBox tbl.Name
 End If
 Next
Set cn = Nothing
Set cat = Nothing
End Sub
```

The first program from Access Help is simple because it just enumerates Access query objects using the AccessObject object within the AllQueries collection. The second program using ADO needs a library reference (notice the comments) to be set to access the ADOX catalog. The Catalog object represents an entire database because it contains references to objects such as tables, views, and stored procedures. In short, it contains all the elements of the database.

Creating a List of Fields

The list boxes you have been examining have performed as pick lists. What if you wanted a pick list of fields for each table in your database? You could enumerate the fields collection in much the same way that you enumerated the tables collection. However, there is a much easier built-in technique for enumerating the fields of any table that is often overlooked. You can use the Field List row source type of a list box to list all the fields of whatever row source table is selected. You can use this option to list the fields of every table in your database at the click of a mouse button. Then simply print the form for a hard copy of your list.

Examine the following simple procedure that lists the fields of every table that you click on in your database:

```
Private Sub lstTables_Click()
Dim iTableIndex As Integer
Dim sTableName As String

iTableIndex = Me.lstTables.ListIndex
sTableName = Me.lstTables.ItemData(iTableIndex)
Me.lstFieldList.RowSource = sTableName
End Sub
```

FieldList is the name of the list box on the right. Tables is the name of the list box on the left. List Index is the number of the item of the list. This is just the index that's needed for the ItemData argument. Next you simply assign the table to the row source of the FieldList list box. Then set the Row Source type to Field List. This has been done for you in this example. Follow these steps to see it in action:

1. Open the FormAndControls database. Under Forms, double-click the Show Fields form to open it.

2. Click on several tables, and watch the field list on the right change to reflect the fields corresponding to the table on the left.

3. Close the Show Fields form; then right-click it, and choose Copy.

4. Open the Northwind database from the AccessByExample folder on your hard drive.

5. Press Ctrl+V to paste the form, and then name the form Show Fields.

6. Double-click the Show Fields form to open the form in Northwind, as shown in Figure 12.8. These tables have more fields from which the list boxes can be filled. You can copy the form to any database that you have created in Access 2002 or Access 2000 and it should function as is.

You have seen how objects can be manipulated and enumerated in both ADO and DAO. You have picked up some tips and techniques such as learning how to use Access built-in functions and properties. You have also learned how to measure performance with a timing device.

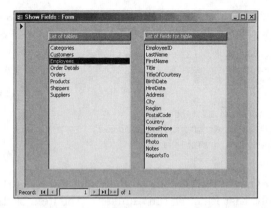

Figure 12.8: *Show Fields for every database table.*

What's Next

You are building a reservoir of tools and techniques that you can use to enhance your applications. These utilities will also come in handy when facing the everyday obstacles that confront developers. The next chapter focuses on Web development and design. You will learn about the various Web page formats and how to convert objects to Web pages.

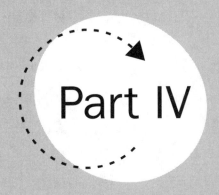

Part IV

Taking Advantage of the Latest Access Features

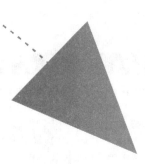

13

Publishing Your Access Database

In simplest terms, the World Wide Web (WWW) is nothing more than a network of networks. The worldwide network is called the Internet, and it has revolutionized the way we do business and access information. Intranets are basically a private or company-wide network of networks. Because databases are the largest repositories of electronic-based information, it naturally follows that databases and the Internet should be integrated.

Access 2002 has added many user-friendly features to make data access easier than ever. Many of these enhancements have focused on Web integration.

In the last chapter, you learned how to program using DAO and ADO. This chapter takes you into the arena of Access Internet integration. In particular, you learn about the following:

- how to convert objects to Web pages
- HTML, XML, and other Web formats
- data Access Pages
- how to create Data Access Pages
- active Server Pages

Converting Objects to Web Pages

The Web page is the vehicle used to display and interact with information on the Web. It contains instructions, called *tags*, to display text and graphics properly formatted and positioned. Hyperlinks are a type of tag that link Web pages together, thus providing the primary navigation tool for the Web. It works as a pointer from one object to another. The destination doesn't always have to be another Web page. It also can be a picture, an e-mail address, a file (such as a Microsoft Office document), or a program. For example, you can use hyperlinks to link text between Office documents.

HTML and XML

One way to create a Web page is to enter these formatting instructions using Hypertext Markup Language, commonly known as HTML. However, Access 2002 has the tools you need to convert objects directly to HTML documents so that they can be viewed on the Web. All you need is a Web browser such as Internet Explorer or Netscape Navigator.

Because of differences in data formats between applications, Internet integration has not always been easy. Although HTML does a good job of providing text and graphics display information for Web browsers, it is limited when it comes to defining data structures. You could call Extensible Markup Language (XML) a specification, a format, and a standard—and you would be correct on all counts. This subset (or simplification) of Standard Generalized Markup Language (SGML) was specifically designed for Web documents.

XML is a data interchange format for creating, delivering, interpreting, validating, and processing Web data. *Data interchange* means that designers can exchange data between dissimilar applications. The two classes of XML applications are data exchange and publishing. In contrast to HTML, which describes the *appearance* of a Web page, XML describes the *data structure* of a Web page. Just as HTML is the standard language for creating and displaying Web pages, XML is the standard language for describing and delivering data on the Web.

At first glance, XML looks like HTML because they were both derived from SGML. However, XML has a different syntax from HTML. It is stricter and has no predefined tags. As HTML has grown, it has become more and more complex because of the addition of more and more tags. In contrast, XML enables you to create your own tags. Although HTML has been a successful language, XML was created to address its shortcomings, which are deemed by some to be major.

As of this writing, HTML is not likely to disappear in the near future. The first working draft of an XML version of HTML, called XHTML 1.0, was released in February, 1999. XHTML looks like an attempt to combine XML and HTML.

Access and XML

Access 2002 provides the tools to both import and export XML data, a feature not available in Access 2000. This means that with version 2002, users can quickly publish forms, reports, queries, or tables to the Web using XML/XSL. The associated XSL file is used for presentation purposes, enabling users to view forms and reports created in Access with any browser that supports HTML 4.0. One of the options available in the export process is to create an XSD file containing schema information accompanying the XML file containing the data. Table 13.1 can be a handy reference for Internet-related acronyms.

Table 13.1: Important Internet Acronyms

Acronym	Stands For
CSS	Cascading Style Sheet
DTD	Document Type Definition
HTML	Hypertext Markup Language
HTTP	Hypertext Transfer Protocol
ISO	International Standard Organization
SGML	Standard Generalized Markup Language
TCP/IP	Transmission Control Protocol/Internet Protocol
URL	Universal Resource Locator
W3C	World Wide Web Consortium
WWW	World Wide Web
XHTML	Extensible Hypertext Markup Language
XML	Extensible Markup Language
XQL	XML Query Language
XSD	XML Schema Definition
XSL	XML Stylesheet Language
XSLT	Extensible Stylesheet Language Transformations

Let's take a closer look at the new XML export option by example.

1. Open the Music Store database from the AccessByExample folder, and under Tables, click the Customers table.

2. Choose File, Export from the menu bar.

3. Choose the folder where you want to save the files; be sure you are pointing to that specific folder. Click the drop-down box of the Save As Type box, and choose XML documents as your file type.

4. Click Export to open the Export XML dialog box, as shown in Figure 13.1. Notice three options in this dialog box.

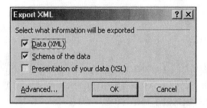

Figure 13.1: *The Export XML dialog box gives you export options.*

5. Select all three options, and click Advanced to open the Export XML dialog box. Click the Schema tab. Notice in Figure 13.2 that a separate schema document named Customers.xsd is set to be created.

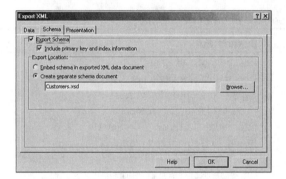

Figure 13.2: *The Schema tab, located on the Export XML dialog box, enables you to create a separate schema document.*

NOTE

When you select all three options, you create four separate files unless you change the preset options from the Export XML dialog box. Two file types, XML and XSL, appear in parentheses in Figure 13.1. The schema file type (XSD) appears on the Schema tab. The HTML file type appears on the Presentation tab.

For additional information about the Schema file type (XSD) while on the Schema tab, click the Help button to open the About XML Data and Access main topic. Click the What Are XML Schemas subtopic. There is also information about XSL file types under the About Extensible Stylesheet Language Transformation subtopic.

---

6. Click the Presentation tab. Notice the options to run from either the Client or the Server, as shown in Figure 13.3.

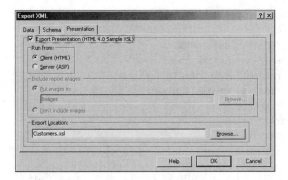

Figure 13.3: *You have the option to export the presentation from the client or from the server.*

NOTE

If you choose the Run From: Server option, you are generating an Active Server Page (ASP). This is popular technology for creating dynamic Web sites. You can tell that it is an ASP by the .asp extension. Look for this extension the next time you surf Web sites.

7. Click OK to create four files.

Now that the page is created, let's examine the page in a browser.

1. Open Windows Explorer, and then open the folder in which you saved the Music Store database files from the preceding steps.

NOTE

Your Windows version must have details turned on so that the file type extensions can be viewed. When you open a file with an extension such as HTML or XML, it opens the file using your browser.

2. Be sure your Details Windows option is activated. Double-click the Customers file with the HTML file type. You should see a representation of the Customers table. Notice that you have opened the file in Internet Explorer.

3. Try to change data in any field. Notice that it doesn't let you make any changes. Close the HTML file.

4. Double-click the Customers file with the type XML. You should see the following listing (only the first record is shown):

```
<?xml version="1.0" encoding="UTF-8" ?>
- <dataroot xmlns:od="urn:schemas-microsoft-com:officedata"
xmlns:xsi="http://www.w3.org/2000/10/XMLSchema-instance"
```

```
xsi:noNamespaceSchemaLocation="Customers.xsd">
- <Customers>
  <CustomerID>101</CustomerID>
  <SortName>Adams</SortName>
  <Customer>Adams High School</Customer>
  <Address>1443 S. Lewis</Address>
  <City>Tulsa</City>
  <State>OK</State>
  <Zip>74136</Zip>
  </Customers>
```

5. Notice that this listing shows the Customers.xsd as the Schema. Close the browser window and Windows Explorer, but leave the Music Store database open.

This exercise took you through some of the options available when you choose the File, Export option from the menu bar to create an XML file. It's one thing to explain the differences between files; it's another thing to see them. The tags in the XML file you examined, such as <State>, are used to delimit the data but leave the interpretation of the data to the application that reads it. A full explanation of the file types created in the exercise is beyond the scope of this book.

NOTE

For a detailed analysis of XML, read *XML By Example* by Benoit Marchal, published by Que Publishing.

Introduction to Data Access Pages

A *Data Access Page* is a Web page stored outside of Access that the user can open with a Web browser or update in Access because it has a connection to a database. For forms and reports, this file is saved in an XML-based language called ReportML, which provides presentation data as well as a data model for creating a Data Access Page.

Web pages can be *static* or *dynamic*. A *static* Web page reflects only the original state of the Access database from which it was created. In other words, no subsequent changes are reflected on the page. In contrast, a *dynamic* Web page is automatically updated every time the Web page is viewed. This means that the current state of the database is reflected each time you view the page.

Data Access Pages are dynamic. You can browse, search, filter, change, and add data to the form, even if you are offline using Internet Explorer 5.0 or greater. This opens up a whole range of possibilities to you, the developer, and your colleagues, the users. Keep in mind, however, that you might not want everyone to see your data. That's precisely why a Data Access Page is a good candidate for an intranet, which typically has tighter security than the Internet.

Before getting into the mechanics of Data Access Pages, consider the following:

- Just because you have created a Data Access Page doesn't mean it will be accessible on the Internet—at least not until you have taken the proper steps to publish it. It does mean that you can view and manipulate the data on the page using Internet Explorer.

- You can click on the Data Access Page from Windows Explorer and use it as if it were an Access form. This opens up your form to people within your organization who don't have a copy of Access. Access doesn't even have to be open to access a page and make changes. Placing the page on a network would open it up to anyone with Internet Explorer 5.0 (IE 5) or greater. After you input new data, you can verify that it has been added by checking it in the Access object from which it was created.

- Just because you have created a Data Access Page doesn't mean that it will be immediately available to anyone on the Internet, even if you have a Web server. This is because Data Access Pages are designed for IE 5 or later. Because they contain Microsoft-specific ActiveX controls, you cannot currently view Data Access Pages from other browsers, such as Netscape Navigator, without a plug-in, which is a software program that extends the capabilities of a browser. In a private network, such as an intranet, you can ensure that everyone has IE 5 or later. Data is shared in much the same way it is shared on the Internet.

- Because the pages are stored outside Access, clicking on icon representations of pages within Access only accesses shortcuts to files stored on your hard drive. That means that any layout changes to the pages are saved on your hard drive; not within the database. However, changes to the data are reflected dynamically in the database. If you try to delete a page, a message asks you if you want to delete the link and the files, or the link only. If you delete the HTML file on your hard drive, you have a shortcut in Access that points to nothing!

- You may choose to convert a database object rather than create a page from scratch or from a wizard. Even if Data Access Pages retain much of the functionality of the original object from which it was converted, don't expect your VBA code to work within Explorer. There are some differences between pages and the database objects that generated the pages that will be addressed.

- Because a page uses Dynamic HTML, access to the database generally is very efficient in a client/server environment. (See the discussion later in this chapter on Active Server Pages for more information related to client/server issues.)

Creating a Data Access Page

Just a few years ago, creating a dynamic, or live, Web page linked to data in a database, even in Microsoft Access, was a daunting task. Data Access Pages have changed all that by streamlining the process enormously. They offer more than just a way to place a form on the Internet. They offer a whole new way for a database user to interact with live data, not only from the local office, but from anywhere in the world.

There are a variety of methods of creating Data Access Pages, so how do you know which is the best method to use? It depends on what you want to do. If you want to create a page that looks like an object (such as a form) that you have previously created, simply click on the object and choose File, Save As. This works great for an address form that you want to publish.

Other methods need to be explored as well. For example, you can use a wizard to create a Data Access Page. Other methods include using an existing Web page from the Internet or using Autopage to create a page. Finally, you can create a Data Access Page from scratch.

Save an Object as a Data Access Page

This is the easiest way to generate a fairly good likeness of your form or report. This doesn't mean that you can't use this technique on tables and queries as well. However, there are some limitations to keep under consideration when converting objects to Data Access Pages. Table 13.2 lists some of those limitations.

Table 13.2: Data Access Page Limitations

Objects Not Supported	Features Not Supported
Bound object frames	Value lists as row sources
Unbound object frames	Multiple columns in list boxes
Toggle buttons	Subform and subreport conversion
Tab controls	Code conversion
Diagonal lines	Expressions that refer to form and subform properties

However, even with these limitations (this list is not comprehensive), the Save As feature is a great way to emulate the functionality of your original object. And remember that you can edit the pages after conversion to better suit your needs. Take the following steps to convert your object to a Data Access Page:

1. In the Music Store Database window under Forms, click the Customers Example form.

2. Click File, Save As. In the box that says Save Form 'Customers Example' To:, type over the suggestion of Copy of Customers Example to read `CustomersExamplePage`.

3. In the As box, click on the down arrow and then choose Data Access Page, as shown in Figure 13.4.

Figure 13.4: *Use the Save As option to convert an existing Access object to a Data Access Page.*

4. Click OK to open the New Data Access Page dialog box. Be sure that you are pointing to your desired folder, and click OK again. Close the page that opens.

5. Under Objects, click Pages. Double-click CustomersExamplePage, as shown in Figure 13.5. (You can just as easily open this page from Windows Explorer.)

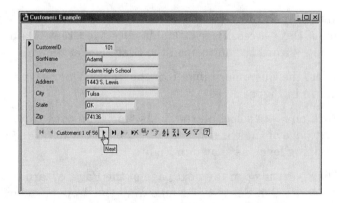

Figure 13.5: *The CustomersExamplePage Data Access Page was created from the Customers Example form in Access.*

6. Click the next record navigation button at the bottom of the form, also shown in Figure 13.5. Notice that you can browse through the form using this button.

7. Click the first navigation button on the bottom left to go back to the first record.

8. Click the `City` field that should say Tulsa.

9. Click the Apply Filter icon that looks like a funnel with a lightning bolt. Notice that the indicator at the bottom changes from 1 of 56 to 1 of 15. Only Tulsa records are available for browsing.

10. To take the filter off, click the funnel without the lightning bolt to the right of the Apply Filter button.

11. Click the `Zip` field, and then click the Sort icon that shows an A with a Z underneath it. Browse the records to see the sorted results.

12. Click the `SortName` field, and sort it. Close the page but stay in the database.

By now, you should appreciate that you have retained some of the functionality of the original form.

Create a Data Access Page Using a Wizard

Notice in the following example that although you select a table, you get a form as a result. That's what a Data Access Page is; a form that can be accessed by a browser. No matter which method you use to create the page, your result will always be a form. The mechanics of the wizard are very similar to a form or a report wizard.

1. In the Music Store database, under Objects, click on Pages to view a list of Data Access Pages. Double-click the Create Data Access Page by Using Wizard option to open the first page of the Page Wizard.

2. Select the Customer table from the Tables/Queries drop-down box, as shown in Figure 13.6.

3. Click on >> to select all the fields, and then click Next to open the next page of the wizard. Select by double-clicking the `State` field for a grouping level, as shown in Figure 13.7.

4. Click Next to open the next page of the Page Wizard in which you set the sort order. Select SortName from the drop-down box for the sort order on this page (see Figure 13.8).

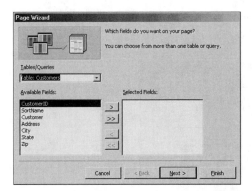

Figure 13.6: You select tables and fields in the Data Access Page Wizard the same way you do with other Access wizards.

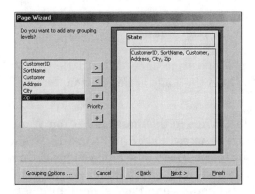

Figure 13.7: You select the State field for the grouping level in the Page Wizard.

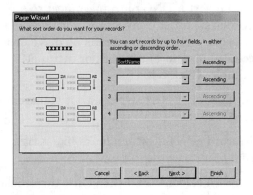

Figure 13.8: The sort order page in the Page Wizard enables you to select a field by which to sort.

5. Click Next to open the last page of the Page Wizard, as shown in Figure 13.9.

Figure 13.9: *The last page of the Page Wizard enables you to open the page immediately or modify the page's design.*

6. Enter Customers Group Page under What Title Do You Want For Your Page? Click the Open the Page option button, and click Finish to open the page.

7. Click Close and then Yes to the message Do You Want to Save Changes to the Data Access Page? As Figure 13.10 shows, when you move your cursor to the File Name box, you get a Control Tips Text message that asks you to input a filename or Web address (http://). However, the Customers Group Page should automatically be entered in the box for you.

8. Click Save. Notice that you get a message, shown in Figure 13.11, which asks you to insert a UNC path to connect to a Network. UNC stands for Universal Naming Convention, such as \\ServerName\ FolderName\FileName. Notice that there is no drive designation. This path can be accessed on a local network or intranet, making it more universally available. Click OK.

9. Double-click the Customers Group Page that you created. Notice that you see only the State field (see Figure 13.12).

10. Click the Next record selector, which looks like a right arrow. Notice that you have only four records to browse.

11. Click the First record selector, and then click the + beside the State label to expand the group.

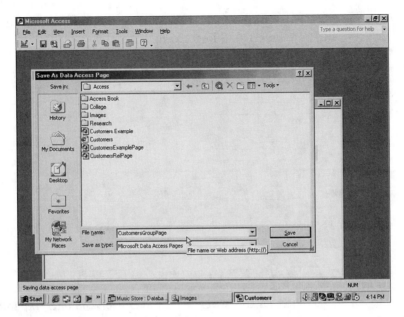

Figure 13.10: *Enter a filename in the Save As dialog box after the wizard has run.*

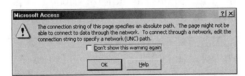

Figure 13.11: *When you click Save to finish the Page Wizard, you get a message warning you to select a UNC path, just in case you want to connect to a network.*

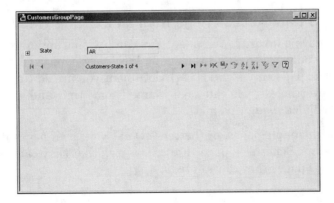

Figure 13.12: *When you open the Grouped Data Access Page, you see only the State field before you drill down.*

12. Click Next on the higher-level navigation toolbar, as shown in Figure 13.13 (it says 1 to 6 for Arkansas).

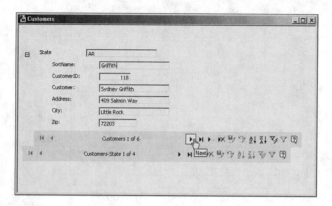

Figure 13.13: *After you expand the group, you see the records for each state.*

13. Click Next on the lower-level navigation toolbar. Expand the next state, and follow step 12.

14. Click the Delete button (with an X) on the higher level, but click No to avoid confirmation and cancel the delete. Close the page. You also can add and edit records because this is a dynamic page.

TIP

You can open your grouped page in Design view and change the default group properties so that, when the form opens, the State field is expanded. Simply right-click anywhere in the top (Customers-State) section, and choose Group level properties. Then change ExpandedByDefault to True. Open the page again, and you immediately see the difference in the page.

Create a Data Access Page from an Existing Web Page

Do you have a favorite Web page? You can use this option to create your own Web page based on a preexisting Web page. One caveat is that you get a dynamic page only if the HTML document you are editing contains XML code. Nevertheless, you can save yourself some time and possibly improve on a good idea using this method.

Start with simple pages, or (better yet) use your own pages if you have created any. Some Web pages are so complex that they can be daunting. Search for pages that contain lists.

The following steps guide you through the process of creating a page using an existing Web page:

1. In the Database window, click Pages under Objects. Click the New button on the Database window toolbar.

2. In the New Data Access Page dialog box, click Existing Web page.

3. Click OK to open the Locate Web Page dialog box; then find the Web page or HTML file that you want to open.

   You can find a Web page by clicking Search the Web (notice the pointing cursor in Figure 13.14) in the Locate Web Page dialog box. You might be able to get a dynamic document, depending on whether there is any XML code contained within the HTML page.

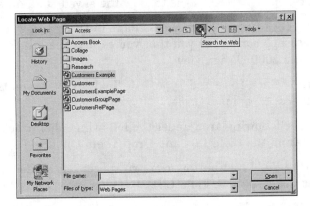

Figure 13.14: *Use the Search the Web button to find an existing Web page.*

NOTE

If you don't have a favorite site, use `http://www.microsoft.com/office/access/using/default.htm`. You might have to connect to the Internet first, depending on what type of connectivity you have.

---

4. Save a copy of the page by using the Save As command on the File menu in Microsoft Internet Explorer, and choose the Edit Web page that already exists under Pages.

5. Choose the folder in which you saved the Web page, and double-click the filename you chose. After viewing the page, when you want to close it, choose Yes to save the page.

6. Microsoft Access creates a shortcut to the HTML file in the Database window.

Create a Data Access Page Using AutoPage

This method is so simple that it is almost a no-brainer. You simply choose New under Pages, and then choose AutoPage: Columnar. (Columnar means Rolodex style.) The benefit of this method is its speed. The drawback is that you must know in advance that you want all the fields from a particular table or query. But then again, you can always use this method to create a quick page to edit. At that time, you can remove any unwanted fields.

Create a Data Access Page from Scratch in Design View

Although this is the most difficult method to use, it is good to get acquainted with the tools available for editing purposes. There might be times when this is the only feasible alternative.

1. Under Objects, select Pages to view the saved Data Access Pages.

2. Double-click Create Data Access Page in Design view. Click OK when the message box warns you that you cannot open the page you create in Access 2000 Design view.

3. Click the Click Here and Type Title Text text box, and then type Customers Relational Page.

4. Click the following area under the following label to select it: Drag Fields from the Field List and Drop Them On This Page.

5. Click the Field List button icon two spaces left of the Toolbox icon (or you can choose View, Field List).

6. If the Tables folder is not expanded, click the + to expand the folder.

7. Expand the Customers table by clicking + to see the Field List, as shown in Figure 13.15. Notice the Related Tables folder.

8. Click the CustomerID field, and then hold the Ctrl key down and click the Customer and Address fields. Now click, hold, and drag the fields down to the Drag Fields from the Field List, and drop them on this page section.

9. While the fields are selected, move them almost as far left as you can drag them in the section.

10. From the Field List, click the City field and, with the Shift key held down, click the Zip field. Drag the fields down to the right of the other fields in the Customers section.

11. Right-click the State field, and then choose Promote, as shown in Figure 13.16. Notice that the State field is promoted to its own section with a Group of State label.

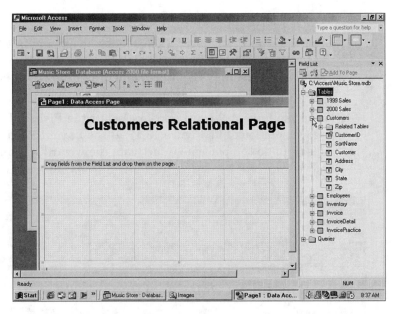

Figure 13.15: *When you click Field List in Design view of a Data Access Page, you view both tables and fields.*

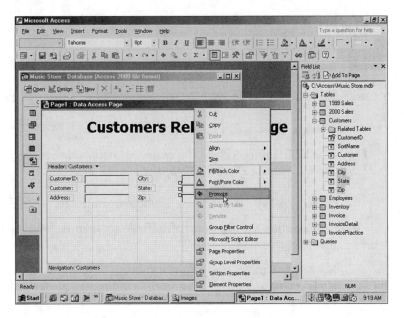

Figure 13.16: *You can promote any field to create a group header for your Data Access Page.*

12. Click the Undo button. (This is just for you to see the results.)

13. Click the + on the Related Tables folder to expand it. Click the + on the Invoice table to expand it. Click the whole table (as opposed to the Field List or the plus or minus), and drag it down to the Customers section.

14. When the Layout Wizard appears, select the Pivot Table option. Your page should look like Figure 13.17. If the Layout Wizard doesn't appear, undo the placement, activate the wizard wand in your toolbox, and retry.

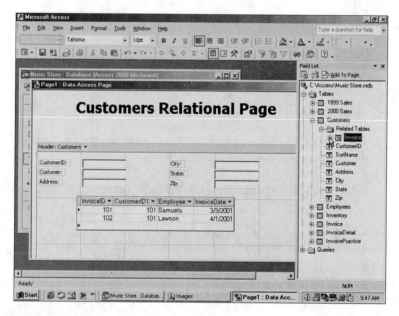

Figure 13.17: *You can drag the entire related table over to the Data Access Page, and select the Pivot Table option.*

15. Close and save the form as CustomersRelPage.

16. Double-click the CustomersRelPage to open it. Your page should look like Figure 13.18.

17. Browse the page, noticing the relational functionality. Close the form. Now you can run the page from Windows Explorer or from Internet Explorer.

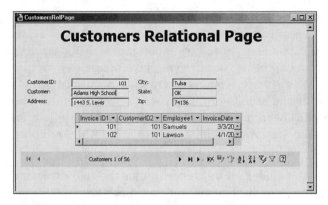

Figure 13.18: *The Customers Relational Page was created from scratch in Design view.*

Active Server Pages

Active Server Pages (ASP) is Microsoft's server-based technology for creating dynamic Web pages. The data they display is often linked to a database through a scripting language such as VBScript. A common use of Active Server Pages is in company intranets. It certainly is one of the most popular ways to build Web pages that display up-to-date server-generated data. For example, Microsoft's Web site has Active Server Pages. An example of a Microsoft Web address using ASP is `www.microsoft.com/biztalk/using/tips/default.asp`.

The following are some of the reasons for the popularity of ASP:

- **Browser Independent**—Because Active Server Pages are executed on the Web server and not within the browser, they are said to be browser-independent.

- **Database Access**—Because Active Server Pages rely heavily on ActiveX Data Object (ADO) technology (which is an important part of Microsoft Access as well as other databases such as SQL Server), integration with the Internet is natural.

- **Easy Maintenance**—Because Active Server Pages are written using scripts, they are easy to maintain. In the event that an Active Server Page bug is detected, you simply open the page with any text editor, such as Notepad, and you can quickly modify the script without having to recompile.

Client-side and server-side script can be mixed when writing ASP pages; because Access can export ASP pages, you can take advantage of this feature even if you don't have any experience writing scripts. But before you think about exporting, be sure you have access to a Web server with the appropriate software, such as Microsoft Internet Information Services (IIS), installed. If you aren't sure, ask your network administrator if Web server software has been installed. If the software is installed, follow these steps (or ask your network administrator to follow them) to prepare for ASP functionality:

1. Create a folder on the server under the root directory where the ASP files can reside. The default root directory is \Webshare\Wwwroot for Personal Web Server and \Inetpub\Wwwroot for Microsoft Internet Information Server.

2. Have your network administrator define the appropriate privileges for the folder.

3. Copy the ASP files to the folder on the server. Copy any related files (such as graphics, linked files, and any folders that might contain these files) to the folder, or be sure the related files can be located by the Web server software.

4. Copy the Microsoft Access database to the folder, or define its network location in the ODBC data source definition.

5. Define the ODBC data source as a System DSN (Data Source Name) on the Web server. (See the next series of steps for information on how to accomplish this.) Be sure the data source name is the same name as the one you entered in the appropriate Output Options dialog box when you exported the ASP files.

6. For a Microsoft Access database, create a user-level security username and password so that users can access the Access database from the Web page. If you do not create a user-level security username or password, the default username is Admin, and no password is needed.

7. For a Microsoft Access project, in the Username and Password boxes, create a database username and password to allow users to access the Microsoft SQL Server database from the Web page. If you do not create a username or password, the default username is Sa, and no password is used.

8. The username and password must match the username and password that you entered in the User to Connect As and Password for User boxes of the Microsoft Active Server Pages Output Options dialog boxes that appear when you output the ASP files.

After these steps are complete, you are almost ready to export. However, if you were not sure how to define the ODBC data source in the previous step 5, follow these steps to be sure you have an active DSN. Again, if you are not sure, ask your network administrator.

1. Open the ODBC Data Source Administrator on your Web server. In Windows 98, click Start, Settings, Control Panel, and then open ODBC Data Sources (32 bit). In Windows 2000 and Windows NT, click Start, Settings, Control Panel; click on Administrative Tools, and open ODBC Data Sources.

2. In the Data Sources dialog box, click the System DSN tab. Click Add if you do not see the name of the System DSN that you used as the DSN in the export process. Click Microsoft Access Driver, and click Finish.

NOTE

If Microsoft Access Driver does not appear, it needs to be installed on your Web server.

---

3. In the ODBC Microsoft Access Setup dialog box, type the requested information. The name that you type in the Data Source Name box is the same name that you use in the Data Source Name box in the Export dialog box.

4. Click OK to close the ODBC Microsoft Access Setup dialog box, and then click OK in the ODBC Data Source Administrator dialog box.

5. If the DSN in the System DSN on your Web server is different from the one you used when you created your Web pages, return to the export process in Microsoft Access, and re-create your Web pages using the correct DSN.

If you do not have access to the Web server, have your network administrator complete the steps. When you export the Access object, choose Microsoft Active Server Pages from the Save As Type: box, and reference the folder you used in step 1 in the Server URL: box on the next screen. For example, if you used the \Inetpub\Wwwroot folder, type http://<server name>/wwwroot/<aspfilename.asp> for the URL.

After you publish your ASP files to a Web server, IIS can run the VBScript code, call the ActiveX server controls, open the database, and send the dynamically created HTML file to the Web browser as a Web page.

Hyperlinks in Access Objects

Hyperlinks in Access are easy to implement. Although there are other ways to create hyperlinks in Access, you can simply create a field in a table and set its data type to hyperlink. To complete the hyperlink to another object, just type the Internet or e-mail address in the hyperlink field. You are not limited to Internet pages and e-mail addresses, however. Through a hyperlink, you can link to database objects such as a table, form or report, Word document, or even an Excel named range. Assuming the link is valid, clicking on the hyperlink opens the linked object.

You can easily use hyperlinks to navigate around your database. They have many advantages over using macros or procedures linked to command buttons to open Access objects. For example, they are easier to create, easier to maintain, and they adapt well to creating menus. But for some people, the best advantage is that they don't have to be Access experts to create or maintain them.

Follow these steps for a glimpse at the power of hyperlinks:

1. Open the FormAndControls database. Under Forms, open the Hyperlink form.

2. Click on a few links to test them. The forms should open for you.

3. Click the View button to enter Design view. Choose Insert, Hyperlink (see Figure 13.19).

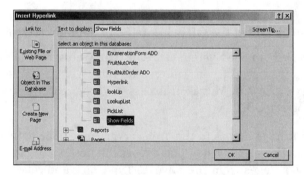

Figure 13.19: *You can insert hyperlinks on forms to open objects in your database so they serve as menu items.*

4. Under Link To: on the left section of the screen, choose Object In This Database to view a list of database objects with expand (drill-down) buttons.

5. Click the + on Forms to drill down. Use the vertical scrollbar to scroll until you see the Show Fields form.

6. Click the Show Fields form, and notice that OK activates. Click OK. A hyperlink to the Show Fields form inserts into the upper-left corner of the form.

7. Place your cursor in the center of the Show Fields hyperlink. When the cursor changes into a hand, position the hyperlink by dragging it directly under the PickList form, as shown in Figure 13.20.

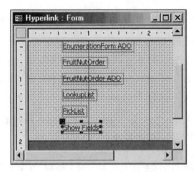

Figure 13.20: *The design window after hyperlink insertion.*

8. Close and save the form. Test your hyperlink by opening the Hyperlink form and clicking your hyperlink.

9. Open the Northwind database. Under Forms, open the Suppliers form, and then click the Home Page field. Click Insert, Hyperlink to open the Insert Hyperlink dialog box.

10. Under the Link To panel, select Existing File or Web Page. Notice the Browse the Web button that looks like a globe with a magnifying glass, as shown in Figure 13.21.

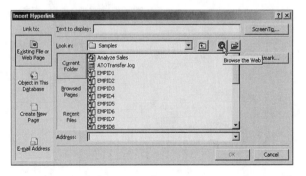

Figure 13.21: *You can click the Browse the Web button to insert a hyperlink, or just click on a favorite page that you already browsed.*

11. Under Look In, click Browsed Pages to see your recently browsed Web sites and files. This option provides an easy way to insert links to your most recently browsed pages.

12. Click your favorite Web page in the list, and then click OK. Notice that a link is automatically inserted into the field.

NOTE

Be sure to choose an Internet link, as opposed to a file. Files have a file:/// prefix in front of the filename.

---

13. With the link still highlighted, type over the link with a friend's e-mail address. Notice that it is underlined as you type. If you double-click on it, you can send your friend an e-mail.

14. After typing the address, right-click on it, choose Hyperlink, and choose Remove Hyperlink. Close the form.

As mentioned previously, hyperlinks provide an excellent alternative to command buttons. Now you know by example that hyperlinks do more than just open Web pages; and they are easy to set up, use, and maintain.

What's Next

You learned about Data Access Pages, Active Server Pages, and hyperlinks in this chapter. You saw that Access 2002 has the capability to integrate with the Internet. In the next chapter, you will examine SQL Server integration. Access is better than ever when it comes to working with sources outside of Access. This flexibility only enhances your ability to expand your horizons as you work with this powerful tool.

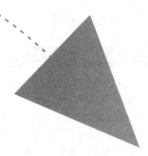

14

SQL Server Integration

In the last chapter, you learned about integrating Access with the World Wide Web. This chapter focuses on integration with SQL Server 2000 using the desktop engine that ships with Access 2002. Now you have an alternative to Microsoft Jet. In particular, you explore the following:

- the history of the Microsoft Data Engine

- how MSDE 2000 compares to SQL Server 2000

- how MSDE 2000 compares to Jet

- how to install MSDE 2000

- how to install a sample Northwind application

- how an Access project compares to an Access database

- how to create stored procedures and triggers

MSDE Upgraded

Microsoft Data Engine (MSDE) was introduced with Access 2000. It offered compatibility with Microsoft SQL Server 7.0 and was an alternative database engine to Microsoft Jet. With Access 2002, Microsoft has upgraded and changed the name of this powerful engine that it continues to offer at no charge as an extra bonus (although it is not part of a standard Access installation). Microsoft SQL Server 2000 Desktop Engine (MSDE 2000) is the new name of the data engine that is completely compatible with SQL Server 2000. This enables users to easily create and modify SQL Server-compatible databases that can be seamlessly deployed on SQL Server 2000 without any modifications.

Because MSDE 2000 is based on the same data engine as SQL Server 2000, most Microsoft Access projects or client/server applications run on either version. This does not mean that the new engine has all the same tools as SQL Server 2000, however. Think of it as a slimmed-down version of SQL Server 2000. Unlike SQL Server 2000, MSDE 2000 has a 2-gigabyte database size limit (the same as Access); it doesn't support Symmetrical Multiprocessing (SMP) on Windows 98 or later; and, when using transactional replication, it can't be a replication publisher (although it can act as a replication subscriber).

Although Microsoft MSDE 2000 is not as powerful as SQL Server 2000, you still can get a great deal of benefit out of this application. As already mentioned, you can use it in place of the Microsoft Jet Engine. One advantage MSDE 2000 has over Jet is that you also can use it to develop and test an Access project or client/server application on a personal computer or workstation, and modify the Access project connection information to connect to a SQL Server database on a remote server for final testing and production. You might not have some of the management tools of SQL Server, but you have plenty of development functionality with MSDE 2000.

When using an Access data project in Access 2002, users can create and modify simple SQL Server stored procedures (a brand-new feature) using the Stored Procedure Designer. This enables users to create stored procedures without having to learn Transact SQL. (See the Transact SQL discussion in the section "Stored Procedures," later in this chapter.) You simply select the Queries tab in the Database Container and double-click Create Stored Procedure in Designer.

What does all of this mean to you, the novice developer? It means that you have a tool that you can use as a small workgroup server database. For example, if you anticipate that your business needs will increase over time until they eventually need the full functionality of SQL Server 2000 running on a larger network server, by all means develop your applications using an Access project connected to the SQL Server 2000 Desktop Engine.

It also means that you will have a SQL platform for testing, learning, and even developing that allows you to get your feet wet in a SQL environment without incurring the expense of a larger system. This will do nothing but improve your resume and expand your horizons regarding job opportunities, not to mention the fun and satisfaction that you will have along the way.

Comparing MSSQL Server 2000 Desktop Engine to Jet

Besides the obvious advantage of the SQL Server compatibility of the desktop engine, some might be tempted to ask, "Why not just stick with Microsoft Access?" You can always upsize later. Both Jet and MSDE 2000 are designed for small workgroup environments. Both technologies have a 2-gigabyte file size limit.

Better Performance

For starters, even in a small workgroup environment, MSDE 2000 has a performance advantage over Jet because the queries are processed on the server rather than on the workstation. Only the data processed from the query is moved to the workstation using the server. In addition to this, in a client/server setting, the server typically is installed on a more powerful machine. Because the server handles the processing requests, the load is shifted from the client machine.

Better Data Integrity

In addition, data integrity and reliability are better using the desktop engine. That's because MSDE 2000 has the same data-integrity features as SQL Server. For example, if a power outage causes the database data to become damaged, SQL Server can repair itself using the transaction log file (every change to the database is logged here). It is used as an automatic recovery mechanism to restore the database to its latest state of consistency in a matter of minutes. This means that time-critical applications can be up and running again right away. In contrast, if the system crashes with Jet, the database can become corrupt, which can force you to revert to your last backup copy.

Tighter Security

The client/server approach also has tighter security. In comparison, Access security is limited. With a SQL Server database, unauthorized users must access the server first instead of accessing the database file directly. Moreover, stored procedures can be a mechanism for additional security options. For example, you can execute built-in SQL Server stored procedures to grant to users access to the database that is based on a specific SQL Server logon. Or, if you prefer, you can base database access on users' Windows network logon.

Because the SQL Server Enterprise Manager that is part of SQL Server 2000 is not included with MSDE 2000, as of this writing, the security tools will not be available when you install MSDE 2000. However, other options for granting database permissions are available, including the following:

- You can use the built-in sa (system administrator) account with a password to allow users to log on as a SQL administrator. The downside is that they will have full administrator access to MSDE 2000.

- If you have NT or Windows 2000, you can use integrated security to add users to the local Windows NT or Windows 2000 Administrators group; but they will have full access to the computer.

- You can purchase and install the Microsoft XP Developer, which includes a developer-only end-user license agreement (EULA) to install SQL Server Personal (including Enterprise Manager, which provides the tools to create user accounts and assign database permissions).

- If you have access to a copy of SQL Server 2000, you can install a copy of SQL Server Enterprise Manager from the CD. This gives you object-level security and the ability to add network domain users.

- You can use built-in SQL stored procedures to grant access to the database to users either based on a specific SQL Server logon or on their Windows network logon.

If you do not have NT or Windows 2000 and do not have access to SQL Server Enterprise Manager, you can use the last option for network security. There are four intrinsic (system) procedures that you can use to grant access rights to the database. The first stored procedure, sp_grantlogin, allows a user to access MSDE 2000. The second stored procedure, sp_default db, specifies the default database for a new user. The third stored procedure, sp_grantdbaccess, gives the user access rights to the database. The last stored procedure, sp_addrolemember, determines what type of access is allowed.

The following stored procedure uses all four intrinsic procedures to prompt the user for <domain>\<user> name and database name:

```
CREATE PROCEDURE GrantAccess
@NewUser      VarChar(30),
@db           VarChar(30)
```

```
AS
    EXEC sp_grantlogin @NewUser
    EXEC sp_defaultdb @NewUser, @db
    EXEC sp_grantdbaccess @NewUser
    EXEC sp_addrolemember "db_owner", NewUser
RETURN
```

For all the reasons just examined and more, MSDE 2000 is a good choice over Jet, especially in a network environment. On the other hand, Jet uses less memory (both disk and RAM) than the desktop engine. For this reason, Jet actually is faster than MSDE 2000 on most older computers with less memory. Creating an application is easier using Access 2000 and Jet because less administrative work is involved.

Installing and Starting the Server

A book could easily be written on this subject alone, but rather than doing that, you can explore MSDE 2000 by example. The first thing you need to do is to install the engine. This couldn't be easier. Simply place your Office XP CD in your computer, and then click Start, Run. When the Open window appears, click Browse. Depending on the drive letter of your CD, substitute the correct drive letter for D: in the following example:

D:\MSDE2000\SETUP.EXE

After returning to the Open window, click OK. After the installation program completes, you are asked if you want to restart your computer to finish the installation. Answer Yes. After your computer reboots, there is still an important step to complete. On the system tray, which usually is at the bottom right of your desktop screen, you see a new icon that looks like a computer tower with a white circle beside it. This white circle has a red dot inside it. Double-click it, and leave it maximized. You should see a screen like that shown in Figure 14.1.

Unless you have another server (such as MSDE) installed on your computer, the installation program should pick up your computer name for the server name. To see if this is the case, right-click your Network Neighborhood or Network Places (or whatever your computer calls it), and choose Properties; then look for an identification tab to check the computer name.

Now that it is installed, you must start the server. Click the Start/Continue button. Notice the Auto-Start Service when OS Starts option. If you choose this option, keep in mind that the server consumes system resources, and there might be times when you want the maximum amount of RAM. If you think that your RAM is low or if you are not sure, don't choose this option. If you have plenty of RAM, it might not be an issue, but keep this in mind.

Figure 14.1: The MSSQL Server Service Manager dialog box.

Installing a Sample Northwind Application

Now that you have finished the installation and startup, you need a project to work with. Open the Northwind database. If you don't have Northwind or if you are not sure, install both options from the Help menu within Access. Simply click Help, Sample Databases. If the program can't find either the Northwind database or the Northwind Project, it will ask you whether you want to install it. Click Yes for either or both options, depending on what you need.

Suppose that a problem occurred in the installation or that you can't find your Office CD. As mentioned before, you can download the Northwind database from the Microsoft Web site. But if you just need the project, there is another option that would be good for you to learn, anyway. You can upsize your Northwind database to a project. (You might have other databases that need to be upsized as well.) If your sample project installed properly, you can delete the resulting upsized project that is just for practice. Otherwise, use the upsized project for the examples in this chapter. Follow these steps to upsize:

1. Open the Northwind database.

2. Choose Tools, Database Utilities, Upsizing Wizard from the menu to open the Upsizing Wizard.

3. When page 1 of the wizard appears, choose Create New Database (see Figure 14.2), and click Next.

4. On page 2 of the wizard, your computer name should have been entered automatically in the box that reads What SQL Server Would You Like to Use for This Database?. If not, be sure that MSSQL Server is started. Hopefully, you won't have to reinstall the server engine again.

Figure 14.2: *On page 1 of the Upsizing Wizard, you can choose to create a new database project based on an existing Access database.*

5. For the login ID, simply type sa (system administrator) with no password for the username. (If you or your client has an NT server, SQL Server can use your NT login to verify your server access, but don't use it for this demonstration.) Go with the default for the SQL Server database name, as shown in Figure 14.3.

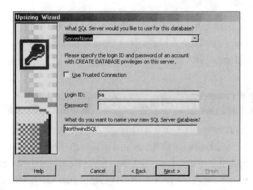

Figure 14.3: *On page 2 of the Upsizing Wizard, simply enter sa with no password.*

6. On page 3 of the wizard, click >> to select all the available tables, and then click Next.

7. On page 4, go with the defaults, as shown in Figure 14.4, and click Next.

NOTE

Notice the options you have for table relationships. The two ways to establish table relationships in SQL Server are DRI (Declarative Referential Integrity) and triggers. SQL Server 2000 supports cascading DRI (similar to Access cascades), which enables you to create a relationship between a master and a dependent table that causes a deletion or update of a record in the master table to automatically cascade to corresponding records in the dependent table.

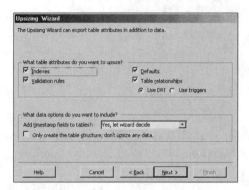

Figure 14.4: *Page 4 of the wizard lets you choose table attributes along with the data.*

8. You can change the directory and filename for the ADP file on the next screen if you like. Click Next.

9. Go with the defaults on page 5, and finish the upsizing. (The last screen defaults open your ADP file.) You should get a report that confirms the options you chose for the upsizing.

Exploring Your Northwind Project

As mentioned earlier, it would take another book for a comprehensive analysis of SQL Server. Therefore, this chapter is just an overview. Even so, you get a taste of what is available to you if you take the time to explore the features of Microsoft SQL Server 2000 Desktop Engine. Actually, the engine has some very basic administrative tools, such as backup, restore, drop, copy, transfer, and SQL security. However, a project's development features are not part of MSDE 2000 at all, but part of Microsoft Access. The bottom line is that, by using an Access project (ADP), you can build client/server applications including triggers, stored procedures, views, transaction logging, rollbacks, and so on, whether you use MSDE 2000 or a full copy of the SQL Server 2000.

Try to separate in your mind the data in a project from the objects that process the data. The files that contain data (or data definitions) reside in a separate file with an .mdf extension. For example, the data file for the Northwind sample file is called NorthwindCS.mdf. The Northwind sample project file is called NorthwindCS.adp. It contains the user interface objects such as forms, reports, data access pages, macros, and modules. There is no need to worry. You can work with the data objects as if they were stored in the Access project file. Table 14.1 compares objects in an Access database and objects in an Access project.

Table 14.1: Object-for-Object Comparison Between an Access Database and an Access Project

Access Database	Access Project
Table	Table
Select Query	View
Action Query	Stored Procedure
Relationships Window	Database Diagrams
Form	Form
Report	Report
Data Access Page	Data Access Page
Macro	Macro
Module	Module

Tables

When you double-click on any Access project table, it looks the same as an Access database table. You see the differences when you click the design button; the differences are mainly between data types. Table 14.2 lists the equivalencies between Access database and SQL Server data types.

Table 14.2: Closest Equivalents Between Access Database and SQL Server Data Types

Access 2002 Database	Access 2002 Project
Text	Varchar, Nvarchar, Char, Nchar
Memo	Text, Ntext
Autonumber	Identity Column
Currency	Money, Smallmoney
Date/time	Datetime, Smalldatetime
Yes/No	Bit
OLE Object	Image
Hyperlink	No equivalent
Long Integer	Int
Integer	Smallint
Double, Single	Float, Real

To examine table properties, take the following steps:

1. In the Northwind project (called NorthwindCS or NorthwindSQL, depending on what method you used to create the project), under Objects, click Tables.

2. Click the Orders table, and then click Design to open the table in Design view. Notice that the OrderID does not have Allow Nulls checked because primary key fields must have unique data without nulls. You should see the screen shown in Figure 14.5.

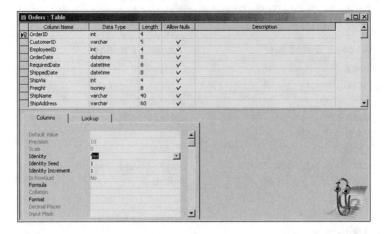

Figure 14.5: *You can view and change table attributes in Design view of the table.*

3. Click the Properties button. You should see the screen shown in Figure 14.6.

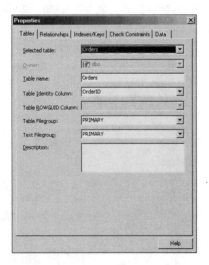

Figure 14.6: *The Properties button in Design view opens property pages organized on tabs.*

4. Click the Relationships tab, and notice that the primary/foreign key relationship is shown.

5. Click the Indexes/Keys tab, click the Selected Index drop-down box, and choose the ShippedDate field. Click Create UNIQUE, and notice that the grayed-out options become active. Uncheck it to the original state.

6. Click the Check Constraints tab, and then click New. Notice that you are prompted for an expression. Click Delete to return to the original state.

NOTE

The Employees table has an example of a constraint, which is similar to a validation rule in an Access database.

---

7. Click the Data tab to finish the tour of the Properties window.

Views

As shown in Table 14.1, the near-equivalent to an Access select query is a SQL Server view. They both work the same way in that they are both essentially a select statement that retrieves data from tables. Among the many similarities are joins. You can create inner and outer joins in SQL Server, just as you can in Access. However, you have a list of operators, such as =, >=, <=, <, that you can use with the joins in SQL Server. The design layout is also very similar. To get you acquainted with views, you will first examine a Northwind view and then proceed to create a view from scratch.

1. While still in NorthwindCS, click Queries. Right-click Sales Total by Amount, and then choose Design View to open the view.

   Notice that two fields have criteria. Also note the way that dates are inserted in the criterion (BETWEEN '19970101' AND '19971231'). In the Subtotal field in the Order Subtotals table, notice the funnel icon that represents a criterion condition.

2. Right-click the join line, and choose Properties to open the Join Line property page, as shown in Figure 14.7.

3. Click the down arrow next to the equal sign. Notice the options for different comparison operators. If you click All Rows from Orders, you create a left outer join. If you click All Rows from [Order Subtotals], you create a right outer join. If you click both boxes, you create a full outer join. Close the join window, and then close the view window. Click No when the message box asks you to save changes.

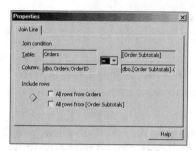

Figure 14.7: *The Join Line property page specifies options for joining tables.*

4. While in Queries, double-click Create View in Designer to open the Add Table dialog box shown in Figure 14.8.

Figure 14.8: *The Add Table dialog box of the Query Designer lets you add tables, views, or user-defined functions to the Diagram pane of your view.*

5. Double-click the Customers, Orders, and Order Details tables to bring them into the Query Designer, and click Close. Notice that the join lines are automatically entered because the relationships are already established.

NOTE

The Query Designer is not to be confused with the Database Designer, which is similar to the Relationships window in a regular Access Database.

---

6. Choose CompanyName and ContactName from the Customers table, OrderDate from the Orders table, and ProductID and Quantity from the Order Details table by clicking the corresponding boxes to the left of each field to check them.

7. In the blank line just under Quantity, type [Order Details].Quantity
   * [Order Details].UnitPrice. In the Alias column, type ExtPrice.

8. Run the view the same way you run a query in Access. The program
   asks you to save the view first. Save it as Sample View. Notice the
   calculated field ExtPrice.

9. Close the view.

Stored Procedures

At first glance, a stored procedure looks a little like a combination of Visual
Basic and SQL. Then again, stored procedures have their own unique characteristics. Transact-SQL (T-SQL) is the SQL Server extension of the SQL
database programming language. *Stored procedures* are precompiled T-SQL
code, which combine collections of SQL statements with optional control-of-
flow (such as if-then-else) statements. You can use input parameters, use
return values, and even call other stored procedures from your T-SQL code.
Although they are similar to Access action queries, they can perform a
much broader array of database operations.

There are many reasons to use stored procedures. Some of their advantages
include the following:

- **Improved Performance**—The stored procedure is compiled on the
  server when it is created, so it executes faster than individual SQL
  statements.

- **Ease Of Use**—You can execute multiple SQL statements from a single stored procedure. You can call other stored procedures from within
  your stored procedure, thus simplifying a series of complex statements. Instead of writing or cutting and pasting SQL statements in
  your VBA code, you can save SQL statements in stored procedures,
  and call them as if they were a function stored in a module.

- **More Security Options**—You can shield users from direct access to
  tables, if necessary. A user can be granted permission to access a
  stored procedure, even if they do not have permission to access the
  tables or views that are referred to in the stored procedure.

You can create and save your own stored procedures in an Access project
using parameters. The following steps guide you through running a para-
meterized stored procedure:

1. Under Queries, click the Sales by Year stored procedure.

2. Click Design. Notice that the title bar says Stored Procedure. Also
   notice the Criteria on the ShippedDate column.

3. Run the stored procedure.

4. At the first parameter prompt, type 3/1/98. At the next prompt, type 3/1/99. You should see the records that match the parameters.

5. Close the stored procedure.

NOTE

You must use a stored procedure if you want to perform operations such as Update, Insert, Append, or Make-Table. In fact, if you upsized these types of queries from an Access database, they would be converted into stored procedures. However, it is wise to test these upsized stored procedures to confirm that they were transferred properly.

Stored Procedures for Beginners

The stored procedures presented here are designed for the Northwind project. Suppose that you have a SQL statement that you want to convert into a stored procedure:

```
Select UnitPrice, Quantity From [Order Details]
```

If you click New under Queries and then click Create Text Stored Procedure, you can create a new procedure that looks something like the following:

```
CREATE PROCEDURE ProcSamp
AS
Select UnitPrice, Quantity From [Order Details]
```

The procedure name can be anything you like—you call it by its name. You can't get much more straightforward than this. Even without a RETURN keyword, you will return two columns. The RETURN keyword will either return a value or exit the program, depending on what you want to do.

Now, add a little functionality without getting too fancy. A variable should make it interesting. Simply precede the variable with an @ sign, the same way you do with a parameter. The difference is that you have to declare it. You need to do something with the variable, so add a WHERE clause so that it looks like this:

```
ALTER PROCEDURE ProcSamp
AS
declare @i as int
select @i=40
Select UnitPrice, Quantity From [Order Details]
Where Unitprice >@i
Return
```

Notice a couple of things here. First, the CREATE in CREATE PROCEDURE was replaced with ALTER. This way, you don't have to drop the procedure only to re-create it later. Second, notice that the WHERE clause used the variable directly, without having to go through the gymnastics of piecing quotes and ampersands together, the way you do when you use SQL statements in VBA. Finally, notice the use of the RETURN keyword. In this case, it only exits the stored procedure, but it could just as easily be used to return a value.

To turn this into T-SQL code using a parameter, you just change a few lines to look like this:

```
ALTER PROCEDURE SampProc
    (
    @i int
    )

AS
Select UnitPrice, Quantity From [Order Details]
Where Unitprice >@i
Return
```

Notice that the AS keyword is on the other side of the parameter. In other words, the variable was *after* the AS keyword, whereas the parameter preceded it. Also notice that there is no value assigned to the parameter because it was only necessary to do so at runtime.

In case you are wondering about flow control, a final stored procedure is examined. It is a little more complicated, but it should be helpful in understanding how flow control works in a stored procedure.

```
ALTER Procedure SelectOwners
@Title char(20)
As
--If records are found that match input parameter, retrieve them and
--set RETURN to 1
--When prompted, type "Owner"
IF (SELECT COUNT(*) FROM Customers WHERE ContactTitle=@Title)>0
      BEGIN
            SELECT ContactName, ContactTitle
            FROM Customers
            WHERE ContactTitle=@Title
            RETURN 1
      END
ELSE
--Otherwise, set RETURN to 0
            RETURN 0
```

This listing demonstrates the use of the RETURN keyword to return a value. It also demonstrates using flow control in conjunction with a SQL statement to evaluate whether another SQL statement will even run. This is the kind of power that is available to you.

Triggers

A *trigger* is a type of SQL Server stored procedure in a class of its own. Just as a Visual Basic programs respond to events, triggers respond to table-level changes. The three types of SQL Server triggers are

- **Insert Triggers**—Fired when a new record is added to a table.
- **Delete Triggers**—Fired when a record is deleted from a table.
- **Update Triggers**—Fired when a record is updated in a table.

To add a trigger to a table, you simply right-click on it, and choose Triggers. Next, click New. You should see the screen shown in Figure 14.9.

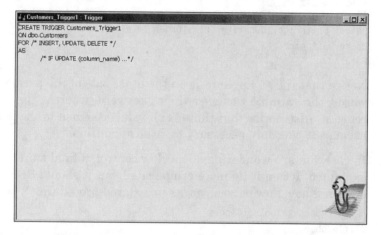

Figure 14.9: *A new trigger is created in the SQL text source editor with the default SQL statements automatically inserted for you.*

After writing and saving your code, you have thereby attached it to your table. If you decide later that you want to edit or delete the trigger, you can right-click on the same table, and choose Triggers. Then, select the trigger from the drop-down box and click the Edit or Delete button.

Messages can be useful to remind the user of the effects of table changes, but keep in mind that PRINT from SQL Server does not work from an Access 2002 project. For example, suppose that you want to send the user a message from a trigger. A PRINT statement would look something like the following:

```
PRINT 'The updated record has been copied into the UpdateTrail table'
```

This trigger fires, but nothing seems to happen because the PRINT statement never sends the message. If you want to relay a message to a user after your trigger fires, you need to use RAISERROR, as the following trigger demonstrates:

```
CREATE TRIGGER NewCount
ON dbo.Customers AFTER DELETE
AS
      DECLARE @RecNum Int
      SELECT @RecNum = COUNT(*) FROM Customers

RAISERROR ('The new record count is %i', 16 , 1 ,@RecNum)
```

The RAISERROR syntax can be quite challenging for a novice, not to mention the fact that it is beyond the scope of this book. For further information, consult SQL Server *Books Online (BOL)*, which you can download from www.microsoft.com/SQL/techinfo/productdoc/2000/books.asp. Be ready to grab a cup of coffee. Depending on your system, it might take a while to download.

For legal purposes, you might want archive tables to track each deletion, insertion, or update performed on a certain table. The following triggers, which use a copy of the Northwind Customers table called NWCustomers, could accomplish this:

```
ALTER TRIGGER TrackDeletes
ON dbo.NWCustomers AFTER DELETE
AS
      INSERT INTO DeleteTrail
      Select CustomerID, CompanyName, ContactName, ContactTitle,
      Address, City, Region, PostalCode, Country, Phone, Fax
      FROM deleted
GO


ALTER TRIGGER TrackInserts
ON dbo.NWCustomers AFTER INSERT
AS
      INSERT INTO InsertTrail
      Select CustomerID, CompanyName, ContactName, ContactTitle,
      Address, City, Region, PostalCode, Country, Phone, Fax
      FROM inserted
GO


ALTER TRIGGER TrackUpdates
ON dbo.NWCustomers AFTER UPDATE
AS
      INSERT INTO UpdateTrail
      Select CustomerID, CompanyName, ContactName, ContactTitle,
      Address, City, Region, PostalCode, Country, Phone, Fax
      FROM deleted
GO
```

These programs use the *deleted* and *inserted* temporary tables that have the same structure (fields and data types) as the originating table. The deleted table is appended into the DeleteTrail table, whereas the inserted table is appended into the InsertTrail table. Notice that the deleted table is also used for the TrackUpdates trigger that populates the UpdateTrail table. Although shown together, they are three separate triggers that can be accessed on the Triggers menu. With the exception of a few words, the triggers are identical. A date can easily be added for each record that is appended to any of the tables.

Try testing the triggers by following these steps:

1. In the Northwind Project, copy the Customer table by right-clicking it and choosing Copy. From the toolbar, click the Paste button to open the Paste dialog box.

2. Choose Structure Only, and give it the table name DeleteTrail.

3. Perform steps 1 and 2 to create two more tables, replacing DeleteTrail with InsertTrail and UpdateTrail, respectively.

4. Right-click the Customers table, and choose Triggers and New.

5. Type in the DeleteTrail trigger from the sample code. Close and save the trigger.

6. Perform steps 4 and 5 for the InsertTrail and UpdateTrail triggers, being careful to enter the appropriate code.

7. Test the code by inserting a dummy record (two fields are sufficient). Close the table.

8. Update the record you inserted by adding a word to one of the fields, and then delete the record you just updated.

9. Look in the DeleteTrail, InsertTrail, and UpdateTrail tables to check the results.

Declarative Referential Integrity

The capability to enforce referential integrity through foreign key constraints that you define is called Declarative Referential Integrity (DRI). DRI actually becomes part of the table definition. You can use other methods, such as triggers, to enforce relationships. This is called *procedural* referential integrity. With Access 2002, you can enforce cascading updates and deletes in Access projects. The following steps describe how to examine a DRI relationship:

1. In the NorthwindCS project under Database Diagrams in the Projects window, choose Relationships and then Design to examine a DRI relationship.

2. Right-click the key between Employees and Orders, and then choose Properties to open Property pages.

3. Click the Relationships tab, and notice that the last two boxes are labeled Cascade Update Related Fields and Cascade Delete Related Fields, as shown in Figure 14.10.

Figure 14.10: *You can use the new Cascade Update or Cascade Delete options for relationships in Access 2002 projects.*

As you can see, Access projects are powerful and practical. Access projects extend the functionality of Access by offering a client/server architecture.

What's Next

Now that you have a taste of what SQL Server integration can do, you can move on to examine integration with other types of programs. The next chapter covers OLE technology and some new features that have been added in Access 2002.

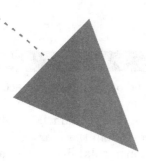

15

User-Friendly Enhancements

In the last chapter, you explored how to integrate Access with SQL Server. This chapter focuses on user-friendly enhancements. Some of these enhancements make it easier to integrate with other applications, such as Microsoft Excel. Specifically, you learn about the following:

- access compact improvements
- why compacting is important
- converting from previous versions of Access
- integrating with other applications
- how to use Object Linking and Embedding
- how to integrate with other applications using code

The Paradox of Databases

Over the years, Microsoft Access has had a myriad of well-deserved accolades from IT professionals and users alike. However, one criticism has hung like an albatross around the neck of Access since its launch in 1992. People were reluctant to take the plunge and move from the limited database capabilities of Excel to more robust and extensive database functionality of Access because of the learning curve associated with such a move. One can only speculate whether Access would have enjoyed the same kind of success without so many user-friendly updates through the years. Nevertheless, although people finally seem to be awakening to the power of Access, some people are still not convinced.

Either you have power or ease of use. Supposedly, you can't have both. This has been the paradox of databases. (That's the rationale for the name of a database that claims to have both.) Access 2002 has addressed this paradox with several "user-friendly" enhancements.

Compact Improvements

It is amazing how a feature so essential can be so often overlooked. So that you don't have to rely on your memory, beginning with Access 2000, the user can choose the Compact on Close option.

After a typical Access session, which usually involves processes such as adding tables, deleting records, and so on, the database begins to grow in size, affecting the space it occupies on the disk. It is important to note that the space that deleted records, tables, or other objects occupied is not automatically made available for new objects. Compacting not only frees up the space for new objects, it makes the overall size of the database smaller. For this reason, you should always compact before zipping.

How often should you compact? It depends on how much work you do. For most users, the Compact on Close option probably is a good idea. Regular compacting ensures updated database statistics and optimal database performance.

You can test how compacting affects the file size of the database by looking at the .mdb file (for example, MyDatabase.mdb) in Windows Explorer before and after compacting. If you have done much database work at all, you definitely will notice a difference. A further benefit is that Access repairs the database simultaneously while compacting. Even if Access doesn't detect that the database is damaged, erratic behavior within Access could be a clear indication of a need for compacting.

If you think you might forget to compact periodically, you can choose the Compact on Close option, which affects only the database you open. The following steps guide you through setting the Compact on Close option:

1. Open the database that you want to compact.

2. Click Tools from the menu bar, and then click Options to open the Options dialog box.

3. Click the General tab in the Options dialog box.

4. Click the Compact on Close option, as shown in Figure 15.1, and then click OK.

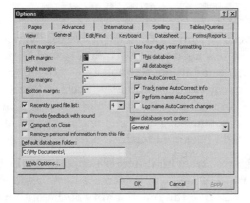

Figure 15.1: *Set the Compact on Close option to automatically compact your database every time you close it.*

Microsoft has announced that Access 2002 has added even greater function-ality to the compact and repair option. For example, it says that files with broken forms and reports are more often recovered with this latest update. To access this feature manually, simply choose Tools, Database Utilities, Compact and Repair Database. Now you can also compact and repair from VBA using the new `CompactRepair` method.

Converting from Previous Versions of Access

If an error occurs when converting a database from previous versions (such as Access 95, Access 97, or Access 2000) to Access version 2002, a table is created that logs information about each error. This streamlines the process of identifying and solving problems in converted databases.

Access 2002 uses the Access 2000 file format as the default file format when you create new databases. This means that Access version 2002 and

Access 2000 can use and modify the same Access 2000 database, thus ensuring compatibility with existing Access 2000 applications when organizations decide to install Access version 2002.

However, if you want to convert to the new optional Access file format, users can enjoy faster data access and processing, especially for larger databases. To summarize, the user now has an option to stay with the default Access 2000 file format or update to the new 2002 file format. This is unprecedented. To update, you simply select Convert Database from the Tools menu. Choose Convert Database, and then select To Access 2002 Format.

Sharing and Integrating with Other Applications

Not only is there a need to convert from earlier Access versions, but increasingly there also is a need to convert data to and from other Office formats, such as Excel. In addition, there is a need to share data with non-Office applications and larger databases, such as Oracle. But Office programs share many of the same features and resources, making the conversion process almost seamless. This functionality makes it particularly tempting to transfer data back and forth.

For example, suppose you know that Access supports mailing labels through its Label Wizard, which can be accessed when you click New under Reports. Then again, you like the functionality of the mail merge feature of Microsoft Word. So, you decide to transfer the Access mailing list to Microsoft Word, which can also handle mailing labels. When you click on Tables under Objects, the Office Links button activates with the Merge It with Microsoft Word option. This option provides an easy way to transfer a mailing list to Word. Just for the record, you can create a mail merge letter in an Access report.

Using Drag and Drop

Microsoft couldn't have made it easier to transfer an Access table to Word for mail-merge purposes. Simply open up both applications at the same time. Maximize a blank new Microsoft Word page, and restore (middle button, top right) a maximized Access window to make it smaller. In the Database window (you don't have to open the table), click, hold, and drag the table to the Word window, and release, as shown in Figure 15.2. Delete the title row by selecting it and choosing Table, Delete, Row from the menu. Save the file, and use it as the data source mail merge file. That's all there is to it, at least from the Access side.

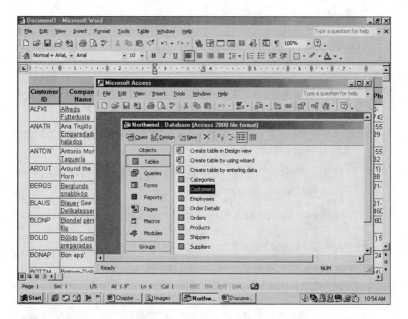

Figure 15.2: *You can drag and drop directly from Access to Word to create a data source for a mail merge.*

From the Word side, you still need to run the Mailing Label Wizard after choosing File, New and then selecting the Letters & Faxes tab. Select the Mailing Label Wizard from the options available, and simply follow the prompts. If you want to create a form letter, choose Tools and Mail Merge from the Word menu, and follow the mail merge helper prompts.

NOTE

This drag-and-drop technique works just as well in Excel.

Copy and Paste

If you want an easier alternative to choosing File, Get External Data and going through the Import Wizard to import Excel data, you might consider just copying and pasting an Excel range (dragging and dropping should work as well). If you use this alternative, be sure you take the following precautions:

- Create column titles (headings) for each field.

- Be sure there are no blank lines between the header row and the first row of data.

- Avoid blank columns.

- Include only the data you need in the range that you copy.

- Answer Yes to the following question: Does the first row of your data contain column headings?

To copy and paste from Microsoft Excel to Microsoft Access, be sure to have both applications open. Then follow these steps:

1. Activate the Excel window, and then select the range of the cells that you want to transfer.

2. Press Ctrl+C to copy. Activate the Access Database window, and then press Ctrl+V to paste.

3. Choose Yes in the message box that displays, as shown in Figure 15.3.

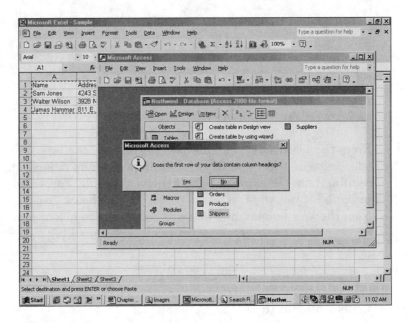

Figure 15.3: *You can copy and paste a database directly from Excel to Microsoft Access.*

Using Object Linking and Embedding

With Access 2002, Microsoft has, to a large extent, concentrated on enhancing Web and SQL Server integration. However, there are other types of integration. The word *integration* generally means to combine parts for the purpose of either forming a whole or working together. When it comes to integrating Access with other applications, integration goes a step further than just making a copy of a table in another application.

NOTE

To learn more about enhancing Web and SQL Server integration, see Chapter 13, "Publishing Your Access Database" and Chapter 14, "SQL Server Integration."

Two types of integration between applications must be understood. When an object created in one application is added to a file created in another application, the process is called Object Linking and Embedding (OLE). You can choose to either *embed* or *link* an object from an outside source. The major difference between an object that is linked and an object that is embedded is where their data is stored. The following points should be helpful:

- With a linked object, a connection is maintained between the source file and the destination file so that the linked object is *updated* when the source data is changed.

NOTE

The *source file* is the file in which the object was created. The *destination file* is the file in which you place the source file object.

- An embedded object becomes part of the destination file and does *not* update if the source file is changed.

- When an object is linked to another application, the object's current data can be viewed from any other applications that contain links to that data.

- When an object is embedded in another application, no other application has access to the data in the embedded object

- When you link an object, you are inserting a placeholder (pointer) for the linked object into your application instead of the data itself.

- When you embed an object, all the data associated with the object is *copied to* and *contained in* the OLE container control.

The last two points have important implications for data storage. Because the embedded data is copied, when you save the contents of the unbound control to an Access (.mdb) file, the saved file contains the name of the application that created the object, the object's data, and a metafile image of the object. Thus, embedded objects can significantly increase file size. In contrast, linked objects do not increase file size as much. To prove this assertion while learning about OLE, you can try the following experiment to insert a Microsoft Word document into a report:

1. Open any access .mdb file from Windows Explorer, and then open any report in Design view.

2. From the Toolbox (with the Control Wizard wand selected), choose the Unbound Object Frame. Draw a rather large box to create the object frame.

3. When the Unbound Object Frame Wizard activates, choose Create from File, as shown in Figure 15.4.

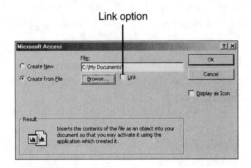

Figure 15.4: *If you choose not to check the Link option when inserting an object into a report, you embed your object.*

4. Click the Browse button, and then choose a word-processing document that is about a page in length.

5. After selecting the file, do not check Link; close and save the report. Compact the database.

6. Close the database to go back to Explorer and write down the size of the file. If you don't see the file size, click Details from the Views drop-down button to show Name, Size, Type, and Modified.

7. Open up the same database again, and follow steps 1 through 6, but this time delete the previous object frame before inserting the new one, and check the Link option.

8. Check the file size again after closing the database. It should be smaller this time.

Because you didn't check Link the first time, the object was embedded. You would notice an even greater difference if the object were a rather large graphics file. If you had copied and opened the Access mdb file containing an embedded graphics object to another computer without the original object, you could still open the report and view the object. However, if you linked the graphics object, you would have been prompted for a disk after trying to open the report because the former is a copy and the latter is a pointer.

For the aforementioned reasons, it might make sense to embed graphics files and link document files. Generally speaking, documents created in programs such as Word and Excel usually need to reflect updates more often than graphics files, making them more adaptable to links. Graphics files, on the other hand, often need to be part of the file in which they are encapsulated, making them more suitable for embedding. However, if the graphics files are huge, you need to keep in mind that the size of your database can increase considerably.

Your situation can vary. You must weigh the pros and cons to decide which to use. If you want the changes made in the source program to be reflected in the destination program, use linking. If you want a copy of the source object in your Access file, use embedding. If you are worried about increasing your Access file size too much, use linking. It just depends on what you want to do.

NOTE

Whether you link or embed an object, you can open the source program simply by double-clicking on the object within Access. This applies only to Design view in a form or report.

One last detail concerning OLE needs to be mentioned before you continue. Sometimes, terms are updated to reflect changes in technology. Dynamic Data Exchange (DDE) is the foundation upon which OLE 1.0 was built (1991). However, even Microsoft had to admit that DDE had its limitations. Along came the Component Object Model (COM), which was the driving force and new standard behind the 1993 release of OLE 2.0. It not only solved many of the problems inherent with DDE, it defined many new advanced and innovative technologies such as ActiveX controls. Even so, you can still find references to DDE in Access help.

All this progress means that the technology behind what they call "compound document objects" has vastly improved over the years. This spells good news to the users. Now you have even more features available to you for integrating applications together. Just be careful, because sometimes these terms are used interchangeably in various textbooks and manuals.

Using Code

Just to give you an idea of application integration through VBA, a look at Excel might be in order. The `Application` object is at the top of Excel's object hierarchy. Through it, you can reference Excel objects, such as `Workbook` and `Worksheet`. The `Workbook` object represents the Excel .xls file in Windows Explorer, whereas the `Worksheet` object represents a sheet in the workbook. The `ActiveCell` object is essential for navigating around the spreadsheet. To move three rows down and one row right, you use the `Offset` property with the `ActiveCell` object:

```
ActiveCell.Offset(3, 1).Select
```

After a selection is made, you can copy the selection, as the following sample code demonstrates:

```
Selection.Copy
```

You can use the `Range` property to copy and the `ActiveSheet` object to paste:

```
Sub SampleXL()
Range("A1:A4").Copy
ActiveCell.Offset(5, 0).Select
ActiveSheet.Paste
End Sub
```

The following procedure selects a range in Excel and then copies the range, cell by cell, into a table called FromExcel in Access. As the comments explain, it should be run from an Excel module.

```
Sub ExcelToAccess()
Dim cn As ADODB.Connection
Dim rs As ADODB.Recordset
Dim rg As Range
'This procedure should be run from an Excel module

Set cn = New ADODB.Connection
Set rs = New ADODB.Recordset
cn.ConnectionString = "Provider=Microsoft.Jet.OLEDB.4.0;" _
& "Data Source=c:\AccessByExample\ExportImport.mdb;"
cn.Open
rs.Open "FromExcel", cn, adOpenKeyset, adLockOptimistic

    For Each rg In Range("a2:a5")
        With rs
            .AddNew
            .Fields("Name").Value = rg.Value
            .Update
        End With
    Next rg

    rs.Close
    cn.Close
    Set rs = Nothing
    Set cn = Nothing
    Set rg = Nothing
End Sub
```

Now that you have had an introduction to Excel, how do you run Excel code from within Access? First, you must set Excel 10.0 Object Library in the References dialog box that you access by selecting Tools, References from the menu bar while you are in an Access module, as shown in Figure 15.5.

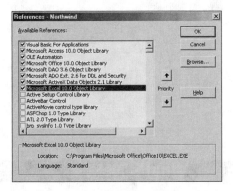

Figure 15.5: *You also can set references to other applications such as Excel when you choose Tools, References in a module.*

Next, declare your variables for the Excel Application object. The following code runs from an Access module using the Excel Application object. Because it sets a range with the intrinsic constant Xldown, if you add values to this range in column A, the range name resets to accommodate the new values. With the exception of naming a range, it performs basically the same operation as the previous procedure, but it runs from Access. The procedure accesses the Excel Range collection and then adds each cell to a table in Access.

```
Sub GetExcelData()
Dim ToAccess As String, rg As Range
Dim ExcelApp As Excel.Application
Dim cn As ADODB.Connection
Dim rs As ADODB.Recordset

Set cn = CurrentProject.Connection
Set rs = New ADODB.Recordset
rs.Open "FromExcel", cn, adOpenKeyset, adLockOptimistic
Set ExcelApp = New Excel.Application

ExcelApp.Workbooks.Open "c:\My Documents\Sample.xls"
ExcelApp.Visible = True
ExcelApp.Range("a2").Activate
ToAccess = ExcelApp.Range(Selection, Selection.End(xlDown)).Address
ActiveWorkbook.Names.Add Name:="ToAccess", RefersTo:="=" & ToAccess
Set rg = ExcelApp.Range("ToAccess") 'Uses the named range "ToAccess"
```

```
      For Each rg In rg
          With rs
              .AddNew
              .Fields("Name").Value = rg.Value
              .Update
          End With
      Next rg
rs.Close
cn.Close
Set rs = Nothing
Set cn = Nothing
Set rg = Nothing

End Sub
```

What's Next

You have discovered methods of integrating other applications with Access. In the next chapter, you learn even more about queries so that you can have techniques to help you overcome development obstacles.

Part V

Overcoming Access Development Obstacles

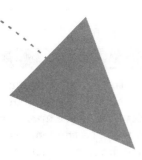

Overcoming the Limitations of Queries

In the last chapter, you learned about integrating Access with other applications. This chapter gives you techniques that you can use to overcome limitations of queries. Because queries are such an important part of Access, you can't go wrong learning as much as you can about them. Specifically, you learn about the following:

- query by table example techniques
- how to use subqueries to overcome query limitations
- more about how to use functions with queries

Query Challenges

Nothing unleashes the power of a database better than a query. Queries are even used behind the scenes in Access to perform many tasks without the user even being aware that they are going on. However, there are situations that can confront the developer that can prove to be challenging, to say the least. The query often is the first place the developer turns to for help. Yet, the best way to apply this powerful tool is not always apparent.

Let's say you are working for an insurance company and your boss approaches you with what they call a "stratification report" in the insurance business. He wants the dollar amounts to be grouped in levels, or "strata," sorted with the smallest levels first. To determine the frequency of the losses, you must show the number of claims in these various levels. To determine the severity of the losses, you must show the dollar amounts for the various levels.

It goes something like this: "How many claims occurred between 1 dollar and 500 dollars, and what were the totals for those numbers? How many claims occurred between 501 dollars and 1000 dollars, and what were the totals for those numbers?" This goes on and on, until the claim dollars are potentially in the millions. You end up with a report that looks something like Table 16.1.

Table 16.1: Loss Stratification Table

Strata Level	Claim Count	Total Incurred
1–500	1,206	248,011
501–1,000	236	156,004
1,001–5,000	269	671,794
5,001–10,000	116	852,609
10,001–25,000	129	2,094,949
25,001–50,000	65	2,272,332
Over 50,001	34	3,440,358

Using Query by Table Example for If Then Scenarios

One solution is to use a string of nested IIF functions in an update query. It would look like the following:

```
IIF([Incurred]>=1 and ([Incurred]<=500,[Level]=1,IIF([Incurred]>=501 and
[Incurred]<=1000,[Level]=501,IIF([Incurred]>=1001 and [Incurred]<=5000,
➥[Level]=1001,IIF([Incurred]>=5001 and [Incurred]<=10001,[Level]=5001,
➥IIF([Incurred]>=10001 and [Incurred]<=25000,[Level]=10001,
➥IIF(Incurred]>=25001 and [Incurred]<=50000,[Level]=25001,
➥IIF([Incurred]>50000,[Level]=50001
```

This solution has several problems. First of all, it is tedious to write and difficult to maintain. Suppose you want to change the levels? The second problem is the following: What would you do if you had 40 levels? You can imagine how long the string of IIFs would be. The third problem is that you are not performing any aggregate functions. You are simply indicating which level each record is in. You would have to come back and "group" the levels while totaling and counting the financial information. There are times when functions are invaluable when working with queries, but this isn't one of them.

Fortunately, there is a better solution. You can create a small table that functions as an example on which you can base your query. Let's explore this easy technique by example.

First of all, you need to build a small table that has two fields, Low and High. Low represents the minimum number for each level, whereas High represents the maximum number for each level. This makes a great basis for a Between...And range in a query. You end up with a table similar to Table 16.2.

Table 16.2: Strata Table

Low	High
1	501
501	1000
1001	5000
5001	10000
10001	25000
25001	50000
50001	100000
100001	250000
250001	500000
500001	1000000

Table 16.2 is in your Claims database, along with a table containing claim values called StratLosses. The following steps unveil this technique:

1. Open the Claims database from your AccessByExample folder.

2. Under Objects, click on Queries to view the stored queries.

3. Double-click Create Query in Design View to open the Show Table dialog box. When the Show Table dialog box appears, double-click the Strata and StratLosses tables, and click Close.

4. In the query design, double-click the Low field from the Strata table, and double-click the Incurred field from the StratLosses table *three times* to bring three instances of the Incurred field to the Query grid.

5. Click the Totals button (the Greek sigma sign) to perform aggregate functions. You should see Group By operators on each field.

6. Change the Group By in the first Incurred total row to Where; change the Group By in the second Incurred total row to Count; change the Group By in the third Incurred total row to Sum.

7. In the Incurred column with the Where operator, enter Between [low] and [high], as shown in Figure 16.1.

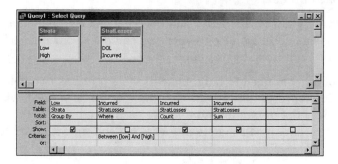

Figure 16.1: *The query by table example design uses relationships without join lines.*

8. Click the Run button to run the query. You should see a screen similar to Figure 16.2. Notice that the Count and Sum numbers are in "buckets" corresponding to the strata numbers. For example, you can tell at a glance that 236 losses occurred between 501 and 1000. You can format the output simply by selecting and right-clicking the appropriate field in Design view and then using the format box.

Low	CountOfIncurred	SumOfIncurred
1	1,206	248,012
501	236	156,005
1001	269	671,795
5001	116	852,609
10001	129	2,094,950
25001	65	2,272,332
50001	34	2,429,847
100001	23	3,440,358
250001	7	2,678,943

Record: 9 of 9

Figure 16.2: *Every level of strata is neatly grouped in the query by table example results.*

9. Close and save the Query as Stratify.

This query works because the Group By operator and Where clause work together. This can be understood better by examining the SQL code behind the design. If the query examined a record that represented a $100 claim, it would first put it in the 1 group because the Where clause points to a range in the same level. The 1 group represents the 1 to 500 range. Thus, the following

```
WHERE StratLosses.Incurred Between [low] And [high]
GROUP BY Strata.Low
```

becomes

```
WHERE 100 Between 1 And 500
GROUP BY 1
```

for that record.

So, where are the limitations of queries? Suppose you take the first approach, and you want to set up an update query that fills a blank field named Level with the proper level designation. Examine Table 16.3, which emulates an Update query grid.

Table 16.3: There Must Be a Better Way than This Query

Update Query Revealing Limitation

Field:	Incurred	Level
Table:	StratLosses	StratLosses
Update To:		1–500
Criteria:	Between 1 and 500	
Or:		

This query works fine for one level, but what if you want more than one? You can't use an Or operator because there is no way to synchronize the if with the then in the added condition. Imagine "Between 501 and 1000" in the Or: row. Where are you going to place the then for this condition? You can't place it in the Update To: row for the Level field. You have already examined why multiple IIF functions would not be advisable. The good news is that the limitation can be overcome with a little innovation.

Just when you thought you had the problem licked, your boss opens up another can of worms. He asks you to group all the claims by policy year. Because the policy year is June 1 through May 31, you can't use the year grouping option in a report to get the report that he wants.

The query by table example can come to the rescue again. All you have to do is add two fields (one from another table) to your original query. Follow these steps to add the fields:

1. From the Claims database, open your Stratify query in Design view.

2. Click the Show Tables button (yellow cross), and double-click the Period table. Click Close to close the Show Table dialog box.

3. Double-click the Date1 field from the Period table and the DOL (Date of Loss) field from the StratLosses table. (Move both fields to the left-most position to sort correctly.)

4. Change the DOL field to a Where clause, and type Between [Date1] and [Date2] in the Criteria row of that field, as shown in Figure 16.3.

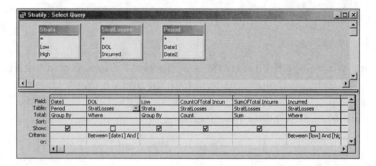

Figure 16.3: *You can add a date grouping in your query by table example to group by nonstandard time spans, such as policy periods.*

5. Run the query. Your query should look like that shown in Figure 16.4.

Date1	Low	CountOfTotal In	SumOfTotal Incl
6/1/1994	1	105	18209.49
6/1/1994	501	13	9287.71
6/1/1994	1001	21	50432.88
6/1/1994	5001	12	90747.35
6/1/1994	10001	13	235953.64
6/1/1994	25001	13	429650.34
6/1/1994	50001	4	311415.98
6/1/1994	100001	6	875436.17
6/1/1994	250001	2	689730.96
6/1/1995	1	225	43899.01
6/1/1995	501	36	24318.79
6/1/1995	1001	42	109616.53
6/1/1995	5001	13	91372.23
6/1/1995	10001	26	447603.18
6/1/1995	25001	11	381248.97
6/1/1995	50001	9	645675.33
6/1/1995	100001	7	1160058.17
6/1/1995	250001	2	770687.39
6/1/1996	1	218	42926.4
6/1/1996	501	25	17335.41
6/1/1996	1001	46	118733.94
6/1/1996	5001	17	116120.04
6/1/1996	10001	19	279752.86

Record: 1 of 52

Figure 16.4: *Notice the groupings for each policy year in the query by table example results.*

6. Close and save the query.

Using Subqueries to Unleash the Power Of Queries

Why not expand your possibilities using subqueries? There are certain scenarios that adopt well to the IN usage of a subquery. If you want to check values against another table, a subquery can be your answer. Think of it as a lookup table. Consider the following SQL example that uses two tables to retrieve all the products that have been sold in quantities over 70:

```
SELECT Products.ProductName
FROM Products
WHERE Products.ProductID
In (SELECT ProductID FROM [Order Details] WHERE Quantity >=70);
```

If you choose Design view on this query, notice that the IN clause becomes the criterion for the ProductID field in the Products table. Along the same lines, you might want to see records from two related tables that don't match. For example, how many records in the Customers table have no matching records in the Invoices table? The following subquery uses the NOT operator to accomplish this:

```
SELECT *
FROM Customers
WHERE CustomerID
NOT IN (SELECT CustomerID
FROM Invoices);
```

You don't have to use two tables to create a useful subquery. Dividing the values comprising a total into percentages is a common request. The following subquery, which uses the Northwind database, handles this task effectively:

```
SELECT [Order Details].UnitPrice,
(SELECT sum(UnitPrice) FROM [Order Details]) AS SumPrice,
[UnitPrice]/[SumPrice] AS [Percent]
FROM [Order Details];
```

Look at this subquery carefully. Notice that it works only with one field in the base table, which is UnitPrice. Yet it creates two fields (SumPrice and Percent) and outputs three fields (UnitPrice, SumPrice, and Percent). The nested Select statement is used as a calculated field and then applied in the division to calculate the percentage. Figure 16.5 shows the Design view of this subquery, whereas Figure 16.6 shows its Datasheet view.

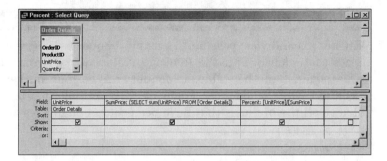

Figure 16.5: *You can create a subquery that becomes a field on which you can calculate.*

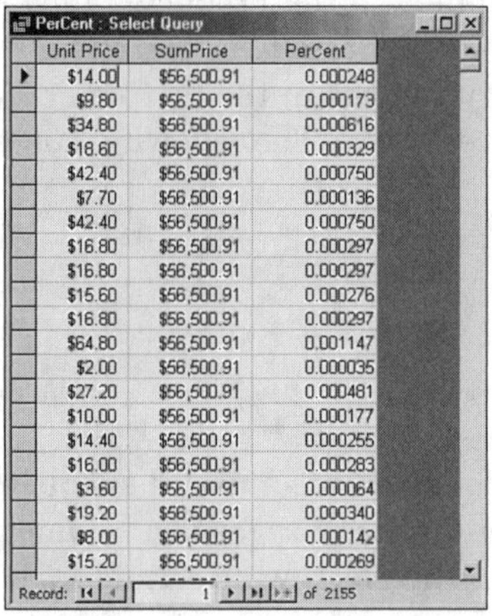

Figure 16.6: *The* SumPrice *field is a total of all the Unit Price values that are used to calculate a percentage.*

Instead of using a subquery as if it were a field, as demonstrated in the last example, you can use the subquery as an element in the WHERE clause (in a little different manner from the WHERE clauses in the first two examples). Notice the next example, which also uses only one table:

```
SELECT [Order Details].UnitPrice
FROM [Order Details]
WHERE UnitPrice>(SELECT Avg(UnitPrice) from [Order Details])
```

This query finds the records in the Order Details table that have a price greater than the average price. It's hard to believe that you can do so much with one table and one field.

There is yet another obstacle to overcome. If you want to delete records in one table based on criteria in another related table, you run into a problem if you try to join the two tables together, select criteria from both tables, and perform the delete. The subquery approach can come to the rescue again. The following query can work without an error message:

```
DELETE Connect.*, Connect.Company, Connect.ID
From Connect
WHERE Company = "Big Heart HMO" AND Connect.ID IN
(SELECT ID from Insureds where Connect.ID=Insureds.ID and Type = "Resident")
```

Using Functions with Queries, Revisited

Sometimes, obstacles are thrown at you for which you are not prepared. Suppose that a client sent you a list of names that was input by two temps. The first temp liked to type everything in uppercase. The second temp typed everything in a combination of upper- and lowercase. After sorting and adding your own primary key, the records were shuffled like a deck of cards. Your boss wants you to find all the records that are uppercase and change them so that the first letter is uppercase and all subsequent letters are lowercase. The following function is Boolean. As you already discovered, the Boolean data type is either true or false.

```
Function ChkUpper(strField As String) As Boolean
Dim i As Integer, chk As String

For i = 1 To Len(strField)
chk = Mid(strField, i, 1)
    If Asc(chk) >= 32 And Asc(chk) < 97 Then
        ChkUpper = True
    Else
        ChkUpper = False
        Exit For
    End If
Next i

End Function
```

If this function finds even one character that is not in uppercase, it exits and returns false. Notice that the If statement uses the ASC built-in function to check for uppercase. Every ASCII character is represented by a number. While in Access, press Ctrl+G to open the immediate window. In the window, type the following:

```
? ASC("A")
```

You should return 65. Now type the following:

```
? ASC("a")
```

You should return 97. At this point, the obvious question should be, "Why not set the range to between 65 and 97?" The answer is very simple.

You have to include spaces, and the number for a space is 32. Another question is the following: "But how are you going to convert the uppercase records to an upper- and lowercase combination?" Do you remember the CapFirstLetter function from Chapter 10, "Using Procedures to Customize Your Database?" It works perfectly in this situation.

The solution is to create a update query that uses both functions. The Claims database has both functions. You can solve this dilemma by example by taking the following steps:

1. Open the Claims database. Under Tables, right-click Clients, and choose Copy.

2. Click the Paste button. Under Table Name, name it Insureds.

3. Double-click the Insureds table, and notice the mixture of records that are all uppercase and those that are not.

4. Click Queries under Objects.

5. Double-click Create Query in Design view to open the Show Table dialog box.

6. Double-click the Insureds table, and choose Close in the Show Table window.

7. Follow Figure 16.7 to set up a update query using both functions.

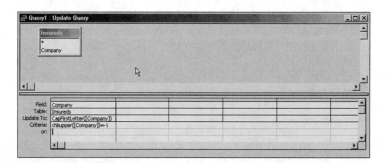

Figure 16.7: *Both the Criteria and the Update To rows use functions to change only the values that meet the criterion.*

8. Double-click Company to bring it to the grid.

9. In the Criteria: row of the Company field, type chkupper([Company])=-1. When you test for Boolean in a query, you must use −1 for true and 0 for false.

10. Click the query type button, and set the query type to Update.

11. In the Update To: section of the `Company` field, type
    `CapFirstLetter([Company])`.

12. Run the query, and click Yes to the warning message that tells you
    that you can't undo. You are only updating the records that are upper-
    case.

13. Close the query, and open the Insureds table to check the results
    shown in Figure 16.8.

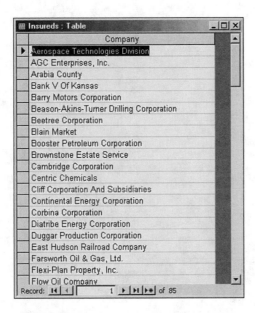

Figure 16.8: The results of the Update query.

Although the results are not perfect, this method is much easier than going
through each record manually. Acronyms are very difficult to determine
through code. How can a program tell whether AON is a company name
that is obtained from the Greek word for "age" or an acronym?
Nevertheless, there is much that a function can do.

What's Next?

In the next chapter, you will continue to look at programming obstacles,
such as slow performance, while getting a firmer grasp on even more query
topics so that you will know which tool to use for a given situation.

17

Getting the Most from Your Queries

In the last chapter, you learned how to overcome limitations of queries. This chapter explores ways to make queries faster and more efficient. You also explore SQL-specific queries. In particular, you learn the following:

- how to optimize your queries
- how compacting optimizes your database
- how indexing speeds up queries
- how to avoid aggregate functions
- how to include only fields that are needed
- why using smaller data types helps optimization
- why using outer joins sparingly helps optimization

Making Your Database More Efficient

A great way to win a client's confidence is to show him or her how to make their application faster or more efficient. As previously mentioned, just because a user has a fast system, it doesn't mean they are getting the optimal performance out of that system. A slow application can discourage users so they start looking for other solutions. Because queries usually are the most common operations in a database, you should be assured that they are fully optimized.

Query Optimization

The Microsoft Jet database engine has a built-in query optimizer that uses statistics to determine which query strategy to use. For this reason, you should open, resave, and run your queries to recompile them if you add a significant number of records to your database—especially if the records are added to the table on which a query is based. You also should recompile them in the event of an index change.

Unfortunately, you can neither view Jet database engine optimization schemes nor specify how you want to optimize a query. However, you can use the Database Documenter to find out whether indexes are present and how unique an index is. Simply choose Tools, Analyze, Performance from the Access toolbar. Because the query performance analysis is closely tied to the Jet database engine, the Performance Analyzer suggests adding indexes only when they actually will be used by the Jet database engine to optimize the query.

Compact Your Access Database

Frequent compacting has many performance benefits. The Microsoft Jet database engine, which uses a cost-based method of optimization, determines the least-expensive list of tasks to perform to generate the intended results. As your database grows, the optimization scheme might no longer be efficient because the statistics have changed and need to be updated. Compacting the database updates the database statistics and reoptimizes all queries.

Also, as your database grows, it will become fragmented. Compacting writes all the data in a table into contiguous pages on the hard disk, improving performance of sequential scans. You also can defragment your hard disk if this is needed.

Index Your Access Fields

Index fields on both sides of a query join or create a relationship between the fields. Jet creates indexes on fields that you join in the relationships window if they are not already there. This can speed query execution by allowing the query optimizer to use a more sophisticated internal join strategy. Try to use primary keys as opposed to unique indexes as much as possible. Additionally, if you index the fields that need to be sorted often, you can maximize query performance.

Avoid Using Domain Aggregate Functions with Queries

Not all criteria expressions are optimizable. Avoid using domain aggregate functions—such as DLookup, Dsum, and Dcount—to access data from a table that's not in the query. Domain aggregate functions are specific to Microsoft Access, which means that the Microsoft Jet database engine can't optimize queries that use them. As an alternative, create a subquery or add the table to the query that the function was accessing.

Use Only Fields that Are Needed

When creating a query, return only the fields that you need. If a field doesn't have to be in the query, don't add it. This ensures optimal speed for your queries, especially when the query is based on a large table. Also, in fields that you use to set criteria, click to clear the Show check box if you don't want to display those fields.

Use Smallest Data Type Necessary for Fields

When defining a field in a table, select the smallest data type that is appropriate for the data anticipated in the field. For example, if you don't need more than 255 characters, don't use a memo field. If you don't need decimals, and the numbers are not anticipated to be huge, use long integers. Also, format fields that you plan to use in joins with the same or compatible data types.

Use Outer Joins Sparingly, If Possible

An outer join requires a complete scan of the left side of the relationship. Therefore, for optimal performance, use them only when absolutely necessary.

Convert to Access 2002 File Format

Using the new optional Access file format, you can enjoy faster access and data processing for large databases. Other advantages include provisions for unknown properties and objects that might exist in future Access versions, the capability to save an Access file as an MDE or ADE while in Access 2002, and improved storage format.

Convert Your Application to an MDE file

Be sure to keep another copy of the database, and weigh the pros and cons before choosing this option. Also, be sure to convert to an Access 2002 file format first. This is a good way to make your database more secure.

When you save your Microsoft Access database as an MDE file, all modules are compiled, all editable source code is removed, and the destination database is compacted. Although your code still runs, it cannot be viewed or modified. Otherwise, your database continues to function normally, which means that you can still update data and run reports. Considering the reduced size of the database due to the removal of the code, memory use is optimized—thus improving overall database performance.

If you want to be sure that nobody views your code, this might be an option for you. Just be aware that saving your Access database as an MDE file prevents the following actions:

- Viewing, modifying, or creating forms, reports, or modules in Design view

- Adding, deleting, or changing references to object libraries or databases

- Changing code (an MDE file contains no source code)

- Importing and exporting forms, reports, or modules (tables, queries, Data Access Pages, and macros can be imported from or exported to non-MDE databases)

Queries Versus Filters

To handle obstacles that occur from day to day, you must be able to know when to use the right tool. A *filter* is a criterion that is applied to current data to obtain a subset of records. You can look at a WHERE clause of a query as a filter. In Access, a filter is a tool that uses criteria to temporarily (unless you save the object you have open) obtain a subset of records that you can view or edit. You apply the filter when the table or form is open. In a query, you apply the filter to the results of the query in Datasheet view.

There are places in Access where the lines between a filter and a query blur. However, it is usually a matter of terminology more than a matter of function. For example, when you use the OpenForm action in a macro, you can fill the Filter box with a query or a filter that is saved as a query. Although both filters and queries can retrieve a subset of data based on criteria, there are some distinct differences. You use filters in the following situations:

- You want a "one-click" (Filter By Selection) method of viewing a subset of records.

- You want a "one-click" method of obtaining a subset of records to edit.

- You want a "one-click" alternative to Find Next (Filter By Selection can use part of a field, and Filter By Form can use wildcards).

- You want a quick way to return a subset of records from only one table (there is a one-table limit with filters).

- You want a mechanism to create a *temporary* subset of records that you can quickly turn on and off. (Unless you save the table, query, or form with the filter applied, it is not available the next time you run the query or open the table or form.)

- You don't need to exclude any fields.

You use queries in the following situations:

- You want to retrieve a subset of records without opening one or more tables.

- You want to perform calculations on fields.

- You want to use functions on fields.

- You want to join two tables to retrieve records.

- You want to sort nonadjacent fields in different directions.

- You want to change table data quickly, with one operation. (You manually change data with a filter *after* the subset is obtained.)

- You want to execute any operation that an action query performs (append, update, delete, make-table).

- You want to exclude fields.

Although Filter By Form has more functionality than Filter By Selection, it still is a far cry from the functionality of a query. And although queries are much more powerful than filters, there are situations in which filters make a lot of sense. Some might argue that you can execute a query with one click, but that's only after you go through the effort of creating it. That's the whole point. You don't have to create anything with the Filter By Selection button. If you want to see all the Colorado records, just click the Filter By

Selection button when you are on a field with that value, and the filter is applied.

Suppose you want to look at anyone from your Customer list who has Sales in his or her title. You also might want to see anyone who was either an owner or manager. Take a closer look by following this example:

1. Open the Northwind database, and open the Customers table.

2. Tab to the Contact Title field, and then find a record in the same field that has Sales in the title, such as Sales Representative.

3. Double-click the word Sales to highlight it.

4. Click Filter By Selection. Notice that any record that starts with Sales in the Contact Title field is selected (see Figure 17.1).

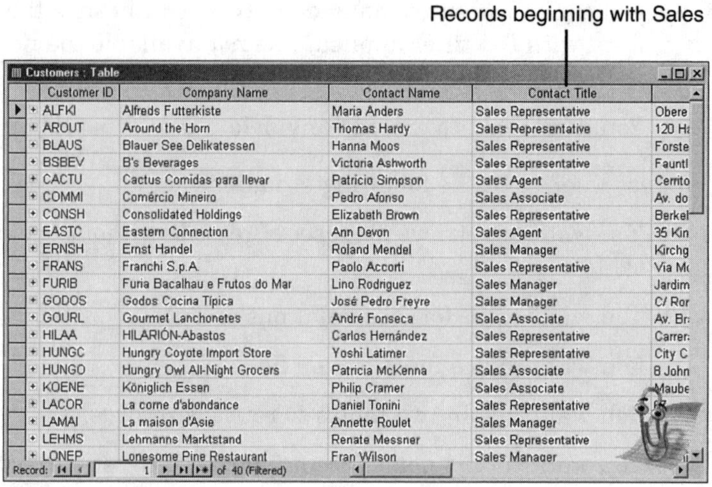

Records beginning with Sales

Figure 17.1: Selecting Sales in the Contact Title field using Filter By Selection retrieves records that begin with Sales.

5. Click the Remove Filter button.

6. To find owners and managers in the Contact Title field, click the Filter By Form button.

7. Click the drop-down box of the Contact Title field and choose Owner.

8. Click the Or box (lower left), and type *Manager in the Contact Title field.

9. From the toolbar, click the Apply Filter button, which looks like a funnel. You should retrieve either owners or managers.

10. Click the Remove Filter button, and then close the table without saving changes to the design of the table.

Special SQL Specific Queries

While you are in the Design view window of a query, you can click Query and then choose SQL Specific. You will notice three options: union, pass-through, and data definition.

These queries cannot be created in the QBE design window; neither can they be upsized. The pass-through query runs on a server, anyway. You can create these queries directly by choosing Create Query in Design view and then clicking Close when the Show Table dialog box appears. Next, click Query and SQL Specific from the menu. Then choose the query type of your choice to create the query.

Union Queries

`UNION` is not a SQL statement or clause, but an operator to combine two or more tables or queries using two or more `SELECT` statements. This type of query produces read-only (non-updatable) recordsets. Duplicate records are removed by default, unless you use the `ALL` keyword after the `UNION` operator.

Compatibility between `SELECT` statements means that they have the same number of columns in the same order. Although you would typically use the same field names and data types between `SELECT` statements, you can use a `Number` and a `Text` field as corresponding fields. The following `UNION` query (results shown in Figure 17.2) uses only two fields:

```
SELECT CompanyName, City, "Customers" as Relationship
FROM Suppliers
WHERE Country="Germany"
UNION SELECT CompanyName, City, "Suppliers"
FROM Customers
WHERE Country="Germany";
```

Customers and Suppliers By Country : Union Query

CompanyName	City	Relationship
Alfreds Futterkiste	Berlin	Suppliers
Blauer See Delikatessen	Mannheim	Suppliers
Die Wandernde Kuh	Stuttgart	Suppliers
Drachenblut Delikatessen	Aachen	Suppliers
Frankenversand	München	Suppliers
Heli Süßwaren GmbH & Co. KG	Berlin	Customers
Königlich Essen	Brandenburg	Suppliers
Lehmanns Marktstand	Frankfurt a.M.	Suppliers
Morgenstern Gesundkost	Leipzig	Suppliers
Nord-Ost-Fisch Handelsgesellschaft mbH	Cuxhaven	Customers
Ottilies Käseladen	Köln	Suppliers
Plutzer Lebensmittelgroßmärkte AG	Frankfurt	Customers
QUICK-Stop	Cunewalde	Suppliers
Toms Spezialitäten	Münster	Suppliers

Record: 1 of 14

***Figure 17.2:** The `UNION` query display the results of merging data from two tables.*

Notice that a field is created on the fly with the name Relationship. You also can use all fields from both tables, provided that they have the same number of fields in the same order. If the Customers and Suppliers tables in Northwind had the same number of fields (actually, they don't), you could write the UNION query as follows:

```
Select * from Customers
UNION
Select * from Suppliers;
```

If you try this query in Northwind, you get a message stating that the number of columns do not match. It works fine if you remove the hyperlink (last) field in the Suppliers table. (You can try it, but use a copy of the Suppliers table instead.) The Customer ID in the Customers table is a text field. The Supplier ID in the Suppliers table is an autonumber field. Yet they are blended in the resulting recordset. If field names don't match, the field name from the first table is used. So, the Customer ID field name is used in the resulting recordset.

How do you use a UNION query? You can use it to feed to a report if you need to see two tables merged together. You can use it as a test before appending two tables together. With the ALL keyword, you can quickly tell whether there are any duplicates. Of course, you also can use the Find Duplicates Wizard for that purpose. You can use it to find out how many customers and suppliers live in the same city, as you did with Northwind. Substitute to suit your need. How many clients and vendors live in the same city? Using your imagination, you can most likely come up with a few examples of your own.

Pass-Through Queries

An Access SQL pass-through query bypasses Microsoft Jet's query processor and sends a SQL statement directly to an ODBC (Open Database Connectivity) data source, such as SQL Server. You must use the appropriate SQL syntax required by the server that you are accessing. You can perform any action supported by that data source, including retrieving records, changing data, or even running a stored procedure or trigger on the server side. You may or may not return records, depending on the operation you want to perform. ADO always saves SQL pass-through queries in the Procedures collection, regardless of whether records are returned or not.

When you create the pass-through query, you normally supply a connection string in the ODBC Connect Str property of the query property sheet. Right-click the title bar of the pass-through query window to access the property sheet. If the string is omitted, you will be prompted for the string when you run the query.

There are two phases to creating a pass-through query. The first phase involves setting up a System DSN (Data Source Name). The second phase involves creating the pass-through query using the DSN that you created. The following steps guide you through the two phases of a pass-through query creation:

1. On the Windows Start menu, point to Settings, and then click Control Panel to open the Control Panel options.

2. Double-click the 32bit ODBC icon (Windows 95) or the ODBC icon (Windows NT). In Windows 2000 or Windows XP, double-click Administrative Tools, and then double-click Data Sources (ODBC). In Windows Millennium Edition, double-click ODBC Data Sources.

3. Click the System DSN tab to view system data sources.

4. Click the Add button to open page 1 of the Create New Data Source Wizard, and select a driver.

5. Select the driver you want to use. For example, select SQL Server. Click Finish to open page 2, as shown in Figure 17.3.

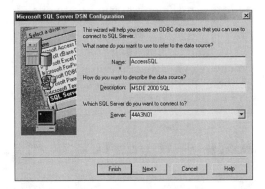

Figure 17.3: *You provide a name, description, and server for the DSN configuration.*

6. In the Data Source Name box, enter a meaningful name for your DSN in the Name box. You may also enter a Description to easily identify your DSN. In the Server box, enter a valid SQL Server name.

7. If you have MSDE 2000 installed on your local machine, you can enter the machine name here. Click Next to open page 3 of the wizard.

8. Select the appropriate logon settings for your machine. Although this page gives you a chance to use NT authentication, choose SQL Server authentication in this case, and click Next.

9. Select the default database to connect to; in this instance, select Northwind. Click Next, and then click Finish.

10. Test your connection by clicking the Test Data Source button, and click OK if the test connection succeeded.

To create a pass-through query, follow these steps:

1. In the Northwind Database window, click Queries under Objects, and click New on the Database window toolbar to open the New Query dialog box.

2. In the New Query dialog box, click Design View, and click OK to open the Show Table dialog box.

3. Without adding tables or queries, click Close in the Show Table dialog box.

4. On the Query menu, point to SQL Specific, and click Pass-Through.

5. On the toolbar, click Properties to display the query property sheet.

6. In the query property sheet, click in the ODBC Connect Str property. Click the Build button at the end of the line to open the Select Data Source dialog box.

7. Click Machine Data Source, and then select the Data Source you created in phase one. Click OK. The connection string will be entered automatically for you, as shown in Figure 17.4.

Connection string

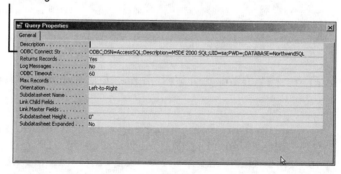

Figure 17.4: You can create the ODBC Connect Str manually, or use the Build button to supply the necessary string.

You also can manually set the ODBC Connect Str property to specify information on the database to which you want to connect. For details on the syntax for your query, see the documentation for the SQL database server to which you're sending the query.

8. In the SQL Pass-Through Query window, enter your pass-through query. For this example, enter the following:

```
"SELECT * FROM [Customers];"
```

NOTE

For information on creating more complex queries, consult SQL Server Books Online (BOL), which you can download from the Microsoft Web site www.microsoft.com/SQL/ techinfo/productdoc/2000/books.asp.

9. From the Query menu, select Run. You should return a result set from the Customers table in Northwind.

Data Definition Queries

You have already been introduced to data definition language (DDL) queries. Although you can do everything that they do manually and more, data definition queries provide a method of automation because they can be run from VBA. Suppose you receive a table from a client every month that must be altered each time you receive it. Let's assume that one of the fields is a text field that has to be used as a date. If the field is only six characters to accommodate dates such as 112289, you must increase the field size two characters to include slashes. This can be done automatically with the ALTER TABLE command. Then, you can add the slashes with a query and convert the text into a date field. This can be accomplished even if there is data in the table.

The following is an example of an ALTER TABLE command:

```
ALTER TABLE Customers
ALTER COLUMN City TEXT(20)
```

You also can create a table with a make-table query or in VBA through the CreateTableDef method. However, when you create a table using a data definition query, some properties can't be set, such as validation rules and nonunique indexes. Yet, it provides a fairly straightforward method to create a table. In contrast to a make-table query, you end up with a table structure with no data. There are times when this is desirable. Just keep in mind that you must conform to SQL data types when you create the query.

The following is an example of the CREATE TABLE command:

```
CREATE TABLE Customers
(CustomerID INTEGER CONSTRAINT PK_Customers, PRIMARY KEY,
LastName TEXT(50) NOT NULL,
FirstName TEXT(50) NOT NULL,
Phone TEXT(10))
```

Data definition queries support any of the following SQL statements:

- CREATE TABLE
- ALTER TABLE
- DROP TABLE
- CREATE INDEX
- DROP INDEX

What's Next

You have learned how to optimize your queries. You should now have a better understanding of query and filter differences. Finally, you examined some special query types that can come in handy in certain development situations. In the next chapter, you will learn how to bring together and separate data by learning about concatenation and parsing. You also will learn how to import and export through code.

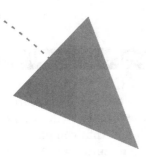

18

Working with Data from External Sources

In the last chapter, you learned how to optimize your database. This chapter brings together elements from other chapters in more ways than one. This means that you will be building on a foundation that was laid in previous chapters. You will see things that are familiar to you either as an expansion or as a different perspective of a previous topic. Seemingly unrelated pieces of information will come together to form a harmonious whole.

Various types of integration have been discussed and shown by example. This chapter delves a little deeper into the issue of how integration (through automating importing and exporting) can help overcome common development obstacles. In particular, you learn the following:

- how to automate importing and exporting
- how to implement error checking in the real world
- how to implement the File Dialog method
- how to handle scalability issues for databases
- the advantages of linked tables
- the advantages of the database splitter
- how to check links when a table opens using an Autoexec macro

Using Automation to Meet Performance Demands

Suppose your boss comes to you, complaining that your Access database is growing too large (some of the tables contain more than 30,000 records). Your company is considering purchasing SQL Server, but it will not happen for at least a year. The users are starting to complain that compacting takes too long, even on their fast machines. To make matters worse, they are beginning to notice degradation in query performance.

You have already implemented the performance tips presented in this book. Although these techniques improved performance, they are insufficient in light of the fact that the database is growing so rapidly. The users explained that, although many of the tables were old, they could possibly be needed from time to time.

The thought occurs to you that the only solution is to create an archive database in which the older tables can be stored. The users like the idea, but complain that exporting and importing the tables manually is too much of a hassle. Besides, the client's data is extremely time-critical.

It becomes clear to you that you must automate exporting and importing tables to and from an archive database. Because there are few graphics objects in the database, you conclude that the tables are consuming the most database space. But how can you make the application that you are about to create "user friendly?"

Suddenly, you remember the query technique presented in Chapter 12, "Access Visual Basic Tools, Tips, and Techniques," which enumerated all the tables in the database. That was fine for the current database, but what about the archive database? How do you query another database for tables from the current database?

Importing and Exporting Data

That is the scenario that you are supposedly facing. You can tackle the last problem first. First of all, your entire solution can be handled with one form. To query another database, consider the IN clause that you can either run from a RunSQL action or directly as a row source. Here is a typical SQL statement:

```
SELECT * from Customers;
```

To make the query run from another database, you simply add the IN clause with the database and path in quotes:

```
SELECT * from Customers IN "C:\AccessByExample\Northwind.mdb"
```

The following is another syntax that produces the same results:

```
SELECT * from [C:\AccessByExample\Northwind.mdb].Customers
```

Applying this to the subject at hand, the following SQL string is the row source for a list box for tables in another database:

```
SELECT MsysObjects.Name AS TableName
FROM [C:\AccessByExample\Archive].MsysObjects
WHERE (((MsysObjects.Name) Not Like "MS*") And ((MsysObjects.Type)=1) And
➥((Left([Name],1))<>"~"))
ORDER BY MsysObjects.Name;
```

Creating Table Names

Recall that the MsysObjects table is a hidden table containing names of various objects in the database. Querying this table can provide a dynamic representation of the tables in the database. If you produce a table of table names, you must constantly update the table each time a table is deleted, added, or renamed. A dynamic list is always current without having to access and refresh a static table for a list of table names. Generally speaking, the more dynamic you can make a form, the better. But this is not always possible.

The other thing you must do is create queues of table names that will be exported or imported. This is handled with two list boxes: one for exporting and one for importing. Because the row source for these tables is created dynamically through code, they are only temporary, which is suitable for your purposes.

Automating the Import/Export Process

In this chapter, you build on the enumeration techniques that you have already learned. However, instead of just enumerating objects, you actually export and import them through code. Start with the TransferDatabase action of the DoCmd object. You can use the methods of the DoCmd object to run Microsoft Access actions (macro commands) from VBA.

If you choose any of the conversion actions, such as TransferDatabase, TransferSpreadsheet, TransferText, and Output To, you are well-advised to create a temporary macro that transfers an object and converts it to a module to examine the correct syntax. Be sure to test it before you convert the macro. The syntax for the TransferDatabase method of the DoCmd object is as follows:

```
DoCmd.TransferDatabase([transfer type],[database type],[database name],_
[object type],[source],[destination],[structure only],[store login]
```

A typical example of a `TransferDatabase` method looks something like this:

```
DoCmd.TransferDatabase acExport, "Microsoft Access",
➥"C:\AccessByExample\Archive.mdb", acTable, _
"Customers", "Customers", False
```

Notice that `"Customers"` is both the source and destination table name. This means that the table will be called `"Customers"` in the destination database, which is a Microsoft Access database (because that's what is specified in the `"database type"` argument) in a different folder. Your only choices for `"transfer type"` are `acImport`, `acExport`, and `acLink`. The object type in the example is `acTable`, and the database name includes the folder with filename and extension (mdb).

Create a subfolder called `AccessByExample`, in which you can copy the Archive database (which contains only two tables) from your download. There are two ways to transfer the tables, whether you export or import. You can choose to copy or move the tables to their destination. Because the move involves a deletion of the source table, a warning message appears, so you can cancel.

Before you look at the form, you are introduced to a new object variable (at least to you) called the `ListBox` object variable. Suppose the name of the list box was ExportList. You can assign a list box variable to the list box this way:

```
Dim Exports as ListBox
Set Exports = Me.ExportList
With Exports
        RowSource = Table1;Table2;Table3
End With
```

This code assumes that the `Row Source Type` property was set to `Value List`. You are now ready to examine the following "by example" application that you can use and modify:

1. Open the ExportImport database from the `AccessByExample` folder. (Be sure you have the Archive table copied to the `AccessByExample` folder.)

2. Under Forms, double-click on ExportImport to open the form shown in Figure 18.1.

3. Notice the screen in Figure 18.1. Click on Customers and Order Details, and then double-click Orders. Notice that the three tables are transferred to the Export list box on the right, as shown in Figure 18.2.

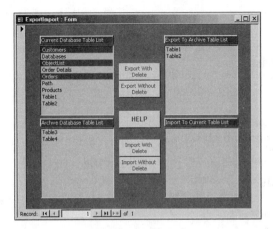

Figure 18.1: *The ExportImport form shows how to use a pick list as a tool to export and import tables.*

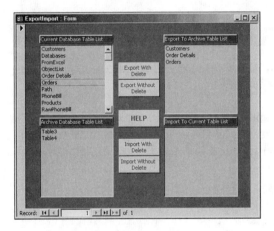

Figure 18.2: *Three tables are transferred to the list box on the right when you double-click.*

4. Click Table1, and then double-click Table2.

   Notice that the previous entries in the right text box are replaced by the new entries. That's why there is no need for a Clear button if a mistake is made.

5. Click the Export with Delete button. Before clicking Yes, notice that the file has been copied in the lower-left (Archive) list box. Click Yes on both messages (one message per table deleted) to delete the two tables after they are copied. Think of the Export with Delete option as a move operation.

NOTE

Table1 through Table4 are empty dummy tables that you can play with. If you receive an error message, you probably have the Archive database in the wrong directory. Remember that the Archive database must be in the `AccessByExample` subfolder on the C drive.

---

6. Reverse the last action by choosing Import with Delete and then clicking Yes to import both tables.

7. Click the Help button in the middle of the form, and read the message shown in Figure 18.3 that explains how to import and export tables. Notice the way in which the text is neatly wrapped. Each line is 70 characters or fewer.

Figure 18.3: *The ExportImport Help message tells the user how to export or import tables.*

The following `WrapString` function uses two arguments. The first argument is the string to wrap, and the second argument is the maximum length of each line to be wrapped. When used in conjunction with the `MsgBox` function, as the Help button demonstrates, it wraps a long message (such as a help message) very nicely. It builds on the technique used in the `CountWord` function from Chapter 10, "Using Procedures to Customize Your Database."

```
Function WrapString(sFullStr As String, iWid As Integer)
Dim sAddWord As String, sNewVal As String
Dim sFrag As String, iNewStrLen As Integer
Dim sBuild As String, sRemnant As String

sRemnant = sFullStr 'only first iteration begins with full string
Do Until Len(sRemnant) < iWid 'exit loop when left over string is less
➥than iWidth
    sBuild = Left(sRemnant, iWid) 'take each line according to specified iWidth
        Do Until Left(sBuild, InStr(sBuild, " ")) = "" 'Build line
            sAddWord = Left(sBuild, InStr(sBuild, " ")) 'get word
            sBuild = Right(sBuild, Len(sBuild) - Len(sAddWord)) 'subtract word
            sFrag = sFrag & sAddWord 'add word to new string
        Loop
    iNewStrLen = iNewStrLen + Len(sFrag) 'calculate length of new string
```

```
    sRemnant = Right(sFullStr, Len(sFullStr) - iNewStrLen) 'adjust left
    ↪over string
    sFrag = RTrim(sFrag) 'get rid of trailer space
    sNewVal = sNewVal & sFrag & vbCrLf 'sBuild line by line word wrap
    sFrag = "" 'initialize sFragment variable to use again
Loop
WrapString = sNewVal & sRemnant ' Add last piece with no carriage return
End Function
```

The following code shows the code behind the Help button:

```
Dim WrapText As String
WrapText = "Just click on the tables that you want to export " _
& "or import and then double click to bring them to the export " _
& "or import queue. The Archive database is another database " _
& "that is reserved for old data. If you need a table from it, " _
& "just import it. You can delete the table to simulate a move " _
& "after it has been safely copied. Deletions will always have a " _
& "warning message so that you can cancel the operation."
MsgBox WrapString(WrapText, 70), , "ExportImport Help"
```

If this were a "real-life" situation, you would want to compact the database immediately after deleting the files that were exported to recover the space. For example, if you export by moving two tables that are both 30,000 records, you will see a major difference in the file size of the Access database (mdb) file after compacting when you look at it in Windows Explorer.

Take a look at the code behind the scenes that makes the transfer process possible. If you right-click the list box labeled Current Database Table List, choose Properties, and select the On Dbl Click event, you see the following VBA code:

```
Dim frm As Form, CurrentList As ListBox, ExportList As ListBox
Dim strChoice As Variant, fillCtl As String

Set CurrentList = Me.Current
Set ExportList = Me.Export
    For Each strChoice In CurrentList.ItemsSelected 'loop through list
        fillCtl = fillCtl & CurrentList.ItemData(strChoice) & ";"
        CurrentList.Selected(strChoice) = False 'turn off selections
    Next strChoice
ExportList.RowSource = fillCtl
```

First, the program loops through the selections using the ItemsSelected property, which is a collection. Notice that strChoice must be a variant. The variable fillCtl is simply a string that is built incrementally. A semicolon is used as a delimiter (separator) between selections to fill the Row Source property of the Export list box on the upper right.

✔ If you need a refresher on collections, refer to "The Database Object" section in Chapter 12.

After the tables have been selected and transferred to the right list box, they are either imported or exported and deleted if the delete option is selected. If you choose the Export with Delete option for importing or exporting tables that are selected, the data definition DROP TABLE query is used to delete each table. Because there is no warning with this query, you must supply it programmatically. You can use a message box to offer the user a choice for confirmation this way:

```
If MsgBox("The table has been successfully copied." & vbCr _
& "Do you want to delete " & strList & " in the Archive " _
& "database?", vbYesNo) = vbYes Then
cn.Execute "drop table " & strList
End If
```

However, because the import program accesses another database, you must have a mechanism to run the query from the ExportImport database. The good news is that the RunSQL method supports Data Definition Language (DDL) queries. The bad news is that, because there is no IN clause for the DROP TABLE query, there is no way to reference another database using this approach.

So what is the solution? ADO is your answer. Simply set a connection to the Archive database, and use the Execute method of the connection object to run the data definition query. You don't need to use a recordset because you are not opening tables or queries. Notice the following code, which is attached to the command button labeled Import with Delete:

```
Dim strList As String, i As Integer
Dim LC As Integer, ImportList As ListBox
Dim cn As ADODB.Connection
'The list in the "Export" listbox is temporary
Set cn = New ADODB.Connection

cn.ConnectionString = "Provider=Microsoft.Jet.OLEDB.4.0;" _
& "Data Source=C:\AccessByExample\Archive.mdb;"
cn.Open
Set ImportList = Me.Import
LC = ImportList.ListCount - 1
    For i = 0 To LC 'i variable represents row data
        strList = ImportList.Column(0, i)
        DoCmd.TransferDatabase acImport, "Microsoft Access", _
        "c:\AccessByExample\Archive.mdb", acTable, strList, strList, False
    If MsgBox("The table has been successfully copied." & vbCr _
```

```
     & "Do you want to delete " & strList & " in the Archive " _
     & "database?", vbYesNo) = vbYes Then
     cn.Execute "drop table " & strList
     End If
     Next i Me.Refresh
```

The `ListCount` property contains the number of items in the value list for the list box. Because it is zero-based, you must count from 0 to `ListCount` - 1. To obtain the row (item) from the column property, you must give the column first, as `ImportList.Column(0, i)` demonstrates. Think of it as a spreadsheet, where 0 = A (first column), and the variable "i" = the consecutive rows (1, 2, 3, and so on). The `DoCmd` object is used to run the `TransferDatabase` macro action from a procedure. Access help says, "The `TransferDatabase` *method* carries out the `TransferDatabase` *action* in Visual Basic."

Notice the use of the `DROP TABLE` data definition query to delete the table. Concatenation, which is detailed in the next chapter, makes it possible to use a variable with the query. Because the `cn` object is pointing to the Archive database, the data definition query is executed on the proper table in that database, which is outside the current database.

✔ For more information about concatenation, see "The Art of Concatenation" in Chapter 19, "Bringing Together and Separating Data."

Export Dilemma

Your form for importing and exporting is a big success, yet the users are still complaining that they want to be able to export to file formats other than Access. Although you can import tables, queries, forms, reports, and other Access objects using File, Import, you can't export multiple objects using File, Export.

The only solution is to accomplish it through VBA. You need only one form with four list boxes. The top-left list box contains the objects to be exported. The top-right list box contains the file format options, such as Excel or HTML. The third text box contains the paths in which the export objects will reside. The fourth text box is visible only if you choose Microsoft Access as a file format. It contains the database name and path options for exporting. When you click on the desired object type, such as table, query, form, or report, the appropriate file formats automatically appear (see Figure 18.4) in the Export Types list box.

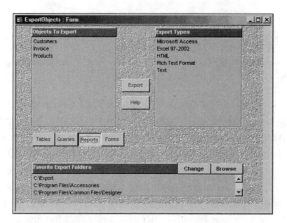

Figure 18.4: *The ExportObjects form shows how you can use a pick list to export various types of Access objects.*

By now, you might be wondering how this form works. After you run the form, you have a chance to see the code behind the form. First, create a folder on the C drive called C:\AccessByExample\Export. Then, follow these steps:

1. Under Forms, double-click ExportObjects to open the form. Click the Help button to get some instructions on how to use the form.

2. Click Tables in the option group of buttons that are side-by-side pointed out by the ControlTip text in Figure 18.5. Notice that both the Objects To Export and the Export Types list boxes are filled.

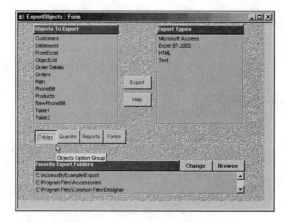

Figure 18.5: *The ControlTip text shows the option group that allows you to select the object type to export.*

3. Under Objects To Export, click on Customers to tag it for exporting.

4. Under Export Types, click on Excel 97-2002 to select this file type for the Customers table export.

5. Next to Favorite Export Folders, click Browse to open the Browse dialog box.

6. Choose C:\AccessByExample\Export, as shown in Figure 18.6, and click OK. (You should have already created this.)

Figure 18.6: *The* `FileDialog` *property of the Application object is used to produce the Browse dialog box in which a user can select a folder.*

7. After selecting the C:\AccessByExample\Export folder and making sure that the screen looks like Figure 18.7, which shows the options that should be selected, click Export. Customers, Excel 97-2002; C:\AccessByExample\Export should be selected.

8. Open Windows Explorer, open the C:\AccessByExample\Export folder, and double-click the Customers.xls file to open it. (If you don't have details activated in Windows Explorer, look for the Excel icon on the document provided by the latest Windows versions.) Notice that the file has been exported, and close the Excel file. Minimize Windows Explorer so that you can see your form again.

9. Click Table1, hold the Ctrl key down, and click Table2.

10. Under Export Types, click Microsoft Access. Notice that the Databases window activates.

11. Click Browse, choose the Archive and Claims databases, and click OK. You can choose more than one file when you browse because the `AllowMultiSelect` property is set to True.

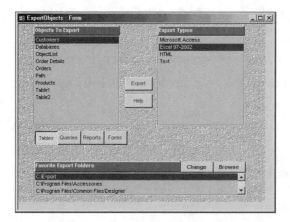

Figure 18.7: *You choose the object to export, the object type, and the folder in which you want the exported object to reside.*

> In contrast with the ExportImport form, you can export more than just tables with this form. Forms, reports, and queries can be exported to other Access databases as well.

12. Try browsing again while selecting the Archive database. You should receive an error message that tells you that you are trying to create a duplicate record.

Now you have a vehicle that your users can implement to export various types of objects. Not only can you use different types of objects, but you can export the object using various file types, such as Excel, HTML, or Rich Text Format (RTF). For example, if a client wants a disk copy of a report you created for them, you can export it in RTF and pull it into Microsoft Word.

Add Error Checking to Your Application

To try to make this application as error-resistant as possible, you try to anticipate the possible errors that could occur. What if the user decides to rename or move a directory that is marked as a favorite? In that event, the user can be prompted to enter another directory. What if the tables containing the objects or pathnames are deleted? You can begin by checking to see if the tables exist. If they don't, they can be created on the fly.

To get started, you can learn how to switch object types with the click of a button. Although you have been introduced to the option group, you have not yet learned to program it. There are four buttons on the option group `WhichObject`. The following code is tied to the `After Update` event of this control:

```
Dim ObjType As Long, TypeName As String
Select Case Me.WhichObject
    Case 1
    ObjType = 1
    TypeName = "Table"
    Case 2
    ObjType = 5
    TypeName = "Query"
    Case 3
    ObjType = -32764
    TypeName = "Report"
    Case 4
    ObjType = -32768
    TypeName = "Form"
End Select

SQLString = "SELECT MsysObjects.Name " _
& "FROM MsysObjects " _
& "WHERE (((MsysObjects.Name) " _
& "Not Like ""MS*"") And ((MsysObjects.Type)=" & ObjType & ") " _
& "And ((Left([Name],1))<>""~""));"

Me.Objects.RowSource = SQLString
Me.Types.RowSource = "SELECT FileType, Object " _
& "FROM ObjectList " _
& "WHERE ObjectList.Object =" & Chr$(34) _
& TypeName & Chr$(34) & ";"
Me.Refresh
```

NOTE

The option group can be created using a wizard. Just be sure the wand is selected before you click the option group tool. When you select the button option, such as a toggle button, the number of buttons you choose becomes a part of the option group.

The Select...Case statement uses the option group's value property to determine which button is clicked. If the first button is clicked, choose tables. If the second button is clicked, choose queries, and so on. The positive and negative values that are set for the various object types are obtained from the MsysObjects table. They are used for a dynamic query by concatenating the values to the SQL string. After the SQLString variable is evaluated to the string, it is assigned to the RowSource property of the Objects list box this way:

```
Me.Objects.RowSource = SQLString
```

After the Objects list box RowSource property is set, notice that the ObjectList table is queried. You can hide and unhide this table by right-clicking on it and choosing Properties. First, choose Tools, Options, View; then check both `Hidden` and `System` objects. Right-click the ObjectList table, and notice that the `Hidden` attribute is checked. If you don't want the user to see a table, you can hide the table to protect it. This table has a `FileType` and an `Object` field. These fields work together in the query. For example, the rich text format shows up only when you click Reports.

After the button is determined, two variables are set—one for the object name (`TypeName`) and one for the object type (`ObjType`). The row sources of two list boxes are then set dynamically with two queries; one for each list box. Because the `After Update` event is used, no default is used for the option group. For example, if the default were set to one, clicking on one would not fire the event because it is not an update. But because no default is set, clicking the first button causes the event to fire immediately.

The list boxes for paths and databases are not dynamic, but neither are favorites set in Windows. The users must remember to go back and change the path if they happen to rename or move a folder. If you try to add an entry that would create a duplicate, you receive a message. The following code, which is attached to the `On Click` event of the Browse button near the Paths list box, deals with the possibility of an attempt to add a duplicate:

```
Dim ItemPicked As Variant
Dim cn As ADODB.Connection
Dim rs As Recordset

'You must set a reference to the Microsoft Office 10.0 Object Library
Set cn = CurrentProject.Connection
Set rs = New ADODB.Recordset
rs.Open "Path", cn, adOpenKeyset, adLockOptimistic
With Application.FileDialog(msoFileDialogFolderPicker)
    If .Show Then
        On Error Resume Next
        For Each ItemPicked In .SelectedItems
            With rs
                .AddNew
                rs("PathName") = ItemPicked
                rs.Update
            End With
            If Err.Number = -2147217887 Then
            MsgBox "Error " & Str(Err.Number) & " was generated." _
            & vbCr & "You have attempted to create a duplicate " _
            & "record. Try another item." & vbCr _
            & "Source: " & Err.Source
            End If
            Next ItemPicked
```

```
    End If
End With
Me.Refresh
```

Using the File Dialog Method

In earlier versions of Microsoft Access, you could not display the File dialog box without either using an ActiveX control or making calls to the Windows API. Microsoft Access 2002 enables you to display the File dialog box used by Microsoft Access. Using the `FileDialog` method, you can determine what files were selected by the user. The `SelectedItems` collection of the `FileDialog` object contains the paths to the files selected by the user. By using a `For...Each` loop, you can enumerate this collection and display each file. Table 18.1 shows the four `DialogType` options that you can use with this object, along with a description of what each dialog type does.

Table 18.1: DialogType Options

Dialog Type	Type Function	Type Usage
`msoFileDialogOpen`	Open dialog box	Allows users to select one or more files (depending on whether `AllowMultiSelect` is set to `True`) that then can be opened in the host application using the `Execute` method.
`msoFileDialogSaveAs`	SaveAs dialog box	Allows users to select a single file that then can be "saved as" using the `Execute` method.
`msoFileDialogFilePicker`	File Picker dialog box	Allows users to select one or more files (depending on whether `AllowMultiSelect` is set to `True`). The file paths that the user selects are captured in the `FileDialog` `SelectedItems` collection.
`msoFileDialogFolderPicker`	Folder Picker dialog box	Allows users to select a path. (`AllowMultiSelect` does not work with this type.) The path that the user selects is captured in the `FileDialog` `SelectedItems` collection.

Remember to set a reference to the Microsoft Office 10.0 Object Library if you want to use this new feature. From a module window, select Tools, References, and scroll the list until you find the library. The `Show` method of the `FileDialog` object returns `True` if the users select one or more files. Because the procedure selects folders, multiple selections are not allowed. Therefore, the `SelectedItems` collection returns only one item.

The procedure for the Browse button near the Databases list box is a little more complicated, but not that difficult. It demonstrates how to use the AllowMultiSelect property to allow the user to select more than one file at a time. The following listing uses ADO to add the selections to the Databases table so the databases can be used again and again as if they are in the Favorites folder:

```
Dim ItemPicked As Variant
Dim cn As ADODB.Connection
Dim rs As Recordset
Dim dlg As Office.FileDialog

Set dlg = Application.FileDialog(msoFileDialogFilePicker)
Set cn = CurrentProject.Connection
Set rs = New ADODB.Recordset
rs.Open "Databases", cn, adOpenKeyset, adLockOptimistic
With dlg
    .AllowMultiSelect = True
    .Show
    .Title = "Please select one or more files"
    On Error Resume Next
        For Each ItemPicked In .SelectedItems
            With rs
                .AddNew
                rs("DbName") = ItemPicked
                rs.Update
            End With
        If Err.Number = -2147217887 Then
            ErrorHandle Err.Number, "You have attempted to " _
            & "create a duplicate record.", Err.Source, _
            "Try another database."
        End If
        Next ItemPicked
End With
Me.Refresh
```

As stated previously, the use of On Error Resume Next should be minimal. However, when you simply want to defer the error message instead of canceling it, you might consider using the Resume Next clause. When properly applied, the error message won't fire until you want it to fire. Multiple error messages are sometimes activated. As you test your procedure, you should comment out the On Error Resume Next statement by placing an apostrophe (') in front of the entire line. After you have read the messages that are generated, you determine what is relevant for your error message. This way, you can choose the message you want the user to see. After placing your error-handling routine in the procedure, simply delete the apostrophe in front of the On Error Resume Next line, and retest the procedure.

When an error occurs, the properties of the Err object are filled with information that uniquely identifies the error. You can use these properties to give the user information about what kind of error occurred and what to do about it. The ErrorHandle subprocedure simply uses the information that is fed to it to send a message to the use without returning a value, as the following listing shows:

```
Sub ErrorHandle(ErrNum As Double, Desc As String, _
Source As String, Solution As String)

MsgBox "Error Number: " & ErrNum & vbCr _
& "Description: " & Desc & vbCr _
& "Source: " & Source & vbCr _
& "Solution: " & Solution

End Sub
```

Scalability

Your boss comes to you a month later with a new problem. Network traffic is increasing because new employees have been hired to accommodate a new client. They, too, must have access to the database. Performance is again decreasing, but for a different reason this time. You have a brainstorming session with other computer professionals, and decide to split the database into two databases: one for the tables and the other for the forms, reports, macros, modules, and other objects.

If this scenario happened in the real world, you would have several options open to you, which would include the following:

- Splitting the database into two databases, as suggested in the scenario.

- Using an Access project.

- Turning your database into an *intranet* application by using a Web server that employees can access with a login and password.

In the computer world, if something is said to be *scalable*, it is adaptable to increased size or growth. For example, if a font can be changed to a larger size, it is said to be scalable. Likewise, if a network or database system can accommodate growth related to factors such as increased file size or larger user numbers, it is said to be scalable. Therefore, the challenge presented in this scenario involves scalability.

Linked Tables

Because the second and third options have already been covered, go with the scenario and assume that you decided on the first option. The first thing that must be addressed is the following: How will you allow your users to access tables from another database as if they were in the local database? Assuming that the tables reside on the file server, you can link the tables to each user's local PC.

Some of the advantages of linked tables include the following:

- You do not increase the size of your database when you add new tables because the data resides somewhere else.

- You can work with tables from other applications, such as Excel, in your Access database without importing them.

Some of the disadvantages of linked tables are as follows:

- If external data is moved to another location, you must use the Linked Table Manager to refresh the links.

- You lose the ability to enforce referential integrity on relationships, unless the linked tables reside in an Access database.

- A linked table performs a little more slowly than a native Access table.

Database Splitter

A split database works well in a network (multiuser) environment. It consists of two database (mdb) files. One of these databases, which is referred to as the *back-end* database, contains only the tables and relationships. This database resides on a network file server. The other database, referred to as the *front-end* database, contains all the other database objects—such as queries, forms, reports, macros, and modules. This database is copied to each user's local computer.

The split database approach has the following advantages:

- Performance is improved because only the application portion of the database resides on the user's local hard disk. The tables reside on the file server.

- Network traffic is reduced because only the data travels over the network. The other objects in the database are local.

- You don't have to interrupt processing to update forms, reports, macros, or modules.

- Users can create their own custom objects, such as queries, forms, or reports, without affecting other users.

Database Splitter Wizard

After the database is split into two separate databases, the two databases perform as one through linked tables. Functionally, the linked tables perform as if they reside in the front-end database, although they are a little slower. Each client computer has its own personal copy of the front-end database that interacts with a single copy of the back-end database located on the file server.

The Database Splitter Wizard automates the splitting process by creating a back-end database and moving every table there. The table links that allow the two databases to communicate are automatically created. Don't worry if you have only one computer; you can still get a feel for how the process works.

Take the following steps to split your database using the wizard:

1. Choose File, Open from the menu bar, and select the AccessByExample folder. Make a copy of the convention database, and call it **Convention Front**.

   You also can right-click the Convention database to open the shortcut menu, and choose Copy, as shown in Figure 18.8. Right-click the large white area to the right of the convention database, and choose Paste. A file called Copy of Convention is created. Rename the copy **Convention Front**.

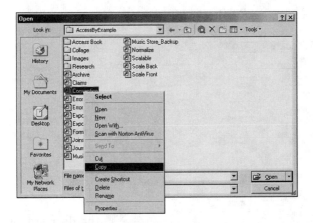

Figure 18.8: *You can copy, paste, delete, and rename databases from the Open dialog box.*

NOTE

You can make the AccessByExample folder the default folder by choosing Tools, Options, General, and setting the Default Database folder box to C:\AccessByExample. You also can increase the recently used file list number from the drop-down box there.

---

2. Double-click the Convention Front database to open it.

3. Choose Tools, Database Utilities, Database Splitter from the menu bar to open the Database Splitter Wizard shown in Figure 18.9.

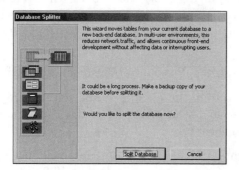

Figure 18.9: *The Database Splitter creates a back-end database containing only the tables to be linked to the front-end database.*

4. Click the Split Database button to open the Create Back-end Database dialog box, as shown in Figure 18.10.

Figure 18.10: *The Create Back-end Database dialog box enables you to name the back-end database and select a folder for the database.*

5. Click on Split to create the Convention Front_BE database (the "BE" suffix stands for back end). The following message appears: Database successfully split.

6. Notice the unique appearance of the tables shown in Figure 18.11 after splitting the database. The large black arrow next to the table name signifies a link.

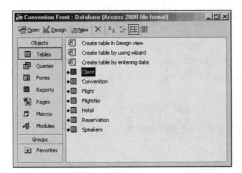

Figure 18.11: *The linked tables have a different appearance in the front-end database, signifying that they are linked.*

7. Open the Client table. Even if it resides in another database, it opens as if it resided in the Convention Front database. Close the table, but stay in the database.

Linked Table Manager

It is best not to move or rename tables or databases associated by linked tables unless absolutely necessary. If you do move or rename either the table or the database, you can use the Linked Table Manager to reestablish the links.

The next example walks you through implementing the Linked Table Manager:

1. In the database open from the last exercise, choose File, Open to display the Open dialog box.

2. Right-click the Convention Front_BE database, and then choose Rename. Change the name to **Convention Back**. Close the Open dialog box.

3. Open the Client table as before. The message shown in Figure 18.12 appears. Click OK.

Figure 18.12: *If a database is moved or renamed, a message informs you of the problem.*

4. Click Tools, Database Utilities, Linked Table Manager to open the Linked Table Manager.

5. Click Select All, as shown in Figure 18.13, and click OK to open the Select New Location of Client dialog box.

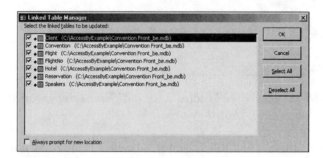

Figure 18.13: *You can select all the linked tables in the Linked Table Manager and refresh the links.*

6. When the Select New Location of Client dialog box appears, click Convention Back, and then click Open. A message tells you that all linked tables are successfully refreshed. Click Close.

7. Open the Client table again, and notice that the link is reestablished. Close the table.

Checking the Links

You can write a program to automatically check the links for you when the front-end file opens. A VBA link-checking procedure can be attached to an Autoexec macro so that the links are verified every time the database is opened. The following code contained in your Scale Front database checks links and sends the user messages, depending on the problem:

```
Function ChkLink()
Dim cn As ADODB.Connection
Dim cat As New ADOX.Catalog 'Must set ADO Ext. 2.5 for DDL
Dim tbl As Table, varTable As Variant, varItem As Variant
```

```
Dim sFolderFile As String, sMsg As String
Dim dlg As Office.FileDialog 'Must set Office 10.0 reference

On Error GoTo ReLink_err
Set cn = CurrentProject.Connection
Set cat.ActiveConnection = cn
    For Each tbl In cat.Tables
        If tbl.Type = "LINK" Then 'Eliminate every type except link
            varTable = tbl.Columns(0) 'Just testing the link
        End If
    Next
cn.Close
Set cn = Nothing
Set cat = Nothing
Exit Function

ReLink_err:
sMsg = "There is a problem with the linkage of the" _
& " table " & tbl.Name & ". Probable cause:  The back end" _
& " database may have been moved or renamed. Please enter" _
& " the name of the source path and database in the next" _
& " screen and an attempt will be made to relink. Otherwise" _
& " choose Cancel and click Tools, Database Utilities, Link" _
& " Table Manager."
If MsgBox(WrapString(sMsg, 52), vbOKCancel) = 1 Then
    With Application.FileDialog(msoFileDialogFilePicker)
        If .Show Then
            For Each varItem In .SelectedItems 'Choose database
                sFolderFile = varItem
            Next varItem
        End If
    End With
Else
    Exit Function
End If
Resume TestAgain:

TestAgain:
sMsg = tbl.Name & " does not exist in back end database." _
        & " Choose OK to open the Linked Table Manager or" _
        & " Cancel to cancel the procedure and find the table."
On Error Resume Next
cn.Execute "SELECT * FROM " & sFolderFile & "." & tbl.Name
If Err.Number = -2147217865 Then
    Select Case MsgBox(sMsg, vbOKCancel)
        Case 1 ' OK
```

```
                DoCmd.RunCommand acCmdLinkedTableManager
        Case 2 ' Cancel
            Exit Function
        Case Else
            Exit Function
    End Select
Else
    DoCmd.DeleteObject acTable, tbl.Name
    DoCmd.TransferDatabase acLink, "Microsoft Access", _
    sFolderFile, acTable, tbl.Name, tbl.Name, False
End If

End Function
```

You should be familiar with most of the coding techniques applied in the ChkLink function by now. The expression varTable = tbl.Columns(0) checks the links by trying to reference the first field in each linked table. If the table or database has been moved or renamed, the link fails, generating an error. The procedure actually checks the links twice. The first time, it checks to make sure the database file has not been moved or renamed, causing the table links to be invalid. The second time, it validates the table links using a query. You finally have an opportunity to run the Linked Table Manager with the action DoCmd.RunCommand acCmdLinkedTableManager. You can run commands from the menu bar this way.

Attaching Code to an Autoexec Macro

You can use the RunCode action from a macro to run a VBA procedure. If you want the procedure to run when the database opens, you must name the macro AutoExec. The following steps guide you through the process of attaching the ChkLink function to a macro:

1. Open the Scale Front database. Under Macros, click New to open a blank macro sheet.

2. Click the drop-down box in the first row of the Action column, and choose RunCode.

3. Press F6 to enter the Function Name box. Type **ChkLink()** in that box.

4. Click Save, and name the macro **Autoexec**. Close the macro.

5. Open the Check Link module to view the code you attached to the macro. If you want to test the procedure, rename Table3 to Table2, and reopen Scale Front. Close the module.

What's Next

This chapter focused on overcoming development obstacles through automation and ingenuity. The next chapter focuses on overcoming obstacles in real-world scenarios by bringing together and separating data. You learn how to problem solve using programming techniques.

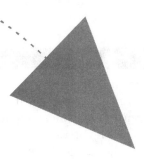

19

Bringing Together and Separating Data

In the last chapter, you learned how to work with data from external sources. This chapter builds on that theme by explaining what to do after you have obtained the data. It is highly likely that, at some point in your experience with Microsoft Access, you will need to obtain data from outside sources. Maybe your friend has an Excel file that he wants you to convert to Access. Or perhaps your company wants you to convert an ASCII (text) file obtained from a client's mainframe to Access. Whatever the situation, you need to understand how to bring together (concatenate) and separate (parse) data. The reason for this is that data obtained from outside sources is not always in the proper format. To be more specific, you learn the following:

- how to concatenate data

- how to parse data

- how to work through a real-world scenario in which you use concatenation and parsing to solve the problem

The Art of Concatenation

For example, it is not out of the ordinary to import a table with a date such as "111197." Assuming that the string has already been parsed out into month, day, and year components, how do you concatenate the string into a date with slashes added? Because it is all text, you can use the plus (+) operator (which works in almost any programming language) to concatenate like this:

"11" + "/" + "11" + "/" + "97"

If every record in the field containing this number has the slashes, you can convert the field to an Access date field. The plus operator behaves differently, depending on what type of data is being referenced. Table 19.1 reveals the different results obtained when working with variables in expressions using the plus operator.

Table 19.1: Different Results Using the Plus Operator

When	What Happens
Both variables are numeric data types (Byte, Boolean, Integer, Long, Single, Double, Date, Currency, or Decimal)	Add
Both variables are string	Concatenate
One variable is a numeric data type, and the other (representing a number) is any variant except null	Add
One variable is a numeric data type, and the other (representing a string) is any variant except null	Type mismatch error
One variable is a string, and the other is any variant (representing a string) except null	Concatenate
Either variable is an empty variant	Return the remaining expression unchanged as *result*
One variable is a numeric data type, and the other is a string	Type mismatch error
Either expression is null	Result is null

Although it is nice to know that you can use the plus operator for more than just adding numbers, there is a drawback to using it. Suppose that you forgot to enclose the last number in quotes in the previous example.

If you press Ctrl+G for the immediate window, type **? "11" + "/" + "11" + "/" + 97**, and then press Enter, you will receive a type mismatch error message. The reason for the error message is that the 97 did not have quotes. In other words, you cannot mix numbers with text using the plus operator. You can use a built-in Access function to mix data types like this:

> ? "11" + "/" + "11" + "/" + cstr(97)

The Cstr function converts the numeric value to a string. If you type **?** **"Today's date " + date**, you will receive another type mismatch error message. But if you type **? "Today's date: " + cstr(date)**, you will return today's date: 06/01/01 (substituting whatever the current date is).

The good news is that there is an easier method of bringing different data types together. This method has been used throughout this book. The ampersand operator converts nonstring data types to string data types when you concatenate. You can combine virtually any data type using this operator.

Concatenating Fields

Concatenation is often used for calculated fields, as the following SELECT statement demonstrates:

```
SELECT FirstName & " " & LastName AS [CustomerName] from Customers;
```

This example shows how you have to insert a space between the two fields being brought together. The AS operator is used to rename the field on the fly. The & operator comes in very handy when you want to use variables with SQL strings. Even table and field names can be represented by variables using this method. This means that if you want to run the same query on a different table with the same field names, you can do it using a variable for the table name. What's more, if you want to run the same query on a different table with different field names, you use variables for the field names as well.

Concatenating Variables

Consider the following listing, which uses a variable with ampersands to access the current certificate number:

```
Dim dCert As Double
dCert = Me.CertNo
DoCmd.RunSql "INSERT INTO Amend SELECT [Clients].* " _
& "FROM [Clients] WHERE [Clients].[CertNo] =" & dCert & ";"
```

This code first stores the current certificate number value from the underlying table in the dCert variable. Then it uses the variable as criterion for an append query. Because the CertNo field is unique, the program selects one record to append into the Amend table, thus providing a history of the amended certificates when they are modified. Notice that the ampersands are used to paste the elements of the string together. It doesn't matter that the dCert variable has a numeric (double) data type.

Using variables, you can even reference multiple occurrences of fields in a string using concatenation. For example, if you had an SQL string that referenced the same field three times (for count, sum, and average), you could search and replace every occurrence of the field with " **& FieldVar &** " (assuming you have declared the FieldVar variable). That way, you could run the same query on another field very easily. It is just as easy to reference a table as it is to reference a field name in an SQL string with a variable. There are some issues using quotes with variables in SQL strings, which will be addressed in the next chapter.

The Art of Parsing

Let's suppose that your boss comes to you with what he thinks is a wonderful idea. The phone company has sent him a disk containing the phone calls for the past month. They can provide this on a monthly basis. He wants you to transfer this list to an Access database so that he can tell who is making the longest calls. When you finally see the phone bill, it looks something like Table 19.2 (minus several thousand records).

Table 19.2: Raw Data Text File for the Phone Bill Table

2790017	9185436525	20001215 351NGTBixby	13538547	24	168
2790017	9184681269	20001129 824DAYBixby	10538547	18	180
2790017	9184681181	20001227 101NGTBixby	3538547	4	28
2790017	9185459191	20001227 102NGTBixby	2538547	2	14
2790017	9185448823	20001227 301NGTBixby	3538547	4	28
2790017	9185452929	20001230 550NGTBixby	8538730	14	98
2790017	9187274948	20001209 1522DAYBixby	15538547	26	260
2790017	9185455118	20001226 2020EVEBixby	2538547	3	24
2790017	9185442288	20001230 56NGTBixby	31538547	55	385

You don't say anything to your boss, but you think to yourself, "How am I going to straighten out this mess?" Through a call to the phone company, you obtain a document showing the field structure along with the beginning and ending character number for each field. When your boss returns, he acknowledges that some fields are not needed.

At this point, you started mulling over in your mind the tools that you have at your disposal. Although you could use the Text to Columns feature in Excel, it would be better to have a tool in Access that could be saved and used again and again. Your boss wants the whole thing automated from start to finish so it can be used every month. This is the scenario you are facing. Now what are you going to do?

Phase I

You can start by writing a program for importing a text file. The best way to accomplish this is to import manually first so that you can create a "specification" name for an import. Then apply the specification to your program. The specification is the table structure that allows Access to know what field names, data types, and field sizes the import table should have.

During your first manual import process, two Access system tables are created in the database to register the field attributes of the fields in the table. These tables contain your specification. All subsequent specifications are also registered in these tables. MSysIMEXColumns is created to record attributes such as field name, field width, and the starting position of each field. The second table, called MSysIMEXSpecs, contains the specification name and file type, among other things.

If you want to import these specifications into another database, simply check Hidden and System objects in Tools, Options, View before importing so that these two system tables can be viewed, selected, and imported. If you have three specifications in the two tables and need only two imported, you can easily delete the unwanted specification after it is imported. The following steps guide you through the manual import process:

1. Open the ExportImport database.

2. Select File, Get External Data, Import to open the Import dialog box shown in Figure 19.1.

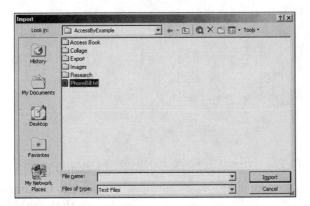

Figure 19.1: *Choose Text Files in the Files of type drop-down box in the Import dialog box.*

3. Select Text Files in the Files of Type drop-down box to set the file type for the import (refer to Figure 19.1).

4. From the AccessByExample folder, click PhoneBill.txt, and then click Import to open the Import Text Wizard shown in Figure 19.2.

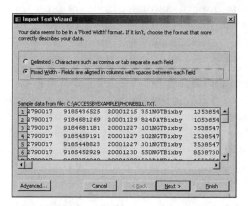

Figure 19.2: *The Import Text Wizard shows you sample data from the file you are importing.*

5. On the first screen, it should have Fixed Width selected. If not, select it, and click Next to open the next page of the wizard shown in Figure 19.3.

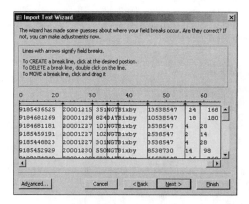

Figure 19.3: *The Import Text Wizard enables you to create templates that can be used over and over.*

6. On the ruler, click 30, 34, and 37 to section off various fields (refer to Figure 19.3); then click Advanced.

7. Place the nine field names and types shown in Table 19.3 and Figure 19.4 in the field information section.

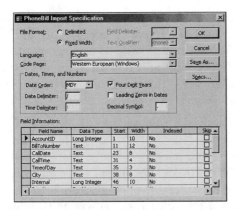

Figure 19.4: *The import specification registers field attributes for the table to be created.*

Table 19.3: Specifications for the Phone Bill Table

Field Name	Data Type	Start	Width	Indexed	Skip
AccountID	Long Integer	1	10	No	0
BillToNumber	Text	11	12	No	0
CallDate	Text	23	8	No	0
CallTime	Text	31	4	No	0
TimeofDay	Text	35	3	No	0
City	Text	38	8	No	0
Internal	Long Integer	46	10	No	0
Duration	Double	56	4	No	0
Cost	Double	60	5	No	0

8. Click Save As, as shown in Figure 19.5.

Figure 19.5: *The Save Import / Export Specification dialog box enables you to save specifications for fields that can be used later.*

9. Keep clicking Next without choosing any primary key. When you get to the Finish screen, click Advanced once more, save the specifications without the primary key, and click OK. Be sure the table name is PhoneBill, and click Finish to import the file. You receive a message informing you that the import was successful.

Now you have a table and an import specification that can be used in other databases. You can automate the import process using the `TransferText` method with the specification functioning as an argument so there's no hit-and-miss. In fact, the whole point of the manual import is to create a specification that can be reused when needed. In Phase II, you learn how to automate the process of importing text files.

Phase II

Although you have done some parsing already, there is more parsing to do—you'll do that in Phase III. In this phase, you concentrate on turning what you just did into a procedure. Working through the previous example accomplished two things. First, it acquainted you with manual importing of text files. Second, it taught you how to set up a specification format for the file, which you should now have in your database. Now you can focus on creating a transfer macro by taking the following steps:

1. Under Macros, click New to open the Macro window.

2. Under Action, choose TransferText from the drop-down box to activate the Action Arguments section for this action.

3. Select the TransferText options in Table 19.4, which coincide with Figure 19.6.

Table 19.4: Arguments for the Transfer Text Action

Transfer Type:	Import Fixed Width
Specification Name:	PhoneBill Import Specification
Table Name:	PhoneBill
File Name:	c:\AccessByExample\phonebill.txt
Has Field Names:	No

4. Save the macro as **Import Phone Bill**, and close the macro.

Now you have a macro that can be converted into a procedure, which serves as a foundation on which to build.

Phase III

This phase of working through the challenge uses queries heavily to both alter table structure and manipulate data. Before tackling the queries, you must convert the Import Phone Bill macro into a module by taking the following steps:

1. Under Macros, right-click Import Phone Bill, and choose Save As from the shortcut menu to open the Save As dialog box.

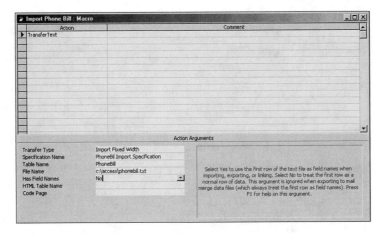

Figure 19.6: *Notice the PhoneBill Import Specification on the second line of the import macro.*

2. Click the As drop-down box, and then choose Module. Click OK to save the macro as Copy of Import Phone Bill, and open the Convert macro dialog box.

3. Click the Convert button when the Convert Macro dialog box appears. Leave both check boxes checked to add error checking and macro comments.

4. After clicking OK on the message that says the conversion is finished, you have access to the Module window.

CAUTION

Whenever you create a module from a macro, the first module in the module list opens. For example, if you create a module from scratch and give it a name that starts with an "a" (making it the first name on the list), this module will open instead of the module you create from a macro. Therefore, you must open the module just created from the Module window. If you don't see the Project-Export window on the left side of the module window, press Ctrl+R. You then can view the module in the Project-Export window and open the module.

---

5. In the Project-Export window, double-click Converted Macro—Import Phone Bill to maximize the Module window shown in Figure 19.7.

6. Insert an underline character after the space following the term `PhoneBill Import Specification,`. Be sure to include the comma. After the underline character, press Enter to make it look like Figure 19.7.

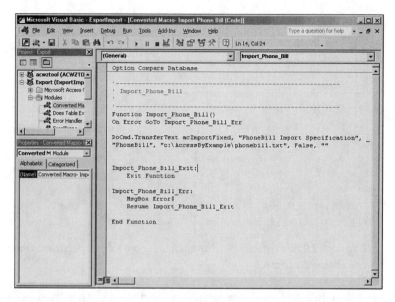

Figure 19.7: *The converted module has the proper arguments inserted in the* TransferText *method for you.*

NOTE

Inserting the underline character simply makes your code more readable. Always include a space before the underline character. Furthermore, be sure the underline character is the last character on the line. The compiler sees this as one long string as if it were still on the same line. However, now you have the string on two lines for better readability, and you don't have to scroll way over to read the entire string.

---

    7. Click the Save button to save the module, and leave the module open for the next exercise.

Although things seem to be going well at this point, there is a problem with two fields that must be addressed. If you go back and examine Table 19.3, you can observe the fact that the CallDate and CallTime fields are too small. CallDate has eight characters, and CallTime has four characters. To convert these fields to date/time data type, they need space to accommodate additional characters. For example, 12/12/2001 has 10 characters, counting the slashes. Likewise, 12:30 has five characters, counting the colon. You can't add the extra characters in the specification file because adding space in one field overlaps into the next. The only option is to change the field size of the table *after importing*, without destroying the data. That way, you have enough space to parse the fields and rebuild the string using concatenation to add the extra characters such as slashes.

The data definition query is just the tool you need to change the table structure for the two fields. Unfortunately, you can't change both fields in one query. The following two data definition queries add the extra characters in the proper fields:

```
ALTER TABLE PhoneBill
ALTER COLUMN CallDate TEXT(10)

ALTER TABLE PhoneBill
ALTER COLUMN CallTime TEXT(5)
```

To automate these queries, you need a mechanism to run them from VBA. As you previously discovered, you can run action queries and SQL-specific queries using the RunSQL method of the DoCmd object. Take the following steps to add the code:

1. In the Converted Macro—Import Phone Bill Module window left open from the last exercise, insert the following code after the two DoCmd.TransferText lines:

```
DoCmd.RunSQL "ALTER TABLE PhoneBill " _
& "ALTER COLUMN CallDate TEXT(10)" 'Expand field 2 characters
DoCmd.RunSQL "ALTER TABLE PhoneBill " _
& "ALTER COLUMN CallTime TEXT(5)" 'Expand field 1 character
```

2. Save and close the module.

The next step involves getting the fields prepared to be converted to a Date/Time data type. The following functions, which are provided in your ExportImport database, do just that:

```
Function MakeDate(strVar As String)
Dim sParse As String
'This function both breaks into pieces and brings together data

    sParse = Mid(strVar, 5, 2) & "/" & Right(strVar, 2) _
    & "/" & Left(strVar, 4)

MakeDate = sParse
End Function

Function MakeTime(strVar As String)
'This program concatenates and sParses
Dim sParse As String
strVar = LTrim(strVar)
    Select Case Len(strVar)
        Case 2
        sParse = "00:" & Right(strVar, 2)
        Case 3
```

```
            sParse = "0" & Left(strVar, 1) & ":" & Right(strVar, 2)
            Case 4
            sParse = Left(strVar, 2) & ":" & Right(strVar, 2)
    End Select
MakeTime = sParse
End Function
```

The first procedure breaks apart the string and reconstructs it using concatenation. For example, take the date 20001227. The first four characters (2000) represent the year. Therefore, you start with the 12 (in the fifth position representing December) after the year by using the Mid string function. Next, you grab the last two characters for the day. Then, you grab the first four-year characters for the year. Between each of these pieces of data, you need to add slashes. You end up with the following piece of code:

```
sParse = Mid(strVar, 5, 2) & "/" & Right(strVar, 2) _
& "/" & Left(strVar, 4)
```

The second procedure is a little more complicated. The arguments for the Left and Right string functions depend on the length of the string. Examine Table 19.2 again. The time values are based on military time. Therefore, 2020 (with a colon separating the 20s) represents 8:20 p.m. Access will take care of the conversion from military time to standard time for you when the field is converted to Date/Time. However, you must add the colon. If this is not done, the conversion fails.

If the size of the string is two characters, you must add two leading zeros followed by a colon. If the size of the string is three characters, you must add one leading zero, followed by the first character, followed by the colon and the last two characters, and so on. You end up with a Select...Case statement like the following:

```
Select Case Len(strVar)
        Case 2
        sParse = "00:" & Right(strVar, 2)
        Case 3
        sParse = "0" & Left(strVar, 1) & ":" & Right(strVar, 2)
        Case 4
        sParse = Left(strVar, 2) & ":" & Right(strVar, 2)
    End Select
```

You can combine the functions with one update query to rebuild the strings on the table. In the ExportImport database, there is a table named RawPhoneBill. The reason for the "raw" prefix is that the date data is unconverted from the import. Double-click the table shown in Figure 19.8.

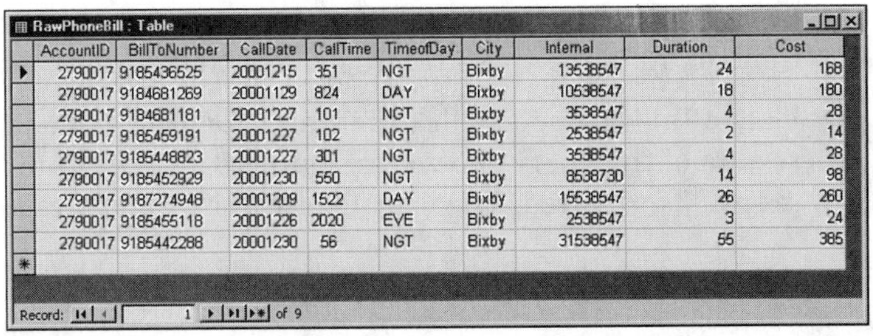

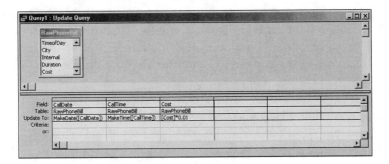

Figure 19.8: *The converted PhoneBill text file (now called RawPhoneBill) after import, but before conversion of date fields.*

To help you understand this part of the conversion process, test the query on a test table before including it in the code. The next steps will guide you through creating the update query:

1. Under Queries, click on Create Query in Design view to open the Show Table dialog box.

2. From the Show Table dialog box, double-click RawPhoneBill to add that table to the Query design, and then click Close.

3. From the RawPhoneBill table, double-click the CallDate, CallTime, and Cost fields.

4. Click the Query Type button drop-down box, and click Update Query.

5. In the UpdateTo: row of the CallDate field, type **MakeDate([CallDate])**.

6. In the UpdateTo: row of the CallTime field, type **MakeTime([CallTime])**.

7. In the UpdateTo: row of the Cost field, type **[Cost]*0.01**. You multiply times .01 to convert the field to dollars and cents. Your query should look like Figure 19.9.

Figure 19.9: *This update query uses functions to rebuild the data in the text fields to accommodate the date data type.*

8. Click the Run button to run the query. Click Yes when prompted to confirm updating these records. Close the query without saving.

9. Under Tables, double-click the RawPhoneBill table to check the results of the query shown in Figure 19.10. The date fields will be properly formatted. The Cost field will be in dollars and cents.

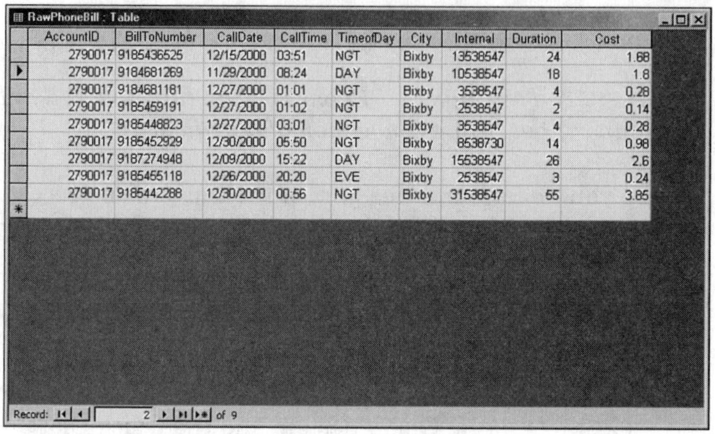

AccountID	BillToNumber	CallDate	CallTime	TimeofDay	City	Internal	Duration	Cost
2790017	9185436525	12/15/2000	03:51	NGT	Bixby	13538547	24	1.68
2790017	9184681269	11/29/2000	08:24	DAY	Bixby	10538547	18	1.8
2790017	9184681181	12/27/2000	01:01	NGT	Bixby	3538547	4	0.28
2790017	9185459191	12/27/2000	01:02	NGT	Bixby	2538547	2	0.14
2790017	9185448823	12/27/2000	03:01	NGT	Bixby	3538547	4	0.28
2790017	9185452929	12/30/2000	05:50	NGT	Bixby	8538730	14	0.98
2790017	9187274948	12/09/2000	15:22	DAY	Bixby	15538547	26	2.6
2790017	9185455118	12/26/2000	20:20	EVE	Bixby	2538547	3	0.24
2790017	9185442288	12/30/2000	00:56	NGT	Bixby	31538547	55	3.85

Figure 19.10: The results of the update query show the data properly formatted.

10. Under Modules, click the Converted Macro—Import Phone Bill, and click Design.

11. Add the following code after the last ALTER COLUMN line, which is the SQL equivalent of the query you created:

```
DoCmd.RunSQL "UPDATE PhoneBill SET PhoneBill.CallDate = " _
& "MakeDate([CallDate]), PhoneBill.CallTime = " _
& "MakeTime([CallTime]), PhoneBill.Cost = [Cost]*0.01;"
```

12. There is no sense in taking the conversion this far just to convert the two fields to Date/Time manually. This can be automated as well. Add the next two data definition queries just after the Update query to take care of the conversion from text to date on the two fields:

```
DoCmd.RunSQL "ALTER TABLE PhoneBill " _
& "ALTER COLUMN CallDate DATE" 'Change data type
DoCmd.RunSQL "ALTER TABLE PhoneBill " _
& "ALTER COLUMN CallTime DATE" 'Change data type
```

After entering the code, the Module should look like Figure 19.11.

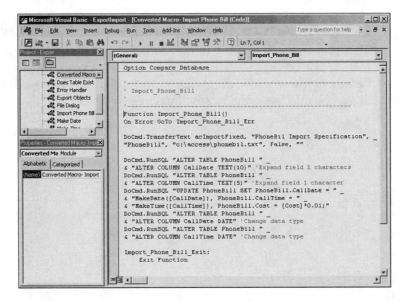

Figure 19.11: *The converted macro with the added lines of code for string rebuilding.*

You are now ready to test the entire procedure. Be sure that the Phonebill.txt file that you downloaded is in the c:\AccessByExample directory or that the program points to the directory in which this file resides. If everything works properly, the program takes the file from a raw text file to a properly formatted Access table.

NOTE

The beauty of this procedure is that it can be run month after month, or whenever your boss requests it. (That is, according to the imaginary scenario.)

Now that the procedure is created, take the following steps to test your code:

1. Choose Debug Compile from the menu to check the code.

2. Place your cursor anywhere on the line that the function is declared, and click the Run Sub/User Form, or press F5.

3. Save and close the module. Open the PhoneBill table to check the date fields.

The scenario that you just worked through is very much like a real-world project. In fact, it was adapted from a real-world project. It proves that you can automate almost any project that involves step-by-step procedures that are repeated from month to month.

What's Next

This project applied many of the skills that you learned in previous chapters. It proved that the best way to learn is by example. The next chapter details how to work with quotes, nulls, and dates. You learn how to conquer big problems that come in small packages.

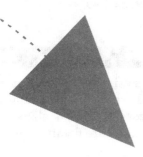

20

Conquering Big Problems that Come In Small Packages

In Chapter 19, you learned about parsing and concatenating data. This chapter deals with other potential pitfalls that a programmer might face that come in small packages. When you know what you are facing and how to face it ahead of time, you can't help but be a better programmer. That's the reason so much space has been devoted to overcoming obstacles. When problems come along, you instinctively know what tools need to be employed to work through the difficulty. Specifically, you learn the following:

- how to master quotes and pounds

- how to use the BuildCriteria function

- how to test quotes and pounds

- what must be done to control nulls

- the difference between nulls and zero-length strings

- how to work with nulls and zero-length strings in fields

- the difference between the Nz and IsNull functions

- how to format dates

- how to calculate time spans between dates

Using Quotes and Pounds

Using variables with quotes and pounds seems so simple at first glance. Yet it is amazing how much havoc and frustration these seemingly simple operations have brought to novice and advanced Access developers alike. Several ways to handle the difficulties that can arise are detailed here.

Quotes

It's ironic that the small things in Access often can be the most difficult to master. Quotes are a prime example. In some situations, quotes don't seem that challenging. For example, if you try to create a filter using a text field, you just use an expression like this:

```
[State] = "Oklahoma"
```

At this point, there is nothing challenging in any way. You get into trouble when you try to embed a string variable inside another string. For example, imagine that you have a variable named strState that you want to use as part of an expression for a filter in a report. If you try to output the variable strState in the immediate window, you get Oklahoma (without quotes), not "Oklahoma" (with quotes). To be able to get the variable to output the string with quotes around it, you have to assign the string to the variable this way:

```
strState = """Oklahoma"""
```

You must put a pair of quotes around the quotes surrounding Oklahoma to get the quotes surrounding the string to output. In other words, you need three quotes on each side of the string. It's starting to get interesting. But there's more.

You want another variable named strWhere to contain the entire expression that is used for the filter. Assuming that strState contains the string "Oklahoma", you try to place the entire where clause expression in a variable, like so:

```
strWhere = "[State] = " strState
```

This generates a compile error due to improper syntax. So, you decide to place the second quote at the end of the line like this:

```
strWhere = "[State] = strState"
```

This approach seems to work at first. The only problem with this method is that you end up with the following being assigned to the strWhere variable:

```
[State]= strState
```

You don't want the literal value of strState in your expression because it is doubtful that you have such a state in your database. So, you get really creative and try concatenating like this:

```
strWhere = "[State]=" & strState
```

At this point, you think you have found success, but it turns out to be a deception. If you run this statement in a procedure, you get the following:

```
[State] = Oklahoma
```

This looks correct, but if you try to insert this expression in a report as a filter through code, you get nothing but disappointment because the report requires that string values be enclosed in quotes. What you want to end up with is this:

```
[State] = "Oklahoma"
```

So how do you get there? Start by enclosing the entire expression that you need in quotes, like so:

```
"[State]=Oklahoma"
```

Now, enclose the embedded string (which is a string within a string) with three quotes (as you did before) like this:

```
"[State]="""Oklahoma"""
```

Remember, the first and last quotes are for the entire expression. Next, concatenate the variable containing "Oklahoma" with ampersands like so:

```
"[State]=""" & strState & """"
```

At last, you have success! Now, assign the entire string to a variable like this:

```
strWhere = "[State]=""" & strState & """"
```

You also can use single quotes for filters, so the following expression also works:

```
strWhere = "[State] = '" & strState & "'"
```

To remember the technique for adding embedded quotes, follow these steps:

1. Begin with enclosing the expression you want in quotes (for example, `"[State] = Oklahoma"`).

2. Insert a set of three quotes (double) on both sides of the embedded string (for example, `"[State]="""Oklahoma"""`).

3. Replace an embedded string with a variable, and place an ampersand on both sides of the variable, separated by spaces (for example, `"[State]=""" & strState & """"`).

4. Assign the entire expression to a variable (for example, strWhere = "[State]=""" & strState & """").

Another method that has merit is using chr$(34) to insert the quote. You might remember from Chapter 16, "Overcoming the Limitations Of Queries," that keyboard characters have corresponding character codes represented by numbers. You can identify what code corresponds to a certain character by using the asc function. For example, to determine the code for a double-quote character, simply type **? asc("""")** in the immediate window, and it will return 34. You must use four quotes to resolve the string down to a single quote. Now you have verified that 34 is the number you use with the chr$ function. If you write the same expression using this method, you end up with the following:

```
"[State]=" & chr$(34) & strState & chr$(34)
```

You also can assign chr$(34) to a variable for better readability. If you assign chr$(34) to sQuote, the expression becomes the following:

```
"[State]=" & sQuote & strState & sQuote
```

Still another alternative is to use a constant to represent the quote. You assign four quotes to a constant, like so:

```
Const strOneQuote = """"
```

Using this method, you end up with the following:

```
"[State]=" & strOneQuote & strState & strOneQuote
```

The BuildCriteria Function

In case you are wondering why there is not an intrinsic Access function that can handle embedding quotes designed for building criteria, the good news is that the BuildCriteria function is ideal for putting the elements of a filter or criteria argument together. Assuming that the value of strState is Oklahoma, you use the function this way:

```
strWhere = BuildCriteria("[State]", 8, strState)
```

The syntax for the function with arguments is the following:

```
BuildCriteria(FieldName, FieldType, Expression)
```

The field type can also be supplied using intrinsic constants. For example, instead of using 8 for the FieldType argument to represent a text field type, you can use the constant adBSTR. Table 20.1 shows the constants that work with the BuildCriteria function and their equivalent table field types and values.

Table 20.1: ADO Data Type Constants

Access Equivalent	Constant	Value
Text	adBSTR	8
Currency	adCurrency	6
Date	adDate	7
Number	adDecimal	14
Number	adDouble	5
Number	adInteger	3
Number	adSingle	4
Number	adSmallInt	2
Number	adTinyInt	16
Any type	adVariant	12

The adBSTR constant can convert date and number values. Keep in mind that the BuildCriteria function only generates criteria. Because you now know techniques that work whether or not you have criteria, you are equipped to handle embedded strings in a variety of ways. For example, if you have a name, such as Charles "Sparky" Mahan, that you want to assign to a variable, you know what to do to embed the nickname. Assuming that the variable strNickName contains "Sparky", the expression looks like this:

```
strFullName = "Charles """ & strNickName & """ Mahan"
```

The technique used should be no surprise to you because you know the principles that make this expression work. After the assignment is executed, the variable strFullName contains Charles "Sparky" Mahan, just as it should.

Pound Signs

As you have learned, pound signs are automatically inserted in the query grid when you type a date expression. But what about when you are not in the query grid? Although pound signs are easier to handle than quotes in a VBA expression, they can still get a little tricky. Assuming you have a string variable named strDate, you need to delimit (separate) the variable with pound signs like so:

```
"[AccidentDate] = # " & strDate &  " #"
```

This expression looks fairly straightforward. It gets a bit more complicated when you work with date ranges in an expression, like this:

```
"[AccidentDate]  Between #" & strBDate & "# And #" & strEDate & "#"
```

You can take this line and use it in a filter by attaching it to the OnOpen event property of a report with a program like this:

```
Private Sub Report_Open(Cancel As Integer)
Dim strBDate As String, StrEDate As String
```

```
Dim strFilter As String

strBDate = "1/1/97"
StrEDate = "1/1/98"
    strFilter = "[AccidentDate]  Between #" & strBDate _
    & "# And #" & StrEDate & "#"
Me.Filter = strFilter
Me.FilterOn = True
End Sub
```

However, because the ampersand operator handles data type conversion, you can rewrite the filter this way:

```
Private Sub Report_Open(Cancel As Integer)
Dim dtmBDate As Date, dtmEDate As Date
Dim strFilter As String

strBDate = #1/1/97#
StrEDate = #1/1/98#
    strFilter = "[AccidentDate]  Between " & strBDate _
    & " And " & StrEDate
Me.Filter = strFilter
Me.FilterOn = True
End Sub
```

Although both procedures work, you can save yourself some trouble by employing the BuildCriteria function, as you did before. Using the adBSTR constant, you don't have to worry about the pound signs; just type the dates as if they were strings, in the following manner:

```
strCrit = BuildCriteria("[AccidentDate]", adBSTR, "Between 1/1/1996
➡and 1/1/98")
```

The value of the strCrit variable becomes the following:

```
[AccidentDate] Between #1/1/1996# And #1/1/1998#
```

If you want to use this technique with variables in a procedure to apply a filter to a report, you end up with this:

```
Private Sub Report_Open(Cancel As Integer)
Dim strBDate As String, strEDate As String
Dim strFilter As String

strBDate = "1/1/96"
strEDate = "1/1/98"
    strFilter = BuildCriteria("[AccidentDate]", _
    adBSTR, "between " & strBDate & " and " & strEDate)
Me.Filter = strFilter
Me.FilterOn = True
End Sub
```

Testing Quotes and Pounds

The moment of truth comes when you apply what you have learned. You can test variables and expressions in a standard module using the immediate window before you insert them into a class module. If you want to test variables in event procedures in class modules, you set breakpoints so that when you run the form or report, you have a chance to examine your code from where the breakpoints are set in the procedure. In contrast, in the standard module, you can test the variables by either using `Print.Debug` statements to view the expressions in the immediate window or by setting breakpoints and watches to view them. Either way, you can view the expressions without ever opening the form or report to which you eventually copy the expressions. The following steps walk you through the testing process:

1. Open the Claims database from the AccessByExample folder.

2. Open the Loss Report report in Design view.

3. Right-click the title bar of the report, and then click Properties to open the Property sheet of the form.

4. Click the Event tab; then click the drop-down box of the `OnOpen` event property, and choose `[Event Procedure]`. Click the Build button.

5. Once in the Visual Basic Editor Module Window, click Insert, Module. If the immediate window is not open, press Ctrl+G.

6. Type the following code in the Module window:

```
Sub Test()
Dim strState As String, strFilter As String

strState = "FL"
strFilter = "[AccidentState]=""" & strState & """"
Debug.Print strFilter

End Sub
```

7. Click Debug, Compile Claims to check for typos.

8. Click the Run Sub/User Form button. Figure 20.1 shows the following results that appear in the immediate window:

```
[AccidentState]="FL"
```

9. Change the line that begins with `strFilter` to the following:

```
strFilter = "[AccidentState]=" & Chr$(34) & strState & Chr$(34)
```

10. Click the Run Sub/User Form button again. The results should be the same.

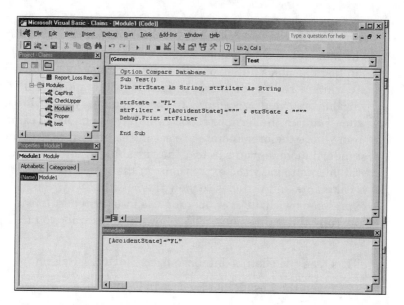

Figure 20.1: *Expressions can be tested in the immediate window before pasting them into another module.*

11. With your mouse, highlight everything between Sub Test() and Debug. Print, as shown in Figure 20.2. Copy the lines by pressing Ctrl+C.

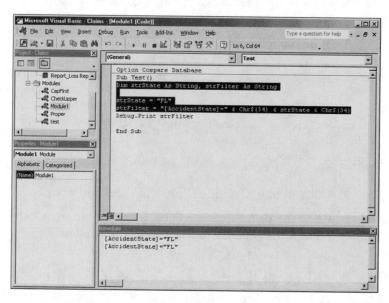

Figure 20.2: *Copy and paste the code from a standard module to a class module.*

12. In the Project window on the left, click the plus sign (+) next to Microsoft Access Class Objects. Double-click Report_Loss Report to open the event procedure tied to the OnOpen event begun in step 4.

13. Paste the copied lines in the procedure on the line immediately following Private Sub Report_Open(Cancel As Integer) by pressing Ctrl+V.

14. Type **Me.Filter = strFilter** on the line immediately following the pasted lines. Next, type **Me.FilterOn = True** on the next line to look like the following:

```
Private Sub Report_Open(Cancel As Integer)
Dim strState As String, strFilter As String

strState = "FL"
strFilter = "[AccidentState]=" & Chr$(34) & strState & Chr$(34)
Me.Filter = strFilter
Me.FilterOn = True
End Sub
```

15. Click Debug Compile Claims to check for errors; then press Alt+F11 to return to Design view.

16. Click the Print Preview button to view the report. Only Florida records appear.

CAUTION

If you get a parameter box for the state field, it is misspelled in the procedure. For example, if you spelled the AccidentState field AcidentState, a parameter box with the incorrect spelling would appear.

17. Close Print Preview. Press Alt+F11 to return to the procedure attached to the OnOpen event property in the Module window.

18. Delete the code between the Sub and End Sub lines, and insert the following code:

```
Dim strBDate As String, strEDate As String
Dim strFilter As String

strBDate = "1/1/96"
strEDate = "1/1/98"
    strFilter = BuildCriteria("[AccidentDate]", _
    adBSTR, "between " & strBDate & " and " & strEDate)
Me.Filter = strFilter
Me.FilterOn = True
```

19. Press Alt+F11 to return to Design view. Click Print Preview to view the records between 1/1/96 and 1/1/98.

20. While in Print Preview, click the drop-down box of the Zoom button, and choose 75% to view the 75% Preview window, as shown in Figure 20.3.

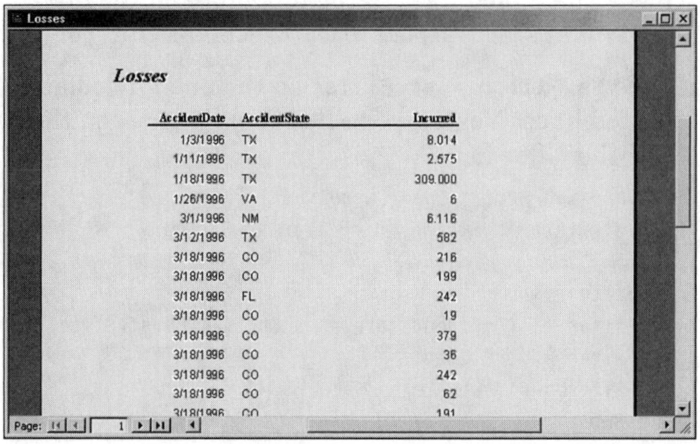

Figure 20.3: *You can view the filtered records in Print Preview to confirm that the filter worked.*

21. Close Print Preview; then close and save the report, but don't save the Standard module, which was just for testing and practice.

Controlling Nulls

One of the common bugaboos that haunt novice Access programmers is working with null values. When a field or variable is Null, it signifies that it has no valid data. This is in contrast to zero-length, which means that the value contains a string that has a zero length, or Empty, which means that a variant variable has not been initialized (assigned a value for the first time). All three values are hard to distinguish because they all represent a non or blank value. To help you differentiate between the three, keep the following in mind:

- Variant is the only data type that can hold the Empty, Null, and Nothing special values.

- The Null, Empty, and zero-length values all have no character that outputs to either a screen or a printer.

- The Null value propagates itself throughout expressions, which means that if any component of an expression contains a Null value, the entire expression evaluates to Null.

- Zero-length strings can be entered into Text, Memo, or Hyperlink fields in an Access database, if the AllowZeroLength field property is set to Yes.

- You can specifically assign Empty, Null, and string values such as Empty string to the Variant data type.

The following procedure sheds some light on this perplexity:

```
Sub NullVal()
Dim varItem As Variant

varItem = Null

Debug.Print varItem

End Sub
```

There are a few interesting points in this procedure. First, notice that the data type of the varItem variable is Variant. If varItem was declared to be a string data type, varItem = Null would have generated an "Invalid use of null" error. This is because variant is the only data type that can contain Null or Empty values. Second, the Debug.Print statement shows the value of varItem to be Null as opposed to zero-length. The next procedure adds one line:

```
Sub NullVal()
Dim varItem As Variant

varItem = Null
varItem = Nz(varItem)

Debug.Print varItem

End Sub
```

The Nz function has two arguments, but the second argument is optional. When you run this procedure with the added line, it evaluates to "" or a zero-length string. Instead of seeing Null in the immediate window as in the first routine, you see nothing. You can prove that it is zero-length with a conditional test such as the following:

```
If varItem = "" Then
Debug.Print "You got zero-length."
End If
```

✔ For more information on the Nz function, see "Nz Versus IsNull" later in this chapter.

What difference does choosing Null or zero-length make? First of all, you test for the two values differently. This variation of your original procedure tests for a Null value and a zero-length string:

```
Sub NullorNot()
Dim varNullTest as Variant, varZeroTest as Variant

varNullTest = Null
        If IsNull(varNullTest) Then
                Debug.Print "This variable is Null"
        End If

varZeroTest = ""
        If varZeroTest = "" Then
                Debug.Print "This variable is zero-length"
        End If
End Sub
```

Notice that varZeroTest is tested differently from varNullTest. If you set varNullTest to "", IsNull(varNullTest) evaluates to False. Likewise, if you set varZeroTest to Null, varZeroTest = "" evaluates to False. The next variation tests for a zero-length string using the Nz function:

```
Sub NullorNot()
Dim varNullTest as Variant, varZeroTest as Variant

VarNullTest = Null
        If Nz(varNullTest)  =  "" Then
                Debug.Print "First pass is zero-length"
        End If

VarZeroTest = ""
        If Nz(varZeroTest)  =  "" Then
                Debug.Print "Second pass is zero-length"
        End If
End Sub
```

This procedure is very interesting because it demonstrates that the Nz function evaluates to "", regardless of whether the variable tested is Null or zero-length. This behavior can be used to your advantage, as you will see.

Nulls Versus Zero-Length in Fields

When you work with field values, another important distinction between Null and zero-length comes to mind. Nulls and zero-length values can be allowed or disallowed in Text, Memo, and Hyperlink field types. Depending on your settings, Nulls and zero-length values can behave totally differently. You can use this distinction to your advantage.

The `AllowZeroLength` property and the `Required` property work independently of each other. The `Required` property only determines whether a Null value is allowed in a field. If the `AllowZeroLength` property is set to `Yes`, a zero-length string will be a valid entry, regardless of the `Required` property setting. Table 20.2 shows the results of various combinations of `AllowZeroLength` and `Required` property settings.

Table 20.2: **AllowZeroLength** *and* **Required** *Property Combinations*

Required	AllowZeroLength	User's Action	Value Stored
No	No	Presses Enter	Null
		Presses spacebar	Null
		Enters a zero-length string	(not allowed)
No	Yes	Presses Enter	Null
		Presses spacebar	Null
		Enters a zero-length string	Zero-length string
Yes	No	Presses Enter	(not allowed)
		Presses spacebar	(not allowed)
		Enters a zero-length string	(not allowed)
Yes	Yes	Presses Enter	(not allowed)
		Presses spacebar	Zero-length string
		Enters a zero-length string	Zero-length string

You can use the `OnLostFocus` event property to distinguish between the display of Null and a zero-length string. Using this property, `"Unknown"` can be displayed when a zero-length string is entered with a procedure such as the following:

```
Private Sub FieldName_LostFocus()
If Me.FieldName = "" Then
    Me.FieldName = "Unknown"
End If
End Sub
```

Of course, this procedure assumes that the `AllowZeroLength` property is set to `Yes`. Nothing happens if you enter a Null value in the `FieldName` field as long as the `Required` property is set to `No`. When you enter a batch of records, a procedure or query can easily distinguish between the Null and zero-length values, whether this procedure has been applied or not.

Why is this important? Imagine that you have a data entry typist who is inputting an employee address list. You want the typist to have a choice in the Fax field because the employee might not have a fax number. For this reason, you set the `AllowZeroLength` property to Yes and the `Required` property to No. The user can leave the field blank to indicate that the employee does not have a fax number. Otherwise, the user can enter a zero-length string to indicate that the employee does have a fax number, but the number was not known at the time of the entry. This way, the user can fill in the unknown numbers at a later time.

When the typist comes to the Social Security Number field, you want to ensure that a value is entered. To accomplish this, you set both the AllowZeroLength property and the Required properties to Yes. The user cannot leave the field blank, but if the Social Security number is not known, a zero-length string can be entered so that it can be supplied later when the number is known. Using either of these methods, you don't have to worry about "unknown" or "none" being printed on a report, but you can still determine which value is entered.

Nz Versus IsNull

The IsNull function returns a Boolean value. It is either True or False, depending on whether the expression argument contains no valid data (Null). The syntax for IsNull is simple:

```
IsNull(expression)
```

If you want a quick way to test for Null, the Nz function is your ticket. As mentioned before, the Nz function has two arguments. The following code shows the proper syntax for Nz:

```
Nz(Value, ValueIfNull)
```

If you use the Nz function in an expression in a query without using the ValueIfNull argument, the results will be a zero-length string in the fields or variables that contain Null values. With the ValueIfNull argument, the function returns the ValueIfNull argument, but only if the Value argument is Null. Consequently, the Nz function can perform as an If...Then...Else construct. In contrast, the IsNull function only returns True if the expression argument is Null, which means that you must use it in a conditional expression, and not by itself. Here is an IsNull example for comparison:

```
varResult = IIf(IsNull(varShipping),  "No Shipping Charge", varShipping)
```

If the value of the varShipping variable is Null, "No Shipping Charge" is returned. Otherwise, the value of varShipping is returned. The next example shows a shorter method using Nz:

```
varResult = Nz(varShipping, "No Shipping Charge")
```

This example performs precisely the same operation as the previous example. If the value of varShipping is *not* Null, varShipping is returned. If it *is* Null, "No Shipping Charge" is returned. In effect, you get an

If...Then...Else operation. If you don't use the second argument and the value is Null, a zero-length string is returned.

There are situations in which using IsNull makes sense. Examine the following procedure:

```
Function MayAddCR(Optional strChkString) As String
'Insert two hard returns if not null

If IsNull(strChkString) Then
    MayAddCR = ""
Else
    MayAddCR = strChkString & vbCrLf & vbCrLf
End If


End Function
```

If you try to use Nz to perform the same operation as this example, you run into a roadblock. Because the Value argument is both the input and return value, whatever is input is also returned when the value is not Null. The next example shows why this won't work:

```
MayAddCR = Nz(strChkString & vbCrLf & vbCrLf, "")
```

If you are trying to check the Value argument, you have already failed because you are checking a non-Null value when you concatenate the vbCrLf intrinsic constant. Even if you discover a way to accomplish this with Nz, chances are good that the IsNull approach is still cleaner and easier to read and maintain.

Only one argument is required when using the IsNull function. Always use the IsNull function to determine whether an expression, as opposed to a single value, contains a Null value. Expressions that you might expect to evaluate to True, such as If Var = Null and If Var <> Null, are always False. This is because any expression containing a Null is itself Null, and therefore is False.

IsNull in Action

Suppose you want to confirm reservations on a database you have created by clicking a button on the record you want to confirm. When the button is clicked, "Confirmed" is entered into the ResNotes (reservation notes) field. That's fine if the field is Null. But what if the field is not Null? If there is already information in the ResNotes field, "Confirmed" can easily get lost in the text if you concatenate it on the end of what's already there, and replace the text if you don't. You want it to stand out by placing it on a separate line.

That involves entering two hard returns before appending "Confirmed" into the field.

The next example shows how to create the program attached to the Confirm button that's already on the form. Before creating the button, you test the function that does the work by taking the following steps:

1. Open the Convention database, and then open the Reservation form in Design view.

2. Click the Confirm button, and press F4 to open the Property sheet.

3. Click the drop-down box of the On Click event box, and choose [Event Procedure]. Click the Build button.

4. From the Project window, double-click the ChkNull module, as shown in Figure 20.4.

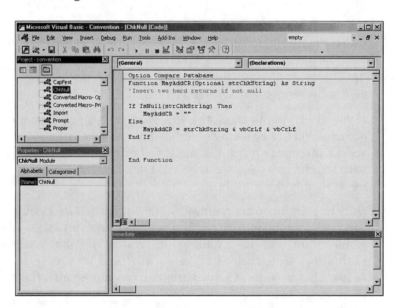

Figure 20.4: *Double-click the ChkNull standard module to test it.*

5. Press Ctrl+G to open the immediate window. Type **? MayAddCR(Null)** in the immediate window, and press Enter. You see nothing. Select and delete everything in the immediate window.

6. This time, type **? MayAddCR("Confirmed")**, and press Enter to see the results shown in Figure 20.5.

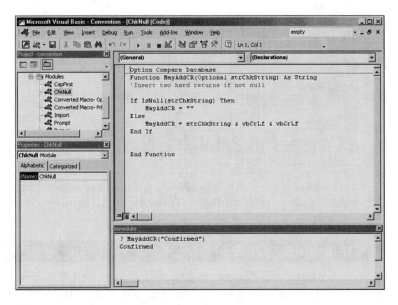

Figure 20.5: *You can test the function by entering an example that's close to the real-life model.*

7. In the project window, double-click Form_Reservation to open the module attached to the Confirm button.

8. Place the following line between the Sub and End Sub lines in the module:

   `Me.ResNotes = MayAddCR(Me.ResNotes) & "Confirmed"`

9. Close the module and property sheet. Click the View button to run the form.

10. Click the Confirm button in the first record. Notice that "Confirmed" is added with no carriage return preceding it.

11. Click the Next Record button to move to ReservationID 2.

12. Click the Confirm button again. Notice that "Confirmed" is added on a separate line separated from the rest of the text by two hard returns, as shown in Figure 20.6.

13. Close the form and save the changes.

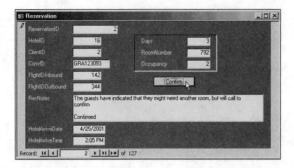

Figure 20.6: *Using the* MayAddCR *function, you can add carriage returns before "Confirmed" if text already exists in the field.*

Conquering Dates

Another hurdle in Access that trips up many a programmer is date calculations. Why should date processing be important to you as an Access programmer? What if you want to know the number of days between two dates, or what if you want to compute the date six months from today? If you are writing an accounting application, you might need to know how long it has been since an item has been ordered. If you are in insurance, you might need to know how long it has been since a claim has been reported. In sales, you might need to track the number of days that have passed since you last called upon a customer. Date processing is an essential part of most applications.

You can begin with some easy intrinsic functions. Table 20.3 shows Access standard date functions.

Table 20.3: Access Standard Date Functions

Function	Returns	Example
Date()	Current date	7/1/1999
Now()	Current date and time	10/25/2001 10:01:39 p.m.
Time()	Current time	08:02:45 p.m.

Formatting Date Functions

Suppose you want to format the date function a different way from that shown in Table 20.3. You can embed (or nest) the date function inside the format function to achieve your desired result. If today is 10/25/2001, the following returns 10:

```
Format(date(),"mm")
```

The following returns 25:

```
Format(date(),"dd")
```

✔ If you want to review custom formats, see "Testing and Using Custom Formats" in Chapter 3, "The Table—The Heart of Any Database."

If you just want the full year, enter the following:

```
Format(date(),"yyyy")
```

However, if you want the full short date, enter the following:

```
Format(date(),"mm/dd/yyyy")
```

The following:

```
Format(date(),"mmmm dd, yyyy")
```

returns

```
October 25, 2001
```

for a full long date, or the following:

```
format(date(),"long date")
```

returns

```
Thursday, October 25, 2001
```

for day of the week, plus a long date.

How Access Stores Dates

Microsoft Access stores the Date/Time data type as a double-precision, floating-point number with up to 15 decimal places. The integer component (before the decimal) of the double-precision number represents the date; the decimal component represents the time.

Valid date values range from -647,434 (January 1, 100 AD) to 2,958,465 (December 31, 9999 AD). Valid time ranges are from .0 (00:00:00) to .99999 (23:59:59). The decimal value represents a fraction of one day. You can convert a decimal value to hours, minutes, and seconds by multiplying it by 24.

If you want to see for yourself how dates are stored, use the CDbl function in the immediate window to convert the date to a double-precision number. Table 20.4 illustrates this.

Table 20.4: Date-to-Number Conversion

Immediate Window Entry	Returns
? CDbl(#10/15/2001 14:00#)	37179.5833333333
? CDbl(#12/15/1889 17:32#)	-3667.73055555556

If you want to reverse this and convert from a double-precision number to Date/Time, use the CVDate function, as Table 20.5 illustrates.

Table 20.5: Number-to-Date Conversion

Immediate Window Entry	Returns
? CVDate(1.5000)	12/31/1899 12:00:00 PM
? CVDate(35000.7812)	10/28/1995 6:44:56 PM

If you multiply the number of years (100) of the 20th century times the number of days in a year (approximately 365.25), the result is 36,525. If you convert that number to a date, you get December 31, 1999, which is the last day of the 20th century. It's not quite that simple because a year is actually 365.2422 days, but you get the idea. Microsoft apparently adjusted for this minor discrepancy by counting from the last day of 1899 instead of counting from the first day of 1900. Table 20.6 shows how the components of the numbers are converted.

Table 20.6: Number-to-Date Conversion Components

Stored Number	Date Component	Date Represented	Time Component	Time Represented
2.50	2	1/1/1900	0.50	12:00:00 PM
36526.75	36526	1/1/2000	0.75	6:00:00 PM

Calculating Time Spans

Although you can convert dates to numbers and use them for calculations, it is difficult to get consistent results with floating-point decimals. For example, if today's date is October 25, 2001, and you type ? Now()=DateValue("10/25/2001") in the immediate window, False is returned. The reason for this is that Now returns a double-precision number, whereas DateValue returns an integer value representing the date only. If this inconsistency isn't reason enough, it is not always easy to cope with potential glitches such as leap years. A better approach is to use Access intrinsic functions to do your work for you.

The DateAdd Function

Use the DateAdd function to add time intervals—such as hours, days, or years—to a Date/Time value. The following syntax for the DateAdd function shows all three required arguments:

```
DateAdd(interval, number, date)
```

Table 20.7 details the arguments for the DateAdd function.

Table 20.7: **DateAdd** *Function Arguments*

Argument	Description
Interval	Required. String expression that is the interval of time you want to add.
Number	Required. Numeric expression that is the number of intervals you want to add. It can be positive (to get dates in the future) or negative (to get dates in the past).
Date	Required. Variant (Date) or literal representing date to which the interval is added.

Table 20.8 shows the settings for the Interval argument and what they represent.

Table 20.8: Settings for the **Interval** *Argument*

Setting	Description
yyyy	Year
q	Quarter
m	Month
y	Day of year
d	Day
w	Weekday
ww	Week
h	Hour
n	Minute
s	Second

NOTE

When working with weeks, w represents workdays minus Saturday and Sunday; in contrast, ww represents weeks.

The following listing shows a procedure that uses the DateAdd function to add 20 years to a date:

```
Sub TestDate()
Dim dBeforeIntv As Date
Dim dAfterIntv As Date

dBeforeIntv = #1/1/1980#
dAfterIntv = DateAdd("yyyy", 20, dBeforeIntv)
Debug.Print dAfterIntv
End Sub
```

This function returns 1/1/2000 in the immediate window. Because the interval argument was set to year, the DateAdd function added 20 years to 1/1/1980. The dBeforeIntv variable is the date to which the 20-year interval was added. To add 20 days to the same date, simply change the "yyyy" interval argument to "d" for day, as shown in the following listing:

```
Sub TestDate()
Dim dBeforeIntv As Date
Dim dAfterIntv As Date

dBeforeIntv = #1/1/1980#
dAfterIntv = DateAdd("d", 20, dBeforeIntv)
Debug.Print dAfterIntv

End Sub
```

The modified function now returns 1/21/1980 because it is adding 20 days instead of 20 years. The next procedure adds a time value to the date before changing the interval, as shown in the following listing:

```
Sub TestDate()
Dim dBeforeIntv As Date
Dim dAfterIntv As Date

dBeforeIntv = #1/1/1980 6:00:00 PM#
dAfterIntv = DateAdd("n", 20, dBeforeIntv)
Debug.Print dAfterIntv

End Sub
```

Notice that the dBeforeIntv variable is evaluated with a time value (6:00 p.m.) added to the date. Also notice that the interval was changed to "n" for minute. This function returns 1/1/1980 6:20:00 p.m. in the immediate window.

The DateDiff Function

The fact that you can add intervals to dates is all well and good, but what if you want to compute the time span between two dates? The DateDiff function is the tool to use. Only the first three of its five arguments are required, shown in the following DateDiff syntax. Optional arguments are shown in brackets.

```
DateDiff(interval, date1, date2, [firstdayofweek], [firstweekofyear])
```

Table 20.9 shows details of the arguments for the DateDiff function.

Table 20.9: **DateDiff** *Function Arguments*

Argument	Description
Interval	Required. String expression that is the interval of time you use to calculate the difference between date1 and date2.
date1, date2	Required; Variant (Date). Two dates you want to use in the calculation. If date1 refers to a later point in time than date2, a negative number is returned.
firstdayofweek	Optional. A constant that specifies the first day of the week. If not specified, Sunday is assumed.
firstweekofyear	Optional. A constant that specifies the first week of the year. If not specified, the first week is assumed to be the week in which January 1 occurs.

Although the Interval argument is the same for the DateDiff function as it is for the DateAdd function, it is repeated here for your convenience. The following procedure shows two date variables as before, but this time both variables are used in the function and assigned to a third variable:

```
Sub TestDate()
Dim dFirstDate As Date
Dim dSecondDate As Date
Dim lDiff As Long

dFirstDate = #1/1/1980#
dSecondDate = #8/25/1980#
lDiff = DateDiff("d", dFirstDate, dSecondDate)
Debug.Print lDiff

End Sub
```

This function returns 237 days, which is the difference in days between the two dates.

What's Next

In this chapter, you have learned how to conquer the common obstacles that trip up programmers. In the next chapter, you learn how to conquer problems associated with forms, but that's not all you learn. In the process, you learn about how to enhance your forms to make them professional looking, user friendly, and efficient.

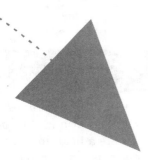

Taking Charge of Forms

In the last chapter, you learned about big problems that come in small packages. This chapter deals with bigger packages by showing you why forms are so powerful.

By now, you have gone well beyond form basics. You can perform operations programmatically now that you had to do manually before. You can change a form's properties, retrieve lookup values, import and export objects, and do the common tasks that you expect to accomplish using forms. But there is still much to learn about multifunctional form objects. In fact, you might be tempted to think that the best was saved until last (well, almost last). In this chapter, you learn the following:

- how query parameters are used with forms

- all about pop-up forms

- how to use PivotTables

- how to control editing, saving, and locking with forms

- how to overcome difficulties with large tables using forms

- how to use tab controls

Using a Parameterized Query As a Form's Record Source

A query that prompts the user to enter information is called a *parameter query*. The information that is entered in turn become criteria in the query. You enter the prompt enclosed in brackets (as if it were a field) in whatever field or fields you want to add criteria. After the query is ready, you can attach it to a form as a record source. Let's say that your coworker wants to add criteria to a query so that the user can open the form displaying the claims for whatever state was selected. You then could add another parameter to make the query select date ranges. After selecting the parameters, the user can browse the records of selected data. All this can be done with very little effort.

Follow these steps to create the query, and then attach the query to a form. Finally, browse the form to verify the data.

1. Open the Claims database from your AccessByExample folder.

2. Open a new query based on the Losses table.

3. Double-click the title bar, and then drag all the fields down to the query grid.

4. In the AccidentState field criteria row, type **[Enter a State]**, as shown in Figure 21.1.

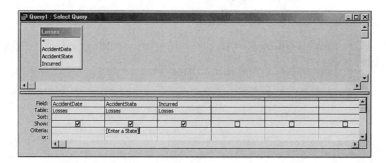

Figure 21.1: *When you enter a parameter in the query grid, you can prompt the user at runtime.*

5. Click the Run button to test the prompt, and view the results of the query.

6. When prompted to enter a state, type **FL** for Florida. The query retrieves the Florida records.

7. Click the View button to switch to Design view. In the AccidentDate field criteria row, type **Between [Date1] And [Date2]**, as shown in Figure 21.2.

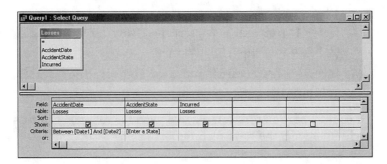

Figure 21.2: *You can insert multiple parameters into the query grid to prompt the user.*

8. Run the query to test the prompt. When prompted for the first date, type **1/1/97**. Next, type **1/1/98** for the second date prompt. When prompted for the state, enter **FL** again. The query retrieves six records, as shown in Figure 21.3.

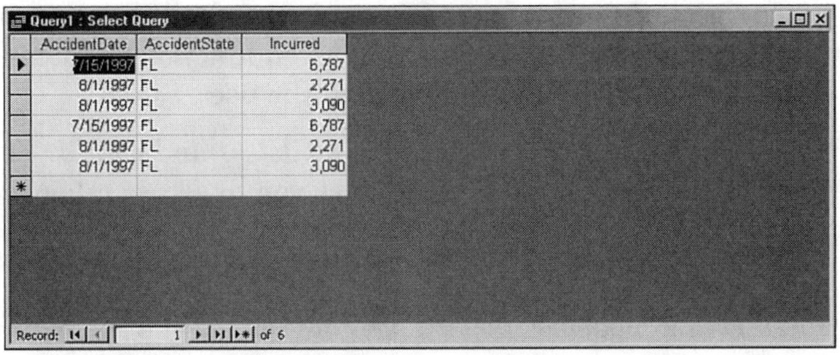

Figure 21.3: *The parameter query only returns records that match the criteria entered using the parameters.*

9. Click the View button to return to Design view; then Close and save the Query as **qryParameter**.

10. Open the LossesParameter form in Design view so that you can change properties.

11. Click the form selector, and press F4 to open the Property sheet of the form.

12. Click the Event tab; then click on the drop-down box of the RecordSource property, and choose qryParameter.

13. Close the Property sheet. Click the View button to switch to Form view.

14. Enter 1/1/96 and 1/1/99, respectively, for the two date prompts. Type FL when prompted for the date.

15. Browse a few records, and close and save the form. Stay in the database.

Of course, parameters can also be used for reports. Contrast the parameter technique with the next technique.

Pop-Up Forms Go Beyond the Message Box

Parameter queries work as record sources for reports as well as forms. However, there are times when your needs go beyond parameters and message boxes. Sure, you can input values using parameters and input boxes, but what if you need 10 items in one field for a report?

How does a pop-up form differ from a regular Access form? Pop-up forms stay on top of all other forms and objects, whether the objects are active or not. Another difference is that record navigation buttons are not as important on pop-up forms because they often function as menus and dialog boxes that request information from the user.

The two types of pop-up forms are *modeless* and *modal*. The difference is that a modeless pop-up form enables you to access other objects, whereas a modal pop-up form doesn't. This means that you must respond to a modal pop-up form before Access releases the form to allow you to continue.

You create a modeless pop-up form by setting the PopUp property to Yes and the Modal property to No. To create a modal pop-up form, set both the PopUp and Modal properties to Yes. If you open a modal pop-up form using the OpenForm method, you must specify the acDialog intrinsic constant in the WindowMode argument.

Pop-up forms give you the functionality to retrieve easily multiple values that can be used as criteria. They can be small enough to not get in the way, and yet powerful enough to give you great flexibility. You can use pop-up forms for calendars, calculators, dialog boxes, pick lists, lookup windows… and the list goes on. For example, if you want to develop a help system but find the message box to be too limiting, pop-up forms are most likely your answer.

Loading a Pop-Up Form

Before talking about the mechanics of creating a pop-up form, let's talk about how to load a pop-up form. If your form was called PopUp, you just insert a line in your code like so:

```
DoCmd.OpenForm "PopUp"
```

So far, it's just like any other form. You are just going with the defaults. As pointed out in the previous section, if you want your program to pause, waiting for the form to be closed or hidden, you must use the acDialog argument of the OpenForm method. This prevents a message box or anything else from opening until the box is closed. Using this approach, the code looks like this:

```
DoCmd.OpenForm "PopUp", , , , , acDialog
```

CAUTION

If you don't use the acDialog constant for the WindowMode argument of the OpenForm method, the default acWindowNormal setting is used, which means that even if you have the Modal property set to Yes, it is overridden by the default. In other words, you think you are getting Modal, but in reality, you are getting the normal Windows setting. This is okay only if you don't want Modal, so just keep this in mind.

If you want to pass a string (or even multiple parameters for that matter) through the OpenArgs argument of the OpenForm method to a pop-up form or any other form, you can easily do so. For example, if you want to pass the name of the state by which you filter a form called LossesArg, you use the OpenArgs argument this way:

```
DoCmd.OpenForm "LossesArg", , , , , , strArg
```

Notice that there are six commas instead of five. The strArg variable is used for the OpenArgs argument. Think of this argument as the quarterback that "passes" the string. The receiver is the OpenArgs property of the receiving form. The following procedure, which can be found in the LossesArg form, demonstrates how you can attach code to the OnOpen event of a form to receive a passed variable:

```
Dim strArg As String

strArg = Nz(Me.OpenArgs)
Me.Filter = "[AccidentState]=" & Chr$(34) & strArg & Chr$(34)
Me.FilterOn = True
```

The procedure in the PassArg pop-up form that calls the LossesArg form and passes the string looks like this:

```
Dim strArg As String
strArg = "CO"
```

```
DoCmd.OpenForm "LossesArg", , , , , , strArg
DoCmd.Close acForm, "PassArg"
```

The variable name does not have to be the same in both procedures for the form that's being called to receive the passed variable. Notice that the PassArg form closes itself.

Take the following steps to see this technique in action:

1. Open the PassArg form.

2. Click the Open Form button to open and filter the LossesArg form. Notice that the Colorado Records are filtered, as shown in Figure 21.4. Close the LossesArg form, and stay in the database.

Figure 21.4: *The* OpenArgs *argument is used to filter the LossesArg form.*

Creating a Pop-Up Form

When you create a pop-up form, keep in mind that you don't need scroll-bars, record selectors, or navigation buttons. You just need a box with a title bar so that you can move it. You don't even necessarily need to have the pop-up form bound to a table or query.

If you only change the first three properties in Table 21.1 to the suggested settings, you end up with the look of a pop-up form. However, setting the PopUp property to Yes assures you that the form is always the top window. Setting the Modal property to Yes causes the form to pause until it is closed. Table 21.1 displays typical settings for a pop-up form. These settings are just for a guide. They are not the only settings that affect pop-up forms, but they are important. You can experiment until you find the right settings for you.

Table 21.1: Typical Pop-Up Form Settings

Property	Setting	Comments
Scroll Bars	No	Whether a form has scrollbars.
Record Selectors	No	Whether a form has record selectors.
Navigation Buttons	Neither	Whether a form has navigation buttons.
Pop Up	Yes	Whether a form opens as a pop-up, which means it is always the top window.

Table 21.1: continued

Property	Setting	Comments
Modal	Yes	Whether a form opens as a modeless object (you can switch to other windows) or a modal object (the form retains the focus until it's closed).
Border Style	Dialog	The type of border and border elements (title bar, Close button, Control menu, Maximize and Minimize buttons) to use for the form. It also determines whether the form is sizable.
Control Box	Yes	Whether a form has a Control menu in Form view.
Min Max Buttons	Both Enabled	Whether a form has Minimize and Maximize buttons in Form view. If you set the BorderStyle property to Dialog, Microsoft Access automatically removes the Minimize and Maximize buttons.
Close Button	Yes	Whether the Close button is disabled.
AutoCenter	Yes	Whether a form is centered automatically in the application window when it is opened.

The following steps guide you through creating a pop-up form:

1. Under Forms, click the Create Form in Design View option to open a blank form in Design view.

2. Click the form selector, and press F4 to open the Property sheet of the form.

3. Click the All tab, and match the 10 settings in Table 21.1. Set the Width property to 2.5. You also can drag the right side of the form over to 2.5 inches on the ruler to set this property.

4. Close the form, save it as **Form1**, and reopen it, as shown in Figure 21.5. Notice the pop-up settings. Delete Form1. Stay in the database.

A blank pop-up form is not too exciting until you do something with it. Use your imagination. You can gather information from users using a pop-up form as a dialog box. A pop-up form can function as a calendar or an appointment manager. You can set report criteria using a pop-up form. The following topics explore some of these applications.

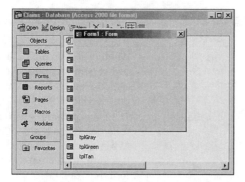

Figure 21.5: *Pop-up forms typically have no scrollbars or navigation buttons.*

Using a Pop-Up Form As a Dialog Box

One of the most interesting applications of a pop-up form is a dialog box. If you examine the Tools Options menus in Access, you see examples of dialog boxes. For example, if you click the View tab, you see option buttons and check boxes.

Perhaps you wonder why there isn't a way to use a template for a form. Instead of changing multiple settings over and over, you save the template with all your desired settings. Then, you can simply specify the template when creating a new form, and you're done.

If you save a form with the name Normal, it automatically functions as a template for any form created from that point forward. If you want, you also can change the Form template in Tools, Options, Forms/Reports from Normal to the name of a form that you created. But that is not very flexible. You might need a variety of templates.

In the Claims database, there is a form called CreatePopup. It uses a template for some settings to be used on the form about to be created and enables you to specify other settings on the fly. In a matter of seconds, you have your blank pop-up form with your desired settings.

This pop-up form has no record source. Therefore, none of the controls on it are bound. This form demonstrates some common controls used for dialog box-style pop-up forms, such as option groups and check boxes. It should be instructive from several perspectives.

First, it demonstrates how to program check boxes. It looks like they are part of an option group, but in reality they just have the appearance of an option group because they are separate controls. Second, it demonstrates how to create a form programmatically using templates. Third, it shows how to work with twips.

NOTE

A *twip* (1/20th of a point) is a measure used in defining objects that are to be displayed on a computer screen or printed. A twip is 1/1440th of an inch or 1/567th of a centimeter. That means that there are 1440 twips to an inch or 567 twips to a centimeter. The twip is 1/20th of a point, which is a standard measure in printing. A point is approximately 1/72nd of an inch. Let's say that you want an object in Access to measure 7 inches. You multiply 7 times 1440 for the total twips.

Follow these steps to examine the form:

1. Open the CreatePopUp form in Design view, as shown in Figure 21.6.

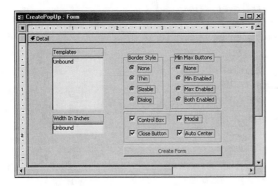

Figure 21.6: *The CreatePopUp form (shown in Design view) uses controls such as check boxes and option groups to display a dialog box-style form.*

2. Right-click the Create Form button, and choose Build Event to open the procedure attached to the OnClick event property. The following code appears. Stay in the module until you finish reading the comments following the procedure. Then close the module, Property sheet, and form. Select No if Access asks you to save changes.

```
Private Sub cmdCreateForm_Click()
Dim iBorder As Integer, iMinMax As Integer
Dim frm As Form, sglWidth As Single
Dim iTplIndex As Integer
Dim sTplName As String

Const TPI = 1440 'TPI = Twips Per Inch
iTplIndex = Me.lstTemplates.ListIndex 'get selection index
sTplName = Me.lstTemplates.ItemData(iTplIndex)
iBorder = Me.optBorder 'Set BorderStyle
'Previous line to set border style could be written:
'Select Case Me.optBorder 'Set BorderStyle
    'Case 0
```

```
'        iBorder = 0
'Case 1
'        iBorder = 1
'Case 2
'        iBorder = 2
'Case 3
'        iBorder = 3
'End Select

iMinMax = Me.optMinMax 'Set MinMaxButtons

sglWidth = IIf(IsNull(Me.txtWidth), 3, Me.txtWidth)
Set frm = CreateForm(, sTplName)
With frm 'PopUp form settings set to dialog box settings
    .BorderStyle = iBorder
    .MinMaxButtons = iMinMax
    .Width = sglWidth * TPI
    .AutoCenter = Me.chkCenter
    .Modal = Me.chkModal
    .CloseButton = Me.ChkClose
    .ControlBox = Me.chkControl
    .PopUp = True
End With

DoCmd.Close acForm, "CreatePopUp"
DoCmd.Restore
End Sub
```

The Select...Case construct is commented out, which makes the text appear green when examined in the form. It is shown only to demonstrate a common method of handling the flow control of the procedure by responding programmatically to the button that was selected in the Option group. In this particular instance, common sense tells you that every "then" is the same as every "if" or case. This is because the values that represent each property setting option are zero-based.

When you create an option group using the Option Group Wizard, each option is sequentially numbered by default. For example, if you have four options, the values assigned to each option is 1 through 4. However, you can change the option values to 0 through 3 to match zero-based numbering schemes. When the optBorder Option group was created, it was set to sequentially number starting at 0 rather than 1 so that the Select...Case values could be in synch. Therefore, the Select...Case code is not needed. You can simply use iBorder = Me.optBorder to handle user selections.

Table 21.2 illustrates by showing the Visual Basic values that correspond to the Border Style settings.

Table 21.2: BorderStyle Property Settings

Setting	Visual Basic
None	0
Thin	1
Sizable	2
Dialog	3

It's only logical. Both the BorderStyle and the MinMaxButtons properties are set up the same way. They both have four zero-based VBA values arranged sequentially, representing the four settings. Therefore, as long as you list the settings in the same order as they are listed on the form, you can get away with a line like this:

```
iMinMax = Me.optMinMax 'Don't need a Select..Case construct
```

Notice that settings are gathered from all over the form. Because both the BorderStyle property and the MinMaxbuttons property have four options, they are perfect for the option group. Only one option per group can be chosen. Four check boxes are used for properties that are either true or false. Any or all of these boxes can be checked or unchecked. They all have a default value of -1, which VBA interprets as True. A value of 0 is interpreted as False. If you uncheck a box, the value of the check box is 0. This value is transferred this way:

```
.CloseButton = Me.ChkClose
```

If the chkClose check box on the CreatePopUp form is unchecked, the CloseButton property of the new form is set to False. If the text box is left blank, a default of 3 is chosen using this line:

```
sglWidth = IIf(IsNull(Me.txtWidth), 3, Me.txtWidth)
```

If you want your form to measure 3.5 inches, enter **3.5** in the box marked Width In Inches. Perhaps the most interesting line in the whole program is this one:

```
Set frm = CreateForm(, sTplName)
```

This line actually creates a form using whatever template you supply, and sets a pointer to the frm variable. You omit the first argument, which is the name of the database, in the CreateForm method, and supply the template on which you want to base the form you are creating as the second argument. The variable sTplName is obtained from the list box using these lines:

```
iTplIndex = Me.lstTemplates.ListIndex 'Get selection index
sTplName = Me.lstTemplates.ItemData(iTplIndex)
```

Because you don't need multiple selections, you don't have to use either Simple or Extended settings in the MultiSelect property of the list box. Leave the default None in this property.

The With construct is used with the `frm` variable to set the properties of the newly created form this way:

```
With frm 'PopUp form settings set to dialog box settings
    .BorderStyle = iBorder
    .MinMaxButtons = iMinMax
    .Width = sglWidth * TPI
    .AutoCenter = Me.chkCenter
    .Modal = Me.chkModal
    .CloseButton = Me.ChkClose
    .ControlBox = Me.chkControl
    .PopUp = True
End With
```

Notice that the `Width` property of the form is set to whatever is entered in inches in the Width In Inches list box contained in the `sglWidth` variable times twips per inch (1440). The `PopUp` property is set to `True` because, after all, this is a pop-up form.

Now that you have an idea of how the procedure behind the form works, let's see it in action by following these steps:

1. Double-click the CreatePopUp form to open it in Form view.

2. In the Templates list box, choose tplGreen. The three templates listed in the Templates box have the `ScrollBars` property set to `Neither` and the `RecordSelectors` and `NavigationButtons` properties set to `No`. The new form will be based on the tplGreen template.

3. Set the Width In Inches text box to 4.5. Uncheck the Control Box check box, as shown in Figure 21.7.

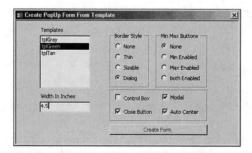

Figure 21.7: *The settings you choose on the controls of the CreatePopUp form are transferred to the new form.*

4. Click the Create Form button. Notice that the form appears in Design view. If the `DoCmd.Restore` line were not there, the form would stay minimized.

5. Press F4 to open the Property sheet of the form, or right-click the title bar and choose Properties. Click the All tab. Be sure the Vertical Scroll Bar slider is at the top. Also be sure that the Property sheet is expanded vertically so that the maximum number of properties can be viewed, as shown in Figure 21.8.

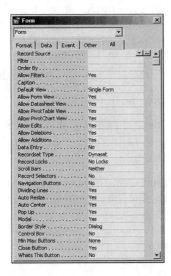

Figure 21.8: *The Property sheet of the newly created form shows that the CreatePopUp form has changed its properties.*

Notice that the ScrollBars, RecordSelectors, and NavigationButtons properties are turned off, reflecting the template. Also notice that the ControlBox property is set to No as you specified.

6. Close the Property sheet. Notice on the ruler at the top of the form that the Width is set to 4.5 as you specified.

7. Close the form, save it as **PopUp**, and reopen it. Notice that it is centered with no control box. Because you can't manually close the form, just right-click it, choose Design view, and close it. There are no user-created controls on the form. However, this is a great way to begin creating your pop-up form. Controls such as check boxes and option buttons can be easily added.

8. Delete the form, and stay in the database.

Using Pop-Up Form Controls to Select Report Criteria

Using a pop-up form to select report criteria is both interesting and fun. You can pass string arguments to the report that is opened, as explained earlier this chapter, or you can supply a SQL string to the `FilterName` argument of the `OpenReport` method. The string can be built piece by piece through strings that are obtained from options that users select on the form.

The next example builds a SQL string containing a date range and a state selection for criteria. You can either type in the date manually or have the date range built automatically from selections on the form.

To try the form by example, follow these steps:

1. Open the CreateCriteria form to view the options available.

2. First, select FL from the Choose a State list box.

3. From the Choose Start Year drop-down box, choose 1996. Notice that the Between list box changes to reflect the year. From the Choose End Year drop-down box, choose 1998.

4. From the Choose Month Option Group, choose Mar, and notice that the month is reflected in both the Between and the And boxes, as shown in Figure 21.9.

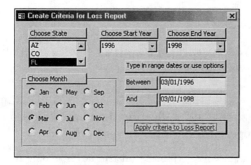

Figure 21.9: *The selections you make using the CreateCriteria pop-up form are used for report criteria.*

5. Click the Apply Criteria to Loss Report button to open the Loss Report in Preview mode, as shown in Figure 21.10. With the magnifying glass cursor, click toward the middle of the report to zoom close enough to verify that the date range and state are what you chose. Close the report.

6. Click the CO (Colorado) State in the Choose State list box. Choose the 1994 and 1995 years, respectively, from the drop-down boxes. Click May in the Option Group.

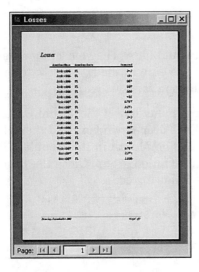

Figure 21.10: *The preview verifies that the report reflects exactly what you chose for criteria.*

7. Click the Apply Criteria to Loss Report button to view the results of changing the criteria. Close the report.

8. Leave the month alone, change the state to AZ, and change both year boxes to 1993.

9. Click the Apply Criteria to Loss Report button to run the report. This time, you get a message because there are no records. Click OK.

10. Close the report and the form, but stay in the database.

By now, you can see that pop-up forms can be very useful. Perhaps you wonder how the CreateCriteria form works. Let's look behind the scenes to view the code that makes it work.

1. Open the CreateCriteria form in Design view to view the code.

2. Click the combo box directly under the Choose Start Year label, and press F4. Click the Event tab, and click the Build button on the After Update event property box to view the following code:

```
Dim sStart As String, iIndex As Integer
Dim sName As String

iIndex = Me.cboStartYear.ListIndex 'Get selection index
sName = Me.cboStartYear.ItemData(iIndex)

sStart = Me.txtStartDate
```

```
Me.txtStartDate = Left(sStart, 6) & sName
End Sub
```

There is nothing too unusual here. The year chosen here is simply concatenated to the end of the date in the txtStartDate text box. The txtEndDate box is set up the same way.

3. Click Edit, Find from the menu bar of the Visual Basic Editor. Type **optMonth** in the Find What drop-down box, and then click Find Next to find the first occurrence of optMonth in the module. This code is attached to the optMonth Option group. Close the Find dialog box, and scroll down to view the following code:

```
Dim ctlMonth As Control, i As Integer
Dim sSDate As String, sEDate As String

Set ctlMonth = Me.optMonth
sSDate = Me.txtStartDate
sEDate = Me.txtEndDate
For i = 1 To 12
    If ctlMonth = i And i < 10 Then
        Me.txtStartDate = "0" & i & Right(sSDate, 8)
        Me.txtEndDate = "0" & i & Right(sEDate, 8)
    ElseIf ctlMonth = i And i >= 10 Then
        Me.txtStartDate = i & Right(sSDate, 8)
        Me.txtEndDate = i & Right(sEDate, 8)
    End If
Next
```

The ctlMonth variable represents the Option Group. The Option Group has 12 values, numbered consecutively from 1 to 12, just as the For...Next loop counts from 1 to 12. The value of ctlMonth will be whatever the user chooses, which happens to correspond to the months of the year. For example, if the user chooses 11, this value represents November.

Nothing happens unless ctlMonth = i, the variable that represents the number of the current loop. If the loop is less than 10, the number will only have a length of 1, which means a zero needs to be concatenated in front of the number. Otherwise, the ElseIf clause concatenates without the zero. To keep the date in the txtStartDate and txtEndDate text boxes showing 10 total characters, a zero must be added before the months that are only one character. The other eight unchanged characters are appended to the month selected.

4. Choose Edit, Find from the menu bar of the Visual Basic Editor. Type **cmdViewReport** in the Find What box, and click Find Next to find the first occurrence of your selection. Close the dialog box. The code you

are viewing is attached to the cmdViewReport command button. Scroll down to view the entire procedure, and stay in the module until you read the comments after the listing.

```
Dim strSQL As String, strWhere As String
Dim iIndex As Integer, sName As String
Dim sStart As String, sEnd As String

iIndex = Me.lstState.ListIndex 'Get selection index
sName = Me.lstState.ItemData(iIndex) 'Get item

sStart = Me.txtStartDate 'Get start date from text box
sEnd = Me.txtEndDate 'Get end date from text box
strSQL = "Select * from Losses Where " 'Build string
strWhere = "[AccidentState] = "
strWhere = strWhere & Chr$(34) & sName & Chr$(34) & " And "
strWhere = strWhere & "[AccidentDate] " & "between #" _
& sStart & "# And #" & sEnd & "#;"
strSQL = strSQL & strWhere
On Error GoTo GetOut 'If no data avoid cancel report error
DoCmd.OpenReport "Loss Report", acViewPreview, strSQL
'DoCmd.Close acForm, "CreateCriteria"
GetOut:
Exit Sub
```

Most of this procedure involves building the SQL string from data obtained from controls. The procedure first grabs the state selection. Then, it grabs the start and end dates for the range. Next, it builds the SQL string. Then, it outputs the report to the screen with the OpenReport method. Notice that the third argument in the method is the SQL string. If the reports return no records, an error routine exits the procedure.

The following steps can help you understand how the PopUp property works:

1. Close the module. Click the Form selector, and press F4 to open the Property sheet. Change the PopUp property to Yes. Click the View button to run the form. Select Colorado (CO), and then select the 1993 and 1999 years respectively. Click the Apply Criteria to Loss Report button to view the report.

   Notice two things. No matter what you do, the form stays on top. Also notice that you can't click on the report underneath the form. Close the form without saving. Now you can click on the report. Close the report. Now you have seen what the PopUp and Modal properties do by example. The PopUp property secured the form as the top window. The Modal property kept you from clicking on another window.

2. Reopen the CreateCriteria form in Design view. Right-click the Apply Criteria to Loss Report button and choose Build Event. Remove the apostrophe (') before the following line:

```
'DoCmd.Close acForm, "CreateCriteria"
```

3. Close the Module window. Click the View button to run the form. Select Colorado (CO), and then select the 1993 and 1999 years, respectively. Click the Apply Criteria to Loss Report button to view the report. Notice that you are asked if you want to save the form. This is because you removed the apostrophe, making the Close method active. Choose No to close the form. Stay in the database.

This exercise taught you that a form can close itself, but more importantly, you learned how to control the interaction of objects. You receive the message because you ran the form before saving the changes to the form. In this case, you want the CreateCriteria form to stay open so you can make another criteria selection after closing the report. At other times, you might want to close the form that called the report immediately after opening the report. Reverse the changes you made by inserting the apostrophe that you removed in the procedure and saving the changes.

How to Tell Whether a Form Is Open

Why do you need to know whether a form is open? If you want to retrieve some data from a form, you might use an expression such as the following:

```
strState = Forms!LossesArg!AccidentState
```

The line runs if the form is open. It fails if the form is closed, whether it is a pop-up form or not. Consequently, there are times when you need a way to determine whether the form is loaded. The following procedure determines whether a specific form is loaded in the database:

```
Function IsFormOpen(frm As String) As Boolean
    Dim objAccess As AccessObject, dbObject As Object
    Set dbObject = Application.CurrentProject
    'Browse AllForms collection for loaded form
    For Each objAccess In dbObject.AllForms
        If objAccess.IsLoaded = True And _
        objAccess.Name = frm Then
            IsFormOpen = True
            Exit Function
        Else
            IsFormOpen = False
        End If
    Next objAccess
End Function
```

Now you have a function that can be called from a procedure to determine whether a particular form is open so that values can be retrieved from the form this way:

```
If IsFormOpen("LossesArg")
    strState = Forms!LossesArg!AccidentState
End if
```

Go Multidimensional with PivotTables

A *PivotTable* is an analysis tool that offers a great deal of flexibility for viewing summary data from different perspectives. You can think of a PivotTable as an expandable summary because it neatly tucks information away to be viewed by expanding your selection. For example, if you view summary information by the year, you can drill down to expand any year to see its details. The capability to "pivot" the perspective of your table by transposing rows and columns gives the PivotTable its name.

PivotTables give new meaning to the term *interactive*, which refers to the capability of users to enter data or commands in programs, as opposed to just viewing data. Tables and forms are interactive to a certain extent. You can sort, filter, and modify data with tables and forms. PivotTables allow users to quickly summarize or cross-tabulate large amounts of data. If you want to rotate rows and columns interactively (on the fly), use PivotTables.

The transformation from PivotTable to PivotChart is only one button click away, making PivotCharts fully interactive. A *PivotChart* is a graph tied to and derived from a PivotTable.

PivotTables go beyond the functionality of Crosstab queries when it comes to viewing data from a variety of different perspectives. Although unavailable in Access 2000, PivotTables make a welcome addition to Access 2002. You can take any existing form and quickly create a PivotTable from it with a few mouse clicks, or you can use the PivotTable Wizard under forms in the Database window. But you are not limited to just forms. You can view any Access table or query; or any Access Project table, view, stored procedure, or form in either PivotTable or PivotChart view. If that's not enough, you can save their PivotTable and PivotChart views as Data Access Pages that can be viewed and manipulated by others using their browsers.

If you double-click on a table or query and then right-click on the title bar, you can choose PivotTable view. After you place the fields you need in the appropriate places, you save the view with the table or query.

To show you how easy it is, let's create a PivotTable by example:

1. Under Forms, click New to open the New Form dialog box.

2. Click AutoForm:PivotTable, and select Losses from the drop-down list of tables and queries. Click OK to open a blank PivotTable view, shown in Figure 21.11.

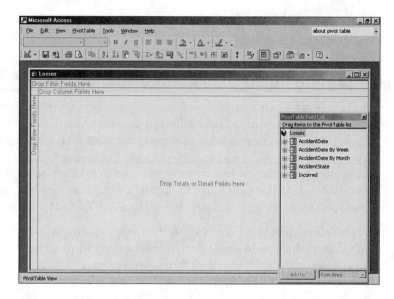

Figure 21.11: *You can drag and drop fields into a blank PivotTable view.*

3. From the PivotTable field list, click the plus sign (+) beside AccidentDate By Month to expand it. Click Years, and drag it over to the section labeled Drop Row Fields Here until you see the section highlighted in blue, as shown in Figure 21.12, and drop it.

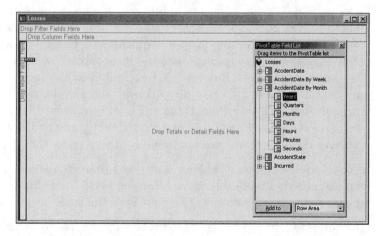

Figure 21.12: *When you drag and release the year field into the section labeled Drop Row Fields Here, it becomes an expandable row.*

4. Right-click the Years row section title you just dropped, and choose Collapse. Drag the unexpanded AccidentDate from the field list over to the right side of Years until you see a blue vertical line, as shown in Figure 21.13, and drop it.

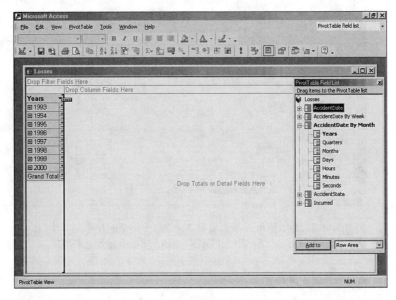

Figure 21.13: *When you see the blue vertical line beside the Years section, you drop the field that you want to see when Years is expanded.*

5. From the PivotTable field list, drag the unexpanded AccidentState over to the section labeled Drop Column Fields Here.

6. Click on (don't drag) the unexpanded Incurred field.

7. At the bottom of the PivotTable Field List, choose Data Area from the drop-down list beside the Add to button.

8. Click the Add to button to add the field with totals to the PivotTable, as shown in Figure 21.14.

9. Right-click the Sum of Incurred field title in the PivotTable, and choose Properties to open the Properties dialog box. Click the Captions tab, as shown in Figure 21.15.

10. Change Sum of Incurred to Incurred Sum, and notice that the field titles change for every column.

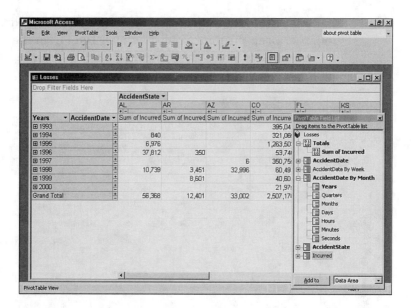

Figure 21.14: *When you use the Add to button to add a financial field to the data area of the PivotTable, totals are added.*

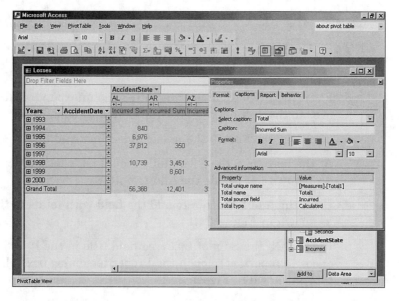

Figure 21.15: *The Captions tab in the Properties dialog box lets you change column titles.*

11. Close the Properties dialog box. Expand year 2000 by clicking the plus sign (+) beside the box. Notice that Colorado is the only state that had any losses reported so far that year. Also notice that you can tell at a glance exactly when the losses occurred.

12. Close the PivotTable and save it as **Loss Years**.

13. Under Tables, open the Sales table just to refresh your memory about how it is arranged. Take special notice of the redundancy. This is the table you use for the next PivotTable, which eliminates redundancy.

14. Under Forms, click New to open the New Form dialog box, and choose AutoForm: PivotTable. Select Sales from the drop-down box, and click OK to open a blank PivotTable.

15. From the PivotTable Field List, drop Regions in the Drop Row Fields Here area. Drop Years in the Drop Column Fields Here area.

16. Click Sales, and then select Data Area from the drop-down list beside the Add to button. Click the Add to button to add it to the PivotTable, as shown in Figure 21.16.

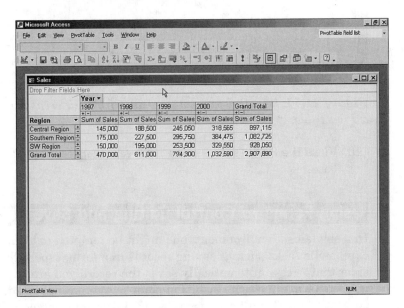

Figure 21.16: *The new PivotTable based on the Sales table eliminates redundancy.*

17. Right-click the Region title in the row section of the PivotTable, and choose Remove.

18. Click the Year title in the column section, and drag it to the row section labeled Drop Row Fields Here.

19. From the PivotTable Field List, drag the Region field to the column section of the PivotTable labeled Drop Column Fields Here, as shown in Figure 21.17.

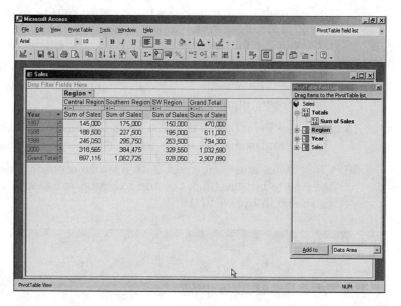

Figure 21.17: *It is easy to view your data from different perspectives using a PivotTable.*

20. Close the PivotTable, saving it as **YearsRegions**, but stay in the database.

Using Forms to Control Editing and Save Records

In a single-user environment, one might be tempted to think that Access can handle tasks such as saving records in a form, especially when you consider that Access automatically saves the record you are adding or editing as soon as you move the insertion point to a different record, or close the current form. This all changes in a multiuser environment. Do you want two or more users to be able to access the same record simultaneously and save their changes? It depends on what you want to do. Table 21.3 explains the differences in the three RecordLocks property settings on a form.

Table 21.3: `RecordLocks` *Property Settings*

Property	Value	Comments
`No Locks`	0	This property often is referred to as *optimistic* locking. It is the default setting. In forms, two or more users can edit the same record simultaneously. If two users attempt to save changes to the same record, Microsoft Access displays a message to the second user who tries to save the record. This user can then discard the record, copy the record to the Clipboard, or replace the changes made by the other user. This setting is typically used in single-user databases or in multiuser databases in which two or more users need to able to make changes to the same record at the same time.
`All Records`	1	All records in the underlying table or query are locked while the form is open in Form view or Datasheet view. Although users can read the records, no one can edit, add, or delete any records until the form is closed.
`Edited Record`	2	This property is often referred to as *pessimistic* locking. A page of records is locked as soon as any user starts editing any field in the record, and stays locked until the user moves to another record. Therefore, a record can be edited by only one user at a time.

Although `No Locks` is the default setting when you first install Access, you can change the default record locking setting in the Advanced tab after selecting Tools, Options from the menu bar. Remember that the default record-locking setting is ignored when you open recordsets using code. Also keep in mind that you can force optimistic record locking by setting the `AllowEdits` property to `False`.

Optimistic Versus Pessimistic Locking

What's the difference between optimistic and pessimistic locking strategies, and which one should you use? *Optimistic locking* refers to the scheme employed by Jet that waits to request a lock on a page of records until the user saves changes to a record. As shown in Table 21.3, Jet uses optimistic record locking by default. Using *pessimistic locking*, the page containing the record being edited is immediately locked, making it unavailable to other users until the user releases the lock by saving or canceling changes to the record. A look at the advantages and disadvantages of both can help.

Pessimistic locking advantages include the following:

- Users don't get messages that could confuse them.

- Users don't have control of what they don't understand.

- Users can't overwrite another user's changes.

Pessimistic locking disadvantages include the following:

- A page of records is usually locked.
- Locks are held for longer periods of time.

Optimistic locking advantages include the following:

- Users have simultaneous individual access to records.
- Locks are held for shorter periods of time.
- Computer-savvy users have a choice when editing conflicts arise.

Optimistic locking disadvantages include the following:

- Users might get messages that confuse them.
- Users are allowed to overwrite another user's changes.

Optimistic locking is generally preferred because it is usually not a good idea to preclude users from being able to make changes to data for potentially long periods of time. If the situation dictates, you can always force pessimistic locking.

Refresh Versus Requery

In an environment in which data is shared on a network, other users can be changing data at the same time that you are viewing the same data in a form. Access updates the data that you see at regular intervals. However, you can force the immediate display of the most current data by refreshing the records. Remember that refreshing records only updates the data that already exists in your form. It doesn't display new records or remove deleted records. To execute those operations, requery the records.

You can change the refresh interval in the Advanced tab after selecting Tools, Options from the menu bar. Some applications might warrant decreasing the 60-second default interval. This provides faster feedback to the user. On the other hand, an interval that is too small could create too much network traffic, especially in larger networks.

If you want to gain a better understanding of locking strategies and forced refreshes/requeries by example, follow these steps:

1. Under Forms, open SaveEdit in Form view, as shown in Figure 21.18.
2. Change the AccidentDate field from 6/29/1993 to 6/29/1994.
3. Change the AccidentState field from MS to MZ.

Figure 21.18: *The SaveEdit form gives you a better understanding of record locking.*

4. From the menu bar, click Records, Save Record (or Shift+Enter). From the toolbar, click Undo. Notice that the changes are undone.

5. Perform steps 2 and 3. Press Page Down to go to the next record. Press Page Up to return to the original record. Click Undo from the toolbar. Notice that the changes are not undone.

6. Change the AccidentDate field from 6/29/1994 to 6/29/1995.

7. Change the AccidentState field from MZ to MY.

8. Click the Save Record button on the form, and then click Undo Record. Notice that the record is not undone, as in step 5. The code behind the Save record button looks like this:

```
If Me.Dirty Then
DoCmd.RunCommand acCmdSaveRecord
Me.Refresh
Me.Requery
End If
```

If you remove the Me.Requery line, the button produces the same results as step 4. The change can be undone. If Me.Dirty is true, which means that the data has changed, the acCmdSaveRecord operation is performed, which is equivalent to choosing Records, Save Records from the menu bar.

9. Change the Accident Date field to 6/29/1993 and the Accident State field to MS.

10. Click the Lock Deletes button to prevent any record deletions. Notice that the button stays depressed because it is a toggle button as opposed to a command button, as shown in Figure 21.19. Also notice that the Delete Record button on the toolbar is disabled. Even if you click on the record selector on the left side of the form and press Delete, nothing happens.

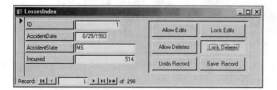

Figure 21.19: *The Lock Deletes toggle button stays depressed until you click the Allow Deletes button.*

NOTE

Although toggle buttons and command buttons look identical when placed side by side, you see the difference after pressing the toggle button. It stays depressed, whereas the command button doesn't depress at all. Unless you have the `TripleState` property checked, toggle buttons are two-state; either on or off. A toggle button can be changed to a check box or an option button.

---

11. Click the Allow Deletes button. Notice that the Delete Record button is activated. Also notice that the Lock Deletes button is no longer depressed.

12. Click the Delete Record button. A message stating that one record is about to be deleted appears. Click No.

13. Click the Lock Edits button on the form. Try to change any field. You can't do it. Try to click Allow Edits. You cannot click on that button or any other buttons on the form. You can get around this by changing the `OnClick` event procedure on the Lock Edits button so that the `RecordsetType` property of the form is set to Snapshot with a line like this:

    ```
    Me.RecordsetType = 2
    ```

    When you use the `Snapshot` data type, you can click any buttons on the form because the data is the only thing that is affected. If you changed the Allow Edit button so that the `RecordsetType` property of the form is set to `Dynaset` (0), the two buttons depress properly. `Dynaset` allows editing, but because `Snapshot` is read-only, it does not allow editing.

14. Close the form but stay in the database.

To get a little better understanding of how the buttons on the SaveEdit form work, let's take a look at the code behind the form:

```
Private Sub cmdSave_Click()
If Me.Dirty Then
DoCmd.RunCommand acCmdSaveRecord
```

```
Me.Refresh
Me.Requery
End If
End Sub

Private Sub cmdUndo_Click()
If Me.Dirty Then
DoCmd.RunCommand acCmdUndo
Me.Refresh
End If
End Sub

Private Sub TogAllowDeletes_Click()
Me.AllowDeletions = True
Me.Refresh
Me.togLockDeletes = False
End Sub

Private Sub togLockDeletes_Click()
Me.AllowDeletions = False
Me.Refresh
Me.TogAllowDeletes = False
End Sub

Private Sub togAllowEdits_Click()
Me.AllowEdits = True
Me.Refresh
Me.togLockEdits = False
End Sub

Private Sub togLockEdits_Click()
Me.AllowEdits = False
Me.Refresh
Me.togAllowEdits = False
End Sub
```

The line Me.TogAllowDeletes = False changes the depressed state of the
Allow Deletes button from the Lock Deletes button. You don't want to allow
both buttons to be depressed at the same time because the depressed state
lets you know whether you can delete records. So, if one button is up, the
other is down and vice versa. The DoCmd.RunCommand options give you a con-
venient way to run menu bar commands such as Undo. Because the Allow
Edits button becomes useless when the Lock Edits button is depressed, you
can change the buttons to set recordset types and test them.

Using Forms to Optimize Large Tables

What do you do when your tables become so large that they are slower than molasses? When tables become large, users start complaining. No matter how creative your application is, if it's slow, it won't be as impressive. If you have applied all the optimization techniques in this book and are still plagued with speed problems, your best option could be to limit the size of the table. You can break up tables that have too many fields by applying the normalization principles from Chapter 1, "Planning and Designing Your Access Database." But assuming that this has been done, there are other alternatives.

Append Obsolete Records into Another Table

One alternative that you might consider is to delete obsolete records. The only problem with that option is that you never know when you might need to access those records for legal purposes. You can create an archive table for obsolete records that can be appended from your form with code like the following:

```
Dim Cert As Double
Cert = Me.CertNo
DoCmd.RunSql "INSERT INTO Amend SELECT [Clients].* " _
& "FROM [Clients] WHERE [Clients].[CertNo] =" & Cert & ";"
```

The archive table doesn't have to be in the same database. You can include the append date along with the creation date of the record. You won't increase the size of the table as rapidly by using this method.

Activate and Deactivate Records

But your business might be different. Suppose you are an administrator for a medical school. Records in the table might need to be activated and deactivated. If you deactivate them by appending them to an archive table, it could end up being more trouble than it's worth because the students are tied to certificates of insurance in a relational database model. A better alternative is to set up a Yes/No field called Activated.

If it's checked, it's activated. Any records that are activated are filtered so that the user never sees the deactivated records. This way, the user works with a smaller amount of records at a time. The deactivated records have a different font color to distinguish them when the All button is pushed.

The following steps show you an application using this technique:

1. Under Forms, open the Insureds form. Click the All button, as shown in Figure 21.20.

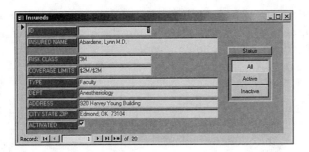

Figure 21.20: *The All button turns the* `FilterOn` *property off so that all the records in the form can be viewed.*

2. Click the Next Record button three times. Notice that the text fields in the third record have a different font color. Click Next Record several times while watching the `Activated` field. Notice that each time an unchecked box appears, the records show a different font color.

3. Click the Inactive button. Six records are filtered. Even though this is a small table, the technique can easily be applied to a large table. If you browse through these records, each record has the same font color.

4. Click the Active button, and notice that the filter is applied and the records change colors again.

5. Close the form.

To understand how the form works, examine the following code, which is attached to the form's `OnCurrent` method:

```
Dim Ctrl As Control
If Me.Activated = False Then
    For Each Ctrl In Me.Controls
        If TypeOf Ctrl Is TextBox Then
          Ctrl.ForeColor = 9474120
        End If
    Next
Else
    For Each Ctrl In Me.Controls
        If TypeOf Ctrl Is TextBox Then
          Ctrl.ForeColor = 10040115
        End If
    Next
End If
```

This procedure demonstrates how you can nest an `If` statement inside a `For...Each` loop that is nested inside another `If` statement. If the `Activated` field, which is a Yes/No field, is False, set all the text boxes on the form to a different forecolor. The filter is set when the form opens using the OnOpen event property with the following code:

```
Me.Filter = "[Activated] = True"
Me.FilterOn = True
```

Fairly straightforward, huh? The programming for the Option group control called optStatus, which keys on the state of the Activated field, is just as easy, as shown in following code:

```
Select Case Me.optStatus
    Case 1
    Me.FilterOn = False
    Case 2
    Me.Filter = "[Activated] = True"
    Me.FilterOn = True
    Case 3
    Me.Filter = "[Activated] = False"
    Me.FilterOn = True
End Select
```

Viewing Sequential Chunks of Data Versus Browsing the Whole Table

Another alternative when considering a method for dealing with huge tables is letting the user see only small chunks of data at a time. The following procedure, which is attached to a button that pages down each time it's pressed, gives you the basic idea that can be expanded:

```
Dim sSQL As String
Dim iMin As Integer, iMax As Integer

iMin = Me.ID + 20
iMax = iMin + 20
sSQL = "Select * FROM Losses"
sSQL = sSQL & "Where [ID] Between " & iMin & " And " & iMax
Me.RecordSource = sSQL
```

The iMax variable is always 20 records ahead of iMin. When you click the command button, you simulate a page down by running a query that grabs the next 20 records from the current position, determined by the ID field. Notice the concatenation of the iMin and iMax variables in the SQL string. Also notice that the record source is changed every time the button is clicked.

Tab Control Benefits

When you have a large amount of data to accommodate, but only a limited amount of space on the form, *tab controls* are probably your answer. They allow you to have many pages worth of data in a small area by grouping similar categories of data on each tab. You navigate between these areas by simply clicking on the appropriate tab. Think of tab controls as electronic file folders in your visual filing cabinet.

Tab controls are excellent for menus, dialog boxes, subforms, images, standard controls, or ActiveX controls. Although you can create the illusion of nested tab controls by setting the visible property programmatically, if you place a tab control on any page of another tab control and then view the form in Form view, the embedded tab control is visible from any page of the main tab control. So, for all intents and purposes, you cannot nest tab controls. Figure 21.21 demonstrates the various ways that tab controls can be formatted.

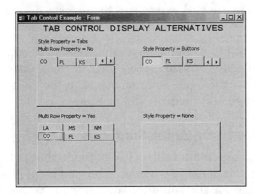

Figure 21.21: *You can show single or multiple rows of tabs on an Access tab control.*

Using Tab Controls As a Substitute for Multipage Forms

Before tab controls arrived on the scene in Access 97, if you had too much data for a single page, you had to resort to creating another form page, which at times can be awkward and confusing. Tab controls provide a way to neatly and systematically arrange your information with a technique that makes sense.

There are two methods of displaying information on a tab control. The first method is to "float" information, which means that you see the same control, such as a subform, or a group of controls, such as text boxes, as you tab from page to page. The second method is to embed the information.

Using this method, every page displays different information as you tab from page to page.

In Design view of the form, you can either place controls directly on a tab control from the toolbox, or cut and paste the controls from a place outside the tab control on the form. If you place them directly from the toolbox, be sure you draw the control directly on the page, which becomes highlighted as you draw, in which you want the controls embedded. Placing the control this way ensures that it is embedded on the page. If you want the control to float, draw the control outside the tab control before dragging it on top of any single page.

If you cut and paste the control (or group of controls) from outside the tab control or from outside the form, be sure that you have the single page in which you want to embed the control selected before pasting the object; otherwise, the object is not embedded on the page. For example, if you have the detail section selected before pasting the control, the object floats when you run the form. Using these techniques, you can control when you embed and when you float. You don't have to run the form to determine whether the control floats or embeds; you can tell from Design view.

If you have the parent table on one page and a subform with the child table on another, you obviously want to embed the controls. However, if you want to use the tabs to filter the same information with the value represented by the selected tab, you should float the information.

Using Tab Controls to Organize Subforms

Suppose you have a large main table with 20 fields that is linked to another table in the relationship window. After you create the form, there is no room on the page for the subform. You can place a tab control on the form, using one page for the parent table and another page for the subform with the child table as its record source.

Let's look at an example of using tab controls for subforms.

1. Open the Convention database from your AccessByExample folder.

2. Under Forms, open One-To-Many Tab Control Example in Form view. Click the Reservation Information tab, as shown in Figure 21.22. Notice that you have two groups of navigation buttons.

3. Click the Next Record button on the lower group of buttons. Notice that the number of records shown depends on the link to the parent table. Also notice that a large amount of information is contained in a small area due to the tab control.

4. Close the form.

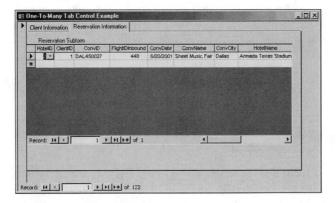

Figure 21.22: *Tab controls are a great way to organize tables that have one-to-many relationships.*

Images can also require a large amount of screen space. You can place a large image on one page in a tab control without dominating the form because the next page can contain supplemental information. An excellent example of using images with the tab control can be found in the Northwind database Employee form.

Using Tab Controls to Organize Menus

If you want your application to be menu-driven, tab controls can provide an alternative to the switchboard. You can set up menus to navigate around your database with hyperlinks or buttons. Tab controls let you organize the user options into categories for easy access. For example, one tab could contain reports to print; another could contain reports to view. Or, you could organize your sales reports on one tab and your expense reports on another. Hyperlinks combined with tab controls are also an excellent way to organize your favorite Web sites.

For an example of a tab control menu, follow these steps:

1. Open the claims database from your AccessByExample folder.

2. Under Forms, open TabControlMenu in Form view, as shown in Figure 21.23.

3. Click on the tabs, and notice that the hyperlink options are arranged into categories.

4. Click any hyperlink to open a form.

5. Close the form, but stay in the database.

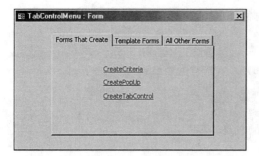

Figure 21.23: *Tab controls are a great way to organize menus for your application.*

Using Tab Controls for Dialog Boxes

If you have some custom dialog boxes that you have saved as forms, you can combine them on one form using tab controls. Use the Select All option from the Edit menu bar option to copy all the controls from the form. Be sure to select the page of the tab control to which you want to paste the controls before pasting. The only caveat is that any code attached to the original form must be pasted separately. That's why it is best to create the dialog boxes after creating the tab controls.

To see an example of custom dialog boxes with tab controls, follow these steps:

1. Open the claims database from your AccessByExample folder.

2. Under Forms, open TabControlDialogBox in Form view, as shown in Figure 21.24.

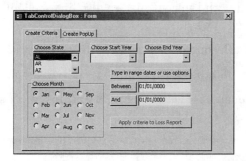

Figure 21.24: *Tab controls are a great way to organize dialog boxes for your application.*

3. The dialog boxes shown on the first page should look familiar. These are "dummy" dialog boxes for example purposes only.

4. Click the Create PopUp tab and close the form. Stay in the database.

Creating Tab Controls Programmatically

Now it really gets interesting. You can actually create your tab control programmatically to save yourself some time. This is especially helpful if you have a large number of tabs to insert. If that's not enough, it gets even better. The tabs can reflect information about what you are organizing. For example, if the tab control is to display information about a loss table, you can have the procedure create a separate tab for each state in the table to act as a filter.

After the tab control is created, you need to know what tab is selected. The tab's name property becomes part of a SQL string that is assigned to the RecordSource property of the subform. The subform floats on top of the tab control so that it appears on each page. Each time you click on a tab, the criteria in the SQL string change, which in turn is reflected in the subform.

The following steps lead you through creating a form and tab control. After the tab control is created, you learn how to program the tab control. Then, you learn how to write the procedure that created the tab control.

1. Under Forms, open CreateTabControl in Form view.

2. Click the Create Tab Control button to create the form and tab control shown in Figure 21.25.

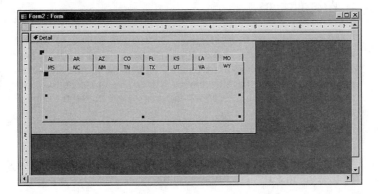

Figure 21.25: *The tab control created when the Create Tab Control button is clicked from the CreateTabControl form reflects every state in the Losses table.*

3. Close the form without saving to show the CreateTabControl form again.

4. This time, click the Pick Tab Control button to choose what states you want for the tab control.

5. From the PickTab form, click AZ, CO, FL, TN, and TX, and then double-click UT to open the form shown in Figure 21.26.

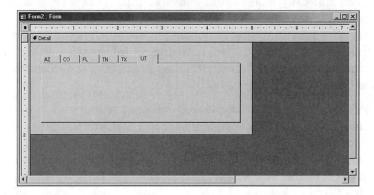

Figure 21.26: *The tab control created when the Pick Tab Control button is clicked from the CreateTabControl form reflects the states in the Losses table that you choose.*

6. Click the Toolbox button to open it. With the wand selected, click the Subform tool, and draw a rectangle slightly smaller than the tab control *below* the tab control, as shown in Figure 21.27. The Subform Wizard opens.

NOTE

This is putting into action what you learned in the section "Using Tab Controls As a Substitute for Multipage Forms," earlier in this chapter. You can embed (lock) the subform on a tab control page by drawing it directly on the page, or you can draw the subform in an area off the tab control and drag it back on the tab control to float the subform.

---

7. On the first page of the wizard, choose the subLosses subform from the list, and click Next. Click Finish on the next page of the wizard to place the subform on the form.

8. Drag the subform to place it on the tab control. Click the subLosses label on the upper-left edge of the subform, and press Delete to remove the label. Click some of the tabs to verify that the subform floats. Drag the bottom edge of the form up to just below the bottom of the tab control.

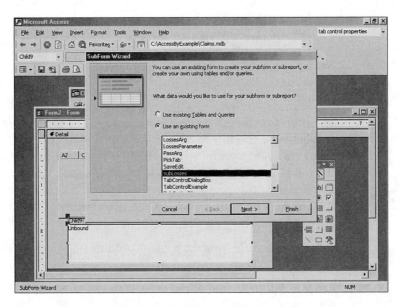

Figure 21.27: *Draw the subform rectangle below the tab control to create a "floating" subform.*

9. Click the tab control, as opposed to one of the pages. You can tell if you have the tab control selected by the fact that the handles are on the very edge of the control, as shown in Figure 21.28.

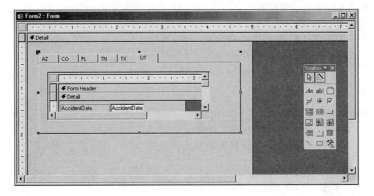

Figure 21.28: *Click the tab control so that you can open its Property sheet.*

10. Press F4 to open the Property sheet of the form. Click the Event tab. Type the following code into the OnChange event's Module window:

```
Dim Pg As String, sSQL As String

With Me.tabOnFly
```

```
        Pg = .Pages(.Value).Name
        sSQL = "Select * from Losses where [AccidentState]=" _
        & Chr$(34) & Pg & Chr$(34)
        Me.subLosses.Form.RecordSource = sSQL
        Me.subLosses.Form.Refresh
    End With
```

The name of the tab control is `tabOnFly`. The `With` clause accesses the properties of the tab control. Every time you click on a tab, the `OnChange` event occurs, which triggers its event procedure. The name of the tab is accessed with the line `Pg = .Pages(.Value).Name`. The last line accesses the subform directly through its control name, which is `subLosses`. The SQL string is then inserted into the control source of the subform.

11. Close the module, property sheet, and form, and save the form as `ControlTabFilter`.

12. Reopen the form, and click on the tabs as you notice the number of records at the bottom of the form.

13. Scroll the subform to verify that the records are there.

14. Close the form.

Let's analyze the procedures that created the tab controls, starting with the procedure that created the tab control with all states:

```
Dim iCount As Integer
Dim frm As Form, iLeft As Integer, iTop As Integer
Dim iWidth As Integer, iHeight As Integer
Dim cn As ADODB.Connection, fld As String
Dim rs As ADODB.Recordset

iCount = 0
Const TPI = 1440 'TPI = Twips Per Inch
    Set cn = CurrentProject.Connection
    Set rs = New ADODB.Recordset
    With rs
     .Source = "States"
     .ActiveConnection = cn
     .CursorType = adOpenKeyset
     .LockType = adLockOptimistic
     .Open
    End With
'Position of Tab Control
iLeft = 0.25 * TPI
iTop = 0.25 * TPI
'Dimensions of Tab Control
```

```
iWidth = 4.5 * TPI
iHeight = 1.5 * TPI
Set frm = CreateForm 'Create form for tab control
With CreateControl(frm.Name, acTabCtl, , _
"", "", iLeft, iTop, iWidth, iHeight)
    .Name = "tabOnFly"
    .MultiRow = True
    Do
        fld = rs.Fields("Code").Value
        rs.MoveNext 'Move through query recordset
            If iCount > 1 Then 'Skip first 2 pages
                .Pages.Add
            End If
        .Pages(iCount).Name = fld 'Tab for each state
        iCount = iCount + 1
    Loop Until rs.EOF
End With
DoCmd.Restore
```

The With clause sets properties for the tab control. The width and height of
the form, along with its position on the form, are set with the CreateForm
function. Notice that the MultiRow property is set to True, which turns it on.
The state abbreviations are obtained from the States table in the Code field.
The pages collection of the tab control is accessed so that new pages can be
added and named. The Restore method makes sure that the window is
restored so that you can see it immediately.

The next procedure, which lets you choose which states you want, is very
similar. It is attached to the OnDblClick event of the PickTab form.

```
Dim iLeft As Integer, iTop As Integer
Dim iWidth As Integer, iHeight As Integer
Dim frm As Form, iCount As Integer
Dim lstSelect As ListBox, vItem As Variant

iCount = 0
Const TPI = 1440
'Position of Tab Control
iLeft = 0.25 * TPI
iTop = 0.25 * TPI
'Dimensions of Tab Control
iWidth = 4.5 * TPI
iHeight = 1.5 * TPI
Set frm = CreateForm 'Create form for tab control
With CreateControl(frm.Name, acTabCtl, , _
"", "", iLeft, iTop, iWidth, iHeight)
    .Name = "tabOnFly"
```

```
        .MultiRow = True
        Set lstSelect = Me.lstPick
        For Each vItem In lstSelect.ItemsSelected
            If iCount > 1 Then
                .Pages.Add
            End If
            .Pages(iCount).Name = lstSelect.ItemData(vItem)
            iCount = iCount + 1
        Next
DoCmd.Restore
DoCmd.Close acForm, "PickTab"
End With
```

This time, the tabs are named from the list box selections. The iCount = iCount + 1 increments the counter for the pages. The name of the list box from which the states are selected is lstPick. The lstSelect variable points to lstPick and is accessed through its ItemsSelected property to determine the selected items in the list box.

CAUTION

Don't use the Dialog setting in the BorderStyle property of the form that creates the form and tab control because it generates an error.

What's Next

This chapter mainly focused on taking charge of forms by making the best use of the tools that are available. The next chapter does the same thing with reports. Reports are about viewing your data from a variety of perspectives. It takes you deeper into some of the principles you learned in Chapter 6, "Exploring Reports."

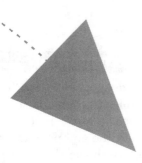

Taking Charge of Reports

Chapter 21, "Taking Charge of Forms," tackled techniques that help you take charge of forms. This chapter does the same with reports.

As of this writing, the paperless office has not yet arrived. Employees and home users are using more paper than ever. As long as paper prevails, reports remain a necessity. With this in mind, you want to be able to get the most out of your reports. This requires moving beyond the basics. Specifically, in this chapter you learn the following:

- how to programmatically handle grouping and sorting
- how to use relationships to control whether data is displayed on a report
- how to remove pesky blank lines on reports
- how to work with multiple column reports
- how to print extra copies of a record on a report

Handling Grouping and Sorting Programmatically

You learned how to manually group and sort records in a report in Chapter 6, "Exploring Reports." Wouldn't it be nice to be able to group and sort on the fly? Having this functionality enables you to see what the report looks like before you go to the trouble of manually setting the grouping and sorting levels permanently in the report. Or, you can use the on-the-fly functionality to preview the report before printing it to see if the groups and sorting levels are satisfactory. Just press a button, and you see the results immediately.

Before you attempt to programmatically create a group level on which to group or sort in your report, you need to determine which group levels already exist. Otherwise, your code could duplicate a group level that is already there. The problem is that Access provides no straightforward method to determine whether a specified group level exists on a report. The same goes for sections. You can access group level properties with code like this:

```
Reports!FlexibleSort.GroupLevel(0).ControlSource = strLevel1
```

However, if you try to access the group level itself, with an assignment such as the following, you generate an error:

```
varGrpLevel = Reports!FlexibleSort.GroupLevel(0)
```

The solution is to let the error determine whether a group level exists. In other words, if an error is generated, the group level doesn't exist. Why not let errors work for you to achieve your desired result? The following procedure does just that:

```
Function LevelExists(objReportName As Object, iLevel As Integer) _
As Boolean

'Don't care about ControlSource except for testing
On Error GoTo Sorry
    If objReportName.GroupLevel(iLevel) _
    .ControlSource <> "" Then
        LevelExists = True
    End If
Exit Function

Sorry:
LevelExists = False

End Function
```

Because you are declaring objReportName as an object variable, you use the function like this:

```
If LevelExists(Reports!FlexibleSorts, 0 ) Then
    Do something ......
End If
```

The report must be open, and the level must be present for the function to return True. Notice that you can't just use the report name in the argument without referencing its collection. The second argument is the group level, which is zero-based. Table 22.1 shows what each group level refers to.

Table 22.1: Group-Level References

Group Level	Refers to
GroupLevel(0)	The first field or expression on which you sort or group.
GroupLevel(1)	The second field or expression on which you sort or group.
GroupLevel(2)	The third field or expression on which you sort or group.

After you determine that a group needs to be created, you use the CreateGroupLevel function to create the various group levels. The syntax of the function is as follows:

```
CreateGroupLevel(ReportName, Expression, Header, Footer)
```

It is used this way:

```
varGroupLevel = CreateGroupLevel("Loss Report", "AccidentDate", True, True)
```

The function needs the name of the report, the field or expression on which to group, and whether you want a header or footer. If you enter True and False (in that order) for the last two arguments, you are specifying a group header but no group footer.

You can attach a toolbar to your report that enables you to group your report according to your specifications. The procedures you create become options on your toolbar. The following example uses toolbar procedures to group the FlexibleGroup report.

Before proceeding any further, let's see what you can do with group levels by example:

1. Open the Claims database from your AccessByExample folder. Under Reports, open the FlexibleGroup report. Notice the toolbar that is attached to the report.

2. Right-click the report title bar in Preview view, and then click the drop-down box beside Zoom, as shown in Figure 22.1. Choose 75%.

3. Expand the right side of the report window. Click OneLevel from the toolbar to group the report, as shown in Figure 22.2.

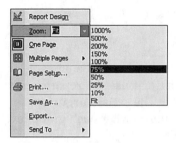

Figure 22.1: *When you right-click the report window in Preview view, you can adjust the zoom percentage.*

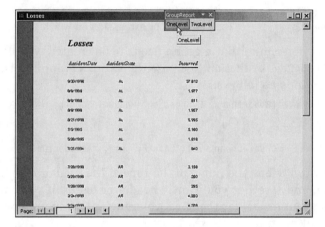

Figure 22.2: *After zooming in on your report, you can run one of the toolbar procedures.*

4. Click TwoLevel to add another level to the report. Your first group level is AccidentState, and your second group level is AccidentDate, but it is rather difficult to determine without at least one group header designation.

5. Right-click the report title bar, and choose Report Design to open the report in Design view. Move the AccidentState field from the Detail section to the AccidentState Header section under the AccidentDate label. Move the AccidentDate field under the AccidentState label in the Detail section, as shown in Figure 22.3.

6. Switch the AccidentDate and AccidentState labels so that the AccidentState label is the first label from the left. Click Print Preview on the toolbar, and then scroll the window until you can see at least two states, as shown in Figure 22.4. Notice how the like values in the

AccidentDate field are grouped. If a date value has no like value with which to group, the record is grouped separately, which explains the extra white spaces.

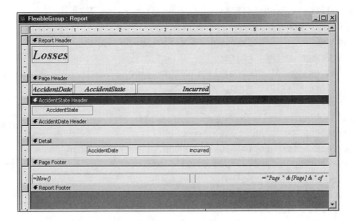

Figure 22.3: *You adjust the positions of the report fields to get a better idea of how the groups work.*

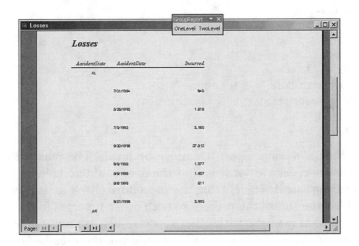

Figure 22.4: *The Print Preview window shows the grouping of the* AccidentState *field and the subgrouping of the* AccidentDate *field.*

7. Close the report without saving. Stay in the database.

The procedure that creates groups and subgroups looks like the following:

```
Public Function GroupLevel(strGroup1 As String, _
Optional strGroup2 As String)
Dim vMakeGroup As Variant
```

```
On Error GoTo ListError
DoCmd.Echo False
DoCmd.OpenReport "FlexibleGroup", acViewDesign

If LevelExists(Reports!FlexibleGroup, 0) = False Then
    'Create group level on strGroup1
    vMakeGroup = CreateGroupLevel("FlexibleGroup", _
    strGroup1, True, False)
    'Set height of strGroup1 header section
    Reports!FlexibleGroup.Section(acGroupLevel0Header) _
    .Height = 400
End If
If strGroup2 <> "" And _
    LevelExists(Reports!FlexibleGroup, 1) = False Then
    vMakeGroup = CreateGroupLevel("FlexibleGroup", _
    strGroup2, True, False)
    Reports!FlexibleGroup.Section(acGroupLevel1Header) _
    .Height = 400
End If

DoCmd.OpenReport "FlexibleGroup", acViewPreview
DoCmd.Echo True
Exit Function

ListError:
DoCmd.Echo True
MsgBox "Error Code: " & Err.number & vbCr _
& "Error Description: " & Err.Description

End Function
```

The FlexibleGroup report has no group levels. The reason the LevelExists
procedure checks anyway is that the user could accidentally click one of the
toolbar options twice. Having the procedure check for group levels also
enables you to use the procedure with other reports. To change this procedure so that it works with other reports, just use a variable to represent
the report instead of specifically referencing the FlexibleGroup report. The
Input function works nicely when you want to ask the user which report
needs to be grouped. The user input is assigned to a variable that the
Openreport method can use instead of a specific report designation. Instead
of calling the function from a toolbar, you can call it from a procedure
attached to a button, if that's your preference.

Let's look at the code more closely. When you open the report, it is already
in Print Preview mode. You switch to Design view because the
CreateGroupLevel function doesn't run in Preview view. So, you use the

`DoCmd` object, such as the following, to switch to Design view and add the group level or levels, whatever the case might be:

```
DoCmd.OpenReport "FlexibleGroup", acViewDesign
```

Then, the same line, with the exception of the second argument, is run again to switch back to Print Preview mode like this:

```
DoCmd.OpenReport "FlexibleGroup", acViewPreview
```

The heart of the procedure lies between these two lines. The first-level variable is `strGroup1`, which is obtained through one of the function arguments. This variable determines on which field the first group level will be based. Notice that `strGroup2` is defined as an optional argument. This means that you don't have to specify a second argument unless you want a second group level. As mentioned earlier, the `CreateGroupLevel` function doesn't even run unless it is first determined that there is no group level that corresponds to the second argument of the `LevelExists` function. For the first level, you end up with this:

```
If LevelExists(Reports!FlexibleGroup, 0) = False Then
    'Create group level on strGroup1
    vMakeGroup = CreateGroupLevel("FlexibleGroup", _
    strGroup1, True, False)
    'Set height of strGroup1 header section
    Reports!FlexibleGroup.Section(acGroupLevel0Header) _
    .Height = 400
End If
```

Because the last two arguments of the `CreateGroupLevel` function are `True` and `False`, respectively, you only create a group header. Aside from a few tweaks, the second `If...Then` construct is much like the first one. You create the group on a different field, and specify the second level in the second argument of the `LevelExists` function. You also specify the second level when setting the section height in the `Section` property with the `acGroupLevel1Header` intrinsic constant.

The FlexibleGroup report example is controlled by a toolbar. The toolbar gives you a mechanism to view the results of your design changes to the report on the fly. The following example demonstrates how to create a sorting procedure and attach the procedure to a toolbar:

1. Under Modules, click New to open a blank module.

2. Type the following after Option Compare Database:

   ```
   Public Function SortLevel(strLevel1 As String, _
   strLevel2 As String)

   On Error GoTo ListError
   ```

```
DoCmd.Echo False
DoCmd.OpenReport "FlexibleSort", acViewDesign

If LevelExists(Reports!FlexibleSort, 0) Then
    Reports!FlexibleSort.GroupLevel(0) _
    .ControlSource = strLevel1
    Reports!FlexibleSort.GroupLevel(1) _
    .ControlSource = strLevel2
Else
    MsgBox "You need to insert groups into " _
    & "your report", vbOKOnly
End If

DoCmd.OpenReport "FlexibleSort", acViewPreview
DoCmd.Echo True
Exit Function

ListError:
DoCmd.Echo True
MsgBox "Error Code: " & Err.number & vbCr _
& "Error Description: " & Err.Description

End Function
```

3. Close the module, and save it as SortReport; then stay in the database.

There are some similarities between this procedure and the last procedure. This time, however, you assign values to the group levels instead of creating them with code like this:

```
Reports!FlexibleSort.GroupLevel(0).ControlSource = strLevel1
```

Again, this expression can never work unless the report is open in Design view. However, because you attach this code to the report using a toolbar, you guarantee that the report will be open when the code is run. Both the strLevel1 and strLevel2 variables are required arguments. They contain the fields by which you want to sort. The order you place them in the function determines the order of sort levels. For example, if you type **?** **SortLevel("AccidentState","AccidentDate")** in the immediate window with the report open, the function sorts first by AccidentState and then by AccidentDate.

NOTE

Be sure to enclose field names with spaces in brackets within the quotes. Turning the Echo off keeps the screen from updating while the program is running.

Because nearly everything else in the procedure has been covered, let's attach this code to a toolbar.

The following example guides you through the process of creating a toolbar, attaching code to it, and attaching the toolbar to a report:

1. Choose Tools, Customize from the menu bar to open the Customize dialog box shown in Figure 22.5.

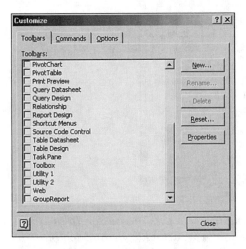

Figure 22.5: *You can add your own procedures to toolbars that can either be run on their own or attached to an Access form or report.*

2. Click the Toolbars tab to view the available toolbar options. Click New to open the New Toolbar dialog box. Type **SortReport** in the box labeled Toolbar Name. Click OK, and notice the toolbar that pops up beside the Customize dialog box, as shown in Figure 22.6.

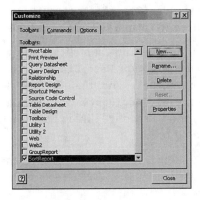

Figure 22.6: *Procedures can be added to the new toolbar that pops up when you click OK.*

3. Click the Commands tab to view the list of command categories. Click File in the Categories box and Custom in the Commands box.

4. Drag the Custom button to the newly created toolbar, as shown in Figure 22.7.

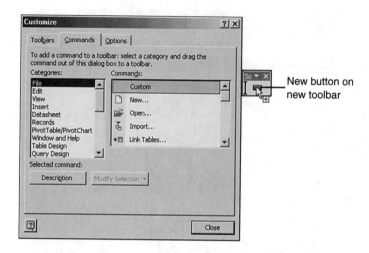

Figure 22.7: *Dragging the new Custom button to the toolbar gives you a blank button to which you can attach code and toolbar tips.*

5. Drag another custom button over to the toolbar. Click the first custom button.

6. Click the Modify Selection button, and then click Properties to view the SortReport Properties dialog box shown in Figure 22.8.

7. In the Caption box, type **State/Date**. In the ScreenTip box, type **Sort first by AccidentState and then by AccidentDate**. In the OnAction box, type **=SortLevel("AccidentState","AccidentDate")**. Don't forget the equal sign. Click Close to return to the Customize dialog box.

8. Click the second custom button, and then click Modify Selection and Properties. In the Caption box, type **Date/State**. In the ScreenTip box, type **Sort first by AccidentDate and then by AccidentState**. In the OnAction box, type **SortLevel("AccidentDate","AccidentState")**. Click Close to return to the Customize dialog box. Click Close again to close the Customize dialog box.

9. Under Reports, open FlexibleSort in Design view so that you can attach the toolbar to the report.

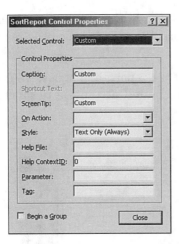

Figure 22.8: *Among other options, the SortReport Control Properties dialog box enables you to specify the procedure to be run when the button is clicked.*

10. Right-click the report selector, and then choose Properties to open the Property sheet. Click the Other tab, and then click the drop-down box of the `ToolBar` property, as shown in Figure 22.9. Select SortReport from the two choices available. Close the Property sheet. Close and save the report.

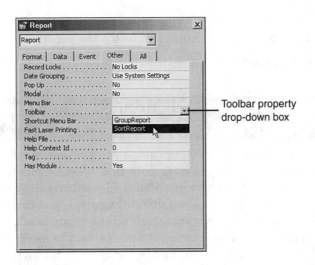

Figure 22.9: *On the Other tab of the Property sheet, choose the toolbar from the Toolbar property drop-down box so that the report will open showing the toolbar.*

11. Reopen the FlexibleSort report in Report view. Drag the toolbar next to the title bar of the report. Close and reopen the report. Notice that the toolbar stays put.

12. Right-click the title bar of the report, and choose 75% zoom again to get a better view. Click the State/Date button to sort the report, as shown in Figure 22.10.

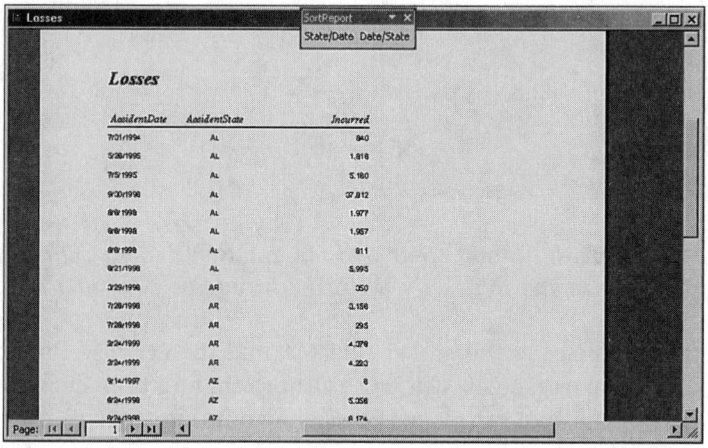

Figure 22.10: *The State/Date button sorts first by* AccidentState *and then by* AccidentDate.

13. Click the Date/State button, and watch the report change again.

14. Close the report without saving changes.

Using Table Relationships to Include or Preclude Entire Sections of Report Data

You have already seen how relationships can provide an effective way to look up data in a form. If you have data that must be conditionally entered into a report, depending on values in a field, table relationships can be an invaluable tool to help you accomplish that goal. If you think of the one side of the relationship as the parent table and the many side as the child table, the technique you are about to see reverses this. The parent table functions as the many side of the relationship, and the child tables function as the one side. However, the goal is the same: to minimize redundant data. The conditional technique is an extra benefit that is often overlooked.

Before getting into the mechanics of this technique, there is another database function that is often overlooked. Although some might argue this point, databases have a definite advantage over spreadsheets, and even word processors, when it comes to preprinted forms. It seems that no matter where you go in the business world, you have to fill out some kind of form. Perhaps you are applying for a credit card or leasing an apartment. If you want to be able to track this information for sorting, calculating, and retrieval purposes, a database is your answer. The report isn't limited to outputting to a preprinted form because it can print the entire form, if necessary.

The following example is not a valid insurance certificate. It is for demonstration purposes only. It does, however, show how to use a database to print an entire form (not to be confused with an Access form), including lines, boxes, and images. It also demonstrates the relational technique previously mentioned.

Take the following steps to discover how conditional controls can operate on a report without any special coding whatsoever:

1. Open the Certificate database from your AccessByExample folder.

2. Under Forms, open Liberty in Form view.

3. Click the View Cert button to open the certificate in Print Preview, as shown in Figure 22.11.

4. The insurance coverage sections of this report are not to be confused with actual Access report sections. Click the Automobile Liability section of the report, in which you see the magnifying glass cursor in Figure 22.11 as shown in Figure 22.12.

   Notice that the entire Automobile Liability (AL) section is blank. All the controls in this section of the report are controlled by the AL control on the form. If there is an X in the AL control on the form, the relational query matches a field in the AL table and pulls in all the pertinent information for the Automobile Liability section.

5. Close the report.

6. Type an uppercase **X** in the AL box. Click the View Cert button again. Notice that the entire AL section appears with everything in the appropriate boxes.

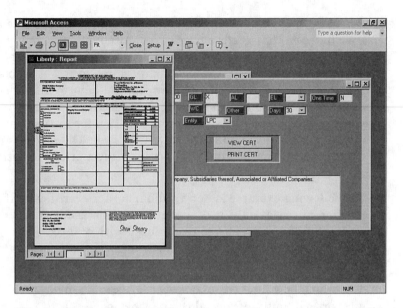

Figure 22.11: *The certificate prints sections according to what is entered in corresponding controls in the Liberty form.*

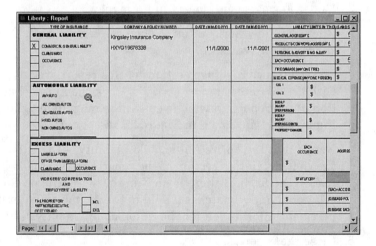

Figure 22.12: *When you zoom, you can verify that the Automobile Liability section is blank.*

7. With the magnifying glass cursor, click the AL section to zoom in, as shown in Figure 22.13.

8. Close the report.

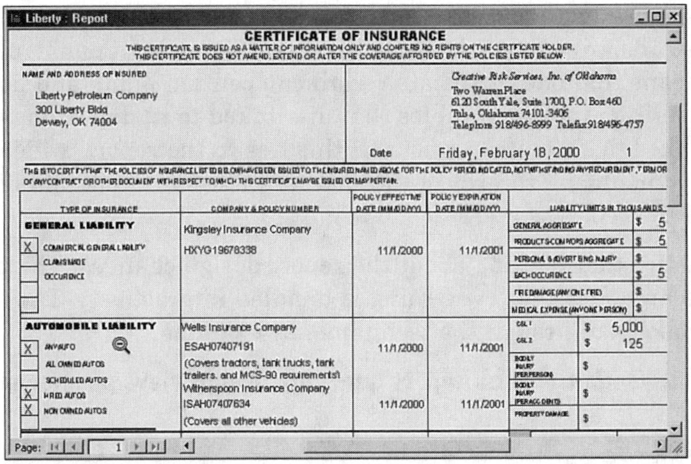

Figure 22.13: *The AL section is pulled into the report because the* AL *field is checked on the Liberty form.*

The procedure behind the View Cert button is very simple. You retrieve the current certificate number in the [Cert No] field, and assign it to a variable. Then, concatenate to the WhereCondition argument of the OpenReport method. The following code is attached to the OnClick event of the View Cert button:

```
Dim cn As String
Cn = Me.Cert_No
Me.Requery
DoCmd.OpenReport "Liberty", acPreview, , "[Cert No]=" & cn
'Me.Requery
```

Notice the Requery lines in the procedure. If you remove the apostrophe in front of the Me.Requery line after the OpenReport method and place an apostrophe in front of the Me.Requery line before the OpenReport method, you get different results. The report does not update to reflect form updates, at least not immediately. This performance demonstrates the importance of order in a procedure.

Understanding the Query Behind the Report

Now that you have seen the technique in action, you have a chance to see how it works. If you look at the relationships between tables in the Relationships window, you discover that the small tables, such as GL and AL, are on the many side of the relationship, whereas the larger certificate table is on the one side of the relationship. The small tables are left joined to the certificate table, which is the only way the technique will work.

Because relationships are all left joins, if the control is left blank, blank records are still retrieved in the query along with nonblank records. That means that one certificate record can contain blank and nonblank information from the small tables that are linked to it, depending on whether the linked fields match or not. All this ties to the report, which shows the blank and nonblank records of the smaller tables as blank and nonblank sections in the report.

Notice that nothing about the report design changes. The beauty of this technique is that everything is handled interactively. The following example walks you through the technique, by example:

1. Open the LinkReport query in Design view, as shown in Figure 22.14.

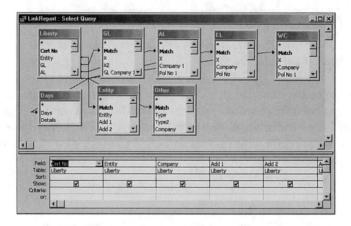

Figure 22.14: *The smaller tables are linked with left outer joins so that records are retrieved, whether they match or not.*

2. Type 1 in the Criteria row of the Cert No field. Using the horizontal scrollbar, scroll right until you see the X field in the GL table. Type an X in the criteria row of the X field, and click the Run button to run the query.

3. Scroll right in the datasheet using your cursor or scrollbar until you see the GL fields, as shown in Figure 22.15. Notice that the GL information is filled in.

   Keep scrolling right until you see the AL information. Notice that the AL information is blank. If you place an X in the proper AL field, that information pulls in, and so on. There is a field called Match in the AL table that has an X in it. When an X is placed in the AL field of the Liberty table, it matches the match field in the AL table.

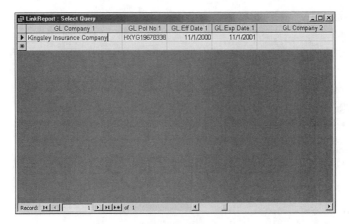

Figure 22.15: *The GL information is pulled in because an X was placed in the X field of the Liberty table.*

NOTE

If you are wondering why a check box field was not used, check boxes are either on or off (unless you set the Triple State property to Yes). Some situations require a large number of matches. For example, the Entity field could contain every branch in the company. If the number of branches was large, a code could represent each entity.

---

4. Click View to switch to Design view. Right-click the line between the GL field in the Liberty table and the Match field in the GL table, and choose Join Properties, as shown in Figure 22.16. The Join Properties dialog box opens. Notice that the second option is checked. This technique works only with a left or right join because equi-joins retrieve only records that match.

5. Close the Join Properties dialog box, and close the query without saving it. Stay in the database.

If you are working in the Human Resources department of a large firm, you might be thinking, "What does this technique have to do with me? I'm not involved with insurance." If you want to create a database of applications, you can include the Education section on the hard copy only if the proper educational level is checked. If you are in retail, you can include only the inventory items that are in stock on the inventory report. Use your imagination to apply this technique to your business or home application.

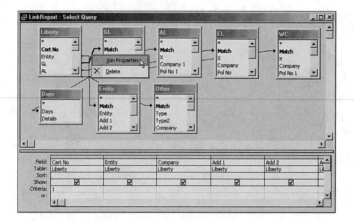

Figure 22.16: *When you check the Join properties of the relationship between the Liberty table and the GL table, you discover that the second option is checked, making it a left join.*

What to Do with Pesky Blank Lines

If you have three address lines and an address needs only two, you don't want an unsightly gap to show up on the report where the address line is supposed to be. Although Access has made provisions for this common problem, it turns out to be a classic good news/bad news situation. The good news is that Access a property that handles blank lines in reports. The CanShrink property can move the control underneath the blank control up so that the blank line is suppressed. The bad news is that this property doesn't work if a label is attached or an image is beside the control.

CanShrink Solution to Blank Lines

However, if you have no labels or images in the part of the report that needs the line suppression, use the CanShrink property. When you set the CanShrink property of a control on the report to Yes, the line is suppressed when the control is blank. When using the CanShrink property, remember the following:

- The property settings don't affect the horizontal spacing between controls. They affect only the vertical space the controls occupy.

- Overlapping controls can't shrink.

- The height of a large control can prevent controls beside it from shrinking. For example, if you have four short text boxes with the CanShrink property set to Yes on the left side of the detail section and one tall text box on the right side of the detail section (which is about the height of the four small text boxes combined), the text boxes on the left side won't shrink.

Another Solution to Blank Lines

Suppose you had an image, such as a .pcx file, on the right side of the controls that has blank lines that need to be suppressed. This image prevents the controls on the left side from suppressing the lines because it nullifies the CanShrink property on the controls. The following expression, entered in the Control Source property of a control, performs the line-suppression operation:

```
=IIf(Not IsNull([Liberty.add 1]) And IsNull([Liberty.add 2]),[City]
➡& ", " & [State] & " " & [Zip],[Liberty.add 2])
```

If the control above the current control in this expression is not Null, and the current control ([Liberty.add 2]) is Null, the expression moves City, State and Zip up to the current control. If [Liberty.add 2] is not Null, use it.

To see this technique in action, take the following steps:

1. Under Reports, open Liberty in Design view to see the design of the report that prints the certificate.

2. Maximize the report window and scroll down to the bottom of the report, as shown in Figure 22.17.

   Notice the signature, which is a .pcx file image to the right of the address controls. The placement of this image cancels any CanShrink operations of the address controls on the left. You might as well leave the default setting of No on the CanShrink property of each control.

   Also notice the way some controls are referenced in the address controls. For example, the [add 1] field is not referenced as [add 1], but as [Liberty.add 1]. This is because there is more than one field on the report with that name. The table name in front of the field name distinguishes it from any other field with the same name. You can avoid this by naming the fields with this in mind, but sometimes duplicate field names are difficult to avoid, especially in a database with a large number of tables.

3. Click the Print Preview button from the toolbar. With the magnifying glass cursor, click the area of the report containing the address lines to zoom in to that part of the report, as shown in Figure 22.18.

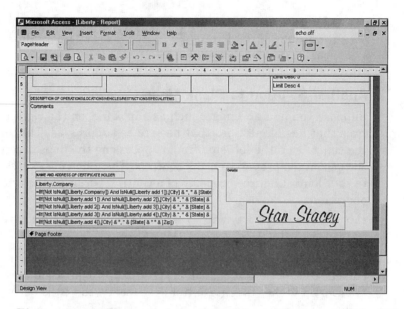

Figure 22.17: *The controls on the left can still suppress blank lines with expressions attached to the control source of each control.*

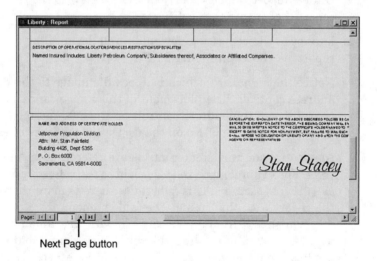

Next Page button

Figure 22.18: *Click the Next Page button at the bottom of the report to page through the report.*

4. Click the Next Page button several times, and notice how the blank lines are suppressed.

5. Close the report but stay in the database.

Multicolumn Reports

A common application for multiple-column reports is mailing labels. Although the procedure to set up labels is fairly straightforward, the implementation can be rather tricky. In the following example, your printer settings might be slightly different because the printer driver you are using is most likely different from the driver used in this example. For this reason, experimentation is recommended to get the proper settings for your printer. However, you can use the example as a guideline.

Take the following steps to create mailing labels:

1. Under Reports, click New to open the New Report dialog box. Select the Label Wizard, and select the Liberty table from the drop-down box. Click OK to open the Label Wizard, as shown in Figure 22.19.

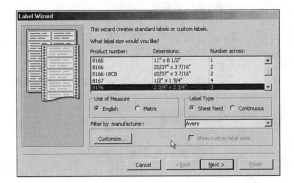

Figure 22.19: *The Label Wizard enables you to set specifications to match various manufacturers of labels.*

2. Select Avery with a Product number 8196, as shown in Figure 22.19, and click Next to open the next page of the wizard.

3. On the second page of the wizard, you select font and color, as shown in Figure 22.20.

4. Click Next to select the defaults and open the page shown in Figure 22.21.

5. Select the Company field by double-clicking, and press Enter so that the next field is added to the next line. Select Add 1, and press Enter. Follow the same procedure as Add 1 for Add 2 through Add 4.

6. Select the City field, and type a comma followed by a space. Select the State field, and press the spacebar twice. Select the Zip field, as shown in Figure 22.22, and click Next to open the next wizard page.

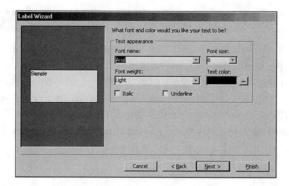

Figure 22.20: *You select the font name, font size, font weight, and color on the second page of the Label Wizard.*

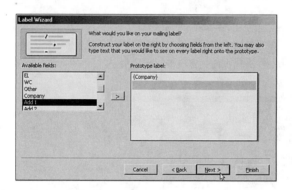

Figure 22.21: *Select the proper field, and press Enter to be sure every field is on a separate line.*

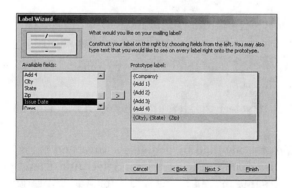

Figure 22.22: *The* City, State, *and* Zip *fields must be on the same line, sep-arated by delimiters.*

7. Double-click Company to select it as a sort field, and click Next to open the next page of the wizard shown in Figure 22.23.

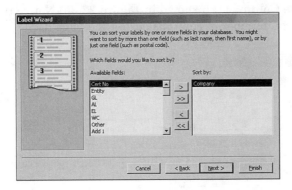

Figure 22.23: *The labels are sorted by the field that you select on the fourth page of the Label Wizard.*

8. Click Finish to preview the report (see Figure 22.24).

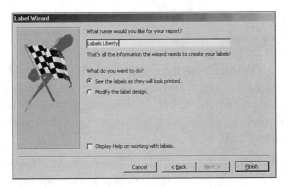

Figure 22.24: *On the final page of the Label Wizard, name the report and choose whether to open the report in Print Preview or Design view.*

9. Depending on your printer driver, you might get a message informing you that the page width is not wide enough. Click OK. Leave the report open, and stay in the database.

Multicolumn Reports

Mailing labels are not the only application of reports using multiple columns. For example, you can print phone book–style reports using more than one column. The place to set up multiple column reports is not where you might expect it to be. The following steps guide you through setting up reports with more than one column:

1. Leaving the report in Preview mode, select File, Page Setup from the menu bar.

2. Click the Columns tab shown in Figure 22.25. Notice that you can change the number of columns across the page here.

Figure 22.25: *The Page Setup dialog box enables you to fine-tune the settings for multiple column reports.*

3. Change the Column Size from 2.75 to 2.25. Click the Margins tab. Change the Left margin setting to .75. Click OK to accept the settings. Notice that the spacing is better (depending on your printer), and you no longer receive the warning message. Your report should look similar to Figure 22.26.

4. Click the View button to switch to Design view. After clicking the top edge of the Page Footer, drag the Page Footer up to decrease the size of the Detail section, as shown in Figure 22.27.

5. Click the Print Preview button, and notice that more labels fit on a page. You might have to make some of these adjustments to make your labels line up properly on your particular printer, but even if you don't, you know how to do it.

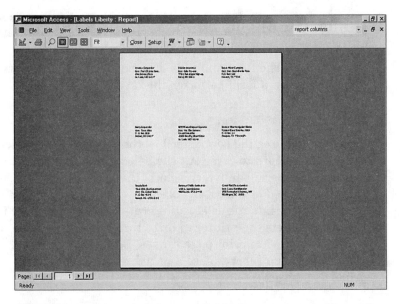

Figure 22.26: *The label report looks better after making adjustments from Page Setup.*

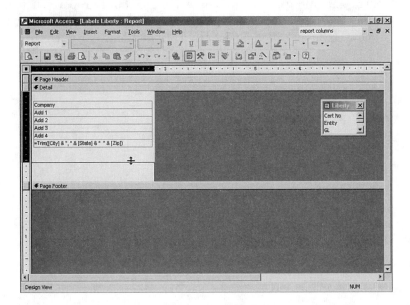

Figure 22.27: *The label report looks better after making adjustments from Page Setup.*

Print Extra Copies

There might be times when you need to print copies of a particular record on your form. The following code attached to the OnClick event of a command button on a form performs the task:

```
RunCommand acCmdSelectRecord
DoCmd.PrintOut acSelection, , , , 3
```

This function uses the RunCommand method with the intrinsic constant acCmdSelectRecord to carry out the Select Record command from the Edit menu on the menu bar, which selects the current record. Then, the PrintOut method of the DoCmd object, having the PrintRange argument set to acSelection, prints the selected record. The fifth argument in the PrintOut method instructs the printer to print three copies. You also can use the PrintOut method to print page ranges. Because you print from a form instead of from a report, place a page break on the form so that the record prints as a page.

What's Next

This chapter concentrated on ways to enhance reports. The next chapter tackles some advanced topics, such as replication. You are introduced to a new acronym called a Globally Unique Identifier (GUID).

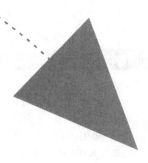

Using Replication

In the last chapter, you learned how to unleash the power of reports. This chapter explains replication. As you have discovered, databases are often concerned with assimilating data from a variety of sources to one central location. Networks and the Internet have resolved many of the issues related to integrating data from various sources. However, users are not always connected to a network when they enter information. Replication often can provide a solution to distributed processing dilemmas. In particular, in this chapter you learn the following:

- why database replication is used

- when you should not use database replication

- how replication works

- how to obtain a list of users in the current database

Database Replication

Database replication is the process of copying a database in a special way so that two or more database copies can exchange updates of data. This exchange between databases is called *synchronization*. This operation is called an exchange because synchronization normally occurs in both directions, though you can choose to synchronize in one direction if you so desire. Each duplicate of the database is called a *replica*, which contains a common set of database objects.

The database with which you start is converted to a Design Master. Each replica is part of a *replica set*, which contains the Design Master and the other replicas. The *Design Master* is the only replica that enables you to make changes to the structure of the database. Any replicas that belong to the same replica set can synchronize with each other.

Why Use Database Replication?

Suppose that your company had three sales representatives (named Roger, Alice, and Mike) covering three different territories. All three sales representatives have laptop computers that they take on the road with them with a copy of a master database from the home office. Because Roger gained customers and orders, he added them to his database. Alice lost a few customers, so she deleted customers from her database. Mike had some address changes for his customers, which he promptly updated on his database.

Tina is the person responsible for updating the database. When the sales representatives return to the central office, can you imagine Tina's frustration as she ponders the task in front of her? First, she has to add Roger's new customers. Even if she copies from Roger's database, his copy of the database has his additions, but doesn't have Alice's deletions and Mike's modifications. Consequently, she then has to look up and delete Alice's customers. Finally, she has to look up and change Mike's customers. To add fuel to the fire, Tina has made updates herself. Her updates, along with the other updates, should also be included in all the database copies.

Tina has a meeting with her boss to discuss the possible solutions. The sales representatives could tie into the home office network with a remote access service (RAS). This involves ordering new phone lines, which is not in the budget. The company president is not open to setting up an Internet database for security reasons, and an intranet might never happen.

Finally, the network administrator walks in and explains the advantages of database replication. Tina doesn't have to manually update any longer. After the databases are copied to the server, she just presses the right buttons and all the additions, deletions, and modifications are instantly updated in the master database and all its replicas.

Other Reasons for Database Replication

The scenario just presented is not the only reason to use replication. Other reasons to replicate include the following:

- **Distribute Updates**—Developers can add new forms and reports to the Design Master and distribute the changes automatically through replication. This means that you can replicate more than just data. You cannot modify forms or reports in a replica as you can with the Design Master. This also gives the developers built-in protection for their applications.

- **Office and Home Synchronization**—A user who takes an office database back and forth between office and home can easily synchronize changes made at home with the office database.

- **Database Backup**—Instead of copying the entire database for a backup, replication is a more efficient backup solution because it copies only the updates.

- **Reduce Network Traffic**—If network response is slow on one database due to increased traffic, replication provides another alternative to the split database approach. Users can make data updates on their local machines instead of the server, and synchronize them with the Design Master at the end of the day.

When You Should Not Use Replication

Although database replication can be a solution to many of the problems inherent in distributed database processing, you should be able to recognize the situations that are not appropriate for replication. You might reconsider replication if the following situations exist:

- **Multiple Replicas and Large Records**—Applications that necessitate frequent updates of large numbers of existing records in multiple replicas are more likely to have record conflicts than applications that simply insert added records to tables in a database. Because the conflicts must be resolved manually, this translates into more administrative time. Therefore, it's probably not a good idea to replicate in this situation.

- **Time-Critical Applications**—Applications that rely on critical information being continuously accurate, such as travel reservations, funds transfers, and shipment tracking, usually are not good candidates for replication. The inherent lag time between the time the data changes and the time the data is synchronized suggests that replicated databases are more appropriate for applications that don't require data to be continuously current. If it's likely that two users will modify data in the same record during the same period of time, the inevitable conflicts must be resolved, which indicates that replication probably is not the best plan. On the other hand, if each user has the complete responsibility for updating a particular set of records, the chances for conflicts diminish, especially in disconnected databases. In this case, replication can be considered.

How Replication Works

At first glance, replication looks easy. You just use the Access menu bar and in a matter of seconds, you have a Design Master with several replicas. However, first impressions can be deceiving. An entire book could easily be written about just one aspect of replication. This does not mean that a comprehensive knowledge of replication is required to be able to use it effectively.

To keep tabs on the complexities of tracking database changes, much activity goes on behind the scenes. When you create replicas, Access creates several new hidden tables in the database. In addition to adding tables, Access adds fields to existing tables to manage synchronization and conflict resolution. Table 23.1 shows the fields that can be added to make the table replicable. Although at least four fields are added, you cannot view them without checking System Objects in Tools, Options, View.

Table 23.1: Replication Fields

Field	Description
s_Generation	Determines whether changes have been made since the last synchronization.
s_GUID	GUID stands for Globally Unique Identifier. It uniquely identifies each record. Because AutoNumber fields can be unreliable for matching records when synchronizing, Access uses GUID instead of AutoNumber.
s_Lineage	Tracks the history of changes in the record and resolves conflicts when an individual record is changed in multiple replicas.
s_ColLineage	Determines who wins a conflict between columns.
Gen_FieldName	Added for each large object (OLE or Memo) field in the table, where FieldName represents the name of the large object field. This field only tracks changes to the appropriate large object field.

AutoNumber Conflicts

AutoNumber fields are designed to increment by one each time you add a record. This does not work in a replication environment. If it did work, each member of the replica set would be adding records independently of each other with identical primary key values, causing conflicts on every synchronization. Therefore, when you create a replica from a database, random incrementing (between -2,000,000,000 and 2,000,000,000) is imposed on the replicas, which greatly decreases the likelihood of two replicas being assigned the same primary key value. If you are using AutoNumber for both uniqueness and sequential numbering, you might need to consider other alternatives before replicating your database. Although you can use a GUID field as a primary key field, it is generally not recommended.

Compacting Before Replicating

Before replication or synchronization, compact the Design Master twice for best results. The first compact flags the replicated objects that need to be deleted, but it doesn't actually delete them. The second compact deletes the flagged objects and recovers space associated with the deleted objects. In general, this is essential only in the Design Master. Ordinary replicas must be compacted only once.

If you compact a replica that is corrupted, it will lose its replicable status. That means that if it's the Design Master, it will lose its Design Master status. Normal corrupted replicas return to a normal, nonreplicable database status. However, all the hidden system tables and fields are still present. Erratic behavior in a database is an indication that the database is corrupted.

Converting a Database to a Design Master

The next example shows how easy it is to replicate a database. You create a Master Design along with two replicas. After making changes, you synchronize the databases and resolve conflicts.

The following steps guide you through the process of replication:

1. Open the Master Sales database in the AccessByExample folder.

2. Choose Tools, Database Utilities, Compact and Repair Database to compact and repair the database; then repeat these choices to compact and repair the database a second time.

3. Select Tools, Replication, Create Replica from the menu bar to begin the replication process. Answer Yes when asked to close the database and create the replica. Answer Yes when asked to back up the

database to open the Location of the New Replica dialog box, shown in Figure 23.1.

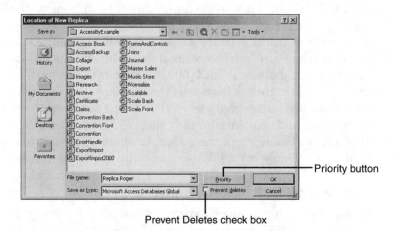

Priority button

Prevent Deletes check box

Figure 23.1: *You enter the location of the replica in the Location of New Replica dialog box.*

Notice the Prevent Deletes check box in the Location of New Replica dialog box. If you are concerned that a user can delete the same record that is important to another user, check this box. But for the purposes of this exercise, leave the box blank.

Also notice the Priority button in the Location of New Replica dialog box. Replicas are assigned a priority, designated by a number between 0 and 100, when the replica is created. For example, when a database is made replicable, the Design Master's priority is set to 90. In the case of a synchronization conflict, the highest priority replica wins.

4. Be sure the AccessByExample folder is selected, and name the newly created database **Replica Roger**, as shown in Figure 23.1, and click OK to create the replica. When the next message informs you that the database structure can be made only at the Design Master, click OK.

5. Repeat steps 3 and 4, but in step 4, name the database **Replica Alice**. Click Yes to close and reopen the database. Notice the new look of your Master Sales database. Specifically, each object in the Database window has a replication graphic beside the icon next to the object name.

6. Open Replica Roger from the AccessByExample folder. Click Forms under Objects. Notice that the New button is disabled. Also notice that both Create Form in Design View and Create Form By Using Wizard are missing, as shown in Figure 23.2.

New button inactive

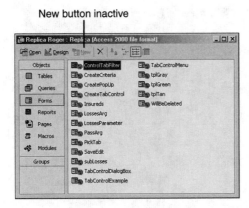

Figure 23.2: *The replica database does not allow you to create a new form.*

NOTE

Also notice that you cannot modify the design of queries, tables, forms, and reports. Neither macros nor modules can be created in replicas.

---

7. Click Queries under Objects. Double-click the AddToReplica query. Click Yes when the message warns you that data will be modified in your table. Click Yes again when the message informs you that you are about to append records. The query adds two records to the LossesIndex table so that you have something to replicate.

TIP

When appending to a table with an autonumber field, don't include the autonumber field in the query. The autonumber takes care of the numbering for you.

---

8. Click Tables under Objects, and open the LossesIndex table. Two records have been added. If you don't see the added records before ID 1 in the LossesIndex table, as shown in Figure 23.3, Press Ctrl+End to go to the last record. If they are positive numbers, they append to the end of the table. Otherwise, you can see the new records when you open the table. Don't worry about whether the Autonumber field shows positive or negative numbers.

9. Choose Tools, Database Utilities, Compact and Repair Database to Compact the database. Choose Tools, Replication, Synchronize Now from the menu bar to open the Synchronize Database dialog box, as shown in Figure 23.4.

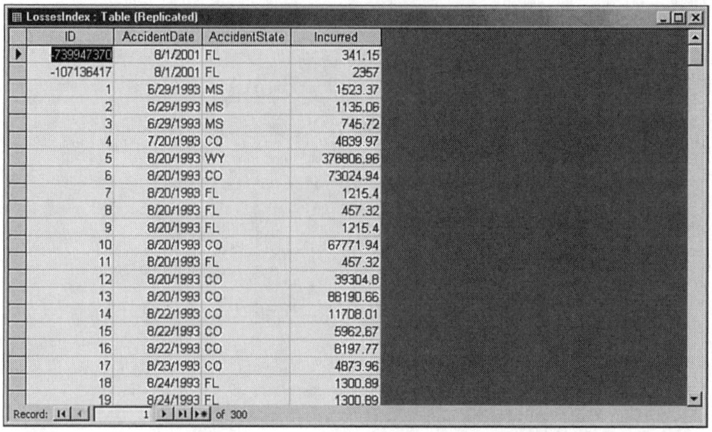

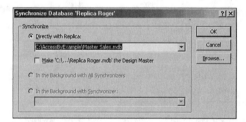

Figure 23.3: *The* Autonumber *field in the replica changes to random incrementing after replication.*

NOTE

When is the best time to replicate? After changes have been made to any of the replicated databases. In the "real world," because of logistical considerations, you might not always be able to replicate immediately after changes have been made.

Figure 23.4: *The drop-down box in the Synchronize Database dialog box shows you the databases that are replicable.*

10. Choose Replica Alice.mdb from the drop-down box, and then click OK to synchronize the databases. If Replica Alice does not appear in the drop-down box, click the Browse button, and then choose Replica Alice in the AccessByExample folder. Click Yes when the message informs you that the database must be closed to synchronize with the replica. You are informed of a successful synchronization.

Now that you have synchronized the databases, the next phase involves verifying that a successful replication has taken place. Although you have been informed that the replication was successful, it is important for you to see the results of the synchronization. More synchronizations, updates, and testing take place with the purpose of giving you a look at what really happens when databases are synchronized. You also discover what happens when conflicts are found. The following steps guide you through the testing process:

1. Open Replica Alice and the LossesIndex table to verify that the records were added. Change MS to WY in the AccidentState field of the ID 1. Close the table and choose Tools, Database Utilities, Compact and Repair Database from the menu bar to compact the database.

2. Open Replica Roger from Windows Explorer in the AccessByExample folder. You should have two Access databases open now as you look at your task bar. If this is not the case, reopen Replica Alice. Open the LossesIndex table and change the AccidentState field of the first record from MS to CO. Close the table and compact the database.

3. From the Replica Roger database, choose Tools, Replication, Synchronize Now from the menu bar to open the Synchronize Database dialog box.

4. Be sure that Replica Alice.mdb is selected, and then click OK to begin the synchronization. Click Yes when the message informs you that the database must be closed to synchronize with the replica. A message tells you that the synchronization was successful. After the successful message, another message appears, as shown in Figure 23.5.

Figure 23.5: *Choose Yes when asked, "Do you want to resolve these conflicts now?"*

5. Click Yes to open the Conflict Viewer dialog box shown in Figure 23.6.

NOTE

If the message appears but the Conflict Viewer Wizard doesn't open, you probably don't have the wzcnflct.exe wizard file on your hard drive. This probably means that you need to reinstall Access 2002.

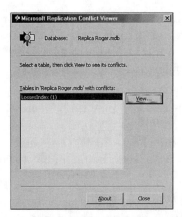

Figure 23.6: *The Conflict Viewer automatically loads when a Yes response is given to the following question: "Do you want to resolve these conflicts now?"*

6. Click View to open the next page of the Conflict Viewer, as shown in Figure 23.7.

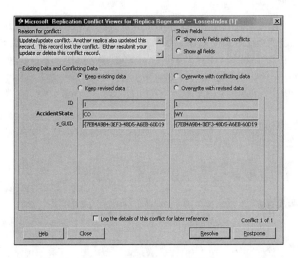

Figure 23.7: *The next Conflict Viewer page lets you decide the best method to resolve synchronization conflicts.*

7. Choose the Overwrite with Revised Data option button, and then click Resolve to resolve the conflict in Replica Roger. You return to the first page of the Conflict Viewer presenting the message <No conflict tables>. Table 23.2 explains the options available in the Conflict Viewer.

Table 23.2: Conflict Viewer Options

Option	Description
Reason for Conflict	View the specific reason for the conflict that occurred and the way in which the conflict was resolved.
Show Only Fields with Conflicts	Display the GUID column and only the fields that have conflicts.
Show All Fields	Display all the fields in the record with conflicts.
Keep Existing Data	Accept the current resolution of the conflict.
Keep Revised Data	Accept the current resolution of the conflict, but include the revisions made in the edit boxes.
Keep Data Deleted	Accept the current resolution of the conflict; data will remain deleted.
Ignore Conflict	Mark the conflict as resolved without making any changes. Because this results in the conflict not being resolved, other means should be taken as soon as possible.
Overwrite with Conflicting Data	Overturn the way the conflict was resolved and keep the conflicting data shown.
Overwrite with Existing Data	Overturn the way the conflict was resolved and keep the existing data shown.
Overwrite with Revised Data	Overturn the way the conflict was resolved with the revisions made in the edit boxes and keep the revised data shown.
Delete Data	Delete the data shown in the fields.
Log the Details of This Conflict for Later Reference	Make a copy of the conflict and store it in a separate log file for later use. The file is stored in *Windows directory*\profiles*user*\Application Data\Microsoft\Database Replication\ UnresolvedConflicts.log.

8. Close and reopen Replica Alice. Notice that the conflict message automatically reappears. Repeat steps 5 through 7 to resolve conflicts in Replica Alice.

9. Open the Master Sales database (Design Master) to synchronize all three databases after making changes to the database. Open the LossesIndex table. Notice that the two records have not been added. Change the Incurred amount of the first record from 1523.37 to 1524.37. Close the LossesIndex table, and compact the database twice.

10. Synchronize the Master database with Replica Roger and Replica Alice by choosing Tools, Replication, Synchronize Now; and using the drop-down box to choose the appropriate table. Open the LossesIndex table, and notice that the two records have been added. Open Replica Roger and Replica Alice, and notice that the Incurred field in the ID 1

record has been changed from 1523.37 to 1524.37. This proves that the synchronization occurred in both directions.

11. Close the table and stay in the database.

Now you have a better idea of what goes on during replication. You have seen that replication does indeed execute in both directions. If you change the same field in the same record two different ways for two replicas, you are creating a conflict. However, you also discovered how to resolve conflicts between replicated tables. Some objects in replicas cannot be created or changed. So far, you have been working with entire tables within databases, but what if you want to work with partial information in one or more tables? The next section describes situations that call for partial replication.

Partial Replicas

You might have an employee, a department, or an entire division in your company that needs to see only part of the database. In this case, a partial replica can be created that provides only a subset of the information from one or more replicated tables. In other words, only the information that is relevant to the individual user or group of users is retained.

For example, salespeople with limited storage capacities on their hard drives can conserve storage space on their hard drives by receiving only a partial replica related to their particular region. The security that this type of replica provides is an extra bonus. This means that sensitive information can be protected by limiting its access to only certain individuals or departments.

A partial replica is created by using the Partial Replica Wizard, which enables you to select only the table (or tables, if there are relationships established) that you need to access, along with a filter expression to determine which records to include in the subset. After a new partial replica has been created, do not delete the full replica on which it was based because it is acting as a sort of backup (though only a partial backup) from before you started creating partial replicas. Furthermore, partial replicas can be synchronized only with full replicas.

If you are wondering what happened to Mike, he is being saved for a partial replication because he only needs Florida claims for his insurance sales. A filter needs to be created for the Florida records. The following example familiarizes you with the process of creating a partial replica, but stops short of actually creating the replica because you learn how to create the partial replica programmatically:

1. From the Master Sales Design Master database, choose Tools, Replication, Partial Replica Wizard to open the first page of the wizard (see Figure 23.8), and begin the creation process.

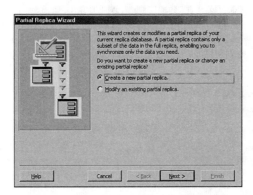

Figure 23.8: *Choose Create a New Partial Replica, which contains only a subset of the full replica, on the opening page of the wizard.*

2. Click Next to choose the Create a New Partial Replica option, and open the next page of the Partial Replica Wizard shown in Figure 23.9. You can choose a global, local, or anonymous replica from this page.

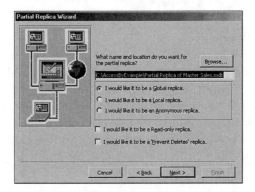

Figure 23.9: *You can make your partial replica global, local, or anonymous on the second page of the wizard.*

Table 23.3 describes the global, local, and anonymous replica choices.

Table 23.3: Replica Visibility

Visibility	Explanation
Global	Can synchronize with all other global replicas and replicas created from it, with some exceptions. From a global replica, you can create a global, local, or anonymous replica.

Table 23.3: continued

Visibility	Explanation
Local	Can synchronize only with its parent, a global replica. Local replicas have a priority of 0, which cannot be changed.
Anonymous	Can synchronize only with its parent, a global replica. Similar to local replicas, but its replica information is not permanently stored in the system table MSysReplicas. Anonymous replicas have a priority of 0, which cannot be changed.

3. Click Next to choose global visibility and open the next page of the wizard (see Figure 23.10).

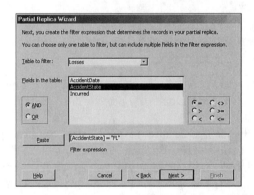

Figure 23.10: *You can create an expression for a filter on the filter page of the Partial Replica Wizard.*

4. Choose AccidentState in the drop-down box next to Table to Filter. Leave = selected from the option buttons, and click Paste to insert the expression [AccidentState]=[Expression] in the Filter expression box. Change [Expression] to FL (to look like Figure 23.10), and click Next to open the next page of the wizard, shown in Figure 23.11.

5. Click Next to open the final page of the Partial Replica Wizard shown in Figure 23.12.

6. On the final page of the wizard, you can choose to create a report, but because you create the wizard programmatically, click Cancel to cancel the replica creation process.

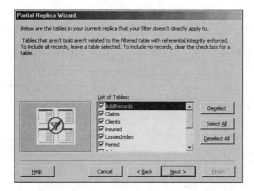

Figure 23.11: *On the page that shows the tables that the filter doesn't apply to, click Next to select the defaults.*

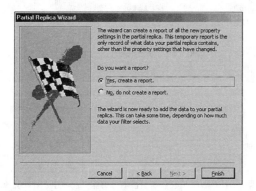

Figure 23.12: *Choose Cancel on the final page of the Partial Replica Wizard.*

Creating a Partial Replica Programmatically

Now that you know how to manually create a partial replica, you can create one programmatically. The following listing creates a partial replica from a Design Master:

```
Public Sub PartialReplica()
Dim rplMaster As New JRO.Replica
Dim rplPartial As New JRO.Replica

'Must set references to Microsoft Jet and
'Replication Objects 2.6 (or latest version)

'Must run from a database other than the Master
'or Replica that the procedure accesses
```

```
'Must set connection to a Design Master
rplMaster.ActiveConnection = "C:\AccessByExample\Master Sales.mdb"

'Create a partial replica from the Design Master
rplMaster.CreateReplica "C:\AccessByExample\" & _
    "Partial Mike.mdb", _
    "Partial Replica For Mike", jrRepTypePartial

'Must create an exclusive connection for PopulatePartial
rplPartial.ActiveConnection = _
    "Provider=Microsoft.Jet.OLEDB.4.0;" & _
    "Data Source=C:\AccessByExample\" & _
    "Partial Mike.mdb;Mode=Share Exclusive"

'Create a filter
rplPartial.Filters.Append "Losses", jrFilterTypeTable, _
    "AccidentState = 'FL'"

'The database from which you get the records to populate
rplPartial.PopulatePartial "C:\AccessByExample\" & _
    "Master Sales.mdb"

Set rplMaster = Nothing
Set rplPartial = Nothing

End Sub
```

The acronym JRO stands for Microsoft Jet and Replication Objects. As the comments indicate, a reference must be set to the JRO 2.6 library in the module in which you type this code. It is to your advantage to type this code into a module in a blank database or any database other than the databases affected by the procedure because you can view the options available as you type, which is very instructional.

The procedure starts by establishing a connection to the Design Master. Next, an empty partial replica (at least as far as table data is concerned) is created from the Design Master. An exclusive connection then is established so that the tables can be populated, but not until a filter is created on the table that is to be partially populated. Finally, the partial replica is populated with records. Run the procedure, and examine the Losses table in the Partial Mike database to verify that only Florida records were copied.

What's Next

What's next for you is enjoying what you have learned by putting the principles into practice. Now you know how to unleash the power of Access.

There are other resources available to you on the Internet.

- The Que Publishing Web site address is `www.quepublishing.com`. Here, you will find information about new releases and free downloadable code.

- Inside Microsoft Access is a helpful journal with a Web site full of tips and techniques. You must be a subscriber to reap the full benefits of this service. The Web site address is `www.elementkjournals.com`.

- The Microsoft Office Developer Web Forum is also helpful, and can be found at `www.msdn.microsoft.com/office`. You can include the Knowledge Base in your advanced searches there.

- Another helpful Microsoft site is called Using Access at `www.microsoft.com/office/access/using/default.htm`. You find tips and tricks, how-to articles, training and certification, newsgroups, and other interesting items there.

- Another subscriber site is the Access VB SQL Advisor, found at `www.advisor.com/www/AccessVBSQLAdvisor`. Click the Microsoft Access Advisor Zone for Access-related articles.

Keep in mind that Web sites can be subject to change, but a search usually can find the desired site.

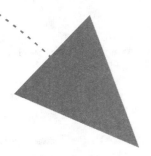

Index